Terrorism

This book adopts an innovative historical approach to Terrorism, focusing on the weaknesses of terrorist states and organizations as reflected in the ideologies, methodologies and propaganda of Russian populist, National Socialist and Islamic Terrorism.

Drawing upon multilingual primary sources, the book challenges the oft repeated claim that the Nazi regime and Islamic State produced propaganda of superior quality, instead arguing that the manipulation of information is the Achilles heel of terrorist organizations. It offers a critical examination of the fears of terrorists themselves, as opposed to the traditional focus on the fear instilled by terrorist organizations in governments and citizens. Taking a multidisciplinary approach and long-term history perspective, the book provides a method for exploring the minds of terrorists and the inner workings of their organizations and traces the evolution of terrorist thought and methodology across time and place.

This is the ideal volume for researchers of Terrorism within the fields of History, Politics, Security Studies, Religious Studies and Legal Studies.

Juan Romero is Associate Professor at Western Kentucky University, USA.

Routledge Studies in Modern History

The Antifascist Chronicles of Aurelio Pego
A Critical Anthology
Edited by Montse Feu

Crafting Turkish National Identity, 1919–1927
A Rhetorical Approach
Aysel Morin

Citizens and Subjects of the Italian Colonies
Legal Constructions and Social Practices, 1882–1943
Edited by Simona Berhe and Olindo De Napoli

Gandhi After Gandhi
The Relevance of the Mahatma's Legacy in Today's World
Edited by Marzia Casolari

The Body in the Anglosphere, 1880–1920
"Well Sexed Womanhood," "Finer Natives," and "Very White Men"
Robert W. Thurston

The Barsden Memoirs (1799–1816)
An Australian Transnational Adolescence
Grant Rodwell

Terrorism
The Power and Weakness of Fear
Juan Romero

For more information about this series, please visit: https://www.routledge.com/history/series/MODHIST

Terrorism
The Power and Weakness of Fear

Juan Romero

LONDON AND NEW YORK

First published 2022
by Routledge
2 Park Square, Milton Park, Abingdon, Oxon OX14 4RN

and by Routledge
605 Third Avenue, New York, NY 10158

Routledge is an imprint of the Taylor & Francis Group, an informa business

© 2022 Juan Romero

The right of Juan Romero to be identified as author of this work has been asserted in accordance with sections 77 and 78 of the Copyright, Designs and Patents Act 1988.

All rights reserved. No part of this book may be reprinted or reproduced or utilised in any form or by any electronic, mechanical, or other means, now known or hereafter invented, including photocopying and recording, or in any information storage or retrieval system, without permission in writing from the publishers.

Trademark notice: Product or corporate names may be trademarks or registered trademarks, and are used only for identification and explanation without intent to infringe.

British Library Cataloguing-in-Publication Data
A catalogue record for this book is available from the British Library

Library of Congress Cataloging-in-Publication Data
A catalog record has been requested for this book

ISBN: 978-1-032-19806-4 (hbk)
ISBN: 978-1-032-19808-8 (pbk)
ISBN: 978-1-003-26094-3 (ebk)

DOI: 10.4324/9781003260943

Typeset in Times New Roman
by codeMantra

Contents

Acknowledgments vii

   Introduction 1

1 Ancient, medieval and early modern extremist movements 10

2 Was Russian terrorism a true instrument of the people? 27

3 Methodology of Russian terrorism 49

4 Ideology of the National Socialist terrorist state 75

5 National Socialist propaganda 98

6 Interpretations of jihad 120

7 Rules of jihad 137

8 Precursors to the Islamic State 154

9 Islamic State media production and Islam 179

10 Islamic State legitimacy and perception of the enemy 200

11 The eleven fears of Islamic terrorist organizations 222

12 A comparative evolution of terrorism 241

   Conclusion 265

Glossary 273
Index 277

Acknowledgments

I am grateful for the generous support of Western Kentucky University in the form of a research grant and a sabbatical leave, without which this book would have taken much longer to see the light of day. This support allowed me during my sabbatical leave to conduct research in the National Archives (US), College Park, the Hoover Institution, Palo Alto and the Library of Congress in Washington, DC.

August 2021

Introduction

Terrorism is an ancient phenomenon which still besets many societies. Unlike other problems, which humanity faces such as diseases to many of which effective treatments have been developed, we have not been very successful in dealing with militant extremist ideologies. In order to treat diseases, doctors study symptoms based upon which a diagnosis can be made. Western medical research has oftentimes developed very aggressive treatments for various diseases, treating illnesses with potent medication which may solve one problem but cause multiple other problems in the form of side effects. Traditional Chinese Medicine (TCM) has over the centuries developed herbal treatments and acupuncture which are very often much less intrusive with less serious side effects, if any. The approach to terrorism adopted in this study resembles TCM in so far as it does not focus on military action to uproot extremist violence but advocates psychological and educational measures to combat terrorism. Having said that, the present author realizes that military action is a part of a comprehensive strategy, but the subject has been explored in detail in military and counterterrorism studies already and does not play a role in this work. Other studies on terrorism have pointed at social inequality, injustice and repression as factors causing radicalization and terrorism.[1] The present volume focuses on inoculation of citizens against terrorism, treating this violent phenomenon as a 'disease of the mind'. The treatment proposed in this volume can be characterized as nonintrusive immunization, that is, unlike treating evil with a minor dose of evil, the problem can be addressed by prescribing a natural solution as protection against the source of contagion. Fortunately, society already possesses the means successfully to achieve this goal – education.

The educational approach may have the best prospects for success if it emulates a natural learning process, relying on two institutions at a minimum – family and school. A problem with society's current approach to education is that certain skills are not acquired by students sufficiently early. Universities make efforts to provide opportunities for students to learn and practice critical thinking, but this is a process which should begin much earlier in order to become not just second nature but 'first' nature in the minds of members of society. This is of particular importance in a modern society

DOI: 10.4324/9781003260943-1

awash with devices which allow individuals of all ages to access all kinds of information for better or for worse. A further challenge to modern societies is the independence of their youth, who unlike earlier historical periods very often do no more remain under the control of families and tradition, partly as a result of spending much time outside their homes and increased mobility. A third problem connected with imparting the concept of critical thinking is the challenge which it poses to societies ruled by authoritarian regimes which are not as keen on exposing their students and other citizens to the process of independent thinking. Moreover, a possible criticism of efforts to teach citizens to think for themselves is that not every individual is prone to engaging in the intellectual exercise involved in critical thinking. This may seem like a valid point. However, a good counterargument is that nobody walks without first learning to walk and no one speaks a language without first learning it. This process involves learning a skill in a natural way by observing and imitating our environment and most likely by an urge to become mobile and to communicate with other individuals. A conclusion which can be drawn from the above discussion is that it should be incumbent upon families and schools to create an environment which enables children and students to develop mental agility.

This book fills a significant lacuna in the literature on terrorism. It is the result of an innovative and multidisciplinary approach to the subject. One aspect of the treatment of the subject presented in this volume is a long-term historical perspective. It examines a number of terrorist movements, representing different societies, time periods and religions/ideologies from the ancient Sicarii to the Islamic State to determine to what extent history reveals continuity and consistency concerning ideology and methodology. An important argument which this study advances is that many aspects of terrorist ideology and methodology have remained unchanged over the course of time despite some differences displayed by individual militant organizations. A second aspect which reinforces the validity of a long-term approach and the findings yielded by such a research method is a detailed analysis of terrorist propaganda published over the course of 150 years by different groups, organizations and states including the Party of Socialist Revolutionaries, the Third Reich, Al-Qaʻida and the Islamic State (Daʻish). Unlike the often repeated opinion that Nazi terrorist propaganda was the product of highly skilled professionals and very effective[2] and the expressions of awe on the part of government officials, researchers and journalists regarding the effectiveness and media acumen of Islamic State propaganda,[3] the findings presented in this study convincingly reveal the many flaws in the attempts of these terrorist states to manipulate information. The second argument advanced in this study is thus that propaganda is a double-edged sword which can very often be used against those who wield it due to weak argumentation and inconsistences. As a result of this circumstance, its 'effectiveness' is explained not by the genius of its authors but rather by the lack of skills in or reluctance to engage in critical thinking on the part of the reader. A third important and innovative aspect of this book is its examination of the nature of fear. Generally speaking, studies in terrorism devote much attention to fear instilled in governments (unless the government itself is terroristic) and civilian populations by terrorist acts perpetrated by extremist groups. This traditional focus on fear as experienced by victims disregards the many fears of the terrorists themselves. The third argument advanced in this work is thus that no real understanding of terrorism can be acquired and no effective countermeasures taken against it without a profound awareness of the terrorists' own fears, which is why a separate chapter has been devoted to this issue.

A plethora of books on terrorism have been published in recent decades, reflecting different methodological approaches. Many works such as those of Michael Weiss and Hassan Hassan, *ISIS: Inside the Army of Terror* and Hisham al-Hashimi, *'Alam Daʿish* have focused on a particular organization. These studies typically provide a good in-depth analysis of a group's methodology and ideological foundation in addition to a brief history of the organization. In *The History of Terrorism: From antiquity to Al Qaeda*, Gérard Chaliand and Arnaud Blin have approached the subject from a long-term historical perspective, producing an excellent overall historical introduction to the phenomenon of terrorism. The authors have drawn attention to the hazard of confusing a terrorist act itself and the moral interpretation of it. Such an act is deemed 'terroristic' when it is perceived as lacking legitimacy.[4] This is an important issue to which I have added a third element in the present volume, namely that terrorists themselves at times violate their own rules or weaken their legitimacy by basing it on unconvincing or confused argumentation. Randall Law's *Terrorism: A History* has adopted an approach somewhat similar to that of my own by emphasizing continuity concerning core features. Law argues that terrorist acts are the result of 'a process of rational and conscious decision-making within particular political and cultural contexts'[5] and that the objective of terrorism is to influence one or several target groups. A non-Western perspective on terrorism is discussed in Haitham ʿAbd al-Salam Muhammad's *Mafhum al-Irhab fi al-Shariʿa al-Islamiyya*, a study in which the author advances the argument that the West has imposed its definition of terrorism on the Islamic world, exploiting it against Muslims.[6] Muhammad contends that Islam has to declare and disseminate its own interpretation of terrorism. This issue is of fundamental importance and will be subjected to a critical analysis in Chapters 6 and 7 of this study. A close reading of sacred texts and the writings of medieval religious scholars and modern militant Islamic ideologues will reveal that this is a formidable task since a scholarly treatment of the issue will produce a multitude of definitions, suggesting as much diversity – including in terrorist ranks – as in the West.

Doctors have a somewhat easier task when making a diagnosis of a disease than scholars who study and analyze terrorism. The reason is that the former have a common terminology and common definitions of diseases.

4 *Introduction*

The latter do not possess a universally adopted definition of terrorism. This constitutes a problem since there is a risk that without a common definition of terrorism, confusion will ensue with respect to what constitutes terrorism, if different legal standards are applied. The Central Intelligence Agency distinguishes between two types of terrorism – international and domestic. Its definition of terrorism is as follows:

> The term 'terrorism' means premeditated, politically motivated violence perpetrated against noncombatant targets by subnational groups or clandestine agents. The term 'international terrorism' means terrorism involving the territory or the citizens of more than one country. The term 'terrorist group' means any group that practices, or has significant subgroups that practice, international terrorism.[7]

A problem with this definition is that it is rather vague. It focuses on violence without distinguishing between physical and psychological violence both of which are resorted to by terrorist groups. Furthermore, the CIA's reference to 'noncombatant targets' needs clarification as well. Do government buildings and hospitals which treat both civilians and military personnel belong in this category? Or job applicants waiting in line to enlist in the armed forces or a police organization? Also, this brief definition makes no reference to printed or visual terrorism. Finally, the definition does not take state terrorism into account. Definitions are helpful when they are sufficiently flexible to include future weapons and methodologies, but should obviously at the same time be sufficiently specific to avoid confusion. These two requirements make it difficult to strike a balance between the two.

Perhaps, due to imperfect definitions, attempts are being made to develop innovative approaches to counterterrorism or even to rethink the meaning of the term terrorism. The French government has realized the danger to national security that extremist propaganda posted to the Internet poses and therefore engages in discussions with other states, the objective of which is to prevent radicalization. France considers such propaganda and incitement to violence terrorism. The solution which it proposes in discussions with digital companies is to withdraw any terrorist content from the Internet within one hour of its posting.[8] If implemented, this would obviously considerably strengthen counterterrorism measures. The educational approach proposed in the present study would, however, be even more effective, since it would make Internet users highly unlikely to embrace terrorist propaganda in the first place, even if they happened to read it before it was withdrawn. Conversely, a proposal most likely unacceptable to Western law enforcement and intelligence officials and legislators alike is one advanced by Haitham 'Abd al-Salam Muhammad. He argues that there are two types of terror – legal and illegal – and formulates a four-pronged method to arrive at a definition of each based upon Quranic texts, the study and analysis of a terror verse, texts relating to Islamic jurisprudence which mention terror and terror in legal praxis (istilah).[9] The problem with an Islamic definition – if one can find universal acceptance among Muslims, which may be as difficult to achieve as in the West – is that Muslims constitute a minority of the world's population. Imposing an Islamic definition on the rest of the world would thus expose it to the same criticism as Muhammad levels at the Western definition. Despite this shortcoming, Muhammad has made a valid point. A solution to the problem of producing a universal definition could be to engage in a cooperative effort launched by the United Nations, taking into consideration different cultural, social, legal and historic perspectives.

The definition of the term terrorism proposed and employed by the present author in this work is as follows: Terrorism is a systematic activity – physical, oral, visual or written – the purpose of which is to instill fear in individuals, organizations or governments, so as to achieve concessions in order to meet certain demands of a group, organization or government, which typically involve restrictions on civil liberties or the authority of a government. Furthermore, terrorism is an activity, which constitutes some form of threat – irrespective of whether an act is actually carried out or not. Terrorism can be selective or indiscriminate as to the implementation of the threat and perpetrated by individuals, organizations or states.[10] Terrorism in this context makes no distinction between cold weapons, fire arms, nuclear, biological, chemical or cyber weapons, but will use any means to achieve a specific end. The number of fatalities resulting from a terrorist attack is important, but it is not necessarily what makes it a terrorist act. When thousands of soldiers die on the battlefield, it does not normally qualify as terrorism; but if wounded soldiers are rounded up and killed after they have surrendered, it could be regarded as a terrorist act which would in a legal context amount to a war crime. Furthermore, it is not difficult to imagine a wealthy terrorist organization acquiring a nuclear weapon or a renegade nuclear scientist teaching it how to build one. A distinction which needs to be drawn, though, is the one between offensive and defensive use of nuclear weapons. If a state is on the verge of collapse as a result of foreign aggression, it will most likely consider resorting to a weapon of mass destruction. Such a situation will, however, probably not occur if a terrorist organization is in possession of a nuclear device, since it would most likely wish to use it offensively, at least if it is fighting a foreign adversary.

The point I am making here is that laws exist for warfare and types of violence which are acceptable. If terrorist groups or states violate such laws, particularly if they are international, they can possibly be labeled terrorists. The Nazi regime in the Third Reich generally did not violate its own laws, but it carried out terrorist acts against Germans and other nationalities in occupied territories, particularly in places where partisans were active.[11] Some scholars might argue that the Holocaust was technically not terrorism because the purpose was not to instill terror in a part of the German population but to eradicate it. However, the Holocaust can be considered terrorism on a uniquely massive scale, if one objective was to set a deterrent example for Germans who contemplated resistance to the Nazi regime or to instill terror in Jewish populations outside Germany. The same can be said about Nazi propaganda, the objective of which was to instill fear in Germans. Genocide was justified by falsely accusing Jews of instigating a worldwide conspiracy to eradicate the 'Aryan' race.[12]

An important purpose of this study is to provide a method to explore the minds of terrorists and the inner workings of their organizations. It does not purport to be a manual for how to defeat terrorism militarily, but rather to explain the arguments advanced by extremist propagandists and identify the weaknesses inherent in their writings. A second rationale for this work is to trace the evolution of terrorist thought and methodology over the centuries. Unlike a focus on one particular organization, society, or time period, a methodology which will most likely limit the applicability of findings and conclusions to a specific era or group, I have chosen an approach which casts the net wide, spanning centuries and different societies, religions and ideologies in order to establish whether any commonalities have withstood the test of time and technological advancements of the modern era. If terrorist groups which have evolved from very different social and cultural milieus evince striking similarities despite intervening centuries, this may be an indication that totalitarian ideologies and extremist interpretations of religions – particularly if certain commonalities pertain to ideology, modus operandi and their strengths and weaknesses – are predictable with regard to the aforementioned aspects. If this turns out to be the case, as argued in this work, it places a powerful weapon in the hands of societies which strive to reduce the appeal and dissemination of extremist ideas. The world's tragic experience with such ideologies, as implemented by organizations and states in the twentieth and twenty-first century, should constitute a very good reason for emphasizing the importance of a long-term historical approach to terrorism as a phenomenon, in particular, if such an approach can increase the preparedness of societies and individuals to neutralize the oftentimes extremely negative consequences of a lack of understanding of the nature and weaknesses of extremist thought. It is the objective of this study, as far as possible, to address these issues and draw attention to existing defects in our system of education.

For this project, I have conducted research in the archives of the Hoover Institution at Stanford University in Palo Alto for the Russian-language material (Okhrana) and in the National Archives in College Park (captured Nazi documents) and the Library of Congress (*Völkischer Beobachter*) for the German-language material. I have drawn upon Arabic-language primary sources such as the works of Abu Musʿab al-Suri, Abu Yahya al-Libi, Abu Bakr Naji, material published on the Internet by Islamic institutions and organizations and additional multilingual primary and secondary sources as well (French, Spanish, Italian, Czech, Danish and Norwegian). The detailed analysis of the ideologies and arguments of Al-Qaʿida and the Islamic State is based upon the contents of their magazines *Inspire* and *Dabiq*.

One strength of this work is that it focuses on a limited number of groups, organizations and states which can be labeled terroristic in accordance with the definition provided above. Instead of a brief discussion of a large number of such entities throughout history, this approach allows the author critically to examine each organization in great detail. Furthermore, the different time periods represented in the selection of terrorist groups ensure that valid conclusions can be reached relating to continuity in ideology and methodology. A third strength of this work is the detailed comparative approach to propaganda. Finally, an advantage which follows from the comparative approach laid out above is that this work will retain its relevance for some time even if some of the modern terrorist organizations examined here will disappear and be replaced by new groups, a claim confirmed by the conclusions drawn regarding continuity and similarities among terrorist groups irrespective of ideology, religion, cultural milieu and historical period.

Notes

1 Rohan Gunaratna, 'Terrorism in Southeast Asia -Threat and Response', in Gérard Chaliand and Arnaud Blin, eds., *The History of Terrorism: From Antiquity to Al Qaeda* (Berkeley: University of California Press, 2009), p. 430; Iain Lauchlan, 'Security Policing in Late Imperial Russia', in Ian Thatcher, ed., *Late Imperial Russia: Problems and Prospects. Essays in Honour of R. B. McKean* (Manchester: Manchester University Press, 2005), p. 46.
2 Nico Voigtländer and Hans-Joachim Foth, 'Nazi Indoctrination and anti-Semitic Beliefs in Germany', *Proceedings of the National Academy of Sciences of the United States of America*, Vol. 112, No. 26, (30, Jun., 2015), pp. 7931–7936, *NCBI Resources*, accessed 26 July 2019, https://www.ncbi.nlm.nih.gov/pmc/articles/PMC4491745/.
3 Greg Miller and Souad Mekhennet, 'Inside the Surreal World of the Islamic State's Propaganda Machine', *The Washington Post*, 20 November 2015, accessed 25 July 2019, https://www.washingtonpost.com/world/national-security/inside-the-islamic-states-propaganda-machine/2015/11/20/051e997a-8ce6-11e5-acff-673ae92ddd2b_story.html?noredirect=on&utm_term=.b962cfdb796c; Romesh Ratnesar, 'Islamic State Is Dying on the Battlefield - and Winning on the Internet', *Bloomberg Businessweek*, 20 July 2017, accessed 25 July 2019, https://www.bloomberg.com/news/articles/2017-07-20/islamic-state-is-dying-on-the-battlefield-and-winning-on-the-internet; Kristina Wong, 'US Officials Warn that IS has Created "Propaganda Machine"', *The Hill*, 4 September 2014, accessed 25 July 2019, https://thehill.com/policy/defense/216601-us-officials-warn-isis-has-created-propaganda-machine; Jane Harman, 'America Is Losing the Digital War against the Islamic State', *The Washington Post*, 17 July 2015, accessed 25 July 2019, https://www.washingtonpost.com/opinions/combating-a-digital-caliphate/2015/07/17/1045d716-2bf5-11e5-a250-42bd812efc09_story.html?utm_term=.09d7c2e10184.
4 Gérard Chaliand and Arnaud Blin, 'Introduction', in Gérard Chaliand and Arnaud Blin, eds., *The History of Terrorism: From Antiquity to Al Qaeda* (Berkeley: University of California Press, 2009), p. 7.
5 Randall D. Law, *Terrorism: A History* (Cambridge: Polity Press, 2009), p. 3.
6 Haitham 'Abd al-Salam Muhammad's, *Mafhum al-Irhab fi al-Shari'a al-Islamiyya* (Beirut: Dar al-Kutub al-'Ilmiyya, 2005), p. 12.

8   *Introduction*

7 Central Intelligence Agency, *News & Information*, accessed 19 June 2019, https://www.cia.gov/news-information/cia-the-war-on-terrorism/terrorism-faqs.html?tab=list-3.
8 'France's International Action against Terrorism', *France Diplomatie*, accessed 19 June 2019, https://www.diplomatie.gouv.fr/en/french-foreign-policy/defence-security/france-s-international-action-against-terrorism/.
9 Muhammad, *Mafhum al-Irhab*, pp. 30–42.
10 Some scholars, such as Ariel Merari, argue that it is important to distinguish between different types of violence or the term terrorism will be equally applicable to nuclear, conventional, and guerilla warfare as well, rendering the term meaningless, Ariel Merari, 'Terrorism as a Strategy of Insurgency', in Gérard Chaliand and Arnaud Blin, eds., *The History of Terrorism: From Antiquity to Al-Qaeda* (Berkeley: University of California Press, 2007), p. 16.
11 United States Holocaust Memorial Museum, 'Operation Anthropoid', *Holocaust Encyclopedia*, accessed 31 May 2019, https://encyclopedia.ushmm.org/content/en/article/lidice; Nick Fagge, 'I Despise them. Germany Is the Enemy: The Greek Survivors of Nazi Massacre Who Say "No" Vote Wasn't Just about Austerity but Continued Resistance against "Occupation"', *Daily Mail*, 8 July 2015, accessed 30 May 2019, https://www.dailymail.co.uk/news/article-3152216/I-despise-Germany-enemy-Greek-survivors-Nazi-massacre-say-No-vote-wasn-t-just-austerity-continued-resistance-against-occupation.html; '1944 Massacre in France: German Police Raid Homes of Six Former SS Soldiers', *Spiegel Online*, 6 December 2011, accessed 31 May 2019, https://www.spiegel.de/international/germany/1944-massacre-in-france-german-police-raid-homes-of-six-former-ss-soldiers-a-802019.html.
12 Adolf Hitler, *Mein Kampf* (Munich: Zentralverlag der NSDAP, Frz. Eher Nachf., G.m.b.H., 1943 first published 1925, Vol. 1 and 1927, Vol. 2), p. 703.

Bibliography

Central Intelligence Agency. *News & Information*. Accessed 19 June 2019. https://www.cia.gov/news-information/cia-the-war-on-terrorism/terrorism-faqs.html?tab=list-3.
Chaliand, Gérard and Arnaud Blin. 'Introduction'. In Gérard Chaliand and Arnaud Blin, eds. *The History of Terrorism: From Antiquity to Al Qaeda*. Berkeley: University of California Press, 2009, pp. 1–11.
Fagge, Nick. 'I Despise Them. Germany Is the Enemy: The Greek Survivors of Nazi Massacre Who Say "No" Vote Wasn't Just about Austerity but Continued Resistance against "Occupation"', *Daily Mail*, accessed 8 July 2015. Accessed 30 May 2019. https://www.dailymail.co.uk/news/article-3152216/I-despise-Germany-enemy-Greek-survivors-Nazi-massacre-say-No-vote-wasn-t-j'st-austerity-continued-resistance-against-occupation.html.
France Diplomatie. 'France's International Action against Terrorism'. Accessed 19 June 2019. https://www.diplomatie.gouv.fr/en/french-foreign-policy/defence-security/france-s-international-action-against-terrorism/.
Gunaratna, Rohan, 'Terrorism in Southeast Asia – Threat and Response'. In Gérard Chaliand and Arnaud Blin, eds. *The History of Terrorism: From Antiquity to Al Qaeda*. Berkeley: University of California Press, 2009, pp. 420–34.
Harman, Jane. 'America Is Losing the Digital War against the Islamic State', *The Washington Post*, 17 July 2015. Accessed 25 July 2019. https://www.washingtonpost.

com/opinions/combating-a-digital-caliphate/2015/07/17/1045d716-2bf5-11e5-a250-42bd812efc09_story.html?utm_term=.09d7c2e10184.

Hitler, Adolf, *Mein Kampf* [My struggle]. Munich: Zentralverlag der NSDAP, Frz. Eher Nachf., G.m.b.H., 1943 (first published 1925, Vol. 1 and 1927, Vol. 2).

Lauchlan, Iain. 'Security Policing in Late Imperial Russia'. In Ian Thatcher, ed. *Late Imperial Russia: Problems and Prospects. Essays in Honour of R. B. McKean*. Manchester: Manchester University Press, 2005, pp. 44–63.

Law, Randall D. *Terrorism: A History*. Cambridge: Polity Press, 2009.

Merari, Ariel. 'Terrorism as a Strategy of Insurgency'. In Gérard Chaliand and Arnaud Blin, eds. *The History of Terrorism: From Antiquity to Al-Qaeda*. Berkeley: University of California Press, 2007, pp. 12–51.

Miller, Greg and Souad Mekhennet. 'Inside the Surreal World of the Islamic State's Propaganda Machine'. *The Washington Post*, 20 November 2015. Accessed 25 July 2019. https://www.washingtonpost.com/world/national-security/inside-the-islamic-states-propaganda-machine/2015/11/20/051e997a-8ce6-11e5-acff-673ae92ddd2b_story.html?noredirect=on&utm_term=.b962cfdb796c.

Muhammad, Haitham 'Abd al-Salam. *Mafhum al-Irhab fi al-Shari'a al-Islamiyya* [The Concept of Terrorism in the shari'a]. Beirut: Dar al-Kutub al-'Ilmiyya, 2005.

Ratnesar, Romesh. 'Islamic State Is Dying on the Battlefield - and Winning on the Internet'. *Bloomberg Businessweek*, accessed 20 July 2017. Accessed 25 July 2019. https://www.bloomberg.com/news/articles/2017-07-20/islamic-state-is-dying-on-the-battlefield-and-winning-on-the-internet.

Spiegel Online. '1944 Massacre in France: German Police Raid Homes of Six Former SS Soldiers', 6 December 2011. Accessed 31 May 2019. https://www.spiegel.de/international/germany/1944-massacre-in-france-german-police-raid-homes-of-six-former-ss-soldiers-a-802019.html.

United States Holocaust Memorial Museum. 'Operation Anthropoid', *Holocaust Encyclopedia*. Accessed 31 May 2019. https://encyclopedia.ushmm.org/content/en/article/lidice.

Voigtländer, Nico and Hans-Joachim Foth. 'Nazi Indoctrination and anti-Semitic Beliefs in Germany'. *Proceedings of the National Academy of Sciences of the United States of America*, Vol. 112, No. 26, *NCBI Resources*, 30 June 2015. Accessed 26 July 2019. https://www.ncbi.nlm.nih.gov/pmc/articles/PMC4491745/.

Wong, Kristina. 'US Officials Warn that IS has Created "Propaganda Machine"', *The Hill*, 4 September 2014. Accessed 25 July 2019. https://thehill.com/policy/defense/216601-us-officials-warn-isis-has-created-propaganda-machine.

1 Ancient, medieval and early modern extremist movements

Introduction

Terrorism in one form or another has been a part of human history since ancient times. From an historical perspective, it is therefore appropriate briefly to touch upon three early movements from very different historical periods, leading up to the main focus of this volume on modern terrorism and extremist ideologies. The three movements examined in this chapter are the Jewish Sicarii of the first century C.E., the Isma'ili Nizaris (Assassins) of the Middle Ages and the Sunni Muhawwid (Wahhabi) movement of the eighteenth century. The comparative analysis offered in this chapter reveals that there are similarities between the Sicarii and Nizaris with regard to methodology. Furthermore, the three movements also display similar exclusivist interpretations of human interaction and religion. Finally, an examination of the Sicarii, Nizari and Muwahhid movements also yields surprising similarities between these militant extremist movements of the past and those of modern times despite the centuries and even millennia which separate us from those periods and notwithstanding the evolution of human societies.

Technological progress and advancements in science and education do not preclude the perpetuation of certain phenomena and the continuous appeal of intolerant and violent ideologies to some human minds. Ironically, human progress in many areas has placed ever more powerful means at the disposal of movements which oppose the moderate interpretations of religions, political ideologies and philosophies embraced by a clear majority of mankind. We know the latter claim to be true even without an opinion poll taken by every individual on this planet since most people have not joined militant organizations, which, in turn, is a major cause of concern for every such group or movement. As the present study progresses, the reader will find convincing evidence of the validity of both these claims, namely, that militant groups benefit from technological progress in society and that violent and exclusivist ideologies do not cease to appeal to certain individuals despite advancements in education. The fact that most human beings do not embrace violence as a lifestyle is without doubt reassuring, but the fact that increasingly powerful means have become easily accessible to adherents to

DOI: 10.4324/9781003260943-2

militant ideologies will appear as a serious challenge to the former assumption since it might actually drastically reduce the importance of numbers. Fortunately, an historical and critical approach to the study of terrorism allows us convincingly to demonstrate that the powerful technologies employed by militants to make the world fit into their ideological Procrustean bed may actually lead to their undoing. The obvious reason for this is that advanced technologies which enable discontented extremists to wage asymmetric warfare against enemies who possess superior resources might lead to an overemphasis on such technologies at the expense of other aspects of their cause and have a detrimental impact on their legitimacy.

The three movements briefly examined in this chapter can be described as revolutionary and traditional at the same time. First, they all resorted to violence in order to realize their political and religious agenda. Second, this militancy was justified by reference to a higher power – God – who had presumably sanctified coercion to rectify what was perceived as serious ills of society and religious misperceptions. Furthermore, the members of these movements saw themselves as guardians of the true religion, a fact which caused them to have very little patience with diversity and pluralism. As a result, they resorted to drastic measures to enforce conformity within each particular movement and the society at large. Moreover, the movements were revolutionary in the sense that they strove to overthrow the existing order by force but not to the extent that they wished to replace the old system with a new one. In this respect, the three movements were revivalist, since they attempted to reintroduce what their leaders believed was the original and unadulterated religion as opposed to the diluted contemporary religion and the immorality of society.

The Sicarii

The most detailed primary source on the Sicarii available to historians is Flavius Josephus's account of the movement. Despite this fact, Western scholars were long at variance over the identity of the Zealots and Sicarii, with traditional scholarship arguing that the two movements were one and the same. In the early twentieth century, some historians gradually came to distinguish between Zealots and Sicarii. Kirsopp Lake contended that Josephus had not used the term 'Zealots' in reference to a political party prior to 66 C.E. Lake therefore concluded that Josephus used the term when referring to a particular party which was not identical with the 'fourth philosophy', a movement founded by Judas of Galilee in 6 C.E., which later became the Sicarii. The misperception that the Zealots and Sicarii were identical probably arose from the term 'zeal' which must have circulated and been applied to individuals who did not belong to the party before the party derived its name from the term.[1] Richard Horsley concurs with the interpretation that Zealots and Sicarii were two different groups and argues that they were active in different parts of Judea and at different times of the Jewish

12 *Early extremist and militant movements*

Revolt against the Roman Empire 66–70 C.E.[2] Discontent with Roman rule and taxation had begun to grow as early as the beginning of the Common Era, when the Romans conducted a census in order to impose taxes on the Judean population. In opposition to these Roman activities, Judas of Galilee formed a protest movement the leadership of which was passed on to his son or grandson Menahem who became the leader of the Sicarii when an open revolt, the so-called Jewish War, erupted in 66 C.E.[3]

The major reasons for the Jewish War were economic, administrative and religious. The unrestrained building projects of the ruler before the Common Era and in the early years of the Common Era together with Roman double taxation and the tithe due to the priests for the upkeep of the Temple created a situation in which the population of Judea suffered greatly.[4] These hardships led Judas the Galilean to incite Jews to resist Roman control and the rule of their high priests in 6 C.E. His primary justification of this call for action was that the census that the Romans had decreed would result in slavery. The only way to prevent this from occurring was to rise up against the Romans. Judas's activities quickly earned him a death sentence, which was carried out.[5] Later in the first century, in the 60s C.E., the attempts of the Roman Procurator to run the affairs of the Temple, the High Priests' exploitation of the Jewish population and their cooperation with the Romans caused a popular uprising supported by the lower priests first against the upper echelons of the sacerdotal establishment and then against the Romans as well in 66 C.E. The main reasons for the Roman intervention in the revolt were the deteriorating security situation in the province and the insurgents' ban on offering sacrifices and gifts to the Roman Emperor in the Temple.[6] Several Jewish factions, amongst which were the Zealots and the Sicarii, were involved in the initial revolt against the high priests. In-fighting among the factions as a result of the oppressive rule of one of the leaders, Menahem, the son or grandson of Judas the Galilean, later led to the Sicarii withdrawing from direct involvement in the Jewish War, limiting their operations to the area surrounding their stronghold on Masada.[7] The religious rationale for Judas's incitement and the Jewish War in the 60s C.E. was the argument that God will not offer assistance unless Jews actively fight to address their suffering.[8] There were thus both religious and secular reasons for the unrest in Judea in the first century C.E.

The fourth philosophy, a doctrine espoused by Judas the Galilean, was the religious and ideological rationale for his movement in the early first century C.E. and his heirs, the Sicarii, of the 60s C.E. The four main pillars of this philosophy were the concept of oneness of God, establishment of the true kingdom of God, the idea that God's assistance in an undertaking can only be expected if the faithful themselves act and the exclusivist approach to anyone who does not embrace this doctrine.[9] The first pillar meant that recognition of the Roman Emperor equaled idolatry. The reason was that such recognition involved offering sacrifice to the emperor in the Temple, which implied usurpation of God's power and idolatry and a violation of God's law which commanded that Jews have no other god besides Yahweh.[10] Exodus states unequivocally that the punishment for such an act is the destruction of whomever offers the sacrifice.[11] According to Judas the Galilean, the second pillar, establishment of the kingdom of God, entailed human agency. If humans insisted on the realization of this notion, then God would see to it that it would come true.[12] The form of government which Judas and the Sicarii envisioned was most likely a theocracy, a conclusion that can be drawn based upon the movement's rejection of worldly rulers. The appointment of a theocratic ruler was clearly democratic in nature since the leader was selected by lot and not based upon hierarchic position or erudition.[13] Since Judas regarded idolatry as a serious sin, he decreed that resistance to alien rulers be considered a religious duty, being the first to do so.[14] In summary, the fourth philosophy constitutes clear evidence of continuity regarding religious doctrine between Judas the Galilean and his heirs the Sicarii, half a century later.

The 'pillars' discussed above harked back to earlier concepts in Jewish religion such as zeal and *herem*. The term zeal can be understood as a duty to implement Jewish law, including readiness to punish Jews who violate God's law. During the Jewish War, this duty was interpreted by many insurgents as a need to 'cleanse the people or the land of "apostate" Jews'.[15] The Old Testament contains precedents for the zeal embraced by the Zealots and Sicarii in the 60s C.E. to the effect that pious Jews were allowed to put to death Jews who disobeyed God's commands in return for which Yahweh promised salvation to the faithful. The difference between how zeal was applied in ancient times and in the mid-first century was, however, that some insurgents in the Jewish War added the interpretation that it could be used against Israel's external enemies as well.[16] Another concept from the Old Testament, closely related to zeal, is *herem*, Holy War. The war which God had commanded Jews to launch against the Canaanites to wrest control from them over the Promised Land. The Bible refers to the terror which *herem* was supposed to unleash on the Canaanites and the duty of Israel to 'destroy all persons with their property who remain in the land...'.[17] The Old Testament thus reveals the precedents for the terrorism of the first century C.E. in Judea.

This brings us to the final aspect of Sicarii motivation and activities – the movement's modus operandi. The Sicarii are generally renowned for their preferred weapon – the sica (dagger) – and infamous for assassinations of prominent citizens. They would assassinate their target in public places during the day and then feign indignation at the victim's death, thereby avoiding discovery. As a result, perpetrators could very often continue their activities undisturbed. After their first assassination, that of a high priest, numerous others followed, sometimes on a daily basis.[18] In addition to assassinations, the Sicarii, prior to abandoning Jerusalem, also resorted to kidnapping in order to force the release of incarcerated militants, and 'expropriation' of the wealth of prominent citizens, justifying these acts by claiming that they were carried out in retribution for the exploitation of the poor by the wealthy. These raids frequently targeted pro-Roman Jews inhabiting the surrounding countryside.[19] A further characteristic of Sicarii attacks was that they were invariably carried out against Jews only; Roman soldiers and civilians were not targeted.[20] Through their acts, the Sicarii expected to evoke sympathy because of the fatal torture they would be subjected to if caught while fighting for the oppressed.[21] Unlike the Sicarii in Jerusalem, those who had seized control of the fortress on Masada exclusively attacked the surrounding countryside, using terrorist tactics. A case in point is the town of Engedi which was attacked by the Masada-based Sicarii who plundered the town, massacring 700 men, women and children.[22]

The Sicarii on Masada turned out to be as willing to turn their weapons on themselves as using them against others. The argument that '[e]veryone who sheds the blood of godless men is like one who offers a sacrifice'[23] was a justification for killing 'violators' of God's law. By extension, offering oneself as a sacrifice was not an idea alien to the Sicarii. When faced with Roman conquest of their fortress, slavery and death, the Sicarii on Masada acted in accordance with other Sicarii who had fallen into the hands of Romans – they chose death. Some women and children who had hidden in the fortress survived the mass-suicide of the other members of the movement. Josephus, who was not present at their leader's speech prior to the suicide, reports that Eleazar encouraged the faithful with the statement that death liberates the soul from its imprisonment in the mortal body, allowing it to depart to a pure realm.[24] Eleazar's statement was consistent with the belief of the Sicarii that the kingdom of God would soon commence with peace and justice imminent.[25] The fact that a small number of survivors lived to tell the story reveals that not everyone in the Sicarii movement embraced the idea of a better existence through suicide.

The Nizaris (Assassins)

The Nizari Isma'ilis have attracted much attention of scholars and the general public since the Middle Ages, most likely as a result of their infamous reputation as drug-addicted assassins led by a morally depraved 'Old Man of the Mountain'. Centuries of Sunni anti-Isma'ili propaganda, Crusader legends and Marco Polo's account of the Nizaris had contributed to this negative legacy in addition to the assassinations carried out by Nizaris themselves during the two centuries of their activities in Persia and Syria. However, more recent scholarship has questioned the accuracy of the traditional account of Nizari history.[26] One scholar has contended that 'Marco Polo's text introduced sex, drugs, and illusion to the myth of the Assassins' Paradise...', and that this description of Nizari Isma'ilism greatly influenced and reinforced the negative Western perceptions of the sect.[27] Another scholar has argued that *hashishun* should not be understood in the way that traditional scholarship has interpreted the term. In the Middle Ages, the term was applied derogatorily without any connotations of drug addiction or use, roughly meaning 'low-class rabble'.[28] One should also add that the increase in terrorism in the Middle East particularly has contributed to the interest in the history, philosophy and methodology of medieval Nizari Isma'ilism.

The exceptional longevity of Nizari Isma'ilism is a clear testimonial to the skilled maneuverings of its leaders and the sect's ability to survive in a hostile political milieu without becoming marginalized. Nizari Isma'ilism emerged as a result of a succession struggle within the Isma'ili Fatimid caliphate. Following the death of the Fatimid caliph-imam in Cairo in 1094 C.E., a succession struggle erupted between two of his sons, al-Musta'li and Nizar. Nizar, the elder brother, was supported by many Persian Isma'ilis, but he was defeated and died in prison without leaving a son to claim the allegiance of the Nizaris who recognized Nizar as the legitimate Isma'ili Imam.[29] As a result, a rumor circulated that a son by a concubine had been born after Nizar's death. According to this story, this son had been taken to the Nizari fortress of Alamut in northern Persia near the Caspian Sea.[30] The rumor guaranteed, at least temporarily, the continuation of the Nizari imamate. With the takeover of the mountain fortress Alamut in 1090 C.E., the Nizaris' first leader Hasan-i Sabbah began to extend Nizari power by taking over fortresses in strategic locations in northern Persia and later in the eastern part of the Seljuq Empire and in Syria. To what degree the Nizaris were successful in their undertaking is evidenced by the fact that they controlled 70 forts in Quhistan (eastern Persia) and 35 in the Alamut region on the eve of the Mongol invasion in 1256 C.E.[31] The Nizaris had by then created their own state, controlling territory from Syria to eastern Persia and posing a serious challenge to other Muslim states in West Asia.[32] The last Nizari stronghold fell to the Mongols in 1270 C.E., and the western (Syrian) branch of Nizari Isma'ilism succumbed to the Egyptian Mamluks in 1273 C.E., 183 years after Hasan-i Sabbah's takeover of Alamut.[33]

The philosophy of Hasan-i Sabbah focused on the role of the Imam as the uncontested authority of the Islamic community. He rejected the Sunni institution of 'ulama (religious scholars and interpreters of Islam), emphasizing the sole authority of the Imam on all matters regarding Islam. Besides the Prophet Muhammad, only the Isma'ili Imam is qualified to fill this function. Furthermore, there is only one Imam in every age who meets the requirements for the position of Imam, and he is appointed by Allah. The problem with this argument with respect to the institution of the imamate is, of course, that an additional authority is needed to identify the Imam.[34] Sabbah attempted to address this weakness in his argumentation by contending that the authority of the Imam can be known by 'the nature of knowledge', not by something beyond the Imam himself. Sabbah's argument that reason ('aql) alone is not sufficient to establish the identity of the Imam leads him to conclude that '[t]he true imam does not seek extrinsic proofs for his authority or imamate, which is proved only by his own existence'.[35] Therefore,

16 *Early extremist and militant movements*

the "Imam" who bases his claim to sole authority on lineage or miracles is an impostor.[36] Sabbah insists that since his Imam is the only one who claims that he is his own *hujja*, proof of God, he is the true Imam.[37]

The weakness of Hasan-i Sabbah's position is, of course, that he does not consider the possibility of several individuals simultaneously advancing the same claim, to be the only true Imam, which is what happened after the death of the Fatimid caliph al-Mustansir. Moreover, his claim that an individual Imam is in no way bound by the decisions of a predecessor[38] has serious implications, at least from a Sunni perspective, since it implies that the Imam potentially has the authority to abrogate statements by the Prophet Muhammad. Finally, the Nizari who realizes the true spiritual nature of the Imam will abandon all his personal views and perceive everything in a way unaffected by his personal senses. He will live a completely spiritual life, which is the experience in the afterlife. This is the Nizari Paradise which is entered into through *qiyama* (resurrection). In this state, the believer experiences *haqiqa*, ultimate reality.

The violent acts of the Nizaris reflected the hostile political environment in the midst of which they lived. Their preferred method of dealing with enemies was to dispatch *fida'iyun* (those who sacrifice themselves) on suicide missions, particularly to assassinate Seljuq officials, a Zaydi Imam who was captured and burned, a Fatimid caliph and an Abbasid caliph. Seljuq counterterrorism measures consisted of massacring Isma'ilis in the cities where they were found in larger concentrations such as Isfahan in 1093 C.E. and 1101 C.E. and Aleppo in 1113 C.E. Furthermore, Nizari leaders who had been captured were sometimes skinned alive. This forceful government strategy was not very successful, however, since it only resulted in more violence.[39] Sometimes the response of the local population to Nizari activities was to massacre them. Such a reaction occurred in Damascus in 1111 C.E.[40] Nizari assassinations were intended to acquire as much publicity as possible, which is why they oftentimes occurred in a mosque or at the court of a prince where large gatherings of people occurred.[41] Another purpose of assassinations was to enable the *fida'iyun* to enter paradise through martyrdom, a fact which explains why the assassins did not attempt to flee.[42] The approach of the Nizaris to terrorism suggests that they were fanatically committed to their cause and that one reason for their zeal was persecution at the hands of other Muslims.

Nizaris applied two methods in particular to achieve their goals – conversion and deception. Assassins would sometimes pose as Turkish soldiers or disguise themselves as Sufis or Christian monks.[43] With respect to Nizari assassinations, one scholar has drawn attention to the moral aspect of this method of terrorism by emphasizing that it caused many fewer casualties than regular warfare and typically targeted individuals in official positions and not the poorer strata of the population.[44] There were, however, exceptions to this rule, for instance, when the Syrian Nizari leader, Sinān, sent *fida'iyun* to set fire to marketplaces in Aleppo.[45] Commenting on assassinations, another scholar has pointed out that they were often used in self-defense since Nizaris were subjected to persecution such as massacres occurring in major cities.[46] It is quite possible that Nizari missionary activities, which were not appreciated by Sunnis, caused some of the backlash against them. One indication of this is Nizari attempts to convert Muslims to their version of Islam based upon the rigid concept of 'total devotion or total enmity',[47] obviously an approach which is often met with resistance, but which nevertheless finds favor with totalitarian regimes. Efforts at converting groups and populations were, however, sometimes quite successful. Conversion of fortress garrisons was a strategy which often enabled the Nizaris to seize control of coveted military strongholds.[48] The Nizaris gradually extended their influence in the Seljuq Empire by organizing cells among sympathizers living in urban centers.[49] Much patience was involved when targeting a victim for assassination. The Nizaris would typically dispatch a *fida'i* to seek employment with an official in his household or office. Once established the agent would then work diligently and patiently to acquire the official's trust, whereupon he would seize a suitable opportunity to carry out his deadly mission.[50]

The Muwahhidun (Wahhabis)

The Muwahhid movement was launched in the Arabian Peninsula by Muhammad Ibn 'Abd al-Wahhab in the eighteenth century. Al-Wahhab's followers are better known under the name Wahhabis, but since this was originally a derogatory term used by their enemies, this study will use the terms Muwahhidun or ahl al-tawhid, which is what al-Wahhab's followers call themselves.[51] Many critical accounts of the movement's history and interpretation of Islam have been written both by Muslim and Western scholars. Not surprisingly, Muwahhid scholars have produced apologetic works on the legacy of their Imam, that is, Muhammad Ibn 'Abd al-Wahhab, but more recently, Western scholars as well have come to adopt a more balanced view on the history of the Muwahhidun and their 'strict' interpretation of Islam. Having initially spread across the Arabian Peninsula in the eighteenth and nineteenth centuries, the ideas of al-Wahhab later reached India and other parts of the world as well. In the twentieth century, many extremist Sunni groups frequently quoted al-Wahhab as justification for their jihad against non-Muslims and Muslims who disagreed with their extreme ideology which bans saint veneration and any form of *bid'a*, innovation, practices which the first generations of Muslims did not follow.

Muhammad Ibn 'Abd al-Wahhab, 1703 C.E.–1792 C.E., was a diligent student and interpreter of Islam and active preacher against any form of 'polytheism'. Following studies under his father, who was an Islamic jurist, he continued his Islamic education in Mecca and Medina, having memorized the Quran at the age of ten.[52] He later studied in Al-Basra, where he began preaching against superstition and intercession. These activities were met with disapproval by the population, as a result of which he was expelled from the city.[53] Following al-Wahhab's return to the Arabian Peninsula, he continued preaching and had to flee from the town where his father had served after the latter's death. He returned to his hometown 'Uyayna, where he was welcomed by the ruler, but had to leave, having incurred the ire of a powerful neighboring ruler who wanted him dead.[54] Al-Wahhab eventually settled in Dar'iyya, where he entered into an agreement in 1744 with the town's ruler, 'Abdul 'Aziz Ibn Sa'ud, guaranteeing al-Wahhab the position of religious leader and Ibn Sa'ud temporal power.[55] This proved a very successful alliance and the two embarked on a religious and political conquest of the Arabian Peninsula.

The conquests allowed al-Wahhab to spread his ideas to other parts of Arabia, converting Bedouins and townsmen to 'true' Islam and simultaneously creating enemies among the 'ulama and other Muslims who opposed his efforts to return Islam to its original 'pure' form. Many religious scholars left the territories controlled by the Muwahhidun for Iraq, where they persuaded Ottoman 'ulama to launch a propaganda war against al-Wahhab.[56] The expansion of Muwahhid-Sa'udi power in the Arabian Peninsula, a result of conquests of Riyadh in 1773, Mecca in 1803 and Medina in 1805, and incursions into Ottoman-controlled Iraq and Syria, eventually caused the destruction of the first Sa'udi state by 1818, since it posed a threat to a powerful enemy – the Ottoman Empire, whose caliph ordered Muhammad 'Ali, Pasha of Egypt, to recover territories lost to the Muwahhidun and eliminate the threat.[57] Having recovered Madina in 1812 and Makka in 1813, Muhammad 'Ali's forces destroyed the Sa'udi state, captured the Sa'udi ruler, Abdullah Ibn Sa'ud, and dispatched him to Istanbul to be beheaded.[58] The Muwahhidun proved quite resilient, however, and founded a second state, which existed between 1824 and 1891, following the Egyptian withdrawal.[59] In 1891, the Sa'ud dynasty was driven out from their capital in Riyadh by the Al Rashid tribe which occupied Najd until the Al Sa'ud regained control of Riyadh in 1902 and initiated a new period of expansion until the Sa'udi state with its present borders was established in 1932.

Like many other controversial figures, al-Wahhab's interpretation of Islam has attracted the attention of apologists as well as detractors. Al-Wahhab's works reflect his lack of patience with Muslims who violated Islam's central concept of *tawhid*, oneness of God. In *Kitab al-Tawhid Explained*, he emphasizes that *shirk*, association of partners with Allah, is 'the most dangerous of all sins',[60] a crime which will not be forgiven by Allah and the punishment for which is a permanent abode in Hellfire.[61] Interestingly enough, al-Wahhab here implies that the punishment for this serious sin is meted out by Allah, not by man. However, another passage in the book refers to a hadith stating that the punishment for adultery, apostasy or murder is death, a clear indication that it is to be carried out by man and not by Allah.[62] One of al-Wahhab's critics was his own brother, Sulaiman, who accused him of engaging in *ijtihad*, independent religious reasoning, without possessing the necessary qualifications.[63] Al-Wahhab responded by condemning Sulaiman as an enemy of religion. Sulaiman's fate – he died while under house arrest – suggests that al-Wahhab allowed Allah to execute the punishment. Another instance of 'leniency' on the part of al-Wahhab is his insistence that *mushrikun*, idolaters, should always be offered the opportunity to embrace true Islam (al-Wahhab's interpretation) before being fought.[64] An important reason why al-Wahhab encountered hostility on the part of many 'ulama was his de-emphasis of *taqlid*, imitation of the past. He argued that *ijtihad*, direct interpretation of the Quran and hadith, should take precedence over tradition.[65] His denunciation of corruption and nepotism in the ranks of the 'ulama further contributed to their hostility toward his teachings.[66]

Critics and apologists of al-Wahhab's teachings have continued their debate over his legacy into the twenty-first century. The Islamic Supreme Council of America has adopted a very critical position on al-Wahhab's interpretation of Islam, arguing that anyone who disagreed with his ideology was excommunicated, 'thus making the shedding of their blood and confiscation of their wealth permitted'.[67] This organization argues that modern extremists have fully embraced al-Wahhab's radical ideology, replacing Islam's traditional tolerance with a rigid ideology which they strive to impose upon Muslim and non-Muslim alike. Conversely, some modern Western scholars have favored a less critical interpretation of al-Wahhab's works, emphasizing that he was reluctant to resort to violence since it would make conversion more difficult, and that trade relations could be maintained with non-Muslims friendly to Muslims since the umma benefits from such interaction.[68] It has also been pointed out that al-Wahhab warned against lightly accusing a Muslim of hypocrisy for personal reasons or just because the accused holds a different opinion.[69] Furthermore, scholars have also emphasized that al-Wahhab did not always support Saudi military operations, and that Muwahhid 'ulama have, over the course of centuries, actually moved away from exclusivism toward a more accommodationist position on certain issues.[70] Finally, apologists of al-Wahhab's teachings have underscored that excesses occurred during Muwahhid-Sa'udi campaigns were not condoned by the religious and temporal leaders.[71] The debate between critics and apologists suggests that a balanced approach to al-Wahhab's teachings needs to be based upon distinguishing between the *'alim* (religious scholar) himself, his followers and the modern extremists who selectively quote al-Wahhab in support of their actions.

Methodology

Critics have argued that al-Wahhab and his followers caused much destruction and suffering as a result of their intolerance toward Muslims who refused to submit to al-Wahhab's version of Islam. It has been pointed out that examples of actions deserving of such criticism are the Muwahhidun's raids against the Iraqi cities of Karbala' and Al-Basra in 1801 C.E. which led to the tearing down of Shi'i shrines and killing of the population.[72] The people of Ta'if suffered a similar fate in 1803 when the Muwahhidun massacred the men of the town and enslaved the women and children.[73] There were, however, instances of relatively peaceful conquest, such as the Muwahhid capture of Riyadh in 1773, where the population was not massacred and forced conversions to al-Wahhab's 'true' Islam did not occur.[74] In territories controlled by the Muwahhidun, they strictly enforced al-Wahhab's ban on celebrating the Prophet's birth, the use of rosaries and constructing minarets and less radical interpretations of Islam.[75] Furthermore, in the nineteenth century, the Muwahhidun discouraged contacts with the Ottomans since they were considered idolaters. It is obvious from the above that critics tried to blame all actions of the Muwahhidun on al-Wahhab, but one should mention that many problematic actions and policies had not been sanctioned by al-Wahhab since they did not occur in his lifetime.

Conversely, apologists have emphasized that al-Wahhab initially used peaceful means to deal with his enemies, but changed tactics when they used violence against his followers. The argument has been advanced that this proves that al-Wahhab and his ally Ibn Sa'ud resorted to violence in order to defend themselves and their followers and that the excesses are blamed on new converts who were not familiar with 'proper Islamic methods of warfare'.[76] Furthermore, the Muwahhid expansion has been justified by the wish to unite Muslims in one Islamic state. It could, however, be argued that it is difficult to reconcile expansion and defensive warfare. One can suspect that Muwahhid leaders had other considerations than purely religious ones. The fact that they remained in occupied territories indefinitely points in this direction despite the claim that expansion occurred for the sake of Islamic unity. Finally, it is worth mentioning that al-Wahhab found the serious accusations leveled at him quite disturbing. He made efforts to dispel misperceptions and false claims advanced by contemporary critics about his teachings. In one letter, he dismisses the accusation that he declares an unbeliever anyone who does not profess obedience to him as mere slander. al-Wahhab underscores that he will declare those who associate others with Allah unbelievers, having first provided evidence to them of their error to offer them an opportunity to realize their error and repent.[77] It should be pointed out that this was indeed mere slander since it would be tantamount to a violation of *tawhid* and a serious case of *shirk*, polytheism, to demand Muslims' obedience to himself. Another false claim which al-Wahhab refuted was the accusation that he excommunicated Muslims who did not violate the concept of *tawhid*, oneness of God, but did not emigrate to Muwahhid-controlled territory.[78]

Similarities and differences

The brief discussion of the Sicarii, Nizari Isma'ilis and Muwahhidun in this chapter has revealed significant similarities and some differences between these three movements. One thing the three have in common is the exclusivist approach to other faiths. The conviction that they represented the only 'true' interpretation of their religion served as a blank check regarding the means they utilized to achieve their goal. This fact, in addition to persecution at the hands of opponents, enabled them to justify what would today be labeled terrorist acts, particularly in the case of the Sicarii and Nizaris, and to a much lesser extent with regard to the Muwahhidun, if at all under their first leader Muhammad Ibn 'Abd al-Wahhab, who emphasized dialogue and education over violence as the best way to leading Muslims gone astray back to the fold of true Islam, that is, *tawhid*. The use of the dagger by the Sicarii and Nizaris as their preferred weapon reveals an amazing consistency in terrorist methodology despite the intervening millennium. Interestingly enough, this 2000-year-old terrorist approach has recently been revived in Europe and Palestine by knife-wielding jihadis.[79] The two movements differed in an important respect, however, namely that the Sicarii 'recycled' their assassins, who often escaped by blending in with crowds, whereas the Nizaris made a point of actually getting caught, since this was a shortcut to martyrdom and a guaranteed place in heaven.[80] Unlike the two previous movements, some Muwahhidun engaged in what can best be described as state terrorism, as evidenced by their massacres of the populations in several cities which they attacked. As has been pointed out above, however, these atrocities were perpetrated by al-Wahhab's followers, who had obviously been radicalized after his death in 1792. The discrepancy between the teachings of the founder of the movement and his radical followers is not a unique phenomenon, a fact which will be discussed in the chapter on jihad in the context of modern extremist Islamic organizations' frequent reference to al-Wahhab's works.

The extent to which the above three organizations controlled territory, enjoyed popular support and cooperated with other extremists are other aspects of their activities worth mentioning. The Nizaris and Muwahhidun controlled actual states over a long period of time, in the case of the former – approximately two centuries and the latter have had their own state with certain interruptions since the mid-eighteenth century. Conversely, the Sicarii did not have a state of their own, but were temporarily part of a coalition which controlled territory during the uprising against the Roman Empire. Like the Sicarii, the Nizaris occasionally were not averse to cooperation, when they could benefit from such ties. The Muwahhidun had formed an alliance with a temporal ruler in 1744 and had no inclination to compromise on their interpretation of Islam for political gain, which effectively excluded cooperation with non-Muwahhidun. All three movements enjoyed popular support to a certain extent, but this did not last very long for the Sicarii, as a result of their terrorist acts against people deemed to be beyond the pale of 'true' Judaism, that is, anyone who happened to disagree with them. Neither the Nizaris nor the Muwahhidun enjoyed significant support in the context of mainstream Islam though the latter have exerted appeal to extremist groups in the twentieth and twenty-first centuries. Later chapters in this volume will demonstrate various degrees of continuity with regard to the similarities and differences between the three movements examined in this chapter.

Notes

1 Morton Smith, 'Zealots and Sicarii, Their Origins and Relation', *The Harvard Theological Review*, Vol. 64, No. 1 (Jan., 1971), pp. 3–4. See also Richard Horsley, 'The Zealots: Their Origin, Relationships and Importance in the Jewish Revolt', *Novum Testamentum*, Vol. 28, Fasc. 2 (Apr., 1986), p. 160.
2 Richard Horsley, 'The Sicarii: Ancient Jewish "Terrorists"', *The Journal of Religion*, Vol. 59, No. 4 (Oct., 1979), p. 436. Solomon Zeitlin drew the same conclusion in his article 'Masada and the Sicarii', *The Jewish Quarterly Review*, Vol. 55, No. 4 (Apr., 1965), p. 316.
3 Horsley, 'The Sicarii: Ancient Jewish "Terrorists"', p. 442.
4 Ibid., p. 446.
5 Martin Hengel, *The Zealots: Investigations into the Jewish Freedom Movement in the Period from Herod I until 70 A.D.*, transl. David Smith (Edinburgh: T. & T. Clark, 1989), p. 76.
6 David M. Rhoads, *Israel in Revolution: 6-74 C.E.: A Political History Based on the Writings of Josephus* (Philadelphia: Fortress Press, 1976), pp. 98–99; Hengel, *The Zealots*, p. 352.
7 Rhoads, *Israel in Revolution*, p. 106.
8 Hengel, *The Zealots*, p. 76.
9 Ibid., pp. 81, 306; Zeitlin, 'Masada and the Sicarii', *The Jewish Quarterly Review*, Vol. 55, No. 4 (Apr., 1965), p. 303.
10 Hengel, *The Zealots*, p. 104; Horsley, 'The Sicarii', p. 443.
11 *Exodus* 22.19, quoted in Hengel, *The Zealots*, p. 107.
12 Rhoads, *Israel in Revolution*, p. 49.
13 Horsley, 'The Zealots', p. 182.
14 Smith, 'Zealots and Sicarii', *The Harvard Theological Review*, Vol. 64, No. 1 (Jan., 1971), p. 5.
15 Rhoads, *Israel in Revolution*, p. 86.
16 Hengel, *The Zealots*, p. 149.
17 David C. Rapoport, 'Fear and Trembling: Terrorism in Three Religious Traditions', *The American Political Science Review*, Vol. 78, No. 3 (Sep., 1984), p. 669.
18 Horsley, 'The Sicarii', pp. 436, 438.
19 Ibid., pp. 440–441.
20 Ibid., p. 439.
21 Rapoport, 'Fear and Trembling', p. 674. Josephus states that the Sicarii preferred torture to death rather than swearing allegiance to the Roman emperor, Josephus, *De Bello Judaico*, 7, 418, in Hengel, *The Zealots*, p. 90.
22 Solomon Zeitlin, 'Masada and the Sicarii', *The Jewish Quarterly Review*, Vol. 55, No. 4 (Apr., 1965), p. 303.
23 Hengel, *The Zealots*, p. 85.
24 Zeitlin, 'Masada and the Sicarii', p. 304.
25 Josephus, *Antiquitates Judaicae* 18.23 and *De Bello Judaico* 7.417–19, in Horsley, 'The Sicarii', p. 443.
26 Shakib Saleh, 'The Use of Bāṭinī, Fidā'ī and Ḥashīshī', *Studia Islamica*, Vol. 82 (1995), p. 41.
27 Bruce Lincoln, 'An Early Moment in the Discourse of "Terrorism": Reflections on a Tale from Marco Polo', *Comparative Studies in Society and History*, Vol. 48, No. 2 (Apr., 2006), p. 253.

28 Farhad Daftary, 'The "Order of the Assassins": J. von Hammer and the Orientalist Misrepresentations of the Nizari Ismailis', *Iranian Studies*, Vol. 39, No. 1 (Mar., 2006), p. 74.
29 Marshall G. S. Hodgson, *The Secret Order of Assassins: The Struggle of the Early Nizari Isma'ilis Against the Islamic World* (Philadelphia, PA: University of Pennsylvania Press, 2005, first published in 1955), p. 62; Daftary, 'The "Order of the Assassins"', p. 73.
30 Hodgson, *The Secret Order*, p. 66.
31 Shafique N. Virani, 'The Eagle Returns: Evidence of Continued Isma'ili Activity at Alamut and in the South Caspian Region Following the Mongol Conquests', *Journal of the American Oriental Society*, Vol. 123, No. 2 (Apr.–June, 2003), p. 365.
32 Rapoport, 'Fear and Trembling', *The American Political Science Review*, Vol. 78, No. 3 (Sep., 1984), p. 664.
33 Farhad Daftary, *The Isma'ilis: Their History and Doctrines* (Cambridge: Cambridge University Press, 1990), pp. 324–325, 429.
34 Ibid., pp. 337, 369; Hodgson, *The Secret Order*, p. 59.
35 Daftary, *The Isma'ilis*, p. 370.
36 Hodgson, *The Secret Order of Assassins*, p. 59.
37 Ibid., 56.
38 Ibid., 59.
39 Daftary, *The Ismailis*, pp. 362, 373; Hodgson, *The Secret Order*, p. 103.
40 Hodgson, *The Secret Order*, p. 93.
41 Ibid., p. 114; Rapoport, 'Fear and Trembling', p. 665.
42 Rapoport, 'Fear and Trembling', p. 665.
43 Daftary, *The Isma'ilis*, p. 376; Bernard Lewis, 'The Ismā'īlites and the Assassins', in Marshall W. Baldwin, ed., *A History of the Crusades* (Madison: University of Wisconsin Press, 1969, I, second edition), pp. 111, 125.
44 Hodgson, *The Secret Order*, p. 84.
45 Lewis, 'The Ismā'īlites', p. 125.
46 Daftary, *The Isma'ilis*, p. 354; Hodgson, *The Secret Order*, 87; Lewis, 'The Ismā'īlites', pp. 113, 117; Shakib Saleh, 'The Use of Bāṭinī, Fidā'ī and Ḥashīshī', p. 36.
47 Hodgson, *The Secret Order*, p. 83.
48 Ibid., p. 85.
49 Rapoport, 'Fear and Trembling', p. 666; Lewis, 'The Ismā'īlites', p. 109.
50 Rapoport, 'Fear and Trembling', p. 666.
51 Talip Kucukcan, 'Some Reflections on the Wahhabiyah Movement', *As-Sunnah Foundation of America*, accessed January 26, 2018, http://sunnah.org/wp/2012/12/26/reflections-wahhabiyah-movement/.
52 Jalal Abualrub, edited by Alaa Mencke, *Wahhab, His Life Story and Mission* (Orlando, Florida: Madinah Publishers and Distributors, 2003), pp. 56–58, 66.
53 Ibid., p. 71.
54 Ibid., pp. 74, 87.
55 Helmtraut Sheikh-Dilthey, 'Dariyyah: Das Herz Saudi-Arabiens', *Anthropos*, Vol. 84, No. 1/3 (1989), p. 142.
56 David Commins, *The Wahhabi Mission and Saudi Arabia* (London: I.B. Tauris, 2006). Accessed January 24, 2018, http://asrdiplomacy.ir/wp-content/uploads/2017/03/The-Wahhabi-Mission-and-Saudi-Arabia-Book-1.pdf, p. 3.
57 Ibid., pp. 33, 40; Jacques Benoist-Mechin, *Arabian Destiny*, trans. by Denis Weaver (London: Elek Books, 1957, pp. 48–54, in Scheikh-Diltey, 'Dariyyah', p. 143); Abualrub, *Wahhab*, pp. 103, 114, 124.
58 John E. Peterson, *Historical Dictionary of Saudi Arabia* (Metuchen, NJ: Scarecrow Press, second edition, 2003, p. 66, in Abualrub, *Wahhab*, p. 180.
59 Sheikh-Dilthey, 'Dariyyah', p. 143.

24 *Early extremist and militant movements*

60 Muhammad Ibn Abdul Wahhab, *Kitab at-Tawheed Explained*, explanation compiled and translated by Sameh Strauch (Riyadh: International Islamic Publishing House, 2000, second edition), p. 29.
61 Ibid., p. 32.
62 Ibid., p. 15.
63 Commins, *The Wahhabi Mission*, p. 22. Also, al-Wahhab's father and grandson rejected his teachings, Commins, *The Wahhabi Mission*, pp. 57–58.
64 Husain Ibn Ghannam, *Tarikh Najd*, p. 477, referred to in Commins, *The Wahhabi Mission*, p. 25.
65 Natana J. DeLong-Bas, *Wahhabi Islam: From Revival and Reform to Global Jihad* (New York: Oxford University Press, 2004), pp. 12–13; John Voll, 'Muḥammad Ḥayyā al-Sindī and Muḥammad ibn 'Abd al-Wahhab: An Analysis of an Intellectual Group in Eighteenth-Century Madīna', *Bulletin of the School of Oriental and African Studies, University of London*, Vol. 38, No. 1 (1975), p. 32.
66 DeLong-Bas, *Wahhabi Islam*, p. 31.
67 Islamic Supreme Council of America, 'Islamic Radicalism: Its Wahhabi Roots and Current Representation', *ISCA*, accessed January 26, 2018, https://www.islamicsupremecouncil.org/understanding-islam/anti-extremism/7-islamic-radicalism.
68 DeLong-Bas, *Wahhabi Islam*, pp. 17–18; Muhammad Ibn 'Abd al-Wahhab, *Kitab al-Jihad*, p. 379, in DeLong-Bas, *Wahhabi Islam*, p. 82.
69 Elizabeth Sirriyeh, 'Wahhabis, Unbelievers and the Problem of Exclusivism', *Bulletin (British Society for Middle Eastern Studies*, Vol. 16, No. 2 (1989), p. 131.
70 DeLong-Bas, *Wahhbi Islam*, p. 35; Abdulaziz H. al-Fahad, 'Commentary. From Exclusivism to Accommodation: Doctrinal and Legal Evolution of Wahhabism', *New York University Law Review*, Vol. 79, No. 2 (May 2004), pp. 487, 516.
71 Abualrub, *Wahhab*, p. 198.
72 Ondrej Beranek and Pavel Tupek, 'From Visiting Graves to their Destruction: The Question of Ziyara through the Eyes of Salafis', Crown Paper 2, July 2009, *Crown Center for Middle East Studies*, p. 20. Accessed January 24, 2018. https://www.brandeis.edu/crown/publications/cp/CP2.pdf; Sheikh-Dilthey, "Dariyyah," p. 143; Kucukcan, "Some Reflections," p. 64.
73 Al-Jabarti, *'Aja'ib*, 3:373, referred to in Commins, *The Wahhabi Mission*, p. 31.
74 DeLong-Bas, *Wahhabi Islam*, p. 36.
75 Kucukcan, 'Some Reflections', p. 64; Commins, *The Wahhabi Mission*, p. 3.
76 Abualrub, *Wahhab*, pp. 101, 172.
77 Muhammad Ibn 'Abd al-Wahhab, *Majmu' mu'alafat al-shaikh Muhammad Ibn 'Abd al-Wahhab*, 7/60, Arabic text reproduced in Abu Iyaad, 'Muhammad Bin Abd Al-Wahhaab and the Claim of Takfir of the Muslim Masses – Part 3: Takfir Based Upon Mere Absence of Obedience', August 22, 2011, *Wahhabis.com*, accessed January 26, 2018, http://www.wahhabis.com/print.cfm?umzta.
78 Muhammad Ibn 'Abd al-Wahhab, *Majmu' mu'alafat al-shaikh Muhammad Ibn 'Abd al-Wahhab*, 'Fatawa wa Masa'il', 4/11, Arabic text reproduced in Abu Iyaad, 'Muhammad Bin Abd Al-Wahhaab and the Claim of Takfir of the Muslim Masses – Part 4: Takfir and Hijrah', 23 August 2011, *Wahhabis.com*, accessed 26 January 2018, http://www.wahhabis.com/print.cfm?qhybo.
79 'Man seriously hurt in Jerusalem knife attack released from hospital', *The Times of Israel*, 12 June 2019, accessed 17 June 2019, https://www.timesofisrael.com/man-seriously-hurt-in-jerusalem-knife-attack-released-from-hospital/.
80 Gérard Chaliand and Arnaud Blin, eds., *The History of Terrorism from Antiquity to Al Qaeda* (Berkeley: University of California Press, 2007), p. 70; Bernard Lewis, *The Assassins: A Radical Sect in Islam* (New York, NY: Basic Books, 2003), p. xii.

Bibliography

Abualrub, Jalal, edited by Alaa Mencke. *Wahhab, His Life Story and Mission*. Orlando, Florida: Madinah Publishers and Distributors, 2003.

Baldwin, Marshall W., ed. *A History of the Crusades*. Madison: University of Wisconsin Press, 1969, I, second edition.

Benoist-Mechin, Jacques. *Arabian Destiny*. Translated by Denis Weaver. London: Elek Books, 1957.

Beranek, Ondrej and Pavel Tupek, 'From Visiting Graves to their Destruction: The Question of Ziyara through the Eyes of Salafis'. Crown Paper 2, July 2009, *Crown Center for Middle East Studies*. Accessed January 24, 2018. https://www.brandeis.edu/crown/publications/cp/CP2.pdf, pp. 1–34.

Commins, David. *The Wahhabi Mission and Saudi Arabia*. London: I. B. Tauris, 2006. Accessed 24 January 2018. https://citeseerx.ist.psu.edu/viewdoc/download?doi=10.1.1.1010.4254&rep=rep1&type=pdf.

Daftary, Farhad. *The Isma'ilis: Their History and Doctrines*. Cambridge: Cambridge University Press, 1990.

Daftary, Farhad. 'The Order of the Assassins: J. von Hammer and the Orientalist Misrepresentations of the Nizari Ismailis'. *Iranian Studies*, Vol. 39, No. 1 (March 2006), pp. 71–81.

DeLong-Bas, Natana J. *Wahhabi Islam: From Revival and Reform to Global Jihad*. New York: Oxford University Press, 2004.

al-Fahad, Abdulaziz H. 'Commentary. From Exclusivism to Accommodation: Doctrinal and Legal Evolution of Wahhabism'. *New York University Law Review*, Vol. 79, No. 2 (May 2004), pp. 485–519.

Hengel, Martin. *The Zealots: Investigations into the Jewish Freedom Movement in the Period from Herod I until 70 A.D.* Translated by David Smith. Edinburgh: T. & T. Clark, 1989.

Hodgson, Marshall G. S. *The Secret Order of Assassins: The Struggle of the Early Nizari Isma'ilis against the Islamic World*. Philadelphia: University of Pennsylvania Press, 2005; first published in 1955.

Horsley, Richard. 'The Sicarii: Ancient Jewish "Terrorists"'. *The Journal of Religion*, Vol. 59, No. 4 (October 1979), pp. 435–58.

Horsley, Richard. 'The Zealots: Their Origin, Relationships and Importance in the Jewish Revolt'. *Novum Testamentum*, Vol. 28, Fasc. 2 (April 1986), pp. 159–92.

Islamic Supreme Council of America. 'Islamic Radicalism: Its Wahhabi Roots and Current Representation'. *ISCA*. https://www.islamicsupremecouncil.org/understanding-islam/anti-extremism/7-islamic-radicalism.

Kucukcan, Talip. 'Some Reflections on the Wahhabiyah Movement'. *As-Sunnah Foundation of America*. Accessed January 24, 2018. http://sunnah.org/wp/2012/12/26/reflections-wahhabiyah-movement/.

Lewis, Bernard. 'The Ismāʿīlites and the Assassins'. In Marshall W. Baldwin, ed., *A History of the Crusades*. Madison: University of Wisconsin Press, 1969, I, second edition, pp. 99–132.

Lincoln, Bruce. 'An Early Moment in the Discourse of "Terrorism": Reflections on a Tale from Marco Polo'. *Comparative Studies in Society and History*, Vol. 48, No. 2 (April 2006), pp. 242–59.

Mencke, Alaa. *Wahhab, His Life Story and Mission*. Orlando, Florida: Madinah Publishers and Distributors, 2003.

Peterson, John E. *Historical Dictionary of Saudi Arabia*. Metuchen, NJ: Scarecrow Press, second edition, 2003.

Rapoport, David C. 'Fear and Trembling: Terrorism in Three Religious Traditions'. *The American Political Science Review*, Vol. 78, No. 3 (September 1984), pp. 658–77.

Rhoads, David M. *Israel in Revolution: 6–74 C.E.: A Political History Based on the Writings of Josephus* Philadelphia: Fortress Press, 1976.

Saleh, Shakib. 'The Use of Bāṭinī, Fidā'ī and Ḥashīshī'. *Studia Islamica*, Vol. 82, No. 2 (1995), pp. 35–43.

Sheikh-Dilthey, Helmtraut. 'Dariyyah: Das Herz Saudi-Arabiens' [Darriyya: Heart of Saudi Arabia]. *Anthropos*, Vol. 84, No. 1/3 (1989), pp. 141–54.

Sirriyeh, Elizabeth. 'Wahhabis, Unbelievers and the Problem of Exclusivism'. *Bulletin (British Society for Middle Eastern Studies*, Vol. 16, No. 2 (1989), pp. 123–32.

Smith, Morton. 'Zealots and Sicarii, their Origins and Relation'. *The Harvard Theological Review*, Vol. 64, No. 1 (January 1971), pp. 1–19.

Virani, Shafique N. 'The Eagle Returns: Evidence of Continued Isma'ili Activity at Alamut and in the South Caspian Region Following the Mongol Conquests'. *Journal of the American Oriental Society*, Vol. 123, No. 2 (April–June 2003), pp. 351–70.

Voll, John. 'Muḥammad Ḥayyā al-Sindī and Muḥammad ibn 'Abd al-Wahhab: An Analysis of an Intellectual Group in Eighteenth-Century Madīna'. *Bulletin of the School of Oriental and African Studies, University of London*, Vol. 38, No. 1 (1975), pp. 32–39.

Wahhab, Muhammad Ibn Abdul. *Kitab at-Tawheed Explained*. Explanation compiled and translated by Sameh Strauch. Riyadh: International Islamic Publishing House, 2000, second edition.

al-Wahhab, Muhammad Ibn 'Abd. *Majmu' mu'alafat al-shaikh Muhammad Ibn 'Abd al-Wahhab* [Collective works of Shaikh Muhammad Ibn 'Abd al-Wahhab], 7/60. Arabic text reproduced in Abu Iyaad, 'Muhammad Bin Abd Al-Wahhaab and the Claim of Takfir of the Muslim Masses - Part 3: Takfir Based Upon Mere Absence of Obedience'. 22 August 2011. *Wahhabis.com*. Accessed January 26, 2018. http://www.wahhabis.com/print.cfm?umzta.

Zeitlin, Solomon. 'Masada and the Sicarii'. *The Jewish Quarterly Review*, Vol. 55, No. 4 (April 1965), pp. 299–317.

2 Was Russian terrorism a true instrument of the people?

Introduction

The 53 years between 1861 and 1914 constituted a period of fluctuating revolutionary activity in tsarist Russia. Ironically, this activity culminated with the assassination of the most reform-minded tsar, Alexander II, in 1881. The tsar had ascended the throne after the death of his arch-conservative and militaristic father, Nikolai I, in 1855. A milestone in his reign was the Emancipation Edict of 1861, the abolition of serfdom in Russia, which earned him the title 'the Liberator'. However, the edict did not result in full economic freedom for the peasantry. Landowners received no compensation from the state for the serfs whom they had lost, which led to peasants becoming indebted to the state for loans to purchase land. Furthermore, many peasants found themselves having access to less land than before the reform because the state allowed landowners to keep land at the expense of the peasants, fearing a backlash from the former if they perceived the redistribution of land as unjust. Despite its numerous defects, most peasants and educated Russians rendered their support for the reform.[1] Conversely, in the cities, criticism of the regime among workers and students increased in the 1860s. Russia's economic backwardness compared to Western Europe, the continued privileges of the aristocracy, discontent among university students and the autocratic system of government were some of the causes of anti-regime sentiments.

In addition to the Emancipation Edict, Alexander introduced educational reform, an initiative which led to higher education becoming much more accessible to young Russians than previously. Unfortunately, for the regime, this had the unintended effect of turning universities into political hotbeds.[2] The fact that students were not free to engage in political activities on campus did not constitute a serious obstacle since they simply formed clandestine groups. This resulted in mass arrests in 1861, but when students were released from prison a few months later, some of them embraced the concept of 'khozhdenie v narod', going to the people,[3] in order to educate the peasants and incite uprisings against the regime, realizing that the prospects for reform were very bleak under the present system of government. However,

DOI: 10.4324/9781003260943-3

the peasants, suspicious of the young people from the cities, were not very susceptible to the students' anti-regime message of *Zemlia i Volia*, land and freedom, which was also the name of the movement. In consequence, the students, temporarily abandoned the idea of a mass uprising, returned to the cities and decided that Russia's peasants needed to be inspired to rise up against the regime by other means than words.[4]

Many young revolutionaries believed that 'propaganda of the deed'[5] was the best way to awaken the masses. One young man, Sergei Gennadievich Nechaev, ardently embraced the concepts of terror and conspiracy, organizing a circle of students before he escaped to Switzerland accused of the murder of a member of his circle in 1869. A decade later, a new organization was formed, *Narodnaia Volia*, the People's Will. Like Nechaev, its members advocated terror as an effective means to achieve regime change in Russia. In 1881, *Narodnaia Volia* appeared to have achieved a great 'victory' with the assassination of Tsar Alexander II.[6] Contrary to the terrorists' expectations, however, the regime did not collapse and Russians did not rise up. The result of the assassination was a government clamp-down on revolutionary organizations, and the movement did not recover until the early twentieth century when a new terrorist party was formed, *Partiia sotsialistov-revoliutsionerov*, the PSR or the Party of Socialist Revolutionaries (PSR).

This chapter examines the concept of violence as a means to achieve political, social and economic objectives, mainly focusing on the populist ideology of *Narodnaia Volia* and the *PSR*. The question whether terrorist ideology changed over the course of the period under discussion will be addressed as well as justifications for terrorism advanced by revolutionary organizations in the latter half of the nineteenth and early twentieth century.

Ideology

A revolutionary pamphlet written in Switzerland in 1869 by the nihilist Sergei G. Nechaev and published under the title *Katekhizis Revoliutsionera*, Catechism of the Revolutionist, constitutes an early reflection of the extreme ideas circulating in parts of Russian society in the 1860s. It is unclear to what extent the noted anarchist Mikhail A. Bakunin contributed to the catechism, but it seems to reflect certain of his anarchist ideas.[7] This is not surprising since Nechaev frequently visited Bakunin during his stay in Geneva. The pamphlet is a 26-point manifesto that lays out the program of a violent revolutionary organization, *Narodnaia Rasprava*, the People's Retribution and the convictions of a young revolutionary who has severed all ties to traditional society and conventional morality:

> (1) The revolutionary is a doomed person. He has no interest of his own, no private affairs, no feelings, no attachments, no property, not even a name. He is completely absorbed by one ... passion—revolution. (2) He has severed all ties with the civil order, the educated world, all laws ...

and morality of this world. He is to it a merciless enemy, and if he continues to live in it, then it is ... to destroy it only. (3) The revolutionary knows one science only, the science of destruction. (4) He despises public opinion ... Moral to him is anything that furthers the revolution. Immoral and criminal is anything which prevents it. (5) He must be prepared to die every day. He must teach himself to endure torture. (6) ...All tender, effeminate feelings of kinship, friendship, love, gratitude, and even honor, must be suppressed in him by the single, cold passion for the revolutionary cause. (9) Revolutionary comrades ... shall, as far as possible, discuss all major affairs together and decide upon them unanimously. (10) When it comes to the execution of a series of destructive acts, each [revolutionary] shall act alone and only resort to the advice and assistance of comrades when this is necessary for the success [of an undertaking].[8]

The *Katekhizis* testifies to the fact that the revolutionary, as Nechaev perceives him, differs from most other human beings.

The excerpt above from the pamphlet gives the reader a general idea of Nechaev's approach to revolutionary activity. It is obvious that revolutionary work should not be undertaken lightly and is not for the faint of heart. The revolutionary has to expel all human feelings from his heart and avoid becoming emotionally attached to anyone. Every activity a revolutionary engages in is for the benefit of the revolution. The expression 'to be married to a cause' truly reflects such a philosophy. Nechaev's hatred for current Russian society seems to equal that of Bakunin for the state, with both focusing on destruction. The rejection of conventional social and moral norms seems to place the revolutionary above censure for 'reprehensible' comportment since such norms apply only to individuals who accept them as guidelines for moral behavior. From the revolutionary's perspective, this is an obvious advantage, which facilitates justification of terrorism, since revolutionary acts can only be judged by those who support them, a conclusion confirmed by point four above. In all honesty, this is a position which any party to a conflict or dispute can take, and does take, and it has not just been exploited by Russian nineteenth-century terrorists. The warning that the revolutionary has to be prepared to die testifies to a revolutionary perception that the movement is involved in a war and is indubitably a reference to future terrorist acts, confirmed by point ten. Point nine stands out in the catechism to the extent that it is a clear reference to a democratic decision-making process within the organization regarding the execution of terrorist acts upon which all members of a group have to be agreed. The ideas expressed in the catechism are not Nechaev's originally, but reflect the contemporary nihilist discourse. Interestingly enough, the author of the pamphlet never carried out a terrorist act against the state himself, though he discussed the execution of such acts.[9] This makes Nechaev an unusual terrorist. Another point on which the pamphlet differs from later terrorist activities is its emphasis on the individualistic approach to terrorism. Later, terrorist acts were generally the result of teamwork and not individualistic operations.[10]

The later points of the Catechism address issues such as assistance, dissimulation and the role of the state. The question of assistance to comrades who have been arrested (point 11), a moral issue for many, is treated from an exclusively utilitarian perspective in the catechism. Personal feelings must not play a role in deciding whether to rescue the revolutionary but only to what extent a rescue would benefit the revolution. Interestingly enough, Nechaev himself did not violate this revolutionary precept. Whilst a prisoner at the Peter-Paul Fortress in St. Petersburg, he actually declined an offer to be rescued, emphasizing that an attempt on the life of the tsar was more important.[11] Point 14 underscores the importance of dissimulation as a means to infiltrate different social classes and government institutions, including the secret police. The impersonal recommendations in the early points make complete sense in the context of revolutionary 'warfare', since the revolutionary is less vulnerable without a true personality and history, something realized and exploited by spies and agents in different eras. The reference to the total destruction of traditional culture and society in the earlier points is deemed deserving of renewed attention, which is why the author returns to this theme in the second half of the catechism – a true revolutionary must strive for the total destruction of the state. As if to dispel suspicions that such an agenda might lead to a totalitarian society, Nechaev reassures the reader that the revolutionaries do not intend to impose a system on the people against its will, explaining that the people itself will build the new society. The issues to which this paragraph has drawn attention suggest that the author of the catechism is much more preoccupied with the revolutionary struggle and the destruction of the current social order than with the task of building the future society.[12]

Some readers will perhaps find the excerpt above reminiscent of Niccoló Macchiavelli's *The Prince*, but there is a fundamental difference between the two. The prince rejects generally accepted norms for human interaction exclusively for the sake of his own benefit, and his overriding objective is to remain in power. The revolutionary rejects generally accepted norms for human interaction because he views these norms as an impediment to the realization of his mission, namely, literally to destroy the old order based upon oppression, injustice and exploitation of the poor and replace it with a new society based upon justice and equality. However, in the case of Nechaev, his intolerance of dissent and suspicion of strong personalities and intellectuals[13] suggest that he, to a certain extent, shared the selfish motivations of Macchiavelli's ruler.

In a co-written article, Nechaev and Vladimir Serebrennikov criticize the old order and European socialists. The two authors convey good tidings to their readers, claiming that a social crisis is approaching in Europe and that the old order is living out its last days.[14] The foundations of the old society are flawed since they are 'false and contrary to human nature. They have merely led to disasters and suffering of the masses, granting happiness and prosperity to a small number of privileged individuals only...'.[15] The justification for revolutionary action against this order is thus that it is based on the whip and the bayonet. However, previously the struggle has not been very successful since it has been more focused on talk than action. The authors conclude that it is not surprising that such incompetence has not yielded positive results. Success is, however, guaranteed because the revolutionaries for whom Nechaev and Serebrennikov speak have adopted a correct approach.[16] According to the two authors, a new era has dawned for the revolutionary struggle, and it will differ from the old approach through its use of terror.

Revolutionaries such as the Russian anarchist Mikhail A. Bakunin drew the public's attention to the important role of the army in the revolution. He depicts the revolutionary struggle in his appeal *To Officers of the Russian Army* as a struggle between the Romanov-Holstein-Gottorp state and the Russian people between the Tatar-German yoke and the Slavic will. Bakunin's interpretation of contemporary Russian history is that the people are fighting against a foreign enemy within the country. For good measure, he links the regime to the much reviled two-century Mongol rule in Russia, implying that the Romanov dynasty has Germany's, not Russia's, best interests at heart and that the tsar's rule is as brutal as that of the Mongols in the thirteenth–fifteenth centuries.[17] This is an appeal playing on suspicion of foreigners and the traumatic experience of Mongol rule, a message meant to persuade nationalist Russian officers to support the revolutionary struggle against the regime. Bakunin emphasizes that no one can remain sitting on the fence because neither side tolerates such individuals, implying that neutrals will be treated as enemies. These will be exiled abroad to 'earn their livelihood in the sweat of their brow', if their 'crimes' are minor.[18] However, 'tormentors of the people' will have to pay the ultimate price for their crimes. If the army stands with the people, the revolution will result in minimal bloodshed. Conversely, if the armed forces side with the 'butchers', the result will be utter destruction. Bakunin argues that the army will play a key role in the future revolution, adding that the future will not hold a pleasant fate in store for those who make the wrong choice or no choice at all.

Bakunin proposes that a secret organization, the Committee, be formed to lead the people toward the revolution since they are not yet aware of the power which they possess, a fact which, in turn, is the reason why the regime has not yet fallen. The Committee's members must renounce their love of power and private property, work exclusively for the benefit of the people and subordinate their own will to that of the collective. It is expected that a member will not withdraw from the organization since this might pose an existential threat if the member is subjected to torture by the regime in order to extract information.[19] It is quite possible that this was Nechaev's justification for the murder of a member of his own organization. However, according to this reasoning, anyone, member or not, is a potential security risk since there is no guarantee that a member will not fall into the hands of the secret police, a fact which obviously completely undermines the validity of the argument. Bakunin also warns against 'the empty talk of parliamentarians' in the Committee because excessive verbosity constitutes an obstacle to quick action.[20] Finally, his vision of the future revolutionary society is of one that grants complete freedom and equality to all men and women, a society based on common social property and common work.

In 1878, the populist organization Zemlia i Volia, Land and Freedom, published a document laying out its political philosophy. The movement's end objectives are stated as 'anarchy and collectivism'. However, realities show that these goals cannot be immediately achieved, a fact which necessitates a transitional period. The movement therefore proposes that all land be transferred to those who work it with their hands and that most land be owned communally. Furthermore, a peasant administrative unit, the *mir*, should play a leading role in determining functions and powers to be transferred to local authorities. Also, Zemlia i Volia realizes that many ethnic groups have been incorporated into the Russian Empire against their will and states that it is the intention of the movement 'to contribute to a division of the current Russian Empire into parts in accordance with local wishes'.[21] It is unclear whether this simply meant far-reaching local autonomy or an actual breakup of the empire with full independence for ethnic minorities. Whatever the intention was, this was a very unusual idea in an age ruled by empires in the West as well as in the East. The program of Zemlia i Volia states that it can only be implemented if the tsarist government is overthrown, arguing that this can be done by helping disaffected groups to organize and unite with revolutionary organizations and by weakening the power of the state. This, in turn, will be achieved by initiating contacts with workers and liberals. Ideological differences should thus not constitute an obstacle to temporary cooperation with other progressive forces. Zemlia i Volia also mentions the importance of establishing cells in the military and converting individual bureaucrats to their program. Terrorism is not emphasized in the program. The only terrorist threat mentioned is the fate that awaits the most harmful regime representatives – elimination.[22]

Organizational structure

Under Narodnaia Volia's (NV) leaders, terrorism was a centrally planned activity. The organization's plan for the revolution was simple and straightforward. The leaders argued that several terrorist attacks shall be coordinated, resulting in the death of 10–15 government officials. This is sufficient to provoke panic in government circles, causing division. The chaos will prompt the 'masses' to take action. Combat groups will launch an uprising, seizing control of key government institutions. A precondition for a successful revolution is a strong presence of the party in the provinces. This will enable the revolutionaries to call upon the 'masses' to rise up at short notice or at least to refrain from supporting the regime during the uprising. NV realizes the importance of preventing intervention of European powers in support of the regime and believes that this can be achieved by massive popular support for the revolution or lack thereof for the regime.[23] The stance of the 'masses' will thus send a clear signal to other powers that intervention is a doomed undertaking.[24] In order to achieve its objectives, NV must thus create a central combat organization (CO), a provincial revolutionary organization, ensure the support of industrial workers, appeal to the armed forces for support, secure the participation of the intelligentsia in the revolution and win over European public opinion to the revolutionary camp.[25] NV's revolutionary plan reveals that its leaders believed that a revolution can be successfully executed only if meticulously planned under the strict leadership of the Executive Committee, an approach to terrorism differing radically from earlier individualistic terrorist acts executed with minimal support of an organization.

NV's successful attempt on the life of Alexander II had serious and unforeseen consequences for the party organization. Contrary to the expectations of the NV, the assassination of the tsar was not the *coup de grâce* to the regime, but, ironically, it was a deathblow to the Executive Committee of the party owing to subsequent arrests.[26] NV activities had been very centralized prior to the assassination, but the control over local groups was now eliminated. To a certain extent, this loss of authority was a positive development since local groups could devote more attention to agitation and share less resources with the center. Furthermore, less centralization made it easier for the revolutionaries to avoid detection by the secret police.[27] Another positive development from the revolutionaries' perspective was also most likely that the secret police had to spend more resources on surveillance than earlier with the disappearance of central NV control.

An Okhrana report on revolutionary parties in Paris reveals the importance the tsar's secret police attributes to the presence abroad and organizational structure of Russian terrorist organizations and parties. The most active of these parties is the PSR. The author of the report, a police agent, describes the PSR as a very violent party, the goal of which is the complete destruction of the Russian regime and current society. The party's means of action are: *action dirècte* (direct revolutionary action), to cause unrest among peasants, workers, students and military personnel and to carry out expropriations assassinations and terrorist acts. The highest organ of the party is the Central Committee (CC), which does not really exist. In reality, the party is headed by the International Delegation based in Paris. Since 1911, it has seven members, one of whom is Mark Natanson. Several non-members assist the party in disseminating its propaganda. Party funds are used to disseminate revolutionary propaganda, facilitate the return to Russia of revolutionaries, provide them with counterfeit passports and plan terrorist acts in Russia. The report concedes that the Okhrana does not possess much information about Russian anarchists. There are four groups in

Paris: the Anarcho-Communists, Yudich-Strechende, the anarchists of the *Anarchist Tribune* and the Anarcho-Syndicalist German Communist Jews of Russia. In addition to the aforementioned, there are groups of independent anarchists.[28] The report suggests that the Okhrana had more agents assigned to surveillance of the PSR than of other revolutionary parties and organizations since it was perceived as a greater threat to the regime. Another possibility is that surveillance and infiltration of the PSR were easier than that of other parties and groups. The fact that the leader of the PSR's CO in Paris had been an Okhrana agent for years seems to corroborate this assumption. It is obvious that the Okhrana focused its attention on the PSR in Paris in the early twentieth century and that the government in St. Petersburg accepted that the Okhrana's office there did not provide very detailed information about other revolutionary groups.

Justification of terrorism

Justifications of terrorism appear with increasing frequency toward the end of the 1870s. In an anonymous apologia for terrorism entitled 'Death for a death', written by Sergei M. Kravchinskii and published by Zemlia i Volia shortly after the assassination of General Nikolai V. Mezentsev, chief of the Third Department (secret police), the author describes his successful attempt on the life of the general. On 4 August 1878, Kravchinskii walked up to the chief of the Third Department, stabbed him in the back and managed to escape.[29] Kravchinskii writes in his piece that the goal of the revolutionary socialists is to eliminate economic inequality, presumably the origin of human suffering. He argues that the party initially did not want to shed blood, but that it was forced by the tsarist regime to tread the path of terror: 'The government itself has placed the dagger and revolver in our hands'.[30] The revolutionaries consider murder to be a terrible act, but have to resort to it to rescue the people from the brutal oppression of the regime. The murder of Mezentsev was not meant to be a demonstration of the capabilities of Zemlia i Volia or a result of the post that he occupied, but a result of his crimes against the people and the abuse suffered by incarcerated revolutionaries at his hands. The implication is that revolutionaries do not kill without a valid reason and that their acts reflect the law of cause and effect. Kravchinskii's justification reveals that, in the 1870s, there were certain moral restraints associated with terrorism. It is important to note that his purpose is to demonstrate that, unlike the representatives of the regime, the revolutionaries possess a sense of morality. The author goes on to warn the regime that it should expect a response from the revolutionaries commensurate with the measures it takes, in other words – the crueler its repression, the more merciless the revolutionary response. Concurrently, the article ends with an olive branch held out to the regime, implying a possible resolution to the problem of terrorism – introduction of freedom of speech and of the press, cessation of administrative arbitrariness and amnesty for all political prisoners, irrespective of type of crime or nationality.[31] The purpose is obviously to demonstrate that the revolutionaries are reasonable and responsible citizens and not bloodthirsty fanatics. The conclusion that the author wants the reader to draw is that the revolutionaries have proposed a resolution to the crisis and that the ball is in the government's court.

There were other voices in Zemlia i Volia whose support for terrorism was much weaker. In an editorial published in the newspaper *Zemlia i Volia*, somewhat after Kravchinskii's anonymous article referred to above, the author discusses the prospect of a victory for the revolution, arguing that socialism is an irresistible force, thus implying an ultimate victory for the popular movement:

> Only the faith in serving all of humanity is able to provoke that ardent and purely religious fanaticism which inspires socialists and makes them irresistible and invincible, because persecution itself turns for them into a source of the highest bliss on earth—the bliss of martyrdom and self-sacrifice.[32]

This quote is reminiscent of much more recent statements made by Islamic extremists, particularly with regard to so-called suicide bombings.[33] However, there is a major difference between the above quote and such statements, namely the absence of a reference to suicide bombings in the quote. Conversely, the reference to martyrdom suggests that the latter is the result of some form of struggle. A subsequent passage clarifies that this is the case:

> By directing all our energy toward the struggle, we will, of course, greatly accelerate its [the regime] fall. But then, lacking roots in the people, we will not be in a position to exploit our victory... At the price of a bloody struggle, and, indubitably, heavy sacrifice, we will not gain anything for our cause.[34]

The passage reveals that the author considers terror to be one means of struggle among many others. There is a great danger associated with an over-emphasis on terror at the expense of efforts intended to create a popular support base. Nothing will be gained from a revolutionary program which focuses exclusively on terror and excludes work among the people.

A leading member of NV who wholeheartedly embraced terror was Nikolai A. Morozov. He contends that

> [p]olitical murder is above all an act of retaliation ... [I]t is the only means of self-defense under current conditions and one of the best agitational approaches. When a blow is delivered at the very center of the government apparatus, it causes, with terrible force, the whole system to shudder... Political murder is the most terrible weapon for our enemies, a weapon against which neither terrible armies nor legions of spies will help.[35]

Morozov appears to make a strong case by arguing that terror constitutes an act of self-defense. The lack of civil liberties, the tsarist regime's brutal suppression of dissent and the economic exploitation of the poorer strata of the population are realities that convincingly confirm the author's claim. When it comes to the presumably seriously negative impact on the regime of terrorist acts, one must conclude, however, that Morozov overstates his case. It is true that assassinations forced the government to introduce martial law, order Cossacks to patrol city streets and dispatch policemen to villages, but terrorist acts did definitely not 'cause the whole system to shudder'.

Morozov's argumentation suffers from other weaknesses as well. Like many other terrorists, he was convinced that terrorism would lead to the collapse of the regime. The assassination of Tsar Alexander II proved that this was an erroneous assumption. Alexander II was a relatively 'liberal' tsar compared to other Russian rulers, and he was succeeded by Alexander III who was convinced that terrorism should be countered with violence administered by the state.[36] The change in head of state thus resulted in a reactionary regime instead of a weakened one inclined to make concessions to the revolutionaries. Another weakness of Morozov's argumentation is the apparent contradiction that in order to protect the Russian people against tsarist oppression the revolutionaries must resort to terrorist acts, a method which, at least in the case of Alexander III, only increased oppression and persecution of revolutionaries. The traditional argument advanced by terrorists is that increasingly repressive measures taken by the state will provoke a backlash among the population and result in the overthrow of the regime, when this policy reaches a breaking point. This might work to a certain extent as long as the revolutionaries enjoy popular support. However, if they resort to indiscriminate violence to fight the regime, there will be civilian victims and if the number of such victims is not kept at a minimum, popular opinion might turn against the terrorists. A potential third weakness in Morozov's and other terrorists' position is that time might actually work against and not for them. If the revolutionaries promise that the increased state repression will only last for a limited time, say a year or two, and then be followed by a system of government based on civil liberties, the public might be persuaded to accept the suffering. Conversely, if the promise of freedom is not fulfilled, the population might not be willing to accept indefinite suffering which could partly be blamed on terrorist acts. Terrorism will then prove to be a double-edged sword, offering the government an opportunity to make its case.

In his pamphlet *Terrosisticheskaia bor'ba*, The Terrorist Struggle, published in Geneva in 1880, Morozov has not changed his optimistic view on terrorism. He draws the reader's attention to the asymmetric power relation between the regime and revolutionaries, with the former having at its disposal enormous resources in its struggle against a small number of revolutionaries. Despite this unequal relationship between the two adversaries, the terrorists possess a clear advantage over the state, namely their 'strong and terrible energy'.[37]

Another strength of the terrorists is their secret societies, against which soldiers and bayonets are presumably useless. This is not a correct statement since the secret police, at least in its Okhrana version, was quite successful in infiltrating revolutionary movements.[38] It is worth mentioning that revolutionary groups were successful in infiltrating government ranks as well. A third advantage of terrorist groups, according to Morozov, is their ability to act with surprise in ways that the regime cannot anticipate. This assumes, of course, that the secret police has not placed its agents in revolutionary groups. Furthermore, Morozov emphasizes the difference between earlier and contemporary terrorist methodology, arguing that terrorists rarely survived an attack in earlier eras, whereas modern terrorists 'disappear without a trace'[39] to carry out many more attacks.[40] The historical dimension also comes to the fore when Morozov pays tribute to the French Revolution and Saint-Just, who argued that 'every man has a right to kill a tyrant'.[41] A 25-year prison sentence made Morozov turn away from his original positive view on terrorism and focus on an academic career in science instead.[42]

The debate about terror continued among revolutionaries of the twentieth century following the forming of the Partiia sotsialistov-revoliutsionerov PSR in 1901.[43] In a statement published in *Znamia Truda* in 1907, the PSR announces that it only recognizes political and no other types of terror as a weapon used against the regime and that it should be directed at government representatives. However, there were exceptions; private individuals who consistently 'violated their neutrality' in the war against the government could occasionally be targeted. The statement clarifies that the exceptions to PSR policy on terror did not include theorists who support the government, even if they have excused violence against the people. Furthermore, terror against private persons is admissible only if it is sanctioned by the party's oblast' [regional] committee. The authors of the statement add that *agents provocateurs* and police spies are exempt from the ban. The statement clearly reflects the PSR's wish to impose restrictions on political violence and its opposition to indiscriminate terror against 'enemies'.[44]

Like political terror, the so-called agrarian and factory terror was a hotly contested issue among Socialist Revolutionaries (SRs).[45] The PSR CC official position was unequivocal. In an announcement in the party organ, *Znamia Truda*, the PSR stated that

> agrarian and factory terror is completely inadmissible ... when undertaken as a means of resolving economic disputes between the working people and exploiters... The destruction and damaging of private property during the economic struggle, with the intention of inflicting economic loss for the opposing side, must not be carried out by party organizations.[46]

This is a clear statement that the party leadership does not condone such acts.[47] A year later, the PSR still found it necessary to clarify its stance on factory terror. The party argued that it was not practical to subject a whole social class to terror because this class occupied a key position in economic life. Accordingly, factory terror could not prevent shutdowns of factories. It would only result in dismissal of workers, depriving them of their livelihood and causing division in their ranks. The PSR recommends strikes or boycotts as weapons in disputes with landowners. It declares that terrorism is part of the PSR's arsenal only when the regime denies the people its civil rights. Therefore, the party only recognizes political terror, but not economic (agrarian and factory) terror as a weapon.[48] Anna Geifman argues that party leaders did not enforce the ban and looked the other way when capitalists were attacked.[49] One has to wonder, however, why the PSR leaders felt that they had to make their position known a second time, if they were not serious. It would have been easier not to remind members of the ban, if it were not intended to be observed. Moreover, the restrictions imposed on political terror referred to above suggest a party line which was not limited to agrarian and factory terror. A possible explanation is that the CC feared that its control over local groups would be undermined, if it did not plan and sanction most terrorist acts. The *raison d'être* of the PSR CC in Paris would disappear, if too much autonomy was transferred to local groups. Furthermore, the CC needed funds to continue its activities, and some of that money came from Russia. If the flow of money dried up, the CC would find it difficult to continue to operate.

The Azef affair of 1909 sparked an intensified debate about terrorism over the next several years. Evno Azef, head of the PSR's terrorist wing, the CO, was exposed as an Okhrana (secret police) agent in 1909. This was a serious blow to the PSR and the CO, which Azef had headed for several years, exploiting his position to inform the Okhrana of planned terrorist acts and provide the secret police with names of revolutionaries involved in terrorist activities. An Okhrana memorandum reports that the CO position, as a result of the Azef affair, has been weakened and that the PSR CC, against the wishes of the CO has attempted to assert control over the terrorist wing, which had enjoyed near complete freedom of action before 1909 and therefore had come to regard terrorist activities as its prerogative. According to the author of the memorandum, numerous arrests and several failed terrorist acts in 1909 had also contributed to the CO's weakened position.[50] In addition, criticism was also directed at Boris Savinkov, a leading member of the CO and Russia's most (in)famous terrorist, for his depiction in his memoirs of terrorists with their flaws, something that would not improve the PSR's image and had prompted the CC to ask him to revise his memoirs or leave the party. Another problem that the CC was facing was the challenge from the Regional International Committee, the leaders of which argued that the Azef affair had completely discredited terrorism as a policy and that there was no guarantee that this would not happen again in the future. A second argument advanced by the group was that the existence of the Duma (Russian parliament) made terrorism an anachronism.[51]

A different approach to terrorism was promoted by Feliks V. Volkhovskii, a member of the PSR CC. He advocated a combined approach to the revolution, involving both terror and uprisings. For this purpose, the party needed to enlist the peasantry and armed forces through propaganda. Furthermore, Volkhovskii proposed that party members undergo training in military skills. This was a popular idea in certain PSR circles in southern Russia and Moscow and had been discussed in the party organ *Znamia Truda*, No. 39 (most likely) 1911 and repeatedly requested in letters to the editor.[52] A PSR member had been dispatched to Russia to meet these requests. Volkhovskii's proposal reveals that there were forces in the party in spite of the pressure in the wake of the Azef affair for a discontinuation of terror that advocated a clear militant component in the war against the tsarist regime. Moreover, the memorandum shows that Okhrana analysts deemed these forces quite active, planning several assassinations of prominent government officials and therefore posing a credible threat despite the anti-terror forces within the party.

The debates about terrorism had by 1912 resulted in the emergence of three different factions in the PSR. Among the leaders of the 'leftist' group were Chernov, Volkhovskii and Savinkov. The 'rightists' were Avksentiev among others. Finally, two of the leaders of the third faction, the so-called 'conciliatory' group were Natanson and Gots. Interestingly enough, two women, Vera Samoilova and Inna Rakitnikova, played a prominent role in this group, but not in the others. The 'leftists' supported the old position on terrorism and repeated the familiar arguments of NV. They refused to abandon terrorism, contending that centrally directed and mass terror will help create a popular mass movement, which, in turn, will lead to uprisings. Terror has so far created uncertainty and disorganization in government circles. Furthermore, terror is of great agitational importance since '[i]t will awaken in all oppressed segments of the people revolutionary energy and power of initiative, and strengthen the striving for struggle'.[53] The old arguments that revolutionary terror against government officials is a defense against government terror and that it will force the government to grant concessions and eventually hand over power to a popular constituent assembly are repeated by the 'leftists'. Conversely, the 'rightists' rejected these arguments, contending that terror has neither a disorganizing nor an agitational function because government supporters do not fear bombs, terror has not caused chaos in the government and the people are not in need of agitation. The last point is not very convincing since the 'rightists' have not provided an explanation.[54]

The 'conciliatory' SRs are, according to the Okhrana report, 'as ardent terrorists as the "leftists"',[55] but they advocate a temporary cessation of terrorist activities since the party has not executed any terrorist acts in a long time and will not do so in a near future, arguing that such an initiative will produce unity in the party. However, this group will consider allowing SRs who are able and wish to carry out terrorist acts to do so in the name of the

'Social-Revolutionary Combat Group', but not in the name of the CO of the PSR.[56] One can conclude from the aforementioned that the purpose of the 'conciliatory' ambiguity is to get the most uncompromising 'leftist' terrorists onboard to display a unified stance on terror. It is, however, doubtful that another combat group than the PSR CO taking credit for terror acts would divert attention away from the PSR. It is difficult to conceive of anyone who would be deceived regarding the responsibility for a terror act since the name of the alternative organization includes 'Social-Revolutionary'. Furthermore, if a terror act were executed in contravention of a temporary ban, it would reveal division instead of unity, an obvious weakness in the eyes of the public or the organization's enemies. It would also indicate lack of authority on the part of the PSR CC. In summary, the arguments advanced by the 'conciliatory' SRs demonstrate the difficulty of adopting an approach based on the saying 'having your cake and eating it too'.

Participation in elections to the Duma was another issue upon which different PSR factions disagreed. The 'leftists' rejected participation because the regime did not allow full freedom of speech, the press and assembly during pre-election campaigns. This would presumably perpetuate the rule of great landowners and capitalists, thus preventing real peasant and workers' representatives from being elected. The main reason for their opposition to participation in elections was, according to the Okhrana report referred to above, that it would result in the imposition of a moratorium on terror, albeit temporary. Like the 'leftists', the 'rightists' had earlier, before the third Duma (November 1907), rejected participation in elections, but were now arguing that the PSR should seize the opportunity the Duma offered to propagate social revolutionary ideas legally. Conversely, the 'conciliatory' camp rejected both participation and boycott, opting for disseminating printed propaganda. The 'rightists' argued that the PSR must change with the times and accept abandoning the status of a conspiratorial underground party with a small group of leaders controlling it. The PSR must now accept becoming a mass-organization and abandon its conspiratorial past for good. Despite the different stances the PSR factions took on terror and the Duma, they had one thing in common – all three agreed on the importance of printed propaganda, already publishing or planning to publish their own periodicals.[57]

If moderate forces were gaining sway in the PSR, they were much less influential in the anarchist movement. The most extreme exponents of anarcho-communism, the so-called *bezmotivniki*, argued that there was no need for justifying terrorism. The goal of these anarchists was the complete destruction of contemporary society, which would be achieved by means of *bezmotivnii terror*. Anyone serving the government, irrespective of function, deserved to die, and so did anyone deemed to be an 'exploiter'. With such an approach to political violence, it comes as no surprise that many anarchists expressed approval of Nechaev's ideas. Had Nechaev not died in jail, however, he might not have reciprocated since many anarchists emphasized collective over individualistic terrorist acts[58] and did not necessarily attempt to rescue incarcerated comrades based on utilitarian considerations, but emotional. A reason for the strong support for terror among anarchists could be that some groups had coopted criminals, who did not necessarily subscribe to the theoretical goals of the anarchist movement. Individuals from a criminal background could have joined the movement for personal and selfish reasons, which, however, was not in consonance with the *Catechism of the Revolutionist*.

The future society

The subordinate role of terror in Zemlia i Volia's program, discussed earlier in this chapter, conceals the divergent views on the issue which existed within the movement and would lead to the forming of a splinter party in 1879, *Narodnia Volia*, a strong advocate of terrorism. In its program, NV states that it will liberate the people from the autocratic regime in a revolution, the aim of which is to transfer power to the people. A constituent assembly elected in free elections will implement the will of the people. Universal suffrage, popular representation, regional autonomy, independence of the *mir*, people's ownership of the land, transfer of factories to the workers and the creation of a territorial army in lieu of the standing army will guarantee the implementation of the will of the people. Additionally, Narodnia Volia envisions a society based on freedom of expression, assembly, the press and to form associations. Terrorism is an integral part of the party's program for achieving these objectives.[59] Generally speaking, the program is quite similar to that of Zemlia i Volia discussed above. Like Nechaev and Serebrennikov's article analyzed above, an article authored by Nokolai Morozov, a NV leader, is imbued with optimism. It agrees with the two authors of the aforementioned article that the monarchy is experiencing its last days and that its brutal rule will soon be over.

Russian terrorists only infrequently provide details on the society they envision after the successful revolution. Lev A. Tikhomirov, a NV leader, states in an article published in the journal *Vestnik Narodnoi Voli* that the party's seizing of power following the revolution is only a temporary measure. The purpose of this step is to create conditions which will allow Russians to build a free society. The provisional government's main task is to prevent forces hostile to the revolution to resume political and economic exploitation of the people. It is obvious from Tikhomirov's justification of a temporary seizing of power that he expects hostile forces to attempt a counter-revolution, an assumption which makes sense and provides a good reason for the measure. Unlike the Bolsheviks, NV does not envision a future where the party would remain in power for the foreseeable future. The party will adopt a hands-off approach to governing and refrain from involvement in the people's efforts to build the new society. Tikhomirov answers the critics who argue that the society which he envisions will eventually collapse and revert to the previous system that 'the relative equality and relative political-economic independence of the people, created by the revolution ... are sufficiently strong to create a fully democratic government'.[60] The NV leader contends that state ownership of the land and the right to use it granted only to those who work it will effectively prevent the nobility and bourgeoisie from regaining control of society. Tikhomirov does not address the possibility of a power grab. All party activities have so far been controlled and organized by the leadership group of the party. What guarantees are there that the group will not wish to continue the system which it has already become accustomed to? The author's failure to go into detail on checks and balances in the new society creates a weakness in his argumentation which can be exploited by his critics.[61]

For obvious reasons, the tsarist regime was even less inclined than the revolutionaries to discuss the shape of future Russian society. The reluctance of the regime to consider reforms, flexibility or even negotiations with the revolutionaries is a clear indication that it considered the tsarist system to be perfectly suited to meet the needs of Russian society. This rigid position had to be temporarily abandoned as a result of the debacle in the Russo-Japanese War 1904–1905, when tsar Nikolai II was compelled to concede a constitution and a parliament, the Duma, to his subjects. Despite these concessions, terrorism continued to plague Russia, but proved unable to overthrow the government. Another disaster, the Great War, eventually brought about the change that terrorism had failed to achieve for five decades – the collapse of the tsarist regime. One could thus argue that it was the failure of the regime despite the benefit of hindsight to learn the obvious lesson of the past, namely, to avoid a repeat of 1905 at any cost and not to be drawn into a new war, which caused the collapse of the tsarist system and not revolutionary terrorism.

Conclusion

We have followed the Russian terrorist discourse over a period of half a century. The examination of the intra-organizational and -party debates during this period has led us to make a number of important observations: First, the brutality of the ideas presented in *Catechism of the Revolutionist* was generally not perpetuated through the decades, except in the case of a small number of anarchist groups, in which criminal elements played an important role. The reason is perhaps that the author, Sergei Nechaev was a nihilist, meaning that he rejected moral values. This gave him complete freedom to act because he was not bound by the same rules and values as the rest of humanity including most fellow revolutionaries. This was his guiding principle, not just in theory, which was the case of nihilist litterateurs, but, in practice, as well, a fact which made him an extremely ruthless individual, basing his actions on utilitarian and not on moral principles. Second, the continued justifications of terrorism in revolutionary pamphlets suggest that the public was not as willing as many revolutionaries to accept terrorism as a means to achieve an end. Third, the great number of attempts to justify terrorism suggests that the proponents of this approach to revolutionary struggle were working very hard to convince the public of the necessity of resorting to political violence in order to build a new society. Fourth, the internal debates in revolutionary organizations regarding the strengths and weaknesses of terrorism reveal continuity over a period of decades as well. Fifth, these ongoing debates also show that proponents and critics of terrorism accepted certain democratic rules of the game and were allowed freely to express their opinion. Sixth, the debates themselves reflect continuity since they lasted throughout the period under discussion. Seventh, the decreasing Socialist Revolutionary support for terrorism, particularly in the wake of the Azef affair in 1909, reflects changing attitudes with respect to terrorism as an effective weapon in the service of the revolutionaries despite the fact that some anarchist groups continued to advocate terrorism. Eighth, in the 1870s, there were certain moral restraints associated with terrorism. It is important to note that Kravchinskii's purpose was to demonstrate that, unlike the representatives of the regime, the populist revolutionaries possessed a sense of morality. In the early twentieth century, such restraints were considerably weakened, only completely to disappear in certain anarchist groups, which expressed admiration for Sergei Nechaev's nihilistic approach to revolutionary activity. Ninth, the detailed examination of Russian terrorist ideology in this chapter has revealed that a basic argument of all terrorist organizations in pre-1917 Russia, that their war against the government would lead to its eventual collapse suffered from a fundamental flaw – it was an erroneous assumption. It took the regime's lack of action and misguided policies, most important of which were the involvement in two wars, to achieve what the terrorists could not achieve – the destruction of the tsarist system. Whether the successor regime was a success or not is another question. Certainly, from the perspective of SRs and anarchists, and perhaps the nihilists as well, the Bolshevik state proved to be an even greater disaster than the ancient regime. Terrorism was possible under the tsarist regime, but it took a revolutionary Bolshevik regime which was willing to unleash state terror to silence all opposition.

In conclusion, to what extent can the question whether Russian revolutionaries were an instrument of the people be answered? The revolutionaries were convinced that they were. The objective of most Russian terrorists, namely, to build a society which ensured and protected the civil rights of every citizen, appears to confirm the conviction that the terrorists were acting in accordance with the wishes and interests of the Russian people. Unlike Nazi and modern Islamic extremists, most Russian terrorists did not advocate the establishment of a dictatorship, but they nevertheless employed similar means to achieve their end. However, in spite of the agenda of Russian extremists, it could be argued that they constituted an elite to a certain degree separated from the majority of Russians living in rural areas, as evidenced by the initial difficulties the revolutionaries had in convincing peasants to rise up against the tsarist regime.

Notes

1 Adam B. Ulam, *Prophets and Conspirators: Prerevolutionary Russia* (New Brunswick and London: Transaction Publishers, 1998, first published in 1977 by Viking Press), pp. 80, 91.
2 Chaliand and Arnaud Blin (eds.), *The History of Terrorism: From Antiquity to Al Qaeda* (Berkeley: University of California Press, 2007), p. 137.
3 Ulam, *Prophets and Conspirators*, p. 99; Chaliand and Blin, *The History of Terrorism*, p. 137. These activists were called *narodniki*, populists. Populism as ideology was embraced by Zemlia i Volia, Narodnaia Volia, and the Party of Socialist Revolutionaries, all of which attributed a central role to the peasant population in the revolutionary movement.
4 Evgenia L. Rudnitskaia, ed., *Revolutsionnii radikalizm v Rossii: deviatnadtsatii vek* (Moscow: Arkheograficheskii Tsentr, 1997), p. 385. Also, Lev Ia. Shternberg, 'Political Terror in Russia', pamphlet disseminated in Odessa in 1885, in Rudnitskaia, ed., *Revolutsionnii radikalizm*, p. 444.
5 The Italian anarchist Carlo Pisacane, who first used this phrase, argued that deeds produce ideas, not the other way around. Therefore, revolutionaries must emphasize conspiratorial work and assassinations, Nunzio Pernicone, *Italian Anarchism, 1864–1892* (Oakland, CA: AK Press, 2009; first published in 1993 by Princeton University Press), p. 13, referred to in Randall Law, *Terrorism: A History* (Cambridge: Polity Press, 2013, first published in 2009), p. 85.
6 Unbeknownst to the revolutionaries, Alexander II had shortly before his assassination appointed a commission to draft a constitution, Chaliand and Blin, *The History of Terrorism*, p. 149. Because of the assassination, Russia had to wait another 25 years for its constitution.
7 Woodford McClellan, *Revolutionary Exiles: The Russians in the First International and the Paris Commune* (Taylor & Francis e-Library, 2005; first published in 1979 by Frank Cass and Company Ltd. in London, U.K.), p. 142.
8 Sergei Gennadievich Nechaev, 'Katekhizis revoliutsionera', in E. L. Rudnitskaia, ed., *Revoliutsionnii radikalizm v Rossii: deviatnadtsatii vek* (Moscow: Arkheograficheskii Tsentr, 1997), pp. 244–245. The nihilists rejected all authority and did not believe in conventional values. Similar ideas gained prominence in the totalitarian movements of the twentieth century, Chaliand and Blin, *The History of Terrorism*, p. 138.
9 Philip Pomper, 'Nechaev and Tsaricide: The Conspiracy within the Conspiracy', *The Russian Review*, Vol. 33, No. 2 (Apr., 1974), p. 127.
10 This will be discussed in detail in Chapter III.
11 Philip Pomper, *Sergei Nechaev* (New Brunswick, NJ: Rutgers University Press, 1979), p. 202.
12 Sergei G. Nechaev, 'Katekhizis revoliutsionera', *Istoricheskie istochniki po istorii Rossii xviii-nachala xx v. na russkom iazyke v Internete* (elektronnaia biblioteka Istoricheskogo fakul'teta MGU im. M. V. Lomonosova), accessed 23 October 2017, http://www.hist.msu.ru/ER/Etext/nechaev.htm.
13 Ulam, *Prophets and Conspirators*, p. 191.
14 The article was published in the newspaper *Obshchina*, No. 1, 1 September 1870, London. Document No. 14, in Rudnitskaia, ed., *Revoliutsionnii radikalizm*, p. 291.
15 Ibid.
16 Ibid., p. 292.
17 Document 12. 'To Officers of the Russian Army'. January 1870, Geneva, in Rudnitskaia, ed., *Revoliutsionnii radikalizm*, p. 279.
18 Ibid., p. 280.
19 Nechaev agreed that the wish to withdraw from a revolutionary organization must automatically incur a death sentence, Pomper, 'Nechaev and Tsaricide', p. 128.

20 Ibid., pp. 281–286; Law, *Terrorism*, p. 78.
21 'Programma Zemli i Voli' [Program of Zemlia i Volia], May 1878, in Rudnitskaia, ed., *Revoliutsionnii radikalizm*, p. 395.
22 Ibid., pp. 395–397.
23 'Preparatory Work of the Party', *1883 Calendar of Narodnaia Volia*, Geneva, 1883, in Rudnitskaia, ed., *Revolutsionnii radikalizm*, p. 421.
24 This strategy was very successful much later in the Iraqi Revolution of 1958, Juan Romero, *The Iraqi Revolution of 1958: A Revolutionary Quest for Unity and Security* (Lanham, MD: University Press of America, 2011), p. 157.
25 'Preparatory Work of the Party', in Rudnitskaia, ed., *Revolutsionnii radikalizm*, pp. 421–422.
26 Chaliand and Blin, *The History of Terrorism*, pp. 151–152.
27 Norman Naimark, 'The Workers' Section and the Challenge of the "Young": Narodnaia Volia, 1881–1884', *The Russian Review*, Vol. 37, No. 3 (Jul., 1978), pp. 274–277.
28 The report, written in French, has no date, and nothing indicates the name of the author. It was most likely sent to the Director of the Department of Police, St. Petersburg. Okhrana files, Box 214, Reel 396, Hoover Institution, Stanford University, Palo Alto, California (henceforth Okhrana Files).
29 Ulam, *Prophets and Conspirators*, p. 294.
30 Sergei Kravchinskii, 'Death for a Death', in Rudnitskaia, ed., *Revoliutsionnii radikalizm*, p. 398.
31 Ibid., pp. 402–403.
32 Editorial published in the newspaper *Zemlia i Volia*, No. 1, October 25, 1878, in Rudnitskaia, ed., *Revoliutsionnii radikalizm*, p. 407 (my translation).
33 Such statements will be analyzed in the later chapters of this work.
34 *Zemlia i Volia*, No. 1, 25 October 1878, in Rudnitskaia, ed., *Revoliutsionnii radikalizm*, p. 408 (my translation).
35 Nikolai A. Morozov, 'The Meaning of Political Murders', *Listok Zemli i Voli*, No. 2–3, 22 March 1879, in Rudnitskaia, ed., *Revoliutsionnii radikalizm*, pp. 413–414 (my translation).
36 Chaliand and Blin, *The History of Terrorism*, p. 145.
37 Walter Laqueur, ed., *Voices of Terror: Manifestos, Writings and Manuals of Al Qaeda, Hamas, and Other Terrorists from around the World and throughout the Ages* (Naperville, IL: Sourcebooks Inc., 2004), p. 76.
38 Anna Geifman, *Thou Shalt Kill: Revolutionary Terrorism in Russia, 1894–1917* (Princeton, NJ: Princeton University Press, 1993), pp. 59, 82. This capability will be analyzed in detail in the subsequent chapter.
39 Laqueur, *Voices of Terror*, p. 78.
40 Another difference was that earlier terrorists had operated on an individual basis, whereas later terrorists were generally supported by organizations planning and supporting their assassinations, Chaliand and Blin, *The History of Terrorism*, p. 147.
41 Laqueur, *Voices of Terror*, p. 79. Simultaneously with Morozov's pro-terrorist writings, there was at least one group within Narodnaia Volia which took an opposite position on terror. One of the leaders of the organization's Workers' Section, Ivan I. Popov, argued that terrorism was a waste of revolutionary lives since it 'evoke[d] no positive response among workers', Naimark, 'The Workers' Section', *The Russian Review*, Vol. 37, No. 3 (Jul., 1978), p. 279. Furthermore, Popov was quite critical of the strict centralization of Narodnaia Volia, which had only resulted in mass arrests.
42 Morozov went as far as taking the uncharacteristic position of a revolutionary of supporting Russia's participation in the Great War, Ulam, *Prophets and Conspirators*, p. 317.

43 Trapeznik argues that the spectacular terrorist acts carried out during the first few years of the PSR's existence did not lead to much debate about terrorism as a weapon, Alexander Trapeznik, 'V. M. Chernov, Terrorism and the Azef Affair', *New Zealand Slavonic Journal*, Vol. 35 (2001), p. 103.
44 'From the Central Committee of the PSR. On the question of agrarian and factory terror', *Znamia Truda*, No. 3, 1 August 1907, in Nikolai D. Erofeev, *Partiia sotsialistov-revoliutsionerov: dokumenty i materialy. V triokh tomakh. T. 2. Iiun' 1907 g. – fevral' 1917 g.* (Moscow: Rossiiskaia politicheskaia entsiklopedia, 2001), p. 35.
45 Agrarian terror is defined as 'the use of violence against the lives and property of the economic oppressors of the people', Maureen Perrie, *The Agrarian Policy of the Russian Socialist-Revolutionary Party: From Its Origins through the Revolution of 1905–1907* (Cambridge: Cambridge University Press, 2009; first published in 1976), p. 94. Agrarian terror included acts such as seizure of the landowner's property, arson, murder of landowners and armed attacks by the peasants. Factory terror is defined as 'the use of coercion against the lives or property of factory owners to promote the workers' cause in the economic struggle', Anna Geifman, *Thou Shalt Kill: Revolutionary Terrorism in Russia, 1894–1917* (Princeton, NJ: Princeton University Press, 1995; first published in 1993), p. 73.
46 'From the Central Committee of the PSR. On the question of agrarian and factory terror', *Znamia Truda*, No. 3, 1 August 1907, in Erofeev, *Partiia sotsialistov-revoliutsionerov: dokumenty i materialy. V triokh tomakh. T. 2. Iiun' 1907 g. – fevral' 1917 g.* (Moscow: Rossiiskaia politicheskaia entsiklopedia, 2001), p. 35 (my translation).
47 It is worth mentioning, however, that a group had been formed within the PSR in 1904 that advocated expanding terrorist activities to include agrarian terror, but the chief PSR ideologue, Chernov, opposed these ideas, Trapeznik, 'V. M. Chernov', p. 103.
48 'Program for Issues and Draft Resolutions Subject to Discussion at the Forthcoming Conference and [Meeting of the] Council', *Protocols of the first PSR All-Party Conference*, Paris, August 1908, in Nikolai D. Erofeev, *Partiia sotsialistov-revoliutsionerov*, pp. 43–46.
49 Geifman, *Thou Shalt Kill*, p. 73.
50 Memorandum, 28 March 1912. From Lieutenant-Colonel von Koten, Okhrana Office, Paris (most likely) to the Director of the Department of the Police. Okhrana Files, Box 191 Reel 345. The weakened position of the Combat Organization was evidenced by a PSR Council meeting in May 1909, which announced that the CO had been dissolved and would remain so until the next party congress, *The Socialist Revolutionary*, No. 2, Paris, 1910, in Erofeev, *Partiia sotsialistov-revoliutsionerov*, p. 352.
51 Memorandum, 28 March 1912. From Lieutenant-Colonel von Koten, Okhrana Office, Paris (most likely) to the Director of the Department of the Police. Okhrana Files, Box 191 Reel 345. Similar views had been expressed by Avksentiev in 1911, according to Okhrana report, No. 1473, Okhrana Office, Paris to Department of the Police, Box 191 Reel 345, Okhrana Files.
52 Ibid. The memorandum of 28 March 1912 does not give the year of the publication, but there is an earlier reference to the same issue of the *Znamia Truda* referring to discussions of terrorism. This leads me to assume that the year is 1911.
53 No. 741, 13 June 1912, Official for Special Missions. From Okhrana Office, Paris to Department of the Police, Okhrana Files, Box 191 Reel 345.
54 For the 'rightist' argument, see also *The Socialist Revolutionary*, No. 2, Paris, 1910, in Erofeev, *Partiia sotsialistov-revoliutsionerov*, p. 319.
55 Ibid.

56 Ibid.
57 Ibid.
58 Geifman, *Thou Shalt Kill*, pp. 128, 130, 131, 135.
59 'Program of the Executive Committee', *Narodnaia Volia* No. 3, 1 January 1880, in Rudnitskaia, ed., *Revolutsionnii radikalizm*, pp. 417–419.
60 From Lev A. Tikhomirov, 'Chego Nam Zhdat' ot Revoliutsii', [What We Should Expect from the Revolution] *Vestnik Narodnoi Voli: Revoliutsionnoe sotsial'no-politicheskoe obozrenie*, No. 2, 18 April 1884, Geneva, in Rudnitskaia, ed., *Revolutsionnii radikalizm*, p. 432.
61 Later in life, Tikhomirow moved to the opposite end of the political specter, embracing conservatism, Ulam, *Prophets and Conspirators*, p. 297.

Bibliography

Bakunin, Mikhail. 'K ofitseram Russkoi armii'. ('To Officers of the Russian Army'.) January 1870. Geneva. In Rudnitskaia, ed., *Revoliutsionnii radikalizm v Rossii: deviatnadtsatii vek*. Moscow: Arkheograficheskii Tsentr, 1997, pp. 279–87.

1883 Calendar of Narodnaia Volia. Geneva, 1883. Podgotovitel'naia rabota partii' [Preparatory Work of the Party]. In Rudnitskaia, ed., *Revolutsionnii radikalizm v Rossii: deviatnadtsatii vek*. Moscow: Arkheograficheskii Tsentr, 1997, pp. 420–27.

Chaliand, Gérard and Arnaud Blin. 'Introduction'. In Gérard Chaliand and Arnaud Blin, eds., *The History of Terrorism: From antiquity to Al Qaeda*. Berkeley: University of California Press, 2009, pp. 1–11.

Geifman, Anna. *Thou Shalt Kill: Revolutionary Terrorism in Russia, 1894–1917*. Princeton, NJ: Princeton University Press, 1993.

Kravchinskii, Sergei. 'Smert' za smert'. [A Death for a Death]. In Rudnitskaia, ed., *Revoliutsionnii radikalizm v Rossii: deviatnadtsatii vek*. Moscow: Arkheograficheskii Tsentr, 1997, pp. 397–404.

Laqueur, Walter, ed. *Voices of Terror: Manifestos, Writings and Manuals of Al Qaeda, Hamas, and Other Terrorists from around the World and throughout the Ages*. Naperville, IL: Sourcebooks Inc., 2004.

Law, Randall D. *Terrorism: A History*. Cambridge: Polity Press, 2009.

McClellan, Woodford. *Revolutionary Exiles: The Russians in the First International and the Paris Commune*. Taylor & Francis e-Library, 2005; first published in 1979 by Frank Cass and Company Ltd., London, U.K.

Morozov, Nikolai A. 'Znachenie politicheskikh ubiistv' [The Meaning of Political Murders]. *Listok Zemli i Voli*, No. 2–3, 22 March 1879. In Rudnitskaia, ed., *Revoliutsionnii radikalizm v Rossii: deviatnadtsatii vek*. Moscow: Arkheograficheskii Tsentr, 1997, pp. 413–16.

Naimark, Norman. 'The Workers' Section and the Challenge of the "Young": Narodnaia Volia, 1881–1884'. *The Russian Review*, Vol. 37, No. 3 (July 1978), pp. 273–97.

Nechaev, Sergei Gennadievich. 'Katekhizis revoliutsionera' [Catechism of the Revolutionist]. In Evgenia L. Rudnitskaia, ed., *Revoliutsionnii radikalizm v Rossii: deviatnadtsatii vek*. Moscow: Arkheograficheskii Tsentr, 1997, pp. 244–45.

Nechaev, Sergei Gennadievich. 'Katekhizis revoliutsionera' [Catechism of the Revolutionist]. *Istoricheskie istochniki po istorii Rossii xviii-nachala xx v. na russkom iazyke v Internete* (elektronnaia biblioteka Istoricheskogo fakul'teta MGU im. M. V. Lomonosova). Accessed 23 October 2017. http://www.hist.msu.ru/ER/Etext/nechaev.htm.

Obshchina. No. 1, 1 September 1870. In Evgeniia L. Rudnitskaia, ed. *Revoliutsionnii radikalizm v Rossii: deviatnadtsatii vek*. Moscow: Arkheograficheskii Tsentr, 1997, pp. 291–301.

Okhrana Files. Hoover Institution. Stanford University. Palo Alto, CA.

Party of Socialist Revolutionaries. 'Programma Voprosov i Proekty Rezoliutsii, Podlezhashchikh Obsuzhdeniiu na Predstoiashchikh Konferentsii i Sovete' [Program for Issues and Draft Resolutions Subject to Discussion at the Forthcoming Conference and [Meeting of the] Council]. *Protocols of the first PSR All-Party Conference*. Paris, August 1908. In Nikolai D. Erofeev, ed., *Partiia sotsialistov-revoliutsionerov: dokumenty i materialy*. V triokh tomakh. T. 2. Iiun' 1907 g. – fevral' 1917 g. Moscow: Rossiiskaia politicheskaia entsiklopedia, 2001, pp. 38–48.

Party of Socialist Revolutionaries. 'From the Central Committee. On the Question of Agrarian and Factory Terror'. *Znamia Truda*, No. 3, 1 August 1907. In Nikolai D. Erofeev, ed., *Partiia sotsialistov-revoliutsionerov: dokumenty i materialy*. V triokh tomakh. T. 2. Iiun' 1907 g. – fevral' 1917 g. [Party of Socialist Revolutionaries: documents and materials in three volumes. Volume 2, June 1907-February 1917]. Moscow: Rossiiskaia politicheskaia entsiklopedia, 2001, p. 35.

Pernicone, Nunzi. *Italian Anarchism, 1864–1892*. Oakland, CA: AK Press, 2009; first published in 1993 by Princeton University Press.

Perrie, Maureen. *The Agrarian Policy of the Russian Socialist-Revolutionary Party: From its Origins through the Revolution of 1905–1907*. Cambridge: Cambridge University Press, 2009; first published in 1976.

Pomper, Philip. 'Nechaev and Tsaricide: The Conspiracy within the Conspiracy'. *The Russian Review*, Vol. 33, No. 2 (April 1974), pp. 123–38.

Pomper, Philip. *Sergei Nechaev*. New Brunswick, NJ: Rutgers University Press, 1979.

Romero, Juan. *The Iraqi Revolution of 1958: A Revolutionary Quest for Unity and Security*. Lanham, MD: University Press of America, 2011.

Rudnitskaia, Evgeniia L., ed. *Revolutsionnii radikalizm v Rossii: deviatnadtsatii vek*. Moscow: Arkheograficheskii Tsentr, 1997.

The Socialist Revolutionary. No. 2, 1910, in Nikolai D. Erofeev, *Partiia sotsialistov-revoliutsionerov: dokumenty i materialy*. V triokh tomakh. T. 2. Iiun' 1907 g. – fevral' 1917 g. Moscow: Rossiiskaia politicheskaia entsiklopedia, 2001, pp. 317–52.

Tikhomirov, Lev A. 'Chego Nam Zhdat' ot Revoliutsii' [What We Should Expect from the Revolution]. *Vestnik Narodnoi Voli: Revoliutsionnoe sotsial'no-politicheskoe obozrenie*, No. 2, 24 April 1884. Geneva. In Evgenia L. Rudnitskaia, ed., *Revolutsionnii radikalizm v Rossii: deviatnadtsatii vek*. Moscow: Arkheograficheskii Tsentr, 1997, pp. 430–32.

Trapeznik, Alexander. 'V. M. Chernov, Terrorism and the Azef Affair'. *New Zealand Slavonic Journal*, Vol. 35 (2001), pp. 101–11.

Ulam. Adam B. *Prophets and Conspirators: Prerevolutionary Russia*. New Brunswick, USA and London, UK: Transaction Publishers, 1998 (first published in 1977 by Viking Press).

'Editorial'. *Zemlia i Volia*, No. 1, 25 October, 1878. In Evgenia L. Rudnitskaia, ed., *Revolutsionnii radikalizm v Rossii: deviatnadtsatii vek*. Moscow: Arkheograficheskii Tsentr, 1997, pp. 404–12.

Zemlia i Volia. 'Programma Zemli i Voli' [Program of Zemlia i Volia]. May 1878. In Evgenia L. Rudnitskaia, ed., *Revolutsionnii radikalizm v Rossii: deviatnadtsatii vek*. Moscow: Arkheograficheskii Tsentr, 1997, pp. 395–97.

3 Methodology of Russian terrorism

Introduction

The previous chapter examined ideologies of Russian organizations and parties involved in political violence in the latter half of the nineteenth century and the early twentieth century. This chapter focuses on terrorist strategies and tactics during the aforementioned period and counterterrorism measures of the Okhrana (political police) to meet the challenge of the revolutionaries.[1] An examination of the open warfare between the two sides reveals that they actually adopted surprisingly similar approaches to defeat the adversary including disinformation, infiltration, surveillance and use of aliases and safe houses.[2] Another thing which particularly stands out in the confrontation between the Okhrana and the militant revolutionaries of the era is the latter's obsession with explosives and firearms. Explosives were considered the miracle weapon of the militants because of the power of bombs to eliminate government officials and even bring down parts of government institutions. They were the weapon *par excellence* to instill fear in the enemy and impress the Russian public by virtue of their destructive power. The message to Russian society was that the revolutionaries had the resources to dispatch the tsarist system to the ash heap of history and that the public should support them in this endeavor for the benefit of all Russians suffering under the present regime. Concurrently, bombs turned out to be an unreliable weapon which caused destruction not only among government officials but also amongst the terrorists themselves as well. The records of the political police abound with reports of militants who accidentally set off bombs tearing off their limbs or blowing up apartments or hotel rooms.

A third issue addressed in this chapter is cooperation among revolutionary organizations on the one hand and European law enforcement agencies on the other. Revolutionaries oftentimes overcame ideological disagreements, engaging in cooperation both abroad and in Russia aiming at the overthrow of the tsarist regime. The Okhrana, for its part, engaged in cooperation with European law enforcement agencies and other government institutions, exchanging intelligence pertaining to the activities of Russian terrorists in Western Europe.[3] This chapter also addresses the question of whether there

DOI: 10.4324/9781003260943-4

was a clear victor in the war between the terrorists and the regime.[4] Both sides suffered from weaknesses in the methods applied to defeat the enemy. These weaknesses were exploited by the belligerents. From the perspective of the revolutionaries, they were engaged in a tit-for-tat fight with the oppressive government, presumably merely defending themselves against the injustice and exploitation imposed on Russian society. The revolutionaries and the government's secret agents were participants in what could best be described as a cat and mouse game to outwit and surprise the opponent.[5] These efforts caused the Okhrana and the militants to take a keen interest in new scientific developments which could be exploited against the enemy, sometimes producing ingenious improvements in tactics and weapons and bold plans. Not surprisingly, with both sides attempting to get the best of one another, the general conclusion one can draw, based upon archival and primary sources, is that both parties were successful at the same time as they experienced their fair share of failure.

Assassination

The preferred terrorist means of fighting the regime was assassination, with regicide made top of the terrorist agenda. Okhrana records are full of reports on conspiracies to assassinate the tsar. As has been pointed out in the previous chapter, the militants believed that the decapitation of the Russian hydra, that is, a successful regicide, would cause panic in the government, incite the population to a general uprising in Russia and result in regime change.[6] Some of the plans to assassinate the tsar were quite elaborate. One example is a plan to assassinate the tsar in Tsarskoe Selo, the location of the tsar's palace outside St. Petersburg, since the monarch rarely left his residence. The conspirators planned to carry out the attempt on the tsar's life when he traveled by rail from Tsarskoe Selo. The plotters had found a few strategically located houses near the railroad and planned to have a revolutionary with a clean record rent one of the houses. Dynamite would then be brought to the house at night and stored in a nearby pond. The author of the report, Ratacv, stated that the conspirators had encountered what appears to be unexpected problems – a shortage in people to execute the plan, possession of an insufficient amount of dynamite and a lack of diving gear. A member of the group was of the opinion that getting the dynamite was the least serious problem since it was abundantly available in Russia.[7] These problems suggest that the plotters had not conducted appropriate research prior to deciding upon execution of the plan. One of the potential suppliers of dynamite had met with a leading PSR member in Paris. This individual was a very wealthy person who had invested money in mining. This might explain his commitment to place a substantial part of his fortune at the disposal of the PSR Combat Organization and supply whatever amount of dynamite was necessary for PSR terrorist activities. The report reveals that the Okhrana had a well-placed informant in Socialist Revolutionary circles, that the revolutionaries had important connections in Russia, that there were wealthy individuals who were prepared to support terrorism and that not all terrorist acts were well thought out and prepared.

There were numerous other plans to assassinate the tsar and government officials in high positions. In January 1905, a revolutionary arrived in Geneva from Russia to discuss with the PSR Foreign Committee a plan hatched by a small circle of intellectuals in St. Petersburg to assassinate the tsar and a number of government officials. The group had set aside 20,000 rubles for the project and already selected members to execute the plan. It asked the PSR to explain in the party press the necessity of assassinating the tsar, and in the event of success, to call for a popular uprising and assist in organizing it.[8] This report shows that the group has the financial resources to carry out a large-scale operation, but it appears not to have the resources to reach a larger audience with a call for an uprising as well as the network necessary to organize such an operation. Another quite spectacular plan had an American connection. According to the Okhrana's military agent in London, terrorists were preparing an attempt on the life of the tsar to be executed by introducing explosives into the imperial palace. The explosives would be brought from the United States, where these were easy to purchase for mining purposes. The explosives would be concealed in iron boxes and have the appearance of charcoal or firewood.[9]

Interestingly enough, a similar plan had already been executed by Narodnaia Volia in February 1880. Explosives had been brought into a workers' dormitory and set off by the terrorist Stepan Khalturin, who had found employment as a worker in the Winter Palace. The explosion killed 11 people, but did not damage the tsar's dining room. Incidentally, the Russian ruler was late for his dinner and was not in the dining room when the bomb exploded underneath it.[10] Over the course of 50 years, numerous plans were drawn up to assassinate three tsars, but only one was successful.

According to an Okhrana report dated July 1914, even the female members of the imperial family were targeted by terrorists. The report states that certain Jews are raising funds to assassinate the widow of Alexander III. The funds necessary for the undertaking will be sent to a professor, his assistant and a Russian émigré in Copenhagen. These three will be assisted by a Pole and a Jew who has escaped from military service. If successful in their mission, each assassin will receive 100,000 for his participation. The Department of Police asks the Okhrana Office, Paris to ascertain the veracity of the information.[11] It is possible that the Department of Police have doubts about this information since they ask the Okhrana Office, Paris to confirm it. It is worth mentioning that it is unusual for a terrorist organization to target a female member of the imperial family, particularly a widow of a former tsar. The author of the present study has not come across any other Okhrana report to the effect that revolutionaries specifically target a woman, with the exception of informants. Furthermore, it is quite unique that the assassins would receive monetary compensation for a terrorist act. Finally, the compensation constitutes an exceptional amount. It is quite possible that it is the aforementioned circumstances which have raised doubts in the minds of the Department of Police.

Like previous generations of conspirators, nineteenth- and early twentieth-century terrorists sometimes planned to make use of poison as a 'weapon' to rid society of its oppressors. In 1912, the Department of Police requested that the Okhrana Office in Paris investigate the accuracy of information stating that anarchists have distributed a toxic substance in Milan, which has caused the death of 200 people. Four years later, in 1916, the Russian embassy in Washington, D.C. received a note to the effect that a group of anarchists in Chicago had attempted to poison the Catholic Bishop at a banquet. The tsar had not been especially mentioned in connection with this group, but the members had stated that they were planning to target all monarchs. The embassy reported that it had asked the consul in Chicago to investigate.[12] Incidentally, anarchists were involved in both instances. These cases could possibly suggest that the conspirators did not have access to explosives or weapons. The second case could possibly indicate that the group had an informant placed in a position where he/she could add poison to food being served, which would explain why the anarchists would prefer poison to explosives. Another possibility is that they wished to target one person only, for which purpose poison would work better than explosives. The second report reveals the international reach of Russian anarchists as late as during the Great War. Finally, the Okhrana obviously take the unspecific threat seriously, partly, perhaps, because it is an indication that some revolutionaries are prepared to use somewhat unusual approaches when targeting a victim, if one considers the fact that most assassinations had been successful as a result of explosives or firearms being used.

Deception and secrecy

Deception and secrecy were part and parcel of revolutionary activities. Due to the nature of terrorism and the efforts of the authorities to prevent it, terrorist organizations resorted to various kinds of deception and secrecy to conceal their activities.[13] Revolutionaries often used invisible ink (*khimicheskii tekst*) to convey secret and sensitive information in letters. They used code phrases, cipher and addresses of individuals beyond suspicion (*chistye adresa*) to correspond with one another and avoid perlustration. The Okhrana had specialists with foreign language skills attached to post offices in major Russian cities to screen letters to and from addresses abroad. Pavel P. Zavarzin, a leading Okhrana official, describes in detail the method used to peruse incoming and outgoing mail. A special machine or steam was used to open letters, which were then copied and forwarded to their destination. However, correspondence written with invisible ink never reached the addressee because a reagent had to be used to analyze it. Zavarzin reveals that the revolutionaries often used lemon juice, milk or saliva to hide the contents of a letter from the watchful eyes of the Okhrana. Unfortunately, for the revolutionaries, these attempts to confuse the adversary were futile since the letters could be easily read, if the paper was exposed to heat.[14] Many letters in Western Europe were perlustrated as well. In Switzerland and Italy, postal employees were paid by the Okhrana to deliver such correspondence. In Paris, concierges bribed by the Okhrana would fill the same function.[15] It is obvious that conspiratorial correspondence, despite the efforts of the revolutionaries, constituted an important source of information for the Russian political police.

Russian terrorists had to maintain a heavy street presence in order to be able to carry out assassinations. An assassination of a high tsarist official was a serious undertaking, and its success was contingent upon painstaking preparation which involved collection of reliable information about the target's background and routines. The task could be achieved through teamwork only, which, in turn, required an organization which could provide critical services. This explains why the PSR Combat Organization had recruited members from all walks of life who could pose as military officers, minor bureaucrats, newspaper hawkers, peddlers, shoeshines, cabbies, etc. The revolutionaries were aware that the latter case could present a problem, if one and the same terrorist dealt exclusively with a particular cabbie over a period of time.[16] The Okhrana used similar methods to surveille the revolutionaries.[17]

Revolutionary ideology and criticism of the tsarist system of government were disseminated through secret printing offices in many Russian cities or printed abroad and smuggled into Russia. A flyer or proclamation would often be printed in one city and allude to another city in order to confuse the Okhrana with respect to the location of the printing press. Much of the illegal literature was printed abroad and then smuggled across the Russian border.[18] The importance of disseminating illegal literature printed abroad to Russian readers is testified to by a special conference that was held in Bulgaria in 1895 to discuss ways of smuggling illegal political literature into Russia.[19] Some publications were smuggled via Finland and some, printed in Leipzig, delivered to smugglers at the Russian border, whence they were distributed to major urban centers.[20] Other revolutionary literature was smuggled from Austria into Russia by Socialist Revolutionaries.[21] *The Russian Free Press Fund*, based in London, distributed tens of thousands of books and pamphlets over a period of two and a half years 1891–1893. This is an indication of the scale of Russian revolutionary printing activities in Western Europe. Only some copies were smuggled into Russia, but travelers who read the revolutionary literature would bring the ideas back with them when they returned to Russia, even if they could not bring the actual copies with them. *Podpol'naia Rossiia* (Underground Russia), authored by Sergei M. Kravchinskii, was an obvious exception since the work circulated widely in Russia.[22] Russian revolutionaries stored Socialist Revolutionary, Social Democratic and anarchist pamphlets in private apartments and distributed them to teachers.[23] Printing was an effective means to spread revolutionary ideology and propaganda, at least until the printing presses were discovered by the Okhrana and shut down.

Russian revolutionaries used many other methods aimed at confusing the political police. In 1913, the Okhrana Office in Paris reported that the former publisher of the satirical journal *Ovod* (Gadfly) had visited Paris and asked two PSR members whether they would accept to carry out terrorist acts. One of them had expressed his interest, whereupon Zel'ts, the former publisher of *Ovod*, had stated that he would make 20,000 rubles available for the execution of terrorist acts. Zel'ts also informed the PSR terrorist that a Russian millionaire would contribute 8,000 rubles per month to the terrorist cause. The author of the report is skeptical about the accuracy of the above information, suspecting that it is a smokescreen invented by the PSR terrorist, intended to confuse the Okhrana and divert their attention away from another operation which was being planned.[24] This could thus be an example of terrorist disinformation intended to lead the Okhrana in a wrong direction to enable the PSR militants to execute a terrorist act. Revolutionaries also made frequent use of false passports, which was not very difficult, since they lacked photos of the holder in those days. Furthermore, militants usually led a secluded lifestyle, reducing meetings with other revolutionaries to a minimum in order not to attract the attention of the tsar's police surveillants. When a police arrest or search was believed to be imminent, the suspected revolutionaries would indicate this by hanging a sign in or outside the window to alert fellow comrades to the danger and warn them to stay away from the apartment in question. Finally, Russian revolutionaries memorized a secret alphabet to enable them to communicate with other inmates in case of arrest through knocks on prison walls.[25]

Escapes

Russian militants often managed to escape from exile and their fellow revolutionaries at large displayed deep solidarity with incarcerated comrades, often going to great lengths to organize jailbreaks. Okhrana reports abound with reports of revolutionaries escaping from prison or exile. In many cases, the prison experience had left inmates completely 'unreformed', as evidenced by their return to terrorist activities. Terrorism had landed them in prison and incarceration contributed to returning them to the path of terror.[26] The failure of the authorities to keep so many dangerous individuals behind bars testifies to a serious weakness in the Russian penal system.[27] Several women were engaged in raising funds intended for the rescue of incarcerated and exiled comrades.[28] One organization, based in Paris, focusing on raising funds for incarcerated and exiled revolutionaries, the Society for Assistance of Political Exiles, was suspected by the Okhrana of being a branch of Vera Figner's society. This society was quite successful raising 60,000–70,000 francs annually. Narodnaia Volia used a very hands-on approach to organizing prison escapes. One of the organization's members was hired as a prison warder and helped three incarcerated comrades escape.[29] It appears that the funds raised were put to good use. Daly writes that escapes from exile were not difficult to arrange, particularly in the period following the 1905 Revolution, thanks to an underground network.[30] The Okhrana's interest in societies and individuals organizing escapes suggests that the latter had a successful record.[31]

Explosives

As has been stated above, explosives were one of the terrorist's preferred tools in the war against the tsarist regime. Okhrana reports reveal that terrorists carefully prepared their operations, often times carrying out test explosions abroad and in Russia of devices they planned to use when targeting tsarist officials.[32] The fact that the Okhrana frequently reported that these tests had been successful[33] must have been quite unnerving to the Department of Police in St. Petersburg. It is obvious from Okhrana telegrams that Russian terrorists were constantly at work improving their explosive devices, making them more powerful or studying the latest scientific and engineering developments and inventions. This work, with the exception of the testing, was normally carried out in bomb factories in apartments both in Russia and abroad.[34] In two such factories located in Finland, explosive devices of simple construction were manufactured. These devices were made of thick paper and filled with dynamite. According to the Okhrana, the advantage of the simple construction was that such bombs could easily be produced in the thousands. In 1895, a 'youth circle' was manufacturing more sophisticated explosive devices in Moscow, using fulminated mercury for a planned assassination of the tsar during his visit to the city the same month.[35] During a search of the apartment of one of the members of the group, the police found a chemical laboratory with substantial volumes of various acids, fulminated mercury and notes regarding the manufacture of explosives. Okhrana reports indicate that international terrorists were sharing among each other knowledge of bomb-making. One example is a Russian terrorist group based in Bulgaria which corresponded with anarchists in Belgium, receiving advice from these. The same group also was in contact with a female doctor in Paris who had access to various chemical preparations. The efforts terrorists made to study, acquire and manufacture powerful explosive devices testify to the importance they attributed to possessing such weapons in their arsenal.[36]

Russian terrorists were very much aware of the risk of detection by the police and therefore made efforts to establish bomb factories abroad. In 1914, a Russian militant in London inquired about the possibility of establishing a laboratory for the manufacture of explosives and bombs in England. Furthermore, the individual in question wished to find out whether it was possible to conduct tests with explosive devices and what legal consequences could be expected if caught by the police. Also, the terrorist asked whether his interlocutor knew people proficient in bomb-making.[37] This suggests that the Russian revolutionary did not himself possess bomb-making skills, or, at least, that he needed assistance. His mission also indicates that Russian revolutionaries in Western Europe were quite confident that they could smuggle bombs into Russia. In addition to the aforementioned individual, the Okhrana was aware of the presence in London of a Russian engineer, a prominent Socialist Revolutionary, who had recently relocated there from Belgium. He previously lived in Brussels in a large villa where visitors used to stay for shorter periods. This revolutionary was in possession of several passports for use in Russia and abroad.[38] One can conclude from the information collected by the Okhrana that the second individual was in charge of some kind of safe house and that his organization had the financial resources to rent a large villa and procure false passports.

Russian militants were quite innovative when it came to where to gain knowledge about bomb-making and where to store their lethal weapons, waiting to be used. Despite the risks involved, a group with terrorist affiliations in Kiev had decided to work right under the nose of the Okhrana, which is most likely why the political police were aware of the revolutionaries' activities. The group's leader, a Jewish doctor, was a friend of the PSR Combat Organization leader Gershuni. These revolutionaries were preoccupied with manufacturing explosives and conducting chemical experiments in the Polytechnical Institute of all places. They probably reckoned that their activities would not attract attention since they occurred in the laboratories of an institution of higher learning. Russian revolutionaries also displayed an ability to find unexpected 'solutions' to the problem of safely storing bombs. Boris Savinkov, a leading member of the PSR Combat Organization, writes in his memoirs that another terrorist had brought six small bombs to Moscow. Evno Azef, the leader of the CO and a double agent, suggested that Savinkov leave the bombs in a very safe place – a bank locker![39] This was obviously not the first place the Okhrana would search for bombs and bank lockers were fireproof. The two instances discussed in this paragraph testify to innovative thinking of Russian terrorists.

Innovative and nefarious thinking also occurred in the scientific and engineering areas. Russian militants in Bulgaria had met to discuss the best way to manufacture a bomb which could be thrown at the target (*metatel'nii snariad*). Having solicited advice from anarchists in Belgium, who had suggested that their comrades in Bulgaria use bombs containing nails, the group voted unanimously for this splendid idea.[40] The reference to nails is clear evidence that the would-be terrorists wished to injure as many people as possible, not just one individual. A more sophisticated approach was being considered by a group of Socialist Revolutionaries in Moscow, who were planning to assassinate the tsar with an explosive device invented by an Italian mining engineer. This particular device was to be attached to the emperor's carriage and explode after a specific number of revolutions of the wheels. This device would obviously cause much less injury to persons who happened to be in the wrong place at the wrong time. Another visionary idea put forward by Azef in 1907 was to use a flying machine which would take off from an air field in Western Europe, fly to Tsarskoe Selo or Peterhof and completely destroy the palace by bombarding it from the air. The only problem was that 20,000 rubles had to be raised for the project. The money was raised, and the inventor began work on the machine in Munich, but nothing seems to have come of it since Savinkov does not mention the project again in his memoirs.[41] Two other ideas must have appeared at the time as if taken from a science-fiction novel. A female terrorist had, according to the Okhrana, discussed as early as 1895 the possibility of building an enormous rocket which would be launched at the imperial palace, causing utter destruction.[42] This futuristic idea predated the Nazi V-1 and V-2 rockets by 50 years. Finally, a visionary project in which the Department of Police took great interest in 1913 was experiments that had been conducted at the University of Heidelberg in Germany by a deceased Russian professor to induce remote detonation of explosive devices by telephone signals and electro-magnetic waves.[43] The department must have prayed to God that the terrorists would never find out about these experiments which would result in a destructive method applied by terrorists at the end of the twentieth century. The ideas discussed above demonstrate that terrorists made great efforts to use to their advantage new and at times not yet existing technology in their war against the tsarist regime.

The danger of handling explosives

The dangers of working with explosives were obvious despite the precautions taken by the terrorists. When handling explosive devices, terrorists at times suffered the fate they had prepared for their targets, setting off explosions that either killed or maimed them. Many such instances, occurring both in Russia and abroad, are discussed in Okhrana reports. Most accidental explosions happened either in apartments or hotels where militants were preparing assassinations. An incident described in detail in an Okhrana report is worth mentioning. An explosion had occurred in an apartment in Geneva occupied by Russian revolutionaries. Several Russians had dispersed in different directions right after the explosion and before the police arrived. Three of these individuals had been injured with blood running down the face. When the Swiss police arrived (three hours later!), a slightly injured woman answered the door. She refused to explain why the explosion had happened and was arrested. A search of the apartment yielded a number of spherical bombs and several cylindrical bombs. Nitroglycerin, gelatin, cotton and various types of reagent required for manufacturing explosives were also found, as was a bottle of poison. In the evening, another Russian arrived at a cantonal hospital. He had lost several fingers on one hand. A large amount of material required for manufacturing explosives was found when police searched his apartment. The task of this terrorist had been to train PSR members in Geneva in bomb-making and reducing the size of bombs. The direct result of the explosion was that all more or less prominent Russian revolutionaries left Geneva.[44] Savinkov describes other fatal accidents in his memoirs and also mentions that some female terrorists incurred severe injuries when arming bombs.[45] Karma appears to have caught up with some terrorists before they could carry out their missions.

Firearms

Despite their preference for explosives, Russian militants tried to procure firearms from Western Europe and smuggle them to Russia for their terrorist activities. In 1905, the Okhrana reported that Russian revolutionaries mainly purchased firearms in Hamburg. A Finnish revolutionary by the name of Johnny Tsiliakus had already purchased 6,000 Mauser pistols which were set to be shipped to Russia via Finland shortly. According to the Okhrana, Tsiliakus was in contact with the Japanese embassy in London which supplied large amounts of money to Finnish and Polish revolutionaries.[46] A year later, the Okhrana Office, Paris, mentions that another Finn, John Mannerstam, lived in Berlin under the assumed name of Karl Berg. Mannerstam, who was rumored to own a store in Helsinki, had announced that unlimited quantities of arms could be shipped to him and that he could send them to Russia unobstructed.[47] Based upon the information provided in the two Okhrana telegrams, one can conclude that the three different names refer to the same individual. Russian revolutionaries also made efforts to procure heavier weapons from abroad. Early in 1906, a revolutionary party in Finland attempted, unsuccessfully, to place an order for 500 machine guns with a German gun manufacturer in Berlin, who refused to deliver the weapons. According to the Okhrana, the reason for the refusal was that the management would have risked losing the Russian government as a very important client, if it had filled the order.[48] Machine guns are obviously heavy to move, so the order is an indication that the revolutionaries were anticipating large-scale operations that required heavier weapons than revolvers. A machine gun is not suitable for targeting one individual only, unless the target is located in the middle of a group of other individuals, and the terrorists are not concerned about the number of casualties such an operation would result in. It is therefore more plausible that the revolutionaries were preparing a general uprising in Russia, capitalizing on the social unrest in the country, following the Russo-Japanese War. Thus, in consideration of the aforementioned, it is not surprising that the Okhrana took an interest in any revolutionary attempt to acquire heavy weapons and went to great lengths to prevent this from happening. The two Okhrana reports discussed above constitute a clear indication that some militants were thinking 'big', not wishing to limit themselves to small-scale attacks.

Women and children

Russian terrorist organizations and parties presented opportunities for women to participate in revolutionary work and in some cases used children as well for non-terrorist tasks. These opportunities enabled some women to advance to leading positions in the revolutionary movement. Female revolutionaries filled different functions in terrorist organizations, including throwing bombs and shooting at government officials. Some were killed on the spot,[49] some were sentenced to death, and others were sentenced to languish for decades in prisons and exile. The importance of women is evidenced by their presence on Narodnaia Volia's early executive committee – they made up one-third of the committee. Female revolutionaries also played a prominent role in PSR terrorist acts. They differed from their male comrades, however, in one important respect – most militant PSR women involved in terrorist acts between 1902 and 1911 had a background in the intelligentsia, and many were Jews.[50] Women sometimes occupied leading positions in unexpected places. One Okhrana report tells of a Socialist Revolutionary group of railroad workers in the city of Penza who were preparing an uprising. The report refers to a woman who was one of the most prominent members of the group.[51] Also, the Armenian Dashnaktsiun Party used old women to assist in revolutionary activities. One such older lady, aged 80, was involved in smuggling weapons and ammunition. The Polish Socialist Party used a 13-year-old girl to carry weapons and steal documents from the Okhrana Office in Warsaw. The leading Okhrana official Zavarzin alleges that there were other cases of children being used by terrorist organizations to deliver guns to an agreed-upon destination, where terrorists would collect the guns and proceed with an attack.[52] A young woman from an aristocratic background who joined the PSR Combat Organization proved particularly useful since she could move in high society circles and provide information about ministers and other high officials without raising suspicion. The Combat Organization was hoping that she would be able to be employed in the imperial palace as a lady in waiting.[53] Women and sometimes children made an important contribution to revolutionary work by performing certain tasks which would have been difficult to carry out for a man who would have attracted much more attention.

Like the revolutionaries, the Okhrana was aware of the advantages of using women for clandestine work. The Okhrana hired women to work as detectives, *filiory*, to surveille suspects. Sometimes these women would employ modern techniques to surveille their suspects, using a camera to take photographs of suspects from a distance. The camera was usually concealed in a package to create the impression of the woman as a regular shopper. Other women were hired to infiltrate Socialist Revolutionary groups. These women were at times confronted with a dilemma – to accept a request to assassinate a tsarist official, or refuse, and jeopardize her position in the group. The Okhrana found an ingenious solution to the dilemma. Their agent would deliver the bomb to the Okhrana Office, where it would be defused and returned to the agent, who would then proceed with her mission and throw the bomb at the target without causing an explosion.[54] However, one could argue that this approach had a very limited applicability. It could most likely not be repeated a second time since the terrorists would find it highly suspicious, if an assassination attempt failed a second time as a result of malfunction. One Okhrana agent in particular, Zinaida Zhuchenko, proved an invaluable asset to the political police who benefited greatly from her contribution to counterterrorist operations. Zhuchenko was able to continue to draw upon her detailed knowledge of the PSR and its leadership even after she had been exposed. She was a convinced monarchist, but argued that Russia needed reforms and that the monarchy would not survive a second revolution after the 1905 one. Unfortunately, for Russia, few of her colleagues and tsarist officials shared her views.[55] The above examples of women's contribution to the work of the political police demonstrate that they constituted a very valuable asset that the Okhrana could draw upon for many of its activities.

Funding

The intensive activities of Russian revolutionary organizations in Russia and Western Europe constitute evidence that there was a steady flow of money into the coffers of these organizations. An Okhrana report states that a certain Socialist Revolutionary, Bartold, had a large sum of money at his disposal for terrorist purposes. The Combat Organization had attempted, unsuccessfully, to establish control over the money.[56] Most likely this shows that the leadership wished to retain control over all activities carried out in the name of the PSR Combat Organization. The former head of the Okhrana Office, Moscow, Zavarzin, writes in his memoirs that the Russian authorities did not always find a good approach to dealing with individuals who financially sponsored terrorist activities. Armenian priests provided money and weapons to the Dashnaktsutyun and were therefore targeted by Russian authorities who confiscated Church property in response to this support for revolutionary activities. As a result, the party resorted to assassination of Russian administrative officials in the Caucasus region. The tsarist regime quickly realized that it had not been a good idea to alienate a whole nation and promptly returned the property to the Church.[57] Savinkov confirms the flow of donations to revolutionary organizations as well. He claims that following the assassination of Plehve, the PSR received donations amounting to tens of thousands of rubles.[58] Furthermore, he states that American millionaires had donated 1,000,000 francs to the Russian revolutionary cause on condition that the money be used to arm the population and distributed among all Russian revolutionary parties. The PSR had received 100,000 francs, all of which was promptly transferred to the Combat Organization. The conservative pro-regime newspaper *Novoe*

Vremia had reported that the money had originated in Japan, which was denied by the person to whom the donations had been entrusted, a Finn by name Tsiliakus. The Combat Organization used the money to purchase arms abroad which were smuggled to Finland by ship. By a twist of fate, the ship ran aground off the coast of Finland. The crew blew up their ship, and the weapons were later found by the border force. Finnish revolutionaries took over the weapons during a period of social unrest and distributed them among Finnish peasants.[59] Okhrana documents and primary sources confirm that wealthy individuals supported Russian revolutionary organizations financially.[60]

Revolutionary cooperation

The Russian revolutionary landscape consisted of a multitude of revolutionary organizations, but their ideological differences did not prevent them from cooperating in the struggle against the tsarist regime. There are many examples of cooperation between the Party of Socialist Revolutionaries and parties of national minorities. In 1905, during the Russo-Japanese War, the PSR Foreign Committee dispatched a member to Baku to organize a local committee. The committee held talks with the Armenian revolutionary Droshakist Party and agreed upon a merger on condition that a planned assassination, possibly of the governor, be successful. The PSR committee was already in possession of revolvers, but was expecting 'better stuff', interpreted by the Okhrana as meaning explosive devices.[61] The same year, a Finnish revolutionary party made efforts to organize a conference in London, to which it intended to invite all Russian revolutionary parties. The goals of this initiative were to unite all revolutionary groups, organize a popular uprising and arm the people with weapons and bombs.[62] The PSR were actively pursuing cooperation with other parties, discussing plans for smuggling arms into Russia from Bulgaria with the assistance of the Armenian Droshakists[63] and meeting with Macedonian revolutionaries in the Bulgarian capital Sofia to study with them the manufacture of recently invented explosive devices.[64] The revolutionary efforts in 1905–1906 to cooperate were not the first of their kind. A few years earlier, Vladimir L. Burtsev, a former member of *Narodnaia Volia*, had advocated cooperation and unity in the revolutionary movement. He argued that all proponents of political terror constitute one family and should merge into a league of political terror.[65]

International cooperation of the Okhrana

Like the terrorists, the Okhrana had its international partners. An Okhrana report from 1913 reveals that the Okhrana cooperated with the French police. The report states that the Okhrana Office, Paris had received information from French police authorities to the effect that Russian customs officials in Baku had informed the French vice-consul there that an anarchist had left for Paris accompanied by another man and a woman, intending to assassinate a member of the Russian embassy in the city. The trio's traveling funds for the journey amounted to 150,000 francs, a detail which suggests that they were not expecting to stay at a flophouse during their sojourn in the French capital. The Okhrana cooperated with Scotland Yard in a similar way before and during the process against the London-based publicist Vladimir Burtsev whose articles, inciting to regicide, landed him a sentence of a year and a half of hard labor. The heads of the Okhrana Office, Paris and Scotland Yard and British government ministers cooperated to get a conviction.[66] The Okhrana, through its office in Berlin, cooperated with the German police and the ties between the Okhrana Office, Paris and the French security police were very close.[67]

Like security and intelligence agencies today, the Okhrana exchanged important intelligence with other security services and authorities in Europe.

Effectiveness of terrorism

The examination of various aspects of Russian terrorism in this chapter allows us to answer the question of whether terrorism was an effective means to fight the tsarist regime both in the affirmative and negative. The reason for the somewhat ambiguous answer is that certain aspects of terrorism were effective at times and less so at others, depending on planning and execution, and the individuals involved. A young artillery officer who joined the PSR was most likely considered an ideal member since he had important contacts in the military and 'at his disposal' a military depot.[68] An Okhrana communication reports that a revolutionary group in Penza was preparing an uprising 'in the same fashion as is done in the Caucasus'.[69] This indicates that uprisings must have happened more than once in the Caucasus or perhaps even from time to time, a fact which reflects a degree of organizational and agitational effectiveness on the part of the militants. Several high-profile assassinations, including that of tsar Aleksandr II, were touted as enormous successes by the terrorists. The publicity the militants gained was certainly a success, but, as has been pointed out already, the following mass arrests of revolutionaries, crushing of Narodnaia Volia and reactionary policies of Aleksandr III can hardly be interpreted as revolutionary successes. In a sense, Narodnaia Volia could argue that the organization had realized one of its fundamental principles with the assassination of Aleksandr II, namely regime change because of the very different rules of Aleksandr II and his successor. The regime change, which, of course, did not amount to the overthrow of the Romanov dynasty and tsarism, resulted in a political climate which made it much more difficult for terrorists to operate, in other words, a change for the worse, not for the better.

Terrorist organizations appear to have been quite effective as to raising funds for their activities and disseminating their ideologies. Several

Methodology of Russian terrorism 63

Okhrana reports discussed in this chapter testify to the proficiency of some militant organizations in raising funds, a skill which enabled them to maintain a strong and continuous presence in Western Europe, where the political climate allowed them to work more effectively toward achieving their goals by planning and organizing political assassinations. The flow of donations to the revolutionary cause enabled revolutionaries to acquire and set up open printing offices in Western Europe and underground ones in Russia, disseminate propaganda to compatriots temporarily visiting the West and smuggle thousands of pamphlets across Russia's borders. The certain degree of financial independence and freedom of speech enjoyed by Russian terrorists in the West thus allowed them to focus fulltime on their work and get their message across to the public.[70]

The Russian historian Oleg Budnitskii paints a somewhat different picture of terrorist effectiveness, emphasizing the successes of the revolutionaries over their weaknesses. He argues that revolutionary terrorism was quite successful since it forced the tsarist regime to make concessions. One of these concessions, according to Budnitskii, triggered by the explosion in the Winter Palace in 1880 described above, was a proposal prepared by Mikhail T. Loris-Melikov, Minister of the Interior, for a very modest 'constitution' in 1881. The project was scrapped by Aleksandr III, following the assassination of his father. Another presumable success was the refusal of the Second Duma to condemn terrorism. The defiant demeanor of early terrorists tried in civilian courts where they could condemn the government's reactionary and oppressive policies and justify their own acts did indeed provoke public sympathy for the accused. However, as Budnitskii also points out, the wave of assassinations and robberies led to a re-assessment, a 'de-heroization', by the public with regard to the terrorists.[71] Among the successes emphasized by Budnitskii, there is not a clearly developed hint at what might have been the real reason for the collapse of the tsarist regime – the long-term consequences of its reluctance to adjust and adapt to changing sentiments in Russian society and to grant Russians a real role in creating a reformed system of government. The weakness of Loris-Melikov's 'constitutional' project was perhaps not so much its very modest reform – the granting to an assembly of indirectly elected members of a mere advisory role[72] – as the tsar's refusal to approve it. Furthermore, the short-term success of the First and Second Dumas was interrupted when the regime dissolved the Second Duma, stuffing the Third Duma with conservatives. One can thus conclude that, from a historical perspective, some of the successes of the militants were short-lived, due to the rigidity of the regime.

Despite the conclusion that important terrorist successes were oftentimes short-term achievements, there were certain areas in addition to those mentioned earlier where Russian militants displayed skills that deserve mentioning. Traveling across borders in Europe without a passport was a daring undertaking which the leading terrorist Boris Savinkov describes in his memoirs. This activity required meticulous planning, coordination with people smugglers and border guards and a bit of good luck.[73] The methodical planning of assassinations was another skill in which terrorists possessed proficiency, though an element of serendipity was often required successfully to execute such an undertaking. Conspirators would meticulously study daily routines of and routes taken by targeted individuals and details of the appearance of carriages, horses, guards and lackeys accompanying the intended victim. Such a team effort would oftentimes include several bomb throwers carrying one to two bombs and lookouts strategically placed to alert the bomb throwers, in case the target chose an alternate route. Unfortunately, for the militants, it was the latter who sometimes benefited from fortuity. One illustrative occasion was where Pyotr N. Durnovo, Minister of the Interior, unexpectedly walked up to a member of the PSR Combat Organization posing as a newspaper hawker to buy a newspaper. One can imagine the enormous frustration the terrorists must have experienced because of this missed opportunity. The explanation is that the newspaper hawker was a PSR Combat Organization surveillant, and surveillants did not carry a gun.[74] The above examples reveal that meticulous planning always had to make allowances for chance in order to be successful.

Both the revolutionaries and Okhrana turned out to be adept at placing informants in enemy organizations. One such informant was the Narodnaia Volia member Nikolai Kletochnikov who over the course of two years reported from inside the Third Department (Tret'e Otdelenie, the Okhrana's predecessor), revealing the identity of over 300 police informants in revolutionary ranks.[75] Vladimir Burtsev was a one-man intelligence agency, working diligently to reveal *agents provocateurs* in revolutionary organizations, one of whom was Evno Azef, who, for five years as the head of the PSR Combat Organization, shared the names of revolutionaries and their plans with the Okhrana. Burtsev's investigations also exposed a female Okhrana informant in the PSR Combat Organization, Maria Tsikhotskaia and the names of approximately 200 Okhrana informants, though many of these were most likely no longer active.[76] Conversely, the Okhrana admitted that revolutionary informants in their midst constituted a problem. In a report to the Department of Police, Leonid A. Rataev, head of the Okhrana Office in Paris, complains about leaks in the Department of Police of information contained in his reports, which have sometimes been almost verbatim published in revolutionary publications. This circumstance has caused the revolutionaries to look for an informant in their midst who conveys information about their activities to the Okhrana.[77] One can draw a convincing conclusion from this paragraph that enemy informants operating in their midst constituted a serious problem for both the terrorists and the Okhrana.

Effectiveness of counterterrorism

The terrorists and the Okhrana were similar in several respects. As has been pointed out above, both had their fair share of successes and failures. One of the most serious blows to the political police was the exposure in 1909 of Evno Azef, its star agent in the PSR Combat Organization. Shortly before his exposure, however, Azef managed to provide information to the Okhrana that led to the arrest of many members of the PSR.[78] Conversely, an operation which was carried out against terrorists in southern Russia must be considered one of the great achievements of the Okhrana. During the operation, a group of terrorists inside an apartment began to throw bombs through the window. The bombs were so powerful that the 'pavement turned into sand'[79] and shattered all windows in adjacent buildings. Two hundred explosive devices and more than 70 pounds of dynamite were confiscated in the search of the apartment. Additionally, a number of addresses in cipher of intended targets all over Russia were found, resulting in the destruction of the Russian Social Democratic Labor Party's technical unit and, according to a leading Okhrana official, saving the lives of hundreds of people.[80] Also, by the own admission of terrorists in Baku, mounted Cossacks searching for weapons were a serious problem for revolutionary organizations operating there.[81] The political police can probably take some credit for this since they had likely provided the intelligence that the Cossacks acted on. The Okhrana's approach to surveillance is another example of effective police work. In a specific case where agents could suspect that several planned terrorist acts actually constituted a coordinated operation, the Okhrana would not make immediate arrests, but be patient in order to build a solid case against the terrorists, whilst receiving intelligence from very well-informed sources. The intention was to strike simultaneously against all conspirators[82] and, most likely, also to collect incriminating evidence against other militants involved of whom the political police were not yet aware. The above thus reveals that the Okhrana, at least at times, were effective in their counter-terrorism efforts.

Some historians take a much more skeptical approach to the effectiveness of the Okhrana. They have emphasized that the political police were unable to prevent the assassination of Aleksandr II and that they failed to prevent Socialist Revolutionary terrorism in the early twentieth century.[83] It has also been argued that the Okhrana was in complete disarray during the First Russian Revolution of 1905, that the political police were too cautious or frightened to take resolute action against the revolutionaries and that officials who disagreed with this lack of action were relocated to other posts and replaced with individuals who lacked the skills successfully to counter terrorism.[84] The former criticism seems to be somewhat unfair, for the obvious reason that, by this standard, any counterterrorism agency, including modern ones, would be considered ineffective since it is, even with the highly sophisticated technical equipment at the disposal of law enforcement agencies today, virtually impossible to prevent all terrorist acts. The latter criticism seems to point to a real problem – the absence of an effective strategy to deal with the political and social unrest of 1905. Despite this valid criticism, which is also partly echoed by a leading Okhrana official,[85] one needs to give due credit to the political police for sometimes preventing, or at least temporarily thwarting terrorist plans which would have resulted not only in the death of certain government officials but also innocent bystanders who happened to be in the wrong place at the wrong time.

Due credit also has to be given to certain individual political police officials, such as one leading Okhrana official with a past as a secret informant in the revolutionary movement, who considered the very perceptive possibility of a Russian defeat in a conflict with Japan and that such an outcome would result in massive revolutionary unrest in the country, which is exactly what happened in 1905.[86] Had this possibility been seriously considered by the regime, it could have taken steps better to prepare for the unrest which erupted in the country in late 1905. Another leading political police official, Georgii P. Sudeikin, managed in 1879 to arrest most active revolutionaries in Kiev, including the members of Narodnaia Volia's Executive Committee, a notable success from counterterrorism perspective.[87] He had repeated this achievement in St. Petersburg in 1882.[88] Sudeikin was also successful in recruiting several revolutionaries to work for the Okhrana as informers. However, Okhrana recruitment of revolutionaries had its risks. One member of Narodnaia Volia, Sergei Degaev, who had been arrested by Sudeikin and then recruited by him, later assassinated the Okhrana chief. Having confessed about his links to the Okhrana to two N.V. leaders, Degaev had to pledge to assassinate Sudeikin in order to avoid exposure.[89] The examples referred to in this paragraph reveal that the Okhrana had some competent officials in its ranks.

In addition to infiltration, which has been discussed above, there were certain other areas and patterns of behavior in which the Okhrana and revolutionaries displayed striking similarities. One such area was propaganda, an instrument which was exploited by both sides, albeit with the political police at a considerable disadvantage. This disadvantage was particularly obvious in Western Europe where the revolutionaries exploited civil liberties to the fullest to publish their anti-tsarist writings and were helped by anti-Russian sentiments. Personal security was another serious concern of both government officials and revolutionaries. As has been discussed already in this chapter, terrorists exposed themselves to great risks such as betrayal by 'comrades' working for the Okhrana, incarceration, exile in Siberia and accidental explosions when handling bombs. An extreme case of the risks to which government officials exposed themselves and their lifestyle is Georgii Sudeikin, whose life as a leading Okhrana official in many respects mirrored that of wanted terrorists. He intentionally changed his routines frequently to prevent his revolutionary enemies from assassinating him. Sudeikin had several passports issued to him in different names, frequently stayed in different residences for a short time only and often changed uniforms to confuse revolutionary surveillants. Also, Sudeikin avoided meeting his agents in his office and apparently housed his family in one of the prisons in St. Petersburg.[90] Ironically, with this lifestyle, he could easily have joined Narodnaia Volia or the Socialist Revolutionaries without too much adjustment. Admittedly, his was an extreme case, but it suggests that other leading government officials had similar concerns, which they shared with their enemies.

Conclusion

The warfare between nineteenth- and early twentieth-century Russian militants and the tsarist regime's political police testify to the fact that both parties were worthy opponents of one another. The evidence in support of this argument presented in this chapter has demonstrated that despite the weaknesses by which their tactics were sometimes marred and the frequent failures of their plans and operations, both participants in this violent cat and mouse game could sometimes score spectacular successes. What frequently contributed to failure and success was the element of chance, which is, of course, very difficult to take into consideration when planning a terrorist act or an Okhrana operation. Despite this difficulty, both adversaries evinced versatility and a talent for innovative thinking, the purpose of which was to remain one step ahead of the enemy in every aspect of terrorism and counterterrorism. One way of gaining an advantage over the adversary or establishing what can be termed strategic depth was cooperation. In both the terrorist and Okhrana cases, cooperation assumed the form of domestic and international cooperation. The terrorists overcame ideological differences for the 'greater good' of the revolutionary cause. This approach held true, to a certain extent, for the Okhrana's cooperation with West European law enforcement agencies as well. There were, however, certain limitations to how close the relationship between Russian and West European security services could grow, owing to political sensitivities with regard to the oppressive nature of the tsarist regime and the democratic system of government in many Western societies. Liberal public opinion in the West would not approve of too close a relationship. Aware of this circumstance, Russian émigré revolutionaries made every effort in their publications to focus on the negative aspects of the tsarist regime. Nevertheless, utilitarian considerations sometimes took precedence over political sensitivities since it was in the interest of Western governments to maintain peace and stability in their own societies, even if it was not their priority to be concerned about similar factors as they pertained to Russia. The presence of Russian terrorists in the West was more or less tolerated, but there was always a risk that the terrorists would take their war against the tsarist regime to the West. Instances of explosions in apartments occupied by Russian revolutionaries in West European cities and plans to assassinate Russian officials serving or visiting abroad bear witness to this reality.

A couple of important conclusions drawn in this chapter concern similarities of certain aspects of terrorist and Okhrana activities and the effectiveness of the approach to the enemy adopted by each side in the conflict.

68 *Methodology of Russian terrorism*

Certain aspects of the war between the political police and the terrorists displayed striking similarities regarding the tactics adopted to fight the enemy, particularly in activities such as surveillance, infiltration and propaganda. The two belligerents oftentimes adapted well to changing tactics of the enemy, but there were clear exceptions to this record, such as the crackdown on terrorism following the assassination of Aleksandr II, the government's reaction to the widespread social unrest in 1905, when it took the leadership of the Russian state a long time to make the decision to enable the Okhrana and the gendarmerie forcefully to deal with the dangerous situation in the country. The second important conclusion drawn in this chapter is that there was no clear winner in the war between the terrorists and the Okhrana. The conflict between the terrorists and the state had an asymmetric aspect to it in the latter's favor, if one takes into account the total resources of the state as a whole. However, the playing field was much more level if one considers the directly affected main protagonists only – the militants and the Okhrana. The limited personnel numbers[91] and budget of this agency, and the less than attractive monetary incentives it could offer, except to the strategically placed informants in the central committees of terrorist organizations,[92] as a matter of fact reduced the asymmetric aspect of the existential struggle between the two camps. The main contributing factor to this reality was the generally rigid and self-defeating policies of the regime. These policies, particularly the decision to enter the Great War, despite the experienced social unrest in the wake of the Russo-Japanese War of 1904–1905, contributed to the fall of the regime to a higher degree than the activities of the terrorists, which certainly reduced the regime's standing among its citizens, but did not cause its collapse. Despite the 50-year struggle against the regime, terrorism could not achieve its goal – a general uprising in the country. In this respect, the Okhrana's record is similar to that of the terrorists – the political police failed to eliminate terrorism in Russian society, though the number of violent actions carried out against the state decreased as Europe approached the catastrophe of the First World War. It took the Russian state itself to play an instrumental role in achieving its own collapse.

Notes

1 The main task of the Okhrana was to prevent political crimes from being committed and that of the Gendarmerie to investigate such crimes when committed, Nurit Schleifman, 'The Internal Agency: Linchpin of the Political Police in Russia', *Cahiers du Monde russe et soviétique*, Vol. 24, No. 1/2 (Jan., - Jun., 1983), p. 154.
2 Jonathan Daly, *Autocracy under Siege: Security Police and Opposition in Russia 1866–1905* (DeKalb: Northern Illinois University Press, 1998), p. 94.
3 Jonathan Daly, *The Watchful State: Security Police and Opposition in Russia 1906–1917* (DeKalb: Northern Illinois University Press, 2004), p. 86.
4 Savinkov's autobiography confirms that PSR terrorists viewed the revolutionary struggle against the state as a war and themselves as prisoners of war, if they

were captured, Boris Savinkov, *Vospominania terrorista* [Memoirs of a Terrorist] (Moscow: Vagrius, 2006, first published in 1909), p. 42, *Lib.ru/Klassika*, accessed 7 September 2015, http://az.lib.ru/s/sawinkow_b_w/text_0010.shtml.
5 The head of the St. Petersburg Okhrana Office, Georgii P. Sudeikin, seems to confirm this view: 'for him the war with the nihilists resembled a hunt ... the contest of skill and cunning, the danger, the satisfaction from success', Aleksandr A. Polovtsov, *Dnevnik gosudarstvennogo sekretaria: 1883–1892* (Moscow: Nauka, 1966), Volume I, p. 157, quoted in Richard Pipes, *The Degaev Affair: Terror and Treason in Tsarist Russia* (New Haven, CT: Yale University Press, 2003), p. 36. Another almost literal example of hide and seek was the revolutionaries' habit of burying compromising material such as domestic passports, letters and chemicals. The Okhrana would use police dogs to find the concealed evidence, Pavel Pavlovich Zavarzin, *Zhandarmy i Revoliutsionery: Vospominaniia* (Paris: Published by the author, [izdanie avtora] 1930), pp. 186–187.
6 Philip Pomper, 'Nechaev and Tsaricide: The Conspiracy within the Conspiracy', *The Russian Review*, Vol. 33, No. 2 (Apr., 1974), p. 132.
7 From the Okhrana Office, Paris to Ministry of the Interior, Officer for Special Missions, rank 5 at the Department of Police, No. 62. Top Secret. 9 May 1905. Box 214, Reel 396, Okhrana Records.
8 From Rataev, Officer for Special Missions, rank 5 at the Department of Police to the Director of the Department of Police, No. 25, 11 February 1905. Box 214, Reel 396, Okhrana Records.
9 From the Ministry of the Interior, Department of Police to the Head of the Okhrana's Office, Paris. No. 8754, 25 October 1907. Box 214, Reel 396, Okhrana Records.
10 Adam Ulam, *Prophets and Conspirators in Prerevolutionary Russia: In the Name of the People* (New York, NY: Viking Press, 1977), p. 340; E. L. Rudnitskaia (ed.), *Revolutsionnii radikalizm v Rossii: deviatnadtsatii vek* (Moscow: Arkheograficheskii Tsentr, 1997), p. 429.
11 From the Department of Police to the officer dispatched abroad by the Ministry of the Interior for contacts between local authorities and Russian diplomatic and consular missions. No. 173657, 1 July 1914. Box 214, Reel 396, Okhrana Records.
12 The Department of Police to the Head of the Okhrana Office, Paris, No. 117519 [?], 14 October 1912. Secret; From the Russian Embassy, Washington, D.C., No. 89, 12 April 1916. Top Secret. Telegram in cipher. Budnitskii mentions a plan to introduce poison into the imperial palace's water pipe discussed by a group of conspirators in 1895, Oleg V. Budnitskii, *Terrorizm: ideologiia, etika, psikhologiia (vtoraia polovina xix – nachalo xx veka)* (Moscow: ROSSPEN, 2000), p. 35.
13 Savinkov, *Vospominania*, p. 13; Broido, *Apostles into Terrorists*, p. 183.
14 Pavel Pavlovich Zavarzin, *Zhandarmy i Revoliutsionery: Vospominaniia* (Paris: Published by the author, [izdanie avtora] 1930), pp. 92, 156–158; Officer for Special Missions, rank 5 at the Department of the Police, Berlin [no addressee, but most likely, the Director of the Department of Police], No. 40, 8 March 1905. Box 214, Reel 396, Okhrana Files.
15 Richard Johnson, 'Zagranichnaia Agentura: The Tsarist Political Police in Europe', *Journal of Contemporary History*, Vol. 7, No. 1/2 (Jan. – Apr., 1972), p. 233. Funding for perlustration in Russia amounted to 92,000 rubles in 1882 and had only marginally increased to 107, 000 rubles in 1909 despite the radical increase in revolutionary activity. Approximately 400,000 letters were opened annually during this period, Daly, *The Watchful State*, p. 105.
16 Savinkov, *Vospominaniia terrorista*, pp. 84, 92, 98.
17 Jonathan Daly, *Autocracy under Siege: Security Police and Opposition in Russia 1866–1905* (DeKalb: Northern Illinois University Press, 1998), p. 80.

70 *Methodology of Russian terrorism*

18 Officer for Special Missions, rank 5 at the Department of Police, Berlin [no addressee but most likely the Director of the Department of Police], No. 40, 8 March 1905. Box 214, Reel 396, Okhrana Files.
19 From the Director of the Department of Police to the Head of the Okhrana's Office, Paris, No. 4475, June 1895. Secret. Okhrana Records, Box 214, Reel 396.
20 Zavarzin, *Zhandarmy*, pp. 165, 172, 188.
21 From Rataev, Officer for Special Missions [no addressee, but most likely the Director of the Department of Police, no date.], Box 214, Reel 396, Okhrana Files.
22 Donald Senese, 'S. M. Kravchinskii and the National Front Against Autocracy', *Slavic Review*, Vol. 34, No. 3 (Sept., 1975), p. 517.
23 Scott Seregny, 'Revolutionary Strategies in the Russian Countryside: Rural Teachers and the Socialist Revolutionary Party on the Eve of 1905', *The Russian Review*, Vol. 44, No. 3 (Jul., 1985), pp. 231–232.
24 From the Okhrana Office, Paris to the Department of Police, No. 1205, 12 August 1913; From the Okhrana Office, Paris to the Department of Police, No. 1258, 17 August 1913. The Okhrana for their part could cause confusion and division in the revolutionary camp by circulating disinformation to the effect that a particular revolutionary was secretly working for the political police, Daly, *Autocracy under Siege*, p. 94; Pipes, *The Degaev Affair*, p. 39.
25 Zavarzin, *Zhandarmy*, p. 93; Pipes, *The Degaev Affair*, p. 44. Savinkov confirms that terrorists used false passports and *nomes de guerre* to make the Okhrana's work more difficult, Savinkov, *Vospominania*, pp. 13, 30; Franco Venturi, *Il Populismo Russo: Dalla Liberazione dei Servi al Nihilismo*, volume 2 (Turin: Giulio Einaudi editore s.p.a., 1972), p. 302.
26 From Harting, Head of Intelligence Section to the Director of the Department of Police, 20 April 1906. Top Secret. Box 214, Reel 396, Okhrana Files; From the Okhrana Office, Paris to the Director of the Department of Police, No. 97, 2 February 1913. Top Secret. Box 214, Reel 396, Okhrana Files; From Rataev, Officer for Special Missions. [No addressee, but most likely the Director of the Department of Police, no date.] Box 214, Reel 396, Okhrana Files; Senese, 'S. M. Kravchinskii and the National Front against Autocracy', *Slavic Review*, Vol. 34, No. 3 (Sept., 1975), n. 5 and 6, p. 507.
27 From Harting, Head of Intelligence Section to the Director of the Department of Police, 20 April 1906. Top Secret. Box 214, Reel 396, Okhrana Records; Officer for Special Missions, rank 5 at the Department of Police, Berlin [no addressee, but most likely the Director of the Department of Police], No. 40, 8 March 1905. Box 214, Reel 396, Okhrana Files.
28 From the Officer for Special Missions, Frankfurt to the Director of the Department of Police, No. 762, 17 August 1910. Top Secret. Box 214, Reel 396, Okhrana Records.
29 Vera Broido, *Apostles into Terrorists: Women and the Revolutionary Movement in the Russia of Alexander II* (New York, NY: Viking Press, 1977), p. 188.
30 Jonathan Daly, 'Political Crime in Late Imperial Russia', *The Journal of Modern History*, Vol. 74, No. 1 (Mar., 2002), p. 92.
31 This conclusion is confirmed in Jonathan Daly, 'Political Crime in Late Imperial Russia', *The Journal of Modern History*, Vol. 74, No. 1 (Mar., 2002), p. 92.
32 From the Okhrana Office, Paris to the Director of the Department of Police, No. 949, 10 August 1915. Top Secret. Box 214, Reel 396, Okhrana Files; From the Director of the Department of Police to Rachkovskii, Head of the Okhrana Office, Paris, No. 4255, 27 May 1895. Box 214, Reel 396, Okhrana Files.
33 From the Director of the Department of Police to the Head of the Okhrana Office, Paris, No. 106245, 16 September 1912. Secret. Box 214, Reel 396, Okhrana Files.

34 Officer for Special Missions, rank 5 at the Department of the Police, Berlin [no addressee, but most likely the Director of the Department of Police], No. 40, 8 March 1905. Box 214, Reel 396, Okhrana Files. Sergei Nechaev seems to have conducted explosives experiments in his apartment in 1868 where men and girls would gather, creating 'fires and shots', Philip Pomper, 'Nechaev and Tsaricide: The Conspiracy within the Conspiracy', *The Russian Review*, Vol. 33, No. 2 (Apr., 1974), p. 135.
35 From the Director of the Department of Police to Rachkovskii, Head of the Okhrana's Office, Paris, No. 4255, 27 May 1895. Box 214, Reel 396, Okhrana Files.
36 From the Director of the Department of Police to the Head of the Okhrana's Office, Paris, No. 4475, June 1895. Secret. Box 214, Reel 396, Okhrana Files.
37 From the State Councilor, Paris, to the Director of the Department of Police, No. 1493, 13 November 1914. Box 214, Reel 396, Okhrana Files.
38 Ibid.
39 Savinkov, *Vospominania*, p. 14.
40 From the Director of the Department of Police to the Head of the Okhrana's Office, Paris, No. 4475, June 1895. Secret. Box 214, Reel 396, Okhrana Files.
41 Savinkov, *Vospominania*, p. 111.
42 Budnitskii, *Terrorizm*, p. 35.
43 From the Department of Police to the Okhrana Office, Paris. No. 105560, 24 October 1913. Secret. Box 214, Reel 396, Okhrana Files.
44 From Arkady Harting, Head of Intelligence Section [temporarily visiting Geneva] to P. I. Rachkovskii, Paris, no date. Box 214, Reel 396, Okhrana Files.
45 Savinkov, *Vospominania*, pp. 12, 81.
46 Officer for Special Missions, rank 5 at the Department of Police, Berlin [no addressee, but most likely the Director of the Department of Police], No. 40, 8 March 1905. Box 214, Reel 396, Okhrana Files.
47 From Harting, Head of Intelligence Section to the Director of the Department of Police, 20 April 1906. Top Secret. Box 214, Reel 396, Okhrana Files.
48 From the Director of the Department of Police to Harting, Collegiate Councilor. No. 9995, 30 June 1906. Box 214, Reel 396, Okhrana Files.
49 From Harting, Head of Intelligence Section to the Director of Department of Police, 20 April 1906. Top Secret. Box 214, Reel 396, Okhrana Files.
50 Amy Knight, 'Female Terrorists in the Russian Socialist Revolutionary Party', *The Russian Review*, Vol. 38, No. 2 (Apr., 1979), pp. 139, 144, 146; Vera Broido, *Apostles into Terrorists: Women and the Revolutionary Movement in the Russia of Alexander II* (New York, NY: Viking Press, 1977), p. 183.
51 From Rataev, Officer for Special Missions [no addressee, but most likely the Director of the Department of Police, no date.] Box 214, Reel 396, Okhrana Files.
52 Zavarzin, *Zhandarmy*, pp. 117–119, 143–144, 148.
53 Savinkov, *Vospominania*, p. 30.
54 Zavarzin, *Zhandarmy*, p. 189.
55 Ibid., p. 192. Zhuchenko initially worked for the Okhrana in Leipzig and Heidelberg until she returned to Russia in the revolutionary year of 1905. She succeeded in occupying a strategic position in the local PSR Combat Organization which allowed her to provide the Okhrana with critical information on terrorist operations and PSR terrorists, Nurit Schleifmann, 'The Internal Agency: Linchpin of the Political Police in Russia', *Cahiers du Monde russe et soviétique*, Vol. 24, No. 1/2 (Jan., – Jun., 1983), pp. 168–169.
56 From the Okhrana Office, Paris to the Director of the Department of Police, No. 1657, 8 November 1913. Box 214, Reel 396, Okhrana Files.
57 Zavarzin, *Zhandarmy*, pp. 121–122.

72 *Methodology of Russian terrorism*

58 Savinkov, *Vospominania*, p. 30.
59 Ibid., p. 48. See Okhrana telegram under sub-heading **Firearms** above, n. 44. Based upon the information provided by the Okhrana and Savinkov, one can conclude, on good grounds, that Tsiliakus, Berg and Mannerstam are one and the same. Another conclusion one can draw is that both sources seem to have gotten some things wrong and some things right. For another example of generous funding, see the report From the Officer for Special Missions, rank 5 at the Department of Police, Berlin [no addressee, but most likely the Director of the Department of Police], No. 40, 8 March 1905. Box 214, Reel 396, Okhrana Files. For the Japanese connection, see also Daly, *Autocracy under Siege*, p. 159.
60 Sigizmund N. Valk, ed., Arkhif 'Zemli i Voli' (The Archive of Land and Freedom) (Moscow: Izdatel'stvo Vsesojuznogo Obshchestva Politkatorzhan i Ssyl'no-poselentsev 1932), p. 224, referred to in Adam B. Ulam, *Prophets and Conspirators; Prerevolutionary Russia*. New Brunswick and London: Transaction Publishers, 1998 (first published in 1977 by Viking Press), p. 320.
61 Officer for Special Missions, rank 5 at the Department of the Police, Berlin [no addressee, but most likely the Director of the Department of Police], No. 40, 8 March 1905. Box 214, Reel 396, Okhrana Files.
62 Ibid.
63 From Rataev, Officer for Special Missions, rank 5 at the Department of Police to the Director of the Department of Police, No. 25, 11 February 1905. Box 214, Reel 396, Okhrana Files.
64 From Rataev, Officer for Special Missions [no addressee, but most likely the Director of the Department of Police, no date] Box 214, Reel 396, Okhrana Files.
65 Vladimir L. Burtsev, *Doloi tsaria!* [Down with the Tsar!] (London, 1901), quoted in Budnitskii, *Terrorizm*, p. 43. Budnitskii also shows the existence of cooperation between Socialist Revolutionaries and Social Democrats who in 1901–1902 formed joint committees in several Russian cities, Budnitskii, *Terrorizm*, p. 101. Savinkov refers in his memoirs to the close ties between the PSR and the Finnish Active Resistance Party, which thanks to its infiltration of all Finnish government institutions and the police was in a unique position to provide various services to PSR terrorists operating from Finland, protecting them from extradition to Russia, Savinkov, *Vospominania*, p. 75.
66 Budnitskii, *Terrorizm*, p. 38. Also, see Daly, *Autocracy under Siege*, p. 45.
67 Daly, *Autocracy under Siege*, p. 159; Daly, *The Watchful State*, pp. 101–102. Ruud and Stepanov also confirm the ties between the Okhrana and the French police, Charles Ruud and Sergei Stepanov, *Fontanka 16: The Tsars' Secret Police* (Montreal: McGill-Queen's University Press, 1999), p. 81.
68 From Rataev, Officer for Special Missions [no addressee, but most likely the Director of the Department of Police, no date]. Box 214, Reel 396, Okhrana Files.
69 Ibid.
70 The PSR saw their fortunes reversing about 1910, however, with party funds declining from 168,000 rubles in 1908 to 36,000 in 1910, Daly, *The Watchful State*, p. 110.
71 Budnitskii, *Terrorizm*, pp. 116–120.
72 Werner E. Mosse, 'Alexander II', *Encyclopaedia Britannica*, accessed 18 June 2019, https://www.britannica.com/biography/Alexander-II-emperor-of-Russia#ref 292204.
73 Savinkov, *Vospominania*, pp. 4, 6, 25.
74 Ibid., pp. 4–10, 17, 91.
75 Pipes, *The Degaev Affair*, p. 56; Ulam, *Prophets and Conspirators*, pp. 306–307.
76 Daly, *The Watchful State*, pp. 98–100.
77 From Rataev, Head of the Okhrana Office, Paris to the Department of Police, No. 62. Top Secret, 9 May 1905. Box 214, Reel 396, Okhrana Files.

78 Daly, *The Watchful State*, p. 84. For a detailed discussion of the Azef Affair, see Savinkov, *Vospominania*, pp. 124–146.
79 Zavarzin, *Zhandarmy*, p. 139.
80 Ibid., p. 140.
81 The Cossacks were elite military units in Russia, but, in this instance, they probably acted on intelligence from the Okhrana.
82 From Rataev, Officer for Special Missions [no addressee, but most likely the Director of the Department of Police, no date.]. Box 214, Reel 396, Okhrana Files.
83 Budnitskii, *Terrorizm*, pp. 9, 27, 116.
84 Zuckermann, *The Tsarist Secret Police*, pp. 145, 148.
85 Zavarzin, *Zhandarmy*, p. 62. Zavarzin lays most of the blame at the door of military and political leaders who were unable to realize that the war against the terrorists had to be accompanied by reform. The head of the Okhrana in the 1880s, Georgii Sudeikin, concurred in this negative view of the regime, Pipes, *The Degaev Affair*, p. 70.
86 Zavarzin, *Zhandarmy*, p. 60.
87 Pipes, *The Degaev Affair*, p. 37.
88 Ibid., p. 59.
89 Ibid., p. 92. Also, exposed Okhrana informants had a tendency not to live very long following exposure, Ulam, *Prophets and Conspirators*, p. 321.
90 Ibid., p. 37.
91 Iain Lauchlan, 'Security Policing in Late Imperial Russia', in Ian Thatcher, ed., *Late Imperial Russia: Problems and Prospects. Essays in Honour of R. B. McKean* (Manchester: Manchester University Press, 2005), p. 44.
92 For a detailed account of the Okhrana's organization and operations, see Pavel P. Zavarzin, *Zhandarmy i revoliutsionery, vospominaniia* [Gendarmes and revolutionaries: a memoir] (Paris: Izdanie avtora, 1930). Zavarzin served as director of several regional Okhrana offices in the pre-revolutionary era, including Warsaw and Moscow.

Bibliography

Broido, Vera. *Apostles into Terrorists: Women and the Revolutionary Movement in the Russia of Alexander II*. New York, NY: Viking Press, 1977.

Budnitskii, Oleg V. *Terrorizm: ideologiia, etika, psikhologiia (vtoraia polovina xix – nachalo xx veka)* [Terrorism: Ideology, Ethics and Psychology (Second Half of the Nineteenth and Early Twentieth Centuries)]. Moscow: ROSSPEN, 2000.

Burtsev, Vladimir L. *Doloi tsaria!* [Down with the tsar!]. London: n.p. 1901.

Daly, Jonathan. *Autocracy under Siege: Security Police and Opposition in Russia 1866–1905*. DeKalb: Northern Illinois University Press, 1998.

Daly, Jonathan. *The Watchful State: Security Police and Opposition in Russia 1906–1917*. DeKalb: Northern Illinois University Press, 2004.

Johnson, Richard. 'Zagranichnaia Agentura: The Tsarist Political Police in Europe'. *Journal of contemporary History*, Vol. 7, No. 1/2 (January–April 1972), pp. 221–42.

Knight, Amy. 'Female Terrorists in the Russian Socialist Revolutionary Party'. *The Russian Review*, Vol. 38, No. 2 (April 1979), pp. 139–59.

Lauchlan, Iain. 'Security Policing in Late Imperial Russia'. In Ian Thatcher, ed., *Late Imperial Russia: Problems and Prospects. Essays in Honour of R. B. McKean*. Manchester: Manchester University Press, 2005, pp. 44–63.

Mosse, Werner E. 'Alexander II'. *Encyclopaedia Britannica*.

Okhrana Files. *Hoover Institution*. Palo Alto, CA: Stanford University.

74 *Methodology of Russian terrorism*

Pipes, Richard. *The Degaev Affair: Terror and Treason in Tsarist Russia.* New Haven, CT: Yale University Press, 2003.

Polovtsov, Aleksandr A. *Dnevnik gosudarstvennogo sekretaria: 1883–1892* [Diary of a Secretary of State, 1883–1892]. Moscow: Nauka, 1966.

Pomper, Philip. 'Nechaev and Tsaricide: The Conspiracy within the Conspiracy'. *The Russian Review*, Vol. 33, No. 2 (April 1974), pp. 123–38.

Rudnitskaia, Evgeniia L., ed. *Revolutsionnii radikalizm v Rossii: deviatnadtsatii vek.* Moscow: Arkheograficheskii Tsentr, 1997.

Ruud, Charles and Sergei Stepanov. *Fontanka 16: The Tsars' Secret Police.* Montreal: McGill-Queen's University Press, 1999.

Savinkov, Boris. *Vospominania terrorista* [Memoirs of a Terrorist]. Moscow: Vagrius, 2006. First published in 1909. *Lib.ru/Klassika*. Accessed 7 September 2015. http://az.lib.ru/s/sawinkow_b_w/text_0010.shtml.

Schleifman, Nurit. 'The Internal Agency: Linchpin of the Political Police in Russia'. *Cahiers du Monde russe et soviétique*, Vol. 24, No. 1/2 (January - June, 1983), pp. 151–77.

Senese, Donald. 'S. M. Kravchinskii and the National Front against Autocracy'. *Slavic Review,* Vol. 34, No. 3 (September 1975), p. 517.

Seregny, Scott. 'Revolutionary Strategies in the Russian Countryside: Rural Teachers and the Socialist Revolutionary Party on the Eve of 1905'. *The Russian Review*, Vol. 44, No. 3 (July 1985), pp. 221–38.

Thatcher, Ian, ed. *Late Imperial Russia: Problems and Prospects. Essays in Honour of R. B. McKean.* Manchester: Manchester University Press, 2005.

Ulam. Adam B. *Prophets and Conspirators: Prerevolutionary Russia.* New Brunswick and London: Transaction Publishers, 1998 (first published in 1977 by Viking Press).

Valk, Sigizmund N., ed. *Arkhif 'Zemli i Voli'* (The Archive of Land and Freedom). Moscow: Izdatel'stvo Vsesojuznogo Obshchestva Politkatorzhan i Ssyl'noposelentsev 1932.

Zavarzin, Pavel Pavlovich. *Zhandarmy i Revoliutsionery: Vospominaniia* [Gendarmes and Revolutionaries: A Memoir]. Paris: Published by the author [izdanie avtora] 1930.

Zuckermann, Fredric S. *The Tsarist Secret Police in Russian Society, 1880–1917.* New York: New York University Press, 1996.

4 Ideology of the National Socialist terrorist state

Introduction

The National Socialists were convinced that they could successfully implement their totalitarian agenda of racism, genocide and brutal aggression against other nations. Interestingly enough, the Nazi plan to a certain degree mirrored the conspiracy which National Socialist ideology and propaganda accused the Jews of hatching, namely, the wish to establish world domination. The question here is why was the National Socialist Workers Party of Germany (NSDAP) so confident that it would achieve this objective? The answer is the miracle weapons – physical and psychological – that the Nazi state possessed or hoped soon to possess. As the former failed to materialize as offensive weapons in the German arsenal, the Nazi regime still believed that it possessed two miracle weapons which had presumably consistently proved very effective and which the Third Reich had exploited since the beginning of the Nazi movement – ideology and propaganda. The power of these two super weapons would, in the mind of the National Socialist leaders, eventually convert erstwhile enemies to the Nazi cause where physical weapons had failed to achieve military victories. I have chosen to treat ideology and propaganda separately, but it is worth noting that, at times, the line between Nazi ideology and propaganda is extremely obscured. The analysis of the Nazi ideology in this chapter will reveal that the reason for this circumstance is that *both* require the existence of the other. When no hard evidence can be found to support a specific argument, ideology has to resort to propaganda and vice versa. In the mind of Nazi ideologues, propagandists, and inattentive readers and listeners, this makes an irrefutable case without the time-consuming effort of having to conduct serious research. The present and the following chapter will reveal the validity of this claim beyond a shadow of a doubt.

Race

The most well-known aspect of Nazi rule is the extreme racism institutionalized by the regime, which resulted in the Holocaust. However, in order

DOI: 10.4324/9781003260943-5

to present a clear picture of ways in which racism permeated German society under the Nationalsozialistische Deutsche Arbeiterpartei (NSDAP), other aspects of Nazi society must be examined as well. This treatment of the subject involves a multi-disciplinary approach which will critically examine the history and ideology of the NSDAP, and the Nazi movement's positions on the functions of the state, role of its citizens, geopolitics and religion. Language is important in any piece of writing, particularly in the context of dissemination of ideology and propaganda. Part of this chapter will therefore be devoted to analyzing the language and the validity of the arguments advanced in Nazi works of ideological nature. A central concept which serves as a foundation to the above aspects of National Socialist ideology is the idea of Volk, the Aryan/German nation (adjective: *völkisch*). The many National Socialist works discussing the völkisch interpretation of human history testify to its importance to Nazi ideology as a concept upon which other aspects of Nazism are based. Once the racist doctrine of the Volk had been defined, it enabled party ideologues to formulate detailed policies and justify any action taken by Nazi leaders, no matter how repulsive. If the doctrine of the Volk is regarded as the Nazi religion, it facilitates our understanding of NSDAP policies and why many Germans supported the new 'religion', at least until the hardships of a lost cause began to sway public opinion.

The importance of the doctrine of the Volk to justify the policies of the Third Reich is clear from a brief introduction to one of the many ideological works published in the Nazi era. An NSDAP official states in this introduction that 'The resolution of the Jewish question is for the German and other peoples a question of life and death. This realization is a foundational pillar in the National Socialist Weltanschauung ... [which] concerns every *Volksgenosse* [citizen]'.[1] This view is also emphasized in a strictly confidential party directive in which the author chillingly concludes that foreign racial elements need to be purged and that this issue is 'closely connected with preventing the dissemination of a genetic make-up [which causes individuals] not to be able to cope with life'.[2] The directive is a result of the Nazi 'realization' that genetics and racial science have discovered that the idea of racial similarities is erroneous, advancing in its stead the National Socialist idea that the peoples of this world are all different. The corollary of this claim is that members of different races cannot be turned into Germans by a process of naturalization, which is why a main concern of the state is to ensure the maintenance of the purity of the German race and its protection against alien genetic dilution. The directive does not provide any evidence in support of the racial theory advanced above, which indicates that party officials at lower levels are already familiar with it. However, the security classification level, strictly confidential, suggests that the Nazis are not prepared quite yet to announce in public their racial policies. Conversely, this information was not considered deserving of the highest security classification level, *streng geheim* (top secret), which suggests that it was not a state secret and that the Nazis were not really concerned about negative fallout. The official announcement was made a month and a half later at a Nazi rally in Nuremberg on 15 September 1935.[3]

Argumentation

The student of the Nazi ideology will oftentimes find Nazi racial argumentation weak and even contradictory. The necessity to purge the Volk of alien racial elements is backed up by the word 'realization', which is meant to cover up the lack of hard scientific evidence in support of the claim. A second piece of 'evidence', the alien Jews, is used to strengthen the weak argumentation. Many Germans would probably be inclined to accept the alien status of German Jews as a result of the barrage of anti-Jewish propaganda in the Nazi press. This brings the author to the final step in the chain of 'evidence' provided: if Germany gets rid of its Jews, the German race will be pure. However, this conclusion disregards the historical fact that German territory, like many other nations, has witnessed invasions of foreign tribes and peoples, and Germanic tribes have migrated and mixed with other peoples in Europe as well.[4] Now, if history provides the answer, it also raises the question: why would the German race become pure if the alien Jews were removed since many other peoples have interacted closely with the Volk? Germany would most likely have become completely depopulated, had the NSDAP followed through on its racial ideology. Nazi ideologues have obviously overlooked the fact that most peoples have interacted closely with neighboring peoples and invaders. This brings us to the conclusion that there are very few 'pure' nations in the world. Tribes and peoples who have lived in centuries of isolation from the rest of the world such as certain Siberian and Polynesian peoples, the native population of Australia, Inuits of Greenland and northern Canada and Indian tribes of the Amazon jungles might be such examples. Among the Western peoples most likely only Icelanders come close to being a 'pure' race in the *völkisch* sense. This is but one, albeit very illustrative, of many similar examples in Nazi ideological works.

An example of contradictory argumentation is an article authored by the leading Nazi ideologue Alfred Rosenberg. In this article, entitled 'Der Weltparasit' (The World Parasite), Rosenberg argues that Jews constitute a mix of races and that their national characteristic is that they do not easily tolerate what they perceive as alien. Rosenberg then makes a strange statement, arguing that biological research has determined that 'not only in the plant and animal realms do parasites exist, but also among humans'.[5] The author concludes that, since Jews cannot be assimilated and are parasites, they need to be exterminated. Apart from the article's reprehensible message, it suffers from a couple of clear weaknesses. Rosenberg initially states that Jews constitute a mix of races only then to claim that they do not easily accept alien influences. The second part of the sentence clearly contradicts the first part. The second problem with this article is the reference to parasites. The first part of this statement is based upon science and makes sense, but the second part is very problematic, not merely owing to the disturbing conclusion, but also since it is based upon obviously deceptive argumentation. In order to justify extermination of Jews, Rosenberg has linked a scientific (biological/botanical) finding to an emotive statement. The purpose of this approach is to cover up the fact that there is no scientific evidence in support of human 'parasites'. The use of this term is intended to provoke a particular emotion in the reader, which is then taken as hard evidence. The race hatred and encouragement of genocide would come back to haunt Rosenberg at the Nuremberg War Crimes Tribunal as a result of which the author of the above lines was sentenced to death by hanging.[6]

In his *Mein Kampf*, Adolf Hitler himself frequently resorts to contradictory, deceptive and emotive argumentation. In his autobiography, Hitler has exerted himself to make a compelling case for the Nazi ideology. In order to captivate the reader's attention, he introduces one of his arguments as follows: 'There are truths which are so obvious that they exactly for this reason are not seen or at least not recognized by ordinary people'.[7] With this sentence, the author signals a couple of things to the reader. First, the reference to a very obvious truth is intended to reduce the reader's wish to question the claim since skepticism would indicate inferior intellectual faculties. Second, the author uses the expression 'ordinary people' to signal to the reader that he (Hitler) is not an ordinary person and that the reader therefore can trust his judgment since he presumably possesses superior intellectual faculties. In a later sentence, Hitler argues that 'Every animal mates only with an individual of the same species'.[8] This claim appears to be based on direct observation. The keyword is 'species', which the author uses to set a linguistic and emotive trap for the reader. What he is aiming for is clear from the next sentence: 'Any cross-breeding between two beings of unequal level results in an individual between the levels of the two parents'.[9] The author wants us to believe that genetic science operates according to the same laws as mathematics. This is a problematic assumption since it ignores the possibility of characteristics that can be inherited from earlier generations and not exclusively from the parents. Furthermore, Hitler avoids taking into account that some characteristics could be stronger than others and therefore play a more prominent role in the genetic make-up of the offspring. One wonders whether Hitler ever contemplated the implications of his theory, were it ever to be applied to himself, which is most likely why he did not raise the question.

A major weakness of Nazi racial theory is that Hitler and other National Socialist ideologues equate race with the term species as is obvious from the above discussion. Human races do not constitute separate species. This is, however, a precondition for NSDAP ideology to appear 'convincing'. Nazi/racial ideology needs to turn races into species in order to emphasize differences, establish a racial 'hierarchy' and be able to ban cross-breeding, 'a sin against the will of the eternal Creator'.[10] Also, this allows Nazi racial theorists to contend that Aryans occupy the highest rung on the racial ladder and that they therefore possess stronger genes and are in need of protection against 'lower' Jewish genes. Hitler's speeches reveal that he easily gets carried away. This characteristic has carried over into his autobiography, in which he claims that almost all art, science and technology are the result of Aryan creativity, a sweeping statement which, of course has very little basis in reality. Had he ventured outside his bunker in the final days of the Third Reich, he could have determined to what degree his claim was correct.

The Untermensch

Other Nazi leaders, such as Reichsführer Heinrich Himmler, also made their own contribution to Nazi ideology. Himmler's discussion of the *Untermensch* (subhuman) in a pamphlet entitled *Der Untermensch* ties well into Hitler's claims as laid out above. Himmler states that *Menschen* (people) and Untermenschen historically have always fought one another. In this war, the Jews have been the commanders of the Untermenschen, who occupy a position below that of animals in the evolutionary hierarchy. These Untermenschen, such as Attila and Genghis Khan, have gathered in the Asian steppes and then raced across Europe with their 'Hun hordes'.[11]

Important is the assertion that the threat against the Aryans has always emanated from the east. This is a veiled reference to the modern world where the menace to culture is represented by the Bolsheviks. The reader might wonder if the Bolsheviks or the Jews constitute the greater threat. Nazi ideologues have a simplistic answer to this question, which is that they are one and the same, since the Jews allegedly control the Bolshevik movement.[12] In order to emphasize the destructive force of the Jews Himmler creates, without presenting any evidence to this effect, a link between Jews and earlier invasions. The alliance with Japan in the 1930s testifies to Nazi flexibility in regard to ideological matters, when strategic considerations could sometimes take precedence over ideology.

When it comes to Jews, however, NSDAP ideology did not evince flexibility. We have already discussed Rosenberg's argument that Jews constitute a parasitic community, but Nazi leaders felt the need to provide further 'evidence' in order to justify the persecution of German and non-German Jews. Thus, it is not surprising often to find in National Socialist writings the argument that the Jewish people have never possessed their own culture and the foundation of their spiritual works has originated in other cultures.[13] This claim passes over in silence that the German nation, like most other peoples, has borrowed, without inhibition, from other cultures, enriching its own society. One obvious example is the German language, which, like English, has been greatly influenced by Greek, Latin and French. Furthermore, the prophet of the faith that most Europeans embrace was a Jew, an embarrassing fact for the National Socialists, which will be discussed below.

Another somewhat surprising Nazi claim is that Jews have never had their own state.[14] It fits well into the National Socialist attempt to depict Jews as parasites since it stresses their statelessness and lack of belonging. The problem is that this statement can be easily refuted by every German who has read the Bible since two Jewish states existed in ancient times – Israel and Judah. Also, it has already been brought to the reader's attention above that Nazi ideologues are quite unscrupulous when it comes to presenting deceptive information to the public, even when a very inattentive reader can see through their attempts to appear logical. One ideological work claims that the Jew has a very tenuous relationship with truth. The ideologue knows that this is not a very convincing statement since no evidence is provided. Incredibly enough, he backs this statement up with an even less convincing claim, namely, that the language of the Jew is 'not a means to express his thoughts, but to conceal them'.[15] In their attempt to justify Nazi persecution of Jews, National Socialist ideologues frequently resort to extremely weak reasoning, apparently oblivious to the fact that some of their claims are fully applicable to their own ideology and its followers.

The Nazi press was the major outlet for Nazi inflexibility on the racial issue, at times clearly hinting at the fate of the Jews. Early in 1943, the *Völkischer Beobachter*, the official organ of the NSDAP, reported on a speech Hitler had delivered in connection with the anniversary of the founding of the NSDAP. Hitler stated that 'This battle [the Second World War] will end with the extermination of European Jewry'.[16] As if fearing that the message was not sufficiently explicit, he added that 'the German people has ... successfully fought the Jewish internal enemy and is about finally to settle the matter'.[17] However, the Führer had more far-reaching plans for dealing with the Jewish 'enemy', expressing the hope that Germany's other enemies would come to their senses and throw in their lot with the Nazis and destroy all Jews. Hitler's statements are of great significance since they constitute evidence of the Holocaust. It appears that reports about the genocide had begun to reach the Allies at least as early as 1942, but that the latter might not have realized the extent of the human disaster until they actually entered the extermination camps in 1945.[18] This should, however, not have been the case since the Führer's speech leaves no doubt about what was transpiring in Germany and Nazi-controlled territories. This information came from the best possible primary source, and it is unlikely that it did not reach the Allies. They might not have had their own correspondents in Germany, but neutral countries such as Sweden and Switzerland did, and they must have read the *Völkischer Beobachter* on a daily basis. Furthermore, the report completely undermines the excuse made by some Germans after the war that they had not been aware of the extermination of the Jewish population. The newspaper was available in all parts of Germany and excerpts from the speech would have been broadcast by radio. The point of Nazi inflexibility with regard to the racial issue was not to keep it secret, but to convey the policy to the public.

In early 1945, when it was obvious that the war would soon be over, some Nazi leaders, Adolf Hitler not included, began to display vacillation regarding the fate of Jews remaining in German extermination camps. As a result, Swiss and Swedish negotiators made efforts to obtain the release of Jews and Scandinavians interned in Nazi extermination camps. Reichsführer Heinrich Himmler was one of the leaders with whom negotiations were conducted. He intimated that he would consider the release of 500,000 Jews to the United States in exchange for 'trucks and cars'. The Swiss negotiator proposed instead that money could be made available to go toward assisting poor Germans. As a result, an American diplomat deposited 5,000,000 Swiss Francs in a Swiss bank. The agreement led to the release of 1,200 Jews in early February. Himmler had agreed to a second release of 1,800 Jews, but the transport did not materialize.[19] Hitler had already issued an order to the effect that prisoners in concentration camps were to be eliminated 'at the approach of the enemy'.[20] The order did, however, not prevent further negotiations from taking place that spring, with Swiss and Swedish officials continuing their efforts to get Jewish internees released if possible, or at least to improve conditions in the camps, if no promise could be extracted from Nazi leaders to release the Jews. The negotiators were aided by Walter Schellenberg, the Nazi Chief of Foreign Intelligence, and Felix Kersten, Himmler's physical therapist. These two put constant pressure on Himmler to agree to the release of the remaining camp inmates. However, the activities of those involved in the negotiations made these a risky undertaking since they could be considered treason. The risk involved became even more obvious with the deteriorating military situation in Germany, which merely further stimulated Hitler's recalcitrance and only strengthened the Führer's determination to follow through on his promise to implement the 'final solution'. As a result, he issued a new order in the spring of 1945, preventing the evacuation of any remaining camp inmates. It took bringing Germany to the brink of total destruction before some Nazi leaders realized that it might be a good idea to evince some flexibility on the Jewish 'issue'.[21]

1918

An important task of Nazi ideology was to explain the reason for Germany's defeat in 1918 and allot blame for this embarrassment. In order to explain the German defeat in the First World War, Nazi leaders had to rewrite history to make this event fit into their ideology. Accordingly, the argument that the German collapse was caused by an economic catastrophe was rejected out of hand by Adolf Hitler as the main reason for the outcome of the war. In its stead, the Nazis created a face-saving myth to the effect that the main factors accounting for the debacle in 1918 were political, moral and blood-related. He also dismisses in so many words the 'Jewish insolence' to attribute the German defeat to the military factor.[22] Hitler's explanation is that a 'moral poisoning' had been undermining the Volk for many years, as well as a lowered instinct for self-preservation, compounded by the 'Jewish-Marxist lie' that General Erich Ludendorff was to blame for the defeat.[23] It is not surprising that Hitler would list race as a factor contributing to defeat in 1918. He states that it was the failure on the part of the Volk to realize this truth that led to the end of the Second Reich. The Führer incorporates in the Nazi ideology the doctrine that events do not happen by chance but by force of instinct for self-preservation and procreation of the race.[24] The two keywords 'self-preservation' and 'procreation' signal that the last corner stone of the ideological structure that is being erected has to do with Jews. And, indeed, Hitler's conclusion is that they are to blame for the German collapse in 1918. A problem with this myth is that it completely leaves out of the equation the war fatigue after four years of suffering. Despite this weakness, Hitler is now ready to close the case of 1918 by declaring that it could not have been the defeats on the battlefield that caused the German collapse since the victories far outweighed the former.

The myth of the reasons for the defeat in 1918, which became an integral part of Nazi ideology, proved to be useful to the regime when disaster struck in 1942–1943 in North Africa and at Stalingrad. Attempting to cover up the serious setbacks on the southern and eastern fronts, the Nazi leaders compared the situation in early 1943 with that of 1918, arguing that Germany's position was much stronger in 1943. The reasons given for this were that the Third Reich controlled Europe's coastline from Nordkapp to the Bay of Biscay, granting it access to the sea. Furthermore, the *Wehrmacht* (German armed forces) had now advanced much deeper into the Soviet Union than its position in 1918. Also, in 1918, the Second Reich had had only weak allies, whereas the Nazis were now allied with a great power in the east – Japan. Moreover, the food supply situation was much more positive than in the Great War, with butter arriving from Denmark, cheese from the Netherlands and fish from Norway. Thus, Germans could rest assured that the 'hunger blockade' imposed by the Entente powers in the former war did not pose a problem this time around.[25] And as if the ideologues doubted that their assurances were enough to convince the public of the rosy picture they had painted, they added on a more somber note to maintain the fighting spirit of the army and the public that the result of a German surrender would be much worse than in 1918 since it would lead to the extermination of their people.[26] For good measure, it was also pointed out to Germans and non-Germans that only the Wehrmacht could guarantee that Europe would not fall into Bolshevik hands.[27] The above reveals that the myth and 'lessons' of 1918 could still be exploited 25 years later.

The state

Hitler and other Nazi leaders were quite explicit about the role of the state in implementing the National Socialist agenda. The best source of information regarding the vision for the Nazi state is Hitler's *Mein Kampf.* In Hitler's mind, the state was merely a means to achieve specific ends, more specifically, his obsessions with race and gaining redress of the insult suffered by Germany in 1918. These objectives were frequently to be achieved through the use of psychological coercion or military force. Hitler underscores that any defeat can be turned into a later victory and spiritual rebirth as long as the blood is kept pure.[28] He explains many pages later in his book that 'only when the ideational urge to [achieve] independence in the form of military instruments of power gains fighting organization, can the pressing wish of the people translate into marvelous reality'.[29] The quote does not leave much to the reader's imagination with regard to how Nazi objectives will be achieved.

The NSDAP knew exactly what a Nazi state was not and what they wanted to establish in place of the old system, frequently leaving to the reader to imagine how the movement's goals would be realized. National Socialist leaders wanted neither a liberal nor a Marxist state since both were class-based in the sense that they guaranteed power to a particular class and would allegedly place world domination in the hands of Jews, a disaster which the state would prevent from occurring through its racial policy, which rejected the concept of equality among the races. Therefore, it was the obligation of the state, 'pursuant to the eternal Will which rules the universe, to further the victory of the better and stronger, and demand the subjugation of the inferior and weaker...'.[30] Culture and civilization were imputed to the Aryan, and as a consequence of this realization, mankind must establish a system ruled by the most advanced race, the *Herrenvolk* (master race), which will address human problems on this planet.[31] Hitler does not provide details as to how this would be achieved, but the reader can deduce from the above that coercion would have to be part and parcel of the Nazi plan for the world, due to the unappealing role envisioned for 'non-Aryans'.

The domestic implications of a Nazi state were far-reaching and would become more obvious with the consolidation of National Socialist rule in Germany. A quote from *Völkischer Beobachter*, the NSDAP official organ, gives the reader a clear hint as to what kind of state the party envisioned: 'National Socialism has elevated the absolute *Führerprinzip* [idea of unconditional loyalty to the Führer] to the level of principle and rejects any [form of] soviet or parliamentary system'.[32] The vehement National Socialist criticism of the Weimar Republic also reflected the party's rejection of democracy. This republic was presumably supported by Germany's enemies, the Jews and the victors in the Great War since it constituted the most effective way to enslave Germans. Furthermore, the task of the state is not to protect the power of a particular class, but to find the most 'capable heads' to fill government positions.[33] Also, Nazi ideologues argued that the strength of a political party was not based on 'independent intellectuality' but on 'disciplined obedience'.[34] Moreover, the argument that debate – even when mistakes have been made – is of evil and has to be avoided since it causes confusion reflects the Nazi aversion to political pluralism. The above quotes suggest that the Nazis were quite open about what kind of society they wished to build, despite the fact that they were not always truthful about certain military developments as shown in the next chapter on propaganda. The above quotes are clear indications that the NSDAP would establish an elitist dictatorship when assuming power, basically turning Germany into a militarized society ruled by a limited group of people, a system banning input from the German people. Finally, the last argument referred to also reflects an important Nazi principle which permeated the Third Reich – never admit a mistake since it might lead to demands for accountability.

The Nationalist Socialist ideology made it clear that the interests of the population were top on its agenda although these interests appeared to differ from those of many other nations. The NSDAP emphasized that it would ensure that only Germans, and only the best Germans, would lead the Volk. The party explained that these promises would be fulfilled by rejecting the policy of Germanization, which would actually lead to the Volk becoming less German by naturalizing non-Aryans/non-Germans.[35] It is not surprising that this ideology appealed to many Germans in the 1920s when the country was experiencing hyperinflation, enormous unemployment and a government which appeared not to be up to the task of resolving these problems. Conveniently enough, Nazi ideologues did not elaborate on the selection process for government appointments, which suggests that they were convinced that the audience would pay more attention to other issues. The only exception seems to be a passage in *Mein Kampf*, when Hitler discusses in an historical context the primacy of the völkisch idea over the individual. It is highly ironic that Hitler argues how unreasonable it would be if an obviously mentally ill prince could not be removed from office.[36] This was probably the best recommendation Hitler ever made. Unfortunately, the Germans did not heed his advice.

Nazi ideology also discussed duties of the individual citizen and the state's responsibilities toward the private citizen. One of its priorities was to purge the institution of marriage of the ongoing 'racial defilement' (the Nazi term for intermarriage) and ensure its sacred duty of 'producing offspring in the image of the Lord and not monsters between man and ape'.[37] Nazi ideologues made allowance for exceptions, contending that there were geniuses with deformed bodies who were not Untermenschen, but stressed that it was not the 'task of the state to rear ... peaceful esthetes and physical degenerates'.[38] The human ideal of the Nazi ideology was not the old spinster or petit bourgeois, but men who reflected physical power and the woman who brings men into the world. Education was another important responsibility of the Nazi state. A main purpose of 'education' was to instill in the mind of Germans a clear sense of superiority over others; they had to regain their faith in the Volk's invincibility. The army was best suited to achieve this goal. It must serve as the highest institution of learning for the citizens, where they will learn to keep silent and even bear wrongs patiently.[39] The above sheds light on how the National Socialist state perceived its citizens, as tools in the hands of the state, even those who were 'Aryans'.

Other ideologues also provide insights into the thinking of the Nazi regime. Alfred Rosenberg's take on gender issues was that the primary role of woman was to maintain the purity of the race. The importance of this role is reflected in Rosenberg's argument that women need to be emancipated from women's emancipation because it will save the foundation of all culture – the concept of the Volk and race – from destruction. In consistent paternalistic spirit, he adds that the functions of judge, soldier and head of state are the exclusive prerogatives of men. From a National Socialist perspective, the validity of this claim is presumably so obvious that Rosenberg finds an explanation of how he arrived at this conclusion superfluous. Furthermore, Rosenberg gives the reader valuable insights into the Nazi succession process. The head of state appoints his successor and informs the *Ordensrat* (Council of the Order). The members of the council rise to this office via prior service in Stadt- and Gauverbände[40] (city and *gau* units), drawn from all strata of the population in correspondence with their achievements. Like Hitler, Rosenberg rejects democracy which is replaced by the 'council of the best' (the Ordensrat). A parliament, dismissed as an institution controlled by money, will not exist in a Nazi state.[41] As the situation in Germany gradually deteriorated and criticism of the NSDAP spread, the regime increasingly resorted to 'terroristic repression',[42] demonstrating that 'Aryans' were not exempt from severe punishment when expressing dissent or opposition to Nazi policies. 'The slightest ill-judged remark or perceived minor opposition ... could prove disastrous for any individual'.[43] State terrorism became the preferred survival strategy of the Nazi regime when facing domestic and external threats.

Geopolitics

The NSDAP's geopolitical agenda was laid out in detail in several Nazi sources. Nazi ideology stressed several geopolitical priorities. One of these was the recovery of lost territories. This reveals the importance of another principle – force. Since former German territories had been ceded to other states in a peace treaty, they could only be recovered by force. Another principle was irredentism, the goal of which was to incorporate all territories with a German population, but controlled by other states, into the Third Reich. However, force was not the only way to achieve this objective; the Sudetenland, which was transferred to Germany following the Munich Conference, was a case in point. An obvious corollary of the two principles referred to was the necessity of a future war with France to recover Elsass and Lothringen/Alsace and Lorraine.

Despite the emphasis on force, peace was not rejected out of hand by the Nazi regime. The two were considered inextricably intertwined in National Socialist ideology since the latter could be established only by first resorting to the former, once the Third Reich had achieved world domination.[44] Nazi references to the belief that 'he who rests, rusts' and 'victory always lies in attack only'[45] testify to the important role coercion, force and aggression played in the National Socialist ideology. However, what the rest of the world considered aggression was by Nazi ideologues depicted as liberation. Three great liberations were stressed – liberation of the peoples of the world from Jewish control, liberation from Bolshevik oppression and liberation of the world from Anglo-American imperialism.[46] Resistance in Nazi-occupied territories is ample evidence that most non-Germans did not view occupation as liberation.

Nazi ideology used additional explanations to justify its worldwide agenda. One way was to argue that the size of a population must be compatible with the size of the territory it controls. According to this contention, the current population could not be sustained within Germany's present borders. This imbalance could only be rectified by means of territorial expansion.[47] Hitler clarified that Germany intended to acquire the new territory in the east, at Russia's expense.[48]

He advanced two arguments in defense of this expansion – borders are drawn by human beings and are also changed by them, and it is the right and duty of a great nation to acquire new territory if it is threatened by extinction without this acquisition.[49] Ironically, the National Socialist ideology itself turned out to pose the greatest threat to the survival of the German Volk. Nazi ideologues also referred to other justifications to make the case for expansion. The American presidency and economy were controlled by Jews and both see a great business opportunity in the Second World War, which is a main reason for why they had to be contained. The Axis powers' alliance should therefore be viewed as an initiative to guarantee peace based upon the naturally allotted *Lebensraum* to which they were entitled.[50] The same argument applied to Czechoslovakia and the Soviet Union.[51] The focus on acquisition of territory in the east did not exclude action against the United Kingdom. The *Sonderfahndungsliste* [a wanted list compiled in preparation for the Nazi invasion of the British Isles] constitutes clear evidence of what would happen to anti-Nazi personalities in occupied territories.[52] The conclusion that the Nazi ideology wants us to draw, based on the justifications provided above, is, therefore, that Germany did not cause the Second World War, but it was a conflict forced upon the country.[53]

Ideological pluralism and political flexibility

In light of the totalitarian nature of the Nazi ideology, the answer in the negative to the question whether pluralism of thought and political flexibility existed in the Third Reich might appear as a foregone conclusion. However, documents, memoirs and contemporary newspaper articles reveal that the NSDAP evinced limited ideological pluralism and political flexibility prior to, as well as after, the Nazi assumption of power in 1933. What can best be described as an internal ideological and power struggle raged in the 1920s between Joseph Goebbels and Otto Strasser, editors-in-chief of *Der Angriff* and *Berliner Arbeiterzeitung*, respectively. This conflict ended with Strasser's resignation from his post. Strasser withdrew from the NSDAP and formed his own political party, Die Kampfgemeinschaft revolutionärer Nationalsozialisten (The Action Community of Revolutionary National Socialists), as a result of Hitler's support for the former.[54] Throughout his career as a member of the NSDAP, Strasser had supported the role of trade unions in society and advocated the nationalization of large corporations, eventually incurring Hitler's ire. Unlike his brother, Gregor Strasser, Otto Strasser managed to survive the Führer's anger by going into exile in Austria, Czechoslovakia, Switzerland and Canada.[55] According to Walter Schellenberg, Head of Foreign Intelligence, Hitler had ordered him to travel to Lisbon and assassinate Strasser there with a lethal substance, but the intended target never showed up.[56] Dissent within the NSDAP sometimes came at a high cost.

Another much more entertaining ideological conflict than the one discussed above was that between Professor Ernest Krieck and Dr. Wilhelm Hartnacke, former Minister of Education in Saxony. The adjective 'hartnäckig' means obstinate in German. It is a suitable description of the two feuding parties. The case of Professor Krieck is of interest in the context of ideological divisions within the NSDAP. He had a long publication record on Nazi ideology and had both supporters and disparagers. Hartnacke belonged in the latter group. In 1937, he had published an article in *Volk und Rasse* not very appreciative of Krieck's work *Völkisch-politische Anthropologie*. Hartnacke criticizes Krieck's argument that the driving force in the current ideological battle stems from an 'unpredictable fate', contending that this force originates in the Volk and its racial power.[57] Hartnacke underscores that it, by contrast, is the power inherent in a particular race that constitutes a precondition for a turn of fate. However, Krieck turns out to be no pushover. In an acerbic response to Hartnacke addressed to the editorial board of *Volk und Rasse*, Krieck argues that Hartnacke's criticism constitutes an attack on key positions of the National Socialist *Weltanschauung*, a fact which he finds strange, since SS Reichsführer Heinrich Himmler is one of the publishers of the journal. For good measure, he adds that Hartnacke has produced no scholarly work whatsoever in his career and that 'Hartnacke as philosopher is like a bull in a china shop'.[58] Krieck most likely won this round on points. It is significant that this feud took place in public on the pages of a scholarly journal, but what is more important is the reference to SS Reichsführer Heinrich Himmler in the context of criticism leveled at an individual linked to the Reichsführer. This is a potentially dangerous situation for which the critic might have to pay dearly. Therefore, Krieck's comments suggest that he enjoys the support of someone in the highest Nazi hierarchy and that the two factions are more or less equal in power.

Ideological flexibility on the part of the Nazi regime is a phenomenon which needs to be touched upon in the context of pluralism since its existence implies some form of the latter. It has been stated earlier in this chapter (note 19) that the Nazi leadership, Hitler not included, could evince flexibility on such an important issue as the fate of the Jewish population in territories controlled by Germany, when the regime could benefit from such action. A major reason for such flexibility was that it did not compromise the National Socialist official position on the status of Jews since the public was not aware of Jews being released from extermination camps. Another explanation for why Nazi leaders contradicted their own public position on the issue is that the war was almost over, and desperate initiatives were taken to gain goodwill among the Western Allies. Another issue on which Nazi leaders displayed flexibility was their version of euthanasia. In the Nazi mind, there was no question of 'mercy killings', which is the modern interpretation of the term. To the Nazi regime, euthanasia was a necessary measure to maintain a healthy purity of the Aryan race, free from mental illness and physical disability. Under the Nazis, diagnoses for mental illness were not based on laboratory tests, a fact which of course makes them highly questionable, even more so because they could lead to the death of the 'patient'. The National Socialist regime pushed for promulgating a law that would allow euthanasia, but never took this step, since it went against public opinion on this matter. Germans found it difficult to accept killings of other Germans. This did, however, not constitute an insurmountable obstacle to Nazi authorities, which, as was their wont in similar situations, resorted to secrecy. When faced with popular opposition, the regime simply implemented its agenda in secret. The euthanasia program began early in 1940 and was discontinued in 1941 due to opposition, which suggests that the secret program had been exposed to the public despite the threat of severe consequences.[59]

A question that needs to be asked is why the dissent of Strasser had to be castigated, while the public debates of Krieck, Hartnacke and others were allowed to go on. A likely answer is that, in the former case, Strasser was regarded by Hitler as a challenge to his exclusive position as the Führer because the former presented his own interpretation of the Nazi ideology and controlled a newspaper, while individuals involved in the other public debates criticized one another and not ideas that could be linked to Hitler himself. Hitler, like some professional politicians, was quite cautious about committing himself to specific policies, particularly if they had the potential of alienating groups whose support he needed.[60] As a result, prior to the Nazi assumption of power in 1933, Nazi ideology was not a fully developed doctrine but continued to evolve during the first decade since the forming of the NSDAP.[61]

Religion

Ideological pluralism was also reflected in Nazism's relationship with traditional religion, a theme the interpretation of which has caused serious divisions among scholars who study the issue. One scholarly view is that Nazism was a 'pagan' religion, developed as an alternative to traditional Christianity.

However, this interpretation appears to be undermined by Hitler's opposition to such a religion.[62] Joseph Goebbels, Minister for Propaganda, Martin Bormann, Chief of the Party Chancellary and Hitler's private secretary, and Hermann Goering, the Commander of the Luftwaffe, also criticized the 'pagans'.[63] The most prominent proponents of 'paganism', or at least strong anti-Christian sentiments, were Heinrich Himmler, Reichsführer SS, Erich Ludendorff, the famous German general from the Great War, and Alfred Rosenberg.[64] Ludendorff was the most radical anti-Christian member of the NSDAP until he was expelled from the party.[65] Himmler's view on Christianity was not unsurprisingly colored by Nazi ideology. As a result, he rejected the idea that Jesus was a Jew, which was consistent with his conviction that Christianity was an 'Aryan' religion, representing good against the evil of the Jews. His attitude to Protestantism was less critical than his view on the Catholic Church. Himmler condemned the latter for its 'Jewish' influences and praised the former for clearly realizing the 'Jewish peril'.[66] Martin Luther's criticism of Jews and his German ethnicity qualified him as an 'Aryan', facts which certainly influenced some Nazi leaders' preference of Protestantism over Catholicism.

Alfred Rosenberg, the leading Nazi ideologue, held a very negative view of traditional Christianity, but was quite impressed with the writings of the great medieval German mystic Meister Eckehart. Rosenberg writes that German mysticism was suppressed by the (Catholic) Church and adopts a more negative attitude toward Protestantism than Himmler, arguing that a serious sin that Protestantism was guilty of was to turn the Old Testament into a popular book.[67] It does not come as a surprise that Rosenberg adds a Nazi touch to Eckehart's mysticism. He argues that the world today needs to add the sense of an iron will to the enlightened mind and elevated spirit that the mystic demanded of his followers. In order to reach a state where soul and God are of equal importance, the mystic must eliminate the world as idea. This is only achievable when the soul has been completely liberated from dogmas, Churches and Popes. In Rosenberg's words, Eckehart announces this state to be the basic commitment of every 'Aryan' being. The will of the Volk is an integral aspect of Nazi ideology. However, the National Socialist concept is fundamentally different from the mystic will which is a spiritual and non-ego-centered force. The *völkisch* will is in Nazi ideology mainly directed at temporal affairs and is reflected in interaction with external entities. The obvious difference does, however, not prevent Rosenberg from giving the impression that Meister Eckehart was preaching the Nazi ideology in the thirteenth and fourteenth centuries.

According to Rosenberg, Meister Eckehart argues that 'the slave of God' is a Jewish concept which must be rejected. The Nazi ideologue contends that the grace present in a soul is a reflection of God, but not dispensed by an absolutist Lord. Grace is thus possible, not because of divine omnipotence, which is the position of the Church, but because of the soul's

90 *National Socialist terrorist state*

state of being the direct image of God.[68] For obvious reasons, Rosenberg links the German mystic's spiritual message to the Nazi concept of völkisch will, which emphasizes the creative and completely independent power of the Volk. A problem with Rosenberg's interpretation of Meister Eckehart's mysticism is the former's acceptance of the idea that grace and mercy in the human soul are direct reflections of God. Now, if that holds true, it means that, like God, humans must show grace and mercy or the human soul will not be a reflection of God. It is indubitably a stretch of the imagination to argue that Nazi ideology and policy represented divine grace even before the Holocaust. The Nazi ideologue believes that he can address this contradiction by reference to Eckehart's argument that an enlightened soul is in need of no grace.[69] However, this escape route does not aid Rosenberg's case since Eckehart is not implying that an enlightened soul should not show grace and mercy to fellow humans and other creatures. A second problem, which is the unaddressed dilemma Rosenberg's argumentation creates, is the emphasis on the freedom from the diktats of an absolutist Lord that the human soul enjoys. It is, of course, a very hard sell to contend that the National Socialist regime secured this freedom for its citizens.

More recently, students of Nazism's attitude to traditional religion have devoted attention to interpretations such as 'German Christianity' and 'secular religion'. One view among scholars is that most Nazis thought of themselves as good Christians and sincere followers of Hitler at the same time. They called themselves 'German Christians'. They subscribed to a form of Nazified Christian religion, rejected traditional Christian teachings about the divine and human nature of Jesus and displayed selectivity regarding scripture. Despite these different interpretations of the Christian message, the Churches in Germany generally supported the regime, particularly after the outbreak of war in 1939. The risk of being branded unpatriotic or even traitors convinced church leaders to support the NSDAP. Furthermore, Hitler realized the importance of a united home front in the Second World War and therefore acted to restrain some of his anti-Church lieutenants, as has already been pointed out above.[70] The seemingly contradictory term 'secular religion' is another way to describe Nazism. It could be defined according to functionality, in which case it would make Nazism 'an irreligious surrogate for Christianity'.[71] This definition applies to Nazism, if it is argued that the latter is based upon non-Christian or anti-Christian ideas. A critic of this interpretation has stressed that it has a significant weakness – its focus on function does not take into account the possibility of Nazism being Christian and secular at the same time. The one does not exclude the other, if one recognizes that the term secularization does not necessarily imply de-Christianization.

In his *Der Mythos des 20. Jahrhunderts*, Rosenberg seems to disagree with both interpretations discussed in the paragraph above, arguing that Meister Eckehart created a new religion, different from the one that non-Aryans and the Vatican have forced upon Germans. The NSDAP ideologue equates Eckehart's 'religion' with Nazism. The former contends that this 'religion' is not suitable for a [racial] bastard, a claim which is supported by the National Socialist concept of Aryan exclusivity, which rejects the unitarianism of traditional Christianity, that is, one religion for all humanity, irrespective of race. The attentive reader will, however, find it hard to reconcile the mystic's emphasis on the spiritual with Nazism's preoccupation with temporal affairs, such as Lebensraum, warfare and racial discrimination. Despite this significant discrepancy and inconsistence, Rosenberg envisions a Volk Church based upon honor, pride and inner freedom as opposed to the materialism which links Liberalism to the dogmas of the [traditional] Church. This Volk Church rejects the Catholic Church's attempt to turn believers into submissive servants and focuses on the living Jesus to a much higher degree than on the dead Prophet. The 'new religion' stresses the role of the mighty preacher and irate Prophet in the temple in lieu of the crucified and humiliated Christ. The former could be interpreted as a reference to the modern 'prophet' of the Third Reich.[72]

Conclusion

This chapter does not purport to be an exhaustive analysis of all aspects of the Nazi ideology which is not within the purview of this study. However, the issues which have been examined suffice for the detailed comparison and analysis of the transtemporal, transcultural and transnational phenomenon of terrorist thought and methodology that will follow in the later chapters of this volume. The critical examination of Nazi ideology in this chapter has enabled the reader to draw a number of important conclusions. First, Adolf Hitler did not realize that there are many different kinds of strengths. This led him to believe that force was a panacea that could resolve all problems facing Germany and the world in the 1920s, 1930s and 1940s. This 'almighty' approach was emphasized at the expense of other policies which could have produced a more positive and long-lasting result. Inner strength in the form of wisdom and mental composure would have stood the German leadership in the 1930s and 1940s in good stead. The Führer's speeches and writings reveal an almost complete lack of these qualities, so important when addressing domestic and international issues. Second, the NSDAP and military leaders in the Nazi state repeated the mistakes made in earlier historical periods as a result of their loyalty to Hitler. Had the general staff as a whole rejected some of their Führer's megalomaniacal ideas, the military might have been able to avert complete disaster. Third, it would not have required a very high IQ to determine that most countries in the world, if not all, would oppose German control. A wise leader would have adjusted plans and policies and modified objectives accordingly. If that was not the case, Hitler himself had recommended that such a leader be removed from power.

Fourth, Hitler made a costly mistake in believing that Germans constituted a master race which would rise to establish world domination. Had he studied history, he would have realized that the race which Nazism had relegated to the lowest rung on the ethnic ladder were not Untermenschen since they had survived two millennia without a country of their own, retaining much of their religion and culture. The Nazis alienated a highly educated minority, which would otherwise have continued to make an important contribution to German society. Fifth, a major weakness of Nazi ideology was that the purest 'Aryans' – according to the Nazis themselves – the Dutch, Danes, Norwegians and Swedes, either resisted or fundamentally disagreed with Nazi ideology.

An oft-repeated accusation in Nazi publications was that communism was a Jewish idea and reflected the typical thinking of Jews. Karl Marx was *one* individual, and there is nothing particularly Jewish in his thinking; if there is, Nazi ideologues certainly did not reveal it. They wanted the public, based upon the faulty premise of their argument, to conclude that all Jews are Marxists because Marx was a Jew. The implication of this argument is that, since Hitler was a German, he is a typical individual of this nation, obviously an argument which cannot be taken seriously.

Even in one of his few enlightened moments, Hitler, when the Führer actually drew a valid conclusion, was unable actually to develop it into a convincing argument. Hitler made his best case (perhaps the only one) when he argued that the Paris Peace Treaty led to the Second World War. However, it was too tempting to add the accusation that the Jews were responsible for this conflict since it would 'support' the Nazi Weltanschauung. Nazi ideologues could instead have focused on other major powers when allotting blame for the outbreak of the Great War – Russia, France and Great Britain. These European imperialist powers had created a very dangerous geopolitical situation in Europe and the rest of the world because of territorial rivalries and efforts to project power. The corollary of this argument is that the Entente powers had contributed greatly to the Great War, which makes it a very questionable, and most likely even unjust, decision to place all the blame on Germany for the outbreak of war in 1914. Hitler failed to make this reasonable argument, instead resorting to blaming the 'evil Jew' for causing the conflagration through a worldwide conspiracy, a claim much less convincing than the argument advanced above. The reason is that one can actually provide evidence in support of the latter, whereas only emotive 'evidence' is available to support the Nazi argument.

A final insight gained from this chapter on Nazi ideology is that the line between ideology and propaganda is quite blurred, since, in the case of the Nazis, the latter is exploited to shore up the former. However, frequently this does not turn out very well – the reason being that weak propaganda is used to support an unconvincing ideology. This will become abundantly clear in the subsequent chapter on propaganda.

Notes

1. Wilhelm Ziegler, 'Foreword', in Hans Gracht, ed., *Alljuda als Kriegstreiber* [Alljuda as War Monger] (Berlin: Theodor Fritsch Verlag, 1939), p. 3, *German Propaganda*, accessed 9 August 2017, http://archive.org/details/Gracht-Hans-Alljuda-als-Kriegstreiber.
2. National Archives and Records Administration (henceforth referred to as NARA), Record Group (RG) 242, T81, Roll 22, Informationsdienst der Dienststelle des Beauftragten des Fuehrers fuer die gesamte geistliche und weltanschauliche Erziehung der NSDAP. Reichsleitung. Jahrgang 1935, Nr. 47. Ausgabetag: 2. August. Streng vertraulich! Nur fuer den Dienstgebrauch! Dr. Werner Huettig, Rassenpolitisches Amt der NSDAP. Rassisches Denken und praktische Politik.
3. United States Holocaust Memorial Museum, 'Nuremberg Laws', *Holocaust Encyclopedia*, accessed 25 August 2017, https://www.ushmm.org/wlc/en/article.php?ModuleId=10007902.
4. 'Barbarian migrations and invasions: the Germans and Huns', *Encyclopaedia Britannica*, accessed 4 July 2019, https://www.britannica.com/topic/history-of-Europe/Barbarian-migrations-and-invasions.
5. Alfred Rosenberg, 'Der Weltparasit', *Völkischer Beobachter*, 6 June 1943.
6. 'What Were They Accused of and What Were Their Sentences?' *Nuremberg Trials*, accessed 17 December 2018, https://wartrials-nurembergtrials.weebly.com/sentences.html.
7. Adolf Hitler, *Mein Kampf* (Munich: Zentralverlag der NSDAP, Frz. Eher Nachf., G.m.b.H., 1943 (first published 1925, Vol. 1 and 1927, Vol. 2), p. 311, accessed 9 August 2017, https://ia802302.us.archive.org/18/items/Mein-Kampf2/HitlerAdolf-MeinKampf-Band1Und2855.Auflage1943818S..pdf.
8. Ibid.
9. Ibid.
10. Ibid., 314.
11. Heinrich Himmler (ed.), *Der Untermensch* (Berlin: Nordland Verlag, n.d., but most likely published after 1935), p. 1.
12. Jeffrey Herf, *The Jewish Enemy: Nazi Propaganda during World War II and the Holocaust* (Cambridge, MA: The Belknap Press of Harvard University Press, 2006), p. 90.
13. Hitler, *Mein Kampf*, p. 330.
14. Ibid., pp. 332–333.
15. Hans-Georg Otto (ed.), *Der Jude als Weltparasit* (Munich: Zentralverlag der NSDAP, Franz Eher Nachf., 1943/1944), pp. 1–2, accessed 15 August 2017, https://germanpropaganda.org/der-jude-als-weltparasit/.
16. 'Proklamation des Fuehrers zur Gruendungsfeier der NSDAP in Muenchen', *Völkischer Beobachter*, 25 February 1943.
17. Ibid.
18. 'When Did the World Find Out about the Holocaust?', *Jewish Virtual Library*, accessed 29 August 2017, http://www.jewishvirtuallibrary.org/when-did-the-world-find-out-about-the-holocaust.
19. Reinhard R. Doerries, *Hitler's Last Chief of Foreign Intelligence: Allied Interrogations of Walter Schellenberg* (London: Frank Cass Publishers, 2003), p. 23, accessed 30 August 2017, https://archive.org/stream/HitlersLastChiefOfForeignIntelligenceAlliedInterrogationsOfWalterSchellenberg/HitlersLastChiefOfForeignIntelligence-AlliedInterrogationsOfWalterSchellenberg_djvu.txt.
20. Ibid., p. 24.
21. Ibid., pp. 134–136.
22. Hitler, *Mein Kampf*, pp. 247–248.

94 National Socialist terrorist state

23 Ibid., p. 252.
24 Ibid., p. 310.
25 'Die Hypotek von 1918', (The Burden of 1918) *Völkischer Beobachter*, 26 February 1943.
26 Wilhelm Weiss, 'Die Lehre von 1918', (The Lesson of 1918), *Völkischer Beobachter*, 1 August 1943.
27 'Die Botschaft', (The Message), *Völkischer Beobachter*, 26 February 1943. Needless to say, Nazi leaders withheld from the public the important information that by early 1943 both Nazi and Japanese fortunes had turned for the worse.
28 Hitler, *Mein Kampf*, p. 359.
29 Ibid., p. 418.
30 Ibid., p. 421.
31 Ibid., p. 422.
32 Reichsorganisationsleiter Robert Ley, 'Die Entwicklung der Parteiorganisation', *Völkischer Beobachter*, 24 February 1943.
33 Hitler, *Mein Kampf*, p. 480.
34 Ibid., p. 510.
35 Ley, 'Die Entwicklung der Parteiorganisation', *Völkischer Beobachter*, 24 February 1943 and Hitler, *Mein Kampf*, p. 428.
36 Hitler, *Mein Kampf*, p. 260.
37 Ibid., p. 445.
38 Ibid., p. 455.
39 Ibid., p. 459.
40 A gau was a regional administrative unit during the Nazi era.
41 Alfred Rosenberg, *Der Mythus des 20. Jahrhunderts: Eine Wertung der seelisch-geistigen Gestaltungskaempfe unserer Zeit* [The Myth of the Twentieth Century: An Assessment of the (or Mind and Spirit-Based) Creativity Struggles of our Time as they Relate to Mind and Spirit] (Munich: Hoheneichen Verlag, 1939), pp. 546–547.
42 Ian Kershaw, *The End: The Defiance and Destruction of Hitler's Germany, 1944–1945* (New York: Penguin Group, 2011), p. 208.
43 Ibid., p. 209.
44 Hitler, *Mein Kampf*, pp. 438–439, 688, 741.
45 Ibid., p. 440.
46 'Das Ziel des Weltkampfes: Die Völker sollen frei von den Bedrücker werden', [The Goal of the Worldwide Battle: The Peoples Shall Be Freed from their Oppressors!] *Völkischer Beobachter*, 26 June 1943.
47 Hitler, *Mein Kampf*, pp. 728, 732.
48 Ibid., p 742.
49 Ibid., pp. 741–742.
50 'Unser Weg', [Our Way] *Völkischer Beobachter*, 8 August 1943.
51 Jeffrey Herf, *The Jewish Enemy: Nazi propaganda during World War II and the Holocaust* (Cambridge, MA: The Belknap Press of Harvard University Press, 2006), pp. 54, 90.
52 Doerries, *Hitler's Last Chief of Foreign Intelligence*, p. 13. The purpose of the list was to cleanse the British population of its 'racial impurities'.
53 'Vorposten des Reichs', [Outposts of the Reich], *Völkischer Beobachter*, 13/14 June 1943.
54 Russel Lemmons, *Goebbels and Der Angriff* (Lexington, Kentucky: The University Press of Kentucky, 1994), pp. 43, 45–46.
55 Wolfgang Saxon, 'Otto Strasser, 76, Theoretician Who Broke With Hitler, Is Dead', *The New York Times*, 28 August 1974.
56 Doerries, *Hitler's Last Chief of Foreign Intelligence*, p. 14.

National Socialist terrorist state 95

57 Wilhelm Hartnacke, 'Bemerkungen zu Ernst Kriek: Völkisch-politischer Anthropologie', *Volk und Rasse*, Vol. 10, 1937, pp. 13, 18. NARA, RG 242, T81, Roll 56.
58 Ernst Krieck to the editorial board of *Volk und Rasse*, 13 October 1937, NARA, RG 242, T81, Roll 56. The correct expression in German is 'ein Elefant in einem Porzellanladen'. However, Krieck does not find this sufficiently insulting, so he substitutes 'Esel' (ass) for 'Elefant'.
59 Karl Kessler, 'Physicians and the Nazi Euthanasia Program', *International Journal of Mental Health*, Vol. 36, No. 1 (Spring 2007), pp. 7–10, 12; Hajo Holborn, 'Origins and Political Character of Nazi Ideology', *Political Science Quarterly*, Vol. 79, No. 4 (Dec., 1964), p. 545.
60 Holborn, 'Origins and Political Character of Nazi Ideology', *Political Science Quarterly*, Vol. 79, No. 4 (Dec., 1964), p. 545.
61 Barbara Miller Lane, 'Nazi Ideology: Some Unfinished Business', *Central European History*, Vol. 7, No. 1 (1974), p. 8.
62 Richard J. Evans, 'Nazism, Christianity and Political Religion: A Debate', *Journal of Contemporary History*, Vol. 42, No. 1 (Jan., 2007), p. 6, accessed 7 September 2017, http://www.jstor.org/stable/30036424.
63 Richard Steigmann-Gall, 'Rethinking Nazism and Religion: How Anti-Christian Were the "Pagans?"' *Central European History*, Vol. 36, No. 1 (2003), p. 79, accessed 7 September 2017, http://www.jstor.org/stable/4547272.
64 Steigmann-Gall, 'Rethinking Nazism and Religion', p. 79.
65 Ibid., p. 82.
66 Ibid., pp. 94, 102.
67 Rosenberg, *Der Mythus des 20. Jahrhunderts*, p. 218.
68 Ibid., pp. 235–236.
69 Ibid., p. 238.
70 Doris L. Bergen, 'Nazism and Christianity: Partners and Rivals? A Response to Richard Steigmann-Gall, The Holy Reich. Nazi Conceptions of Christianity, 1919–1945', *Journal of Contemporary History*, Vol. 42, No. 1 (Jan., 2007), pp. 28, 31–32, accessed 8 September 2017, http://www.jstor.org/stable/30036426; Richard Steigmann-Gall, 'Christianity and the Nazi Movement: A Response', *Journal of Contemporary History*, Vol. 42, No. 2 (Apr., 2007), p. 186, accessed 8 September 2017, http://www.jstor.org/stable/30036441.
71 Milan Babik, 'Nazism as a Secular Religion', *History and Theory*, Vol. 45, No. 3 (Oct., 2006), p. 376, accessed 9 July 2017, http://www.jstor.org/stable/3874131.
72 Rosenberg, *Der Mythus des 20. Jahrhunderts*, pp. 239, 258, 604, 608.

Bibliography

Babik, Milan. 'Nazism as a Secular Religion'. *History and Theory*, Vol. 45, No. 3 (October 2006). http://www.jstor.org/stable/3874131.
Bergen, Doris L. 'Nazism and Christianity: Partners and Rivals? A Response to Richard Steigmann-Gall, The Holy Reich. Nazi Conceptions of Christianity, 1919–1945'. *Journal of Contemporary History*, Vol. 42, No. 1 (January 2007). http://www.jstor.org/stable/30036441.
Doerries, Reinhard R. *Hitler's Last Chief of Foreign Intelligence: Allied Interrogations of Walter Schellenberg*. London: Frank Cass Publishers, 2003. https://archive.org/stream/HitlersLastChiefOfForeignIntelligenceAlliedInterrogationsOfWalterSchellenberg/HitlersLastChiefOfForeignIntelligence-AlliedInterrogationsOfWalterSchellenberg_djvu.txt.

Encyclopaedia Britannica. 'Barbarian Migrations and Invasions: The Germans and Huns'. Accessed 4 July 2019. https://www.britannica.com/topic/history-of-Europe/Barbarian-migrations-and-invasions.

Evans, Richard J. 'Nazism, Christianity and Political Religion: A Debate'. *Journal of Contemporary History*, Vol. 42, No. 1 (January 2007). http://www.jstor.org/stable/30036424.

Gracht, Hans. *Alljuda als Kriegstreiber*. Berlin: Theodor Fritsch Verlag, 1939.

Hartnacke, Wilhelm. 'Bemerkungen zu Ernst Kriek: Völkisch-politischer Anthropologie' [Comments on Ernst Kriek: Völkisch-political Anthropology]. *Volk und Rasse* Vol. 10 (1937), pp. 1–44.

Herf, Jeffrey. *The Jewish Enemy: Nazi Propaganda during World War II and the Holocaust*. Cambridge, MA: The Belknap Press of Harvard University Press, 2006.

Himmler, Heinrich, ed. *Der Untermensch* [The subhuman]. Berlin: Nordland Verlag, n.d., but most likely published after 1935.

Hitler, Adolf. *Mein Kampf* [My Struggle]. Munich: Zentralverlag der NSDAP, Frz. Eher Nachf., G.m.b.H., 1943; first published 1925, Vol. 1 and 1927, Vol. 2.

Holborn, Hajo. 'Origins and Political Character of Nazi Ideology'. *Political Science Quarterly*, Vol. 79, No. 4 (December 1964), pp. 542–54.

Jewish Virtual Library. 'When Did the World Find out about the Holocaust?' Accessed 29 August 2017. http://www.jewishvirtuallibrary.org/when-did-the-world-find-out-about-the-holocaust.

Kershaw, Ian. *The End: The Defiance and Destruction of Hitler's Germany, 1944–1945*. New York: Penguin Group, 2011.

Kessler, Karl. 'Physicians and the Nazi Euthanasia Program'. *International Journal of Mental Health*, Vol. 36, No. 1 (Spring 2007), pp. 4–16.

Lemmons, Russel. *Goebbels and Der Angriff*. Lexington, Kentucky: The University Press of Kentucky, 1994.

Ley, Reichsorganisationsleiter Robert. 'Die Entwicklung der Parteiorganisation' [Development of the Party Organization]. *Völkischer Beobachter*, 24 February 1943.

Miller Lane, Barbara. 'Nazi Ideology: Some Unfinished Business'. *Central European History*, Vol. 7, No. 1 (1974), pp. 3–30.

National Archives and Records Administration (NARA, USA). Record Group (RG) 242, T81, Roll 22.

Nuremberg Trials. 'What were they Accused of and What Were Their Sentences?' Accessed 17 December 2018. https://wartrials.nuremberg trials.weebly.com/sentences.html.

Otto, Hans-Georg, ed. *Der Jude als Weltparasit*. Munich: Zentralverlag der NSDAP, Franz Eher Nachf., 1943/1944. Accessed https://germanpropaganda.org/der-jude-als-weltparasit/.

Rosenberg, Alfred. *Der Mythus des 20. Jahrhunderts: Eine Wertung der seelischgeistigen Gestaltungskaempfe unserer Zeit* [The Myth of the Twentieth Century: An Assessment of Creativity Struggles of Our Time as They Relate to Mind and Spirit]. Munich: Hoheneichen Verlag, 1939.

Rosenberg, Alfred. 'Der Weltparasit'. *Völkischer Beobachter*, 6 June 1943.

Saxon, Wolfgang. 'Otto Strasser, 76, Theoretician Who Broke With Hitler, Is Dead'. *The New York Times*, 28 August 1974.

Steigmann-Gall, Richard. 'Rethinking Nazism and Religion: How Anti-Christian were the "Pagans"?' *Central European History*, Vol. 36, No. 1 (2003), pp. 75-105. Accessed 7 September 2017. http://www.jstor.org/stable/4547272.

Steigmann-Gall, Richard. 'Christianity and the Nazi Movement: A Response'. *Journal of Contemporary History*, Vol. 42, No. 2 (April 2007), pp. 185-211. Accessed 8 September 2017. http://www.jstor.org/stable/30036441.

United States Holocaust Memorial Museum. 'Nuremberg Laws'. *Holocaust Encyclopedia*. , Accessed 25 August 2017. https://www.ushmm.org/wlc/en/article.php?ModuleId=10007902.

Völkischer Beobachter (Berlin), Newspaper published by the German National Socialist Workers' Party.

Weiss, Wilhelm. 'Die Lehre von 1918' [The Lesson of 1918]. *Völkischer Beobachter*, 1 August 1943.

Ziegler, Wilhelm. 'Foreword'. In Hans Gracht, ed., *Alljuda als Kriegstreiber* [Alljuda as War Monger]. Berlin: Theodor Fritsch Verlag, 1939. Accessed 9 August 2017. http://archive.org/details/Gracht-Hans-Alljuda-als-Kriegstreiber.

5 National Socialist propaganda

Introduction

The rule of the Nazi regime in Germany left a legacy as one of the darkest chapters in human history. The genocidal policies against its own citizens and citizens of occupied states, war crimes perpetrated against populations in conquered territories and violent suppression of political opposition in Germany by the Nazis have been meticulously recorded and analyzed by historians. These policies, officially sanctioned by the political leadership, qualify Nazi Germany as a terrorist state. Some goals of the regime were forcefully to discourage opposition and non-conformity, exterminate 'alien' elements in order to avoid the dilution of the 'Aryan' race, justify hatred of 'non-Aryans' by categorizing those who did not fit the description of a 'pure' race as *Untermenschen*, or subhumans and disseminate Social Darwinist ideas of the right of the strong to eliminate the weak. It is in the context of an extremely coercive implementation and dissemination of its violent and often dehumanizing propaganda that the Nazi state will be analyzed and, in later chapters, compared with the militant propaganda of terrorist organizations of earlier and subsequent historical periods. This chapter draws mainly upon captured documents in the holdings of the National Archives and Records Administration and issues of the official mouthpiece of the Nationalsozialistische Deutsche Arbeiterpartei (NSDAP), *Völkischer Beobachter*, available at the Library of Congress. The aforementioned sources reveal the crucial role Nazi propaganda played in creating and maintaining support for the regime through what frequently amounted to extreme manipulation of information. Manipulating information proved to be the last powerful weapon in the Nazi arsenal, as the expected successes on the battlefield increasingly failed to materialize. Subsequent chapters on terrorist propaganda in this volume reveal important similarities irrespective of whether the author represented a state or non-state actor and a secular or religion-based organization.

Two superweapons

In the Nazi state, propaganda and terrorism constituted two sides of the same coin. Both were frequently resorted to simultaneously, particularly

DOI: 10.4324/9781003260943-6

in hate propaganda targeting 'non-Aryan' populations. A major aspect of propaganda is the importance attributed to it by states and organizations alike. This chapter reveals that, in the case of the Nazi regime, manipulation of information was believed – particularly after the catastrophe at Stalingrad – to be a panacea to resolve all problems faced by the government, and later, even the key to the survival of not only the *Volk*, the German nation, but European culture, and the 'Aryan' race as well.[1] These and other themes to be discussed in the present chapter demonstrate the degree to which the National Socialist leadership realized the value of propaganda as a survival strategy. Nazi era sources reflect the conviction that propaganda could always cover up any undesired developments – domestic as well as international. Terrorism, as exploited by the Nazi state, had two aspects to it – propagandistic and physical, which at times went hand in hand. Furthermore, terrorism in the form it was applied in Nazi Germany sets it apart from terrorist violence of militant organizations; the enormous resources placed at the disposal of a great power enable a terrorist regime to unleash a reign of terror on the world with millions of victims as a result, a record which can be replicated by a non-state actor only with the acquisition of nuclear capability or the ability to cause mass epidemics or poison food or water resources on a massive scale. Had the Nazis had access to such weapons of mass destruction, or decided to use them, the outcome would have dwarfed the actual casualty numbers of the Second World War. In the absence of or unwillingness to use such weapons, propaganda was believed to be a superior approach to make realities fit the Procrustean Nazi ideology.

As has been pointed out previously in this study, propaganda is a double-edged sword, which is why this chapter assesses both weaknesses and strengths of the activities of the Reichsministerium für Propaganda, the Nazi Ministry of Propaganda. The support for the German National Socialist Workers Party (NSDAP) at the polls and mass rallies has created the impression that Nazi propaganda was well crafted. The research findings presented in this chapter, however, have led the author to conclude that NSDAP propaganda frequently suffered from serious flaws in its attempts to present a convincing case to the German public. One could, of course, argue that Joseph Goebbels and other Nazi propagandists were highly skilled because their message seems to have been embraced by many Germans, but a cogent counter-argument would be that this fact speaks volumes about the target audience and perhaps less so about the quality of Nazi propaganda.

The conspiracy theory

Like in the context of ideology, the Jewish 'question' was a leading theme in Nazi propaganda. Jews in Germany and abroad were subjected to a constant barrage of extreme vilification in German media. They were invariably treated as a monolithic group. The advantage of such an approach is that it facilitates criticism of all members of a nation, faith or group since the propagandist can disregard individual characteristics and idiosyncracies. Conversely, a problem with this approach was that the German National Socialist Workers Party (NSDAP) expected the German public to believe that poor Jews with socialist leanings had much, if not everything, in common with upper-class wealthy Jews, without providing any hard evidence in support of this claim. Nazi popularity based on domestic and initial military successes such as a dramatic reduction in the unemployment rate and quick acquisition of new territory through Blitzkrieg, indubitably facilitated the public's willingness to disregard the flaws of the official propaganda. Furthermore, Nazi propagandists often built the case they were attempting to make on a very limited number of selected sources, arguing that these sources represented a general phenomenon without any exceptions. An example of such a phenomenon was the purported quest for world domination, which was the alleged ultimate goal of all Jews. This *Weltherrschaft* was frequently referred to in Nazi propaganda and documents, such as a circular from SS Reichsführer Heinrich Himmler and a propaganda pamphlet published in 1939 under the title *Alljuda als Kriegstreiber* (Alljuda as Warmonger).[2] One can deduce from the frequency with which this accusation occurs in Nazi-inspired writings that propagandists believed it to serve the Nazi cause very well. On the surface, the latter conclusion appears convincing. The conspiracy theory can indeed be exploited to cover up any invented or manipulated information since it is very general. In this way, it can function as a type of *perpetuum mobile*, allowing the Nazis continuously to end each installment of their anti-Jewish propaganda linked to the theory with the words 'to be continued'.

In addition to strengths, however, the conspiracy theme also had its weaknesses. A major problem is, even with the enormous resources at the disposal of the Reichsministerium für Propaganda, it is very difficult for authors to keep track of all manipulations they present to the readership. Anyone who has watched a crime film appreciates the difficulty the screen writer is faced with to remember all details in a plot and treat them in a consistent way throughout the story. Propagandists encounter the same problem, particularly when their writings are based, to a large extent, on figments of their mind. Incidentally, this weakness also is a strength since the inattentive reader fails to keep track of all inconsistencies, which places the propagandist in an advantageous position. However, a problem arises when an attentive reader actually takes the time to analyze arguments and expose their flaws. Again, this might have been a problem in the Weimar era, but less so under Nazi rule, when the state was willing to use extreme coercion to silence critical thinkers. The powerful repressive tools at the disposal of the Nazi state helped 'convince' Germans of the accuracy of the conspiracy theory. A practical way of achieving this was severely to punish those who dared tune in to 'enemy' news broadcasts.[3] Again, the conspiracy theory appears to be a strength, but it involves a weakness as well. The strength of the conspiracy theory is that it lasts as long as Nazi successes on the battlefield continue. When reality reaches a point where theory and propaganda appear unconvincing, it leads to their downfall. The NSDAP made a concerted effort to describe the deteriorating military situation in rosy terms until the bitter end, when many civilians and soldiers realized that Nazism had been a catastrophic project. Interestingly, Nazi leaders had realized this long before the German collapse in May 1945. In a circular to party members dated 1 October 1944, Himmler draws the conclusion that the war is lost, an obviously explosive piece of news, which warrants the instruction to destroy the communication after reading it.[4]

The *Völkischer Beobachter* was one of the leading fora for the dissemination of the Jewish conspiracy theory, drawing the reader's attention to its domestic and international ramifications. The newspaper 'confirmed' the existence of the conspiracy by contending that, in the Weimar Republic, all parties with the exception of the National Socialist Party were controlled by Jews.[5] This was not an unrealistic argument since Germans could draw the conclusion that criticism of the Nazis might suggest Jewish influence. The accusation that all German political parties but one were controlled by Jews is, however, problematic, for the reason that it contradicts the basic Nazi assumption that all Jews are the same. If they were, why would they support and control different parties which did not cooperate with one another against the Nazis and which subjected one another to criticism? Furthermore, had there been some truth to the Nazi argument, the Jews would have been powerful enough to prevent the Nazi takeover in 1933. Moreover, had a Jewish group opposed its 'own' party, which they would have had to do in order successfully to coordinate with other Jewish groups and implement their 'conspiratorial plan', such action would have raised suspicion and been counter-productive, as it might have posed a threat to their alleged control of the party. Finally, in order to assume power in 1933, the National Socialists had to form a coalition government with the Deutschnationale Volkspartei (German National People's Party). If all parties, except that of the Nazis, were controlled by Jews, this meant that Hitler's coalition partner was controlled by Jews and that the Nazis cooperated with the archenemy. The *Völkischer Beobachter's* propagandists had obviously made an embarrassing mistake in 1943, which possibly went unnoticed by many readers, since it referred to events that had transpired a decade earlier, but critical readers would certainly have noticed the blunder. The aforementioned example confirms that it is easier to tell the truth than to tell a lie because an action does not occur in a vacuum and has consequences.

Several other aspects of the main conspiratorial theme figured prominently in Nazi propaganda as well. The continuous effort to establish a link between Jews and war[6] was a clever stratagem, which could be embellished upon in eternity, a major advantage being that it worked equally well in good times and bad times. Before the outbreak of the Second World War, Nazi propaganda consistently attributed responsibility for the Great War to the Jews. The democratic states were all allegedly controlled by Jews and

102 *National Socialist propaganda*

therefore wanted war. One can easily assume that this made perfect sense in the Nazi mind – non-Jews would perish, thereby paving the way for Jewish world domination. Ironically, in accordance with Nazi thinking, the corollary was that, since the Jews were responsible for the eruption of war in 1914, they were also depicted as perpetrators of genocide (*Völkermord*), a future crime of the Nazis themselves.[7] But why stop at one genocide? If Nazi propaganda could establish one link between Jews and genocide, that would be a great achievement. However, if a second example could be found, it would be even more convincing since it could be argued that the urge to perpetrate repeated genocides constituted a typical aspect of the Jewish racial character. Therefore, the Jews were blamed for the genocide against Native Americans for good measure. It is obvious that Nazi propagandists must have gotten carried away by their 'discoveries', when, as an afterthought it seems, it was contended that Gavrilo Princip, the assassin of the Austrian heir to the throne, Erzherzog Franz Ferdinand, was a Jewish mercenary.[8] Princip was an ethnic Serb from Bosnia and did not advocate Jewish world domination but Serb irredentism and the establishment of a Greater Serbia. The Nazis could possibly have argued that Jews had supplied the bombs and handguns used by the Black Hand (Tserna Ruka) organization for the assassination, but no such information has been unveiled. Propagandists, in their attempt to make their case as persuasive as possible, at times, lose sight of what is obvious manipulation of information and should be excised from a piece.

Calumny and denigration of Jewish individuals was a common approach adopted by the Nazis to argue that the negative news that they reported about these individuals for some unexplained reason applied to Jews as a nation. Jewish doctors in Germany constituted a case in point. The 3 August 1943 issue of *Völkischer Beobachter* breaks the 'shocking' news to the German public that 13 percent of German doctors were Jews before the Nazi takeover in 1933, a percentage which was ten times higher than the Jews' share of the total population.[9] A population that has been exposed to vicious anti-Jewish propaganda for a decade might not find this statistic suspicious, which had most likely been taken into account by the author. The report continues:

> [Considering t]he perverted preference of the Jew - based upon his racial predisposition - to occupy himself with all kinds of sexual perversions, it is no mere coincidence that Jewish physicians [select] a specialization as an expert in skin and venereal diseases.[10]

If the reader has accepted the statistics presented above as true, he/she will be more inclined uncritically to accept the emotional claim that comes next. No scientific data is provided in support of the claim regarding sexual perversions. The unattentive reader is, however, not looking for a scientific confirmation and is therefore prepared to accept the third manipulation of information: Germans should be outraged at the fact that their children were at least sometimes examined by Jewish doctors, who were all perverts because of their 'racial predisposition'. Some people may agree that the propagandist has done an excellent job in this particular case based upon the likelihood that many readers will fall for his argumentation. The method applied by the author is to create trust by advancing a correct initial argument, only subsequently to introduce a highly suspicious claim. It is difficult to categorize this method as high quality propaganda, which needs to be much more sophisticated to trick the perspicacious reader.

A person prone to critical thinking will notice the glaring absence of pertinent questions in the above article. One such question is whether most patients of the 'perverted' Jewish doctors were Jews or 'Aryans'. If the latter is the answer, which is highly likely, considering the low Jewish percentage of the total German population, the question arises: Why do 'Aryans' suffer from the same diseases as Jews, who are racially predisposed to be perverts? However, the most important question which the article leaves unanswered is how Jewish doctors acquired their license to practice medicine. Most likely the same way as 'Aryan' doctors, namely, because they were deemed qualified by peers. The article's failure to address this question undermines its veracity. The reason for not raising the question is obvious since the answer would contradict the basic argument that Jews are inherently perverts and therefore unfit to serve as physicians. The Nazi author of the article has in this case adopted a common strategy in propaganda – divert the reader's attention away from the propagandist's own group or nation and focus the attention on one particular target of criticism. From the perspective of manipulating information, a simplistic argument is easier to make and creates less 'confusion' in the mind of the reader by exposing her/him to a less nuanced argument. Unfortunately, for the propagandist, the critical reader will most certainly also want to know whether there are more 'Aryan' than Jewish specialists in skin and venereal diseases, and if so, whether the 'Aryans' are or are not considered perverts and the reasons for the answers to these questions. Moreover, there are a number of possible reasons for why a doctor chooses a career as a specialist in skin and venereal diseases: monetary incentives, job opportunities, scientific (non-perverted) interest, prospect of research funding, etc., none of which are discussed in the article. Finally, since there were no legal obstacles barring Jews from a career as a specialist in skin and venereal diseases in the Weimar Republic, they were deemed qualified by the same criteria as non-Jewish doctors in Germany. The questions raised in this paragraph constitute a clear indication as to why the propagandist avoided them.

The war on the airwaves

Early on in the Second World War, keeping the United States out of the war was a Nazi priority. Germany's international radio broadcasts played a prominent role in this effort. A German-American by the name of Frederick Wilhelm Kaltenbach had been hired by the Reichsministerium für Propaganda to influence American public opinion.[11] Transcripts of a number of his broadcasts were published in an English-language periodical entitled *News from Germany*. In a broadcast on 17 June, Kaltenbach assures the American public that Germany has no designs on the American continent and that the Nazi leaders expect the United States to leave Europe to the Europeans.[12] Kaltenbach follows up with another argument designed to strengthen the first one, contending that Germany was not an aggressor in the war since it was Britain and France that had declared war on Germany.[13] Furthermore, the British had imposed a hunger blockade on Germany, evidence of the inhuman intention to starve German non-combatants.[14] Another broadcast of 26 June 1940, entitled 'Armistice, Model 1940', reflects the Nazi obsession with the defeat in 1918. It was crucial to the Nazis to restore German honor and this was achieved by describing in detail the French surrender in the famous railroad carriage that had served as the place of German surrender in November 1918. Kaltenbach's comment on the event was 'the stain on the good name of the German army of 1914–1918 was wiped out'.[15] It is doubtful whether the above broadcasts had any impact in the United States, where the public had access to alternative news sources over which the Nazis exerted no control, a circumstance to which Nazi propagandists appear to have been oblivious. Furthermore, it is inconceivable that any Americans would be concerned with German honor, except, perhaps, for a small number of German-Americans. Reading the transcripts of Kaltenbach's broadcasts one wonders what kind of counsel he gave his superiors since the contents of the broadcasts display a lack of understanding of American culture and public opinion. Perhaps the answer is that Kaltenbach's supervisors would not pay heed to his advice since they had a set agenda that they were unwilling to modify.

Dealing with adversity

With the Soviet Red Army's advance toward Germany's borders after the Nazi disaster at Stalingrad in early 1943 and the intensifying allied bombings of German cities, it became increasingly important to boost the population's morale. In a highly symbolic speech at the 23rd anniversary of the founding in München in 1920 of the National Socialist Party, Hitler conjured up the magic and myths of the party's early days. Hitler had chosen Munich as the venue since it symbolized the beginning of a new Germany and the struggles of the Nazi party against a hostile world.[16] The purpose was to infuse hope in the minds of a guaranteed friendly audience of party members. Now, in 1943, as then, in 1920, the party and Germany were involved in an existential struggle and the party had to encourage Germans to continue and eventually bring the war to a successful end 'by creating new energy for the present and the future'.[17] The Führer emphasized the importance of the total war that Germany needed to wage against 'Bolshevism, the Jewish world pest and its plutocracies in England and the United States'.[18] In the early days of the party, Hitler recalled that he and a few supporters had faced an overwhelmingly superior enemy. The past had thus resembled the situation in 1943, but the lesson to be learned was that through perseverance he and the party had prevailed and so they would now. Hitler avoided, however, to discuss the critical situation in detail.

The Führer had made the calculation that ignoring the problems Germany was facing was the best approach. However, problems have a tendency not to go away by themselves, and this turned out to be the case in Germany, where the situation continued to deteriorate between 1943 and 1945. Hitler most likely believed that since the Nazis were in complete control of the media, no unadulterated information would reach the public in Nazi-controlled territory and that it would be sufficient to wield his magic wand, that is, propaganda, in order to persuade the German people to continue to fight. It is astounding to learn that Hitler failed to prepare Germans for the significance of the defeats in North Africa and at Stalingrad, instead stressing that Germans must have confidence in their Führer who has always been victorious, like Germany in the last three-and-a-half years. Germans must also place their trust in the Nazi party, which has consistently come out stronger from every crisis it has faced. Hitler talks about the glories of the past and compares the present situation to difficulties he and the party have overcome in the past. This is mildly put an exaggeration, since now (1943), Germany stands more or less alone against the rest of the world, with the enormous resources of her enemies dwarfing those of the Nazis. It is easier to go on the offensive verbally than on the battlefield, which is most likely the reason why Hitler and the National Socialist Party intensified their propaganda efforts in this difficult situation. The Führer is convinced that he can ignore discussing the crisis because he has a *Wunderwaffe* (miracle weapon) up his sleeve. This weapon is the Nazi ideology, and it will presumably thwart the Jewish dreams of world domination and eradication of the 'Aryan' race. The war will instead end with the eradication (*Vernichtung*) of all Jews in Europe. Hitler's magic weapon will eventually be embraced by all peoples, including Germany's enemies, who will throw their lot in with the Nazis in their war against the Jews.[19] The Nazi leader's speech suggests that he had spent too much time in his bunker in Berlin and lost touch with reality.

At a meeting attended by the upper party echelons, more than seven months later in October 1943 and a separate conversation in Hitler's headquarters the next day, not much has changed in the Führer's mind: he is still convinced that the German will (Wille) can overcome any obstacle and lead to an eventual Nazi victory in the war. A number of things mentioned in *Völkischer Beobachter* about the two meetings are quite revealing. Even without a verbatim transcript of the conversations during the two meetings, the critical reader can draw certain interesting conclusions. First, with so many attendees, something important must have been discussed and what could be more important than the war? This suspicion is strengthened by the fact that, unlike the anniversary in Munich, no such reason was mentioned for the two meetings in October. The confirmation of this conclusion is the caption 'The Führer: German victory contingent upon our will'.[20] This is a clear indication that things are going less than well for Germany in the war. Were the opposite true, there would be no need for such a statement, for, unlike the reason for Hitler's speech of February 23 in Munich, the October meetings were not part of a celebration or anniversary. Second, it is obvious that Hitler and the other Nazi leaders by now have realized that Germany is in a crisis, despite Hitler's refusal to admit this. If that is the reason for the meeting, the purpose must be to boost the morale of the leaders and the country. This, in turn, reveals to the critical thinker that the situation is very bad. Third, how bad the crisis is, is clear from the mentioning of defeatism in the article and that this crime carries the death penalty.[21] Fourth, this tells the reader that some Germans have realized that the Nazis will lose the war and that the latter want to nip such sentiments in the bud. The Nazi leaders believe that the crisis can be covered up and resolved with threats of punishments, encouragements and positive coverage of war developments.

The final aspect of this propaganda strategy is an article published on the same page as the article above in the *Völkischer Beobachter* entitled 'Our Armament constantly better and stronger'.[22] The thinking reader will of course wonder why this does not translate into successes on the battlefield and will most likely infer that the report is untrue. The alternative conclusion is that the report is true, which would mean that the German war effort is conducted by incompetent leaders, which would certainly be even more damaging than the first conclusion. Given the repressive nature of the Nazi regime, the main purpose of the propaganda strategy – to prevent the public from realizing the truth about the war – is not surprising. The problem is that despite major efforts to convey to the public only what the regime wanted, an attentive reader without access to alternative sources could, as demonstrated above, still figure out much information that the Nazis wanted to conceal from the public.

A propaganda technique often used by the Nazis was to identify a foreign source to strengthen an argument advanced in a particular article. One example of this approach is a report in the 14 March 1943 issue of the *Völkischer Beobachter* with the caption 'Finstere Judashände am Werk' (Dark Judas Hands at Work). This is in reference to British and American bombings of German cities, condemned by the Nazis as barbaric crimes against Europe's cultural heritage.[23] The Nazi mouthpiece has found several European newspapers (a Spanish, a Hungarian and a Swedish newspaper) echoing its condemnation of the allied air raids. The Hungarian newspaper *Függetlenseg* reports that 'dark Judas hands' behind Stalin and the western democracies are to blame for the air raids. The Spanish *El Alcazar* and the Swedish *Helsingborgs Dagblad* newspapers have omitted any reference to a Jewish world conspiracy, but otherwise agree that the bombings are barbaric acts. What stands out is the anti-Jewish propaganda in the Hungarian newspaper, which makes no attempt to provide evidence in support of its claim. This circumstance could raise questions as to why the other newspapers have left out such an important detail. The reason is, of course, that Hungary was a Nazi ally during the Second World War, and that the newspaper referenced was a Nazi-inspired one, a circumstance which might detract from a particular contention. The intention of referencing the international press is indubitably to create the impression that Nazi sources are diversified, and they are both domestic and international.

The second purpose of using foreign sources is to make the reader believe that there is international support for Nazi policies in general, not just one particular issue. A potential problem is that whenever the international press is not referenced, it could cause doubts to arise in the mind of the reader, prompting her/him to ask why foreign sources have not been quoted on a particular issue, which might limit the effectiveness of a Nazi argument. A propagandist certainly does not want the reader to ask questions that are left unanswered A major rationale for propaganda is to instill so much confidence in the reader's mind that no questions are asked. Another potential problem is the Spanish newspaper, which is published in a fascist country with strict censorship and a regime which, on account of its ideology, is bound to agree with certain aspects of Nazism. This could, of course, in a different context, somewhat detract from the effectiveness of a Nazi contention. The strongest link in the argument is the Swedish newspaper, published in a neutral country that does not support the Nazi ideology. This particular example of Nazi propaganda shows that propagandists at times were fairly effective in their selection of an issue to comment on and sources to strengthen a particular argument. To focus on the topic of indiscriminate allied bombings of civilian targets was a very effective approach since it is difficult to defend the intentional killing of civilians, the destruction of churches and the targeting of hospitals, which is bound to result in international expressions of sympathy.[24] The main weakness of the report is that the Nazis made the mistake to blame the Jews since most of the world disagreed with their anti-Jewish policies.

Enemy propaganda

For obvious reasons, it proved much harder for the National Socialists to direct people in occupied territories how to think. Belgium and Poland are cases in point. An internal report from the Nazi propaganda unit in occupied Belgium reveals some of the difficulties the regime's propagandists were encountering. Encouraging Belgian workers to volunteer for work in German factories was an important task. However, it was not always easy to achieve success, as the report evidences. It states: 'The advertising for [job openings in German factories] has recently, despite an intensive campaign,

108 *National Socialist propaganda*

not achieved the previous success'.[25] Despite the drop in the number of Belgian workers willing to relocate to Germany, the propaganda unit expects the numbers to reach 300,000 by early April. One phenomenon that the Nazis had to contend with in occupied territories which constituted a much less serious problem at home was hostile counter-propaganda. One example is an illegal flyer of the Flemish Communist Party appealing to Brussels workers to prevent, by force, new deployments of the Walloon Legion to the eastern front. This was obviously a serious threat to Nazi attempts to make up for losses in the east by recruiting volunteers. The underground newspaper *La Voix des Belges* announces to Belgians that 'Hitler will be driven back to Berlin'.[26] A third example of enemy counter-propaganda is the German-language periodical, *Die Wahrheit* (Truth), which warns soldiers that the enemy is in their own country and that no soldiers should volunteer to go to the eastern front. The Nazi propaganda unit in Belgium also let the Reichsministerium know what they were up against in the occupied country, where 'wide circles [of the population] are eagerly waiting for the Anglo-American forces to land'.[27] How difficult the task of the Nazi propagandists in Belgium is is clear from a report to the Reichsministerium to the effect that 'the lack of decisive [German] action in Russia and North Africa is interpreted as a weakness'.[28] Some of the reports convey the frustration of the propaganda unit in Belgium. Their job is not made easier by developments beyond their control, and they are clearly struggling to counter some of the hostile propaganda of the enemy.

Labor recruitment

A report on propaganda strategy for communication with populations in occupied territories clearly demonstrates the importance the Nazi regime attributed to such efforts. The report proposes to publish a brochure on labor recruitment in which a worker has signed up to work in Germany. His decision is being criticized by family members and friends. The worker returns home after several months in Germany and talks about his positive experience in the country, refuting in conversations with friends the British propaganda. The author of the report also proposes to counter enemy propaganda aiming at frustrating National Socialist labor recruitment by interviewing vacationers in Germany and reading in radio broadcasts letters from workers extolling their experience in Germany. Another idea being discussed is the publishing of a 32-page political brochure entitled *Who should shape the future of Europe?*[29] The question that will be posed in the pamphlet is whether a Belgian worker should entrust Britain, America, the Soviet Union or Germany with shaping his future. The proposal reflects an incredible lack of understanding of the situation of workers in Nazi-occupied countries. Why would a worker place her/his future in the hands of a foreign power, particularly one that has occupied the home country? The Nazi premise is that great powers should control small countries, an idea that would most likely not be embraced by targeted populations. The Nazi propagandist appears to be completely oblivious to the existence of nationalism, a powerful force which led to the unification of Germany in 1871 and the political successes of the Nazi party in the early 1930s. From a propaganda perspective, this is a disastrous approach since it proves to the reader that the Nazis are preoccupied with promoting their own agenda only, not the welfare of non-German workers and their country. The proposed product does not reflect the importance attributed to it.

The proposal examined above also suffers from other weaknesses. With regard to labor recruitment, the Nazis may offer certain incentives such as higher pay, but a critical-minded individual will realize that working in Germany will benefit the German economy and possibly perpetuate Nazi occupation of the home country, a prospect which makes the idea slightly less attractive. The proposal is somewhat more creative when it comes to dealing with enemy propaganda. It is obvious that enemy propaganda targeting labor recruitment is a thorn in the side of the Nazis, which is why the author suggests that it be neutralized. This is to be achieved by retaining some of the enemy propaganda and inconspicuously manipulating it through 'gross exagerrations' and insertion of mocking remarks. Finally, the propagandist suggests that censors photocopy worker letters that can be exploited for Nazi propaganda and reward those describing the most positive experiences in Germany.[30] It is not clear how the author envisioned how to achieve the propagandistic miracle of 'inconspicuously manipulating' a text through 'gross exagerrations'. Perhaps by blaming the Jews. Whatever the result achieved, it would most certainly have been less successful than in Germany because of alternative sources of information being readily available in occupied territories. Generally speaking, the proposal is fraught with serious weaknesses.

Nazi reports from Poland show that some Poles were not very susceptible to German propaganda. The Nazi propaganda unit in Krakow, Poland, reports that Ukrainian small farmers with communist leanings in Poland are providing refuge to escaped Bolshevik prisoners of war. These escapees have formed a gang under the leadership of a Bolshevik officer in southern Poland. One learns from the weekly report that a sabotage act had been carried out in which tens of tons of straw intended for the Wehrmacht (army) had been burned at a railroad station. The swift punishment for this act – ten hostages executed by firing squad – reveals how seriously the Nazi regime looked upon sabotage and resistance, and that innocent civilians had to pay the ultimate price for opposition to occupation. Such retaliation must have been very unpopular, but it did not discourage the Germans from attempting to raise an auxiliary army of Poles to be deployed to the eastern front. The author of the report also points out that the recruitment of labor has encountered temporary difficulties as a result of the wintry road conditions, but that the result prior to the winter had been good. The reason for this is very positive reports about living conditions in Germany from Polish vacationers who have visited the country.³¹ Volunteer labor recruitment most likely became much more difficult when allied bombings of German cities intensified, and this would have led to forced recruitment instead. With changing fortunes in the west and east, the Nazis decided that more 'resolute' action was called for since they no longer could depend on volunteers. As a result, the Polish population was forced to build fortifications against the approaching Red Army in 1945 and German citizens did not escape regime oppression either. East Prussians were conscripted for fortification construction in their province the same year in an effort to boost public morale.³² Generally speaking, as the world conflagration wore on, and Germans and non-Germans alike became less susceptible to Nazi propaganda, the regime increasingly relied on repressive measures to prevent chaos and collapse.³³

Boosting morale

One reason why totalitarian regimes and organizations are obsessed with propaganda is that it can fill most functions when communicating with enemies, civilians in occupied countries and the population in the homeland. The Nazis consistently referred to 1918, the defeat and unconditional surrender in the Great War, as a mistake and humiliation that would never again be repeated. The slogan was 'Nie wieder ein 1918', never again 1918.³⁴ To Germans who had experienced the country's economic collapse, hyper inflation and mass unemployment, Hitler's promise must have been very appealing. The lesson to be learned is that Germany cannot surrender ever since the consequences would be even worse than in 1918. As if this warning was not enough, an article in the *Völkischer Beobachter* explains that the goal of the victorious powers in 1918 was to establish economic control over Germany, whereas '[t]he war aim of the Jewish and democratic world powers [in 1943] is to exterminate and annihilate the middle European peoples ... The Axis powers merely want to determine their national destiny by themselves'.³⁵ In the context of 1918, this appears to be a somewhat convincing argument, at least to a German audience. The Second World War is, however, a very different conflict than the Great War. The Nazi egregious attempt to rewrite history is not very effective outside Germany where non-Germans will contend that the Nazis have passed over in silence the fact that no one wishes to deny them the right to exercise self-determination. The problem is that the Nazi regime wishes to deny other peoples this right and make it an exclusively German right. The National Socialist conclusion that the Paris Peace Treaty eventually led to the Second World War is, unlike the preceding claim, quite convincing, but this conclusion is followed by another unconvincing statement, namely, that '[t]he task to let this war be followed by a real and lasting peace will fall to cleaner and stronger hands this time around'.³⁶ Again, Nazi propagandists have not produced convincing propaganda, since by August 1943 it was obvious that there would be no peace until Germany surrendered.

National Socialist propaganda 111

From the perspective of a government, propaganda offers excellent opportunities to explain away embarrassing mistakes and adversity, something the Nazis greatly came to appreciate as their fortunes reversed in the Second World War. We will focus on a limited number of examples. A report in the *Völkischer Beobachter* of 6 August 1943 carries the caption 'Onslaught of Soviets without Consideration of Losses'.[37] The caption suggests that the focus is on the enemy, which is an attempt to divert the reader's attention away from German activity or inactivity. Either there is not much to report about German operations in the vicinity of the Soviet city Orel, or the result of German operations is too embarrassing to report. Either case is bad news because the Germans have been on the retreat since the Stalingrad debacle in early February 1943. The propagandist believes that he has achieved the purpose of omitting any reference to the Wehrmacht by focusing on Soviet losses. Unfortunately, his choice of one word and its position in the caption plant doubts in the mind of the critical reader. 'Onslaught' clearly suggests that the initiative on the eastern front has slipped into Soviet hands since it does not refer to the Wehrmacht but to the Red Army. Furthermore, its position as the first word will, owing to its strong connotations, most likely create a negative reaction in the mind of the reader when he/she figures out that it refers to the enemy and not the performance of the Wehrmacht. The second important word in the caption is 'losses'. This would normally be a wise choice when used in propaganda since it refers to the enemy. However, in the present context, 'onslaught' in combination with 'losses' has a synergistic effect since it creates an image of inevitability because the Red Army steamroller unwaveringly continues to push the Nazis back toward German borders. Also, the position of 'onslaught' diverts the reader's attention away from what the Nazi propagandist wants to emphasize, which is the losses suffered by the Soviets. This caption fails to achieve an important function of propaganda – to turn unfavorable news into positive news.

In the report referred to above, the author provides data that the Germans have destroyed thousands of Soviet armored vehicles over the past month as well as many aircraft and artillery pieces, but this still does not convince the attentive reader that the German armed forces are doing a good job in the east. The numbers presented sound reassuring, but they nevertheless suggest that the Wehrmacht is only defending itself. This is disappointing news since the German public, undoubtedly as a result of enemy air raids and mounting civilian and military casualties in the war, most likely wants to bring the war to an end quickly, something which Nazi propaganda in the early stages of the conflict had suggested was possible with its reports about astounding victories. Despite the difficulties he is facing, the propagandist makes a last ditch effort to win the reader over:

> Under these circumstances [Soviet attacks] it is of decisive importance for the assessment of the fighting on the Eastern Front, that the German armies generally hold their positions and prevent operative [enemy]

breakthroughs ... If individual positions must be abandoned every now and then is an issue of secondary importance.[38]

The author wants the reader to draw the positive conclusion that a minor retreat is not necessarily of great importance. The reader is most likely inclined to agree with this statement, which is what the propagandist has been waiting for. He now goes on the offensive in an effort to strengthen his case by arguing that the German forces have abandoned the Soviet city of Orel as part of a tactical operation aiming at a shortening of the front line. Militarily, this makes sense and could quite possibly be deemed to be a wise move on the part of the Wehrmacht. Generally speaking, however, the overall impression of the report is not a positive one. Hitler always tells the German people to fight the enemy with fanaticism and perseverance and that this approach will lead to eventual victory. If the reader has not forgotten Hitler's advice, it will most likely have an undesired consequence, namely, the conclusion that Soviet soldiers are fanatic fighters who have one goal only, which is to defeat the Nazis irrespective of losses. This is the true fanaticism that Hitler is talking about, but, unfortunately, for the Germans, it is the enemy displaying it.

A second example of how the Nazis reported military setbacks dates back to 26 March 1945. The source is a newspaper for soldiers of an army division. It describes the situation accurately to the soldiers, explaining that the enemy, despite heavy casualties, has gained territory due to a massive superiority in numbers, which has enabled him to gain territory in the east. However, the propagandist makes every effort to put a brave face on the desperate situation by referring to the action of the people's militia which has forced the enemy to postpone a full-scale attack on Berlin. There is bad news in the west as well, where Anglo-American bombers have attacked cities. According to the newspaper, however, German anti-aircraft batteries have proved very effective, preventing the enemy from hitting most of his military targets. The propagandist adds that German retaliatory V-2 strikes against London continue. These strikes will, however, not change the outcome of the war. By now it is clear to most Germans that the war has been lost, but the Nazi leaders still cannot bring themselves to admit this, so propagandists continue to manipulate information. However, using words such as 'forced' and 'postpone' to describe German successes at this late stage of the war will not sway anyone's opinion despite the possibility that they might reflect realities on the ground, that the Nazis can still muster sufficient energy to go on a very short-lived desperate 'offensive'. Forcing the Soviets to postpone a full-scale attack on Berlin is obviously good news, but Germans understand that this gives them a temporary respite only before they have to face the end.[39]

A third example of how the Nazi regime conveyed negative news is a circular sent by the SS Reichsführer Heinrich Himmler to party members in October 1944. It is obvious why the contents of the circular warrant 'immediate destruction' after reading it, which is the instruction to recipients. First, Himmler, in a candid moment, explains why Germany has lost the war. It is because of '[c]owardly treason, malicious subversive activities at the front and at home, and the overwhelming superiority in numbers of our enemy'.[40] Treason and subversive activities at the front are definitely problems with which a commander does not want his soldiers to be preoccupied, since such information could easily undermine morale. Furthermore, Himmler has not realized that if treason and subversive activities are reasons for losing the war, it raises potentially embarrassing questions. In order for treason and subversive activities to cause Germany's defeat in the war, these phenomena must have been quite widespread and not isolated occurrences. Now, if sentiments leading to such events were widespread, it would most likely indicate that Nazi policies have caused them, something that regime leaders obviously do not want party members or the public to believe. The negative news conveyed to party members is clearly more candid than news reported to the German public and military personnel on active duty.

Himmler appears to be playing a dangerous game since his openness might have undesired consequences. Expressing defeatist ideas is a serious crime by Nazi standards and carries severe punishment.[41] Before we proceed to provide a possible explanation for Himmler's seemingly counterproductive approach, we first need briefly to discuss a third reason that he gives for the German defeat. This reason, according to the Reichsführer, is 'overwhelming superiority in numbers'. A problem with this statement is that this superiority of the enemy could be blamed on the Nazis themselves since it was clear from the beginning of the war that most of the world did not embrace the Nazi ideology. The Nazis were of course aware of this, so their leaders were clearly responsible for the disastrous results of their aggressive policies. Himmler appears to have painted himself into a corner with this statement, so he resorts to an argument which resolves any Nazi problem at least as effectively as Alexander the Great's approach to the Gordian knot – the worldwide Jewish conspiracy is the reason. The Nazi leader then moves on to a typical psychological approach, he ends the list of negative news on a positive note:

> The war is lost, but the real struggle has only just begun! The reason is that National Socialism is not a political system, but a faith, and as such it can neither be defeated nor destroyed. So long as there are Germans, National Socialism will exist.[42]

So, why did Himmler share such explosive thoughts with party members? He was seeking the easy way out, which is blaming others, because he believed that this approach would ensure that he and the party would not have to take responsibility for the defeat. This is probably the reason why he sent the circular in the first place. Party members will most likely want to hear that they are not at all responsible for the disaster. The problem with this approach is that, at this point of the war, it might not even work in the alternative universe of the Nazis.

The deteriorating situation on the western and eastern fronts compelled the Nazis to plan for a future following defeat. Characteristic of this bright future was that Nazi Germany, like a magic phoenix, would rise again. When Nazi power was still in the ascendance, Joseph Goebbels had predicted in June 1941 that the British would capitulate in fall of that year.[43] Also in June, Hitler had predicted that the Soviet Union would fall within four months.[44] Perhaps there seemed to be some merit to these predictions at the time, but the situation had deteriorated catastrophically by the end of 1944. In the western part of Germany, reports informed Goebbels in November 1944 that the public doubted the veracity of Nazi propaganda reports of British and American atrocities presumably committed on German soil. Germans in these parts of the country wanted peace.[45] These sentiments were obviously quite alarming to Nazi leaders, who wanted Germans to continue fighting until the bitter end. However, like in similar situations, the Nazi regime continued in internal party documents to attempt to divert party officials' attention away from the abysmal present toward an imaginary bright future. In a circular to party members dated 1 October 1944, Himmler laid out his plans for continued resistance. He recommended that party members temporarily surrender to the 'despicable Americans and English' in order to prepare for the future struggle. To continue fighting at this point would not make sense since precious Nazi talent (meaning future leaders) would be wasted. Surrender is the only way to ensure that the hated enemy is dealt a decisive blow in the future. Like a phoenix, Germany will rise again as the Fourth Reich.[46] The first part of the Nazi prophecy has been fulfilled, but Germans have no appetite for repeating their mistake with Nazism.

A survival strategy

A National Socialist Party document of October 1944 provides insights into Nazi survival strategy during foreign occupation. It states:

> It is at this moment impossible to eject them [the Bolshevik plutocratic mercenaries], but this must not mean the end of the war. The war must continue, as long as we do not succeed in ... defeating the enemy permanently ... Certainly, the bands of enemy soldiers will continue successfully to occupy our cities and villages on account of their cowardly superiority in people and materiel, but what does that matter?[47]

Unlike Himmler's circular, this document does not inform party members that the war has been lost, and there is no talk of surrender. Instead, the war must continue. A possible explanation of this seeming divergence between the two documents is that the former is directed at party officials in higher positions, whereas the latter document targets low-ranking party members, hence the different instructions – preparatory/passive resistance in the former case and active resistance in the latter case. The goal is, of course, the same, but this is an important difference. However, at the same time, a fundamental similarity exists between the documents, which is that they both express hope for the future. It is clear from both documents that the Nazi leaders are desperately seeking excuses for their military setbacks which can be exploited in their propaganda. This effort results in a strange interpretation of what is a just war. The view presented in the second document is that the enemy is not waging a just war since he possesses superiority in numbers, which is the way cowards wage war. If this were the standard for a just war, the Nazis themselves have broken the rule every time they invaded a country since they possessed overwhelming superiority in people and materiel, particularly when they attacked smaller countries. Without noticing it, Nazi leaders have set a trap that they themselves have walked straight into. According to their argument, a war is fair only if both sides in the conflict have the exact number of soldiers, aircraft, artillery pieces, submarines, etc., which is, of course, a highly unlikely scenario. Furthermore, according to this contention, one could argue that hostilities have to be initiated at exactly the same time by both belligerents, which, of course, makes the Nazi concept of Blitzkrieg a cowardly approach to warfare since it gives the attacker an advantage over the attacked, by virtue of the element of surprise.

The above document addresses two main issues – just war and the strategy for a continuation of the war. A corollary of the contention that the Second World War is not a just war, since one side possesses a superiority in numbers, is that what determines whether a conflict is just or not is if the definition is provided by the Nazis. Based upon the conclusions advanced in the above paragraph, it is obvious that 'cowardly' is the term that best characterizes enemy military operations when the Nazi regime suffers defeat. This selective and arbitrary argumentation is hard to sustain, but that is, as has been pointed out above, not a major concern of the propagandist since the audience is a friendly one. The second issue addressed in the document – the strategy for a continued war – reveals much about National Socialist thinking in the waning days of the Third Reich. Nazi leaders stress the feasibility of a continued struggle. Again, convincing arguments are not a major concern. The main point is to enthuse party members and other Germans to continue the fight, a task which can presumably be achieved by understating the difficulties of such an effort. Since the enemy is in control of cities and villages, resistance must be transferred to mountains and forests, where it can continue for years. The struggle must involve women and children who will shoot approaching enemy soldiers down or stab them. Through a few weeks of training, German girls will acquire the skills to pretend interest when invited by lecherous enemy soldiers, only to await the opportunity when they can castrate the enemy with a dexterous cut of the knife. The Nazi leadership has obviously not for a moment considered the danger to

116 *National Socialist propaganda*

which German girls would be exposed, including the terrible punishment of a successful or unsuccessful execution of such an act. The document also discusses survival strategies for unconventional warfare, encouraging party members to acquire the survival skills of their ancestors. This entails surviving on berries and herbs of the forest.[48] The Nazi leadership seems to have overlooked the change of seasons, which would leave party members very hungry during the winter season. The general impression of the document in question is that it has not been well thought through.

Conclusion

This chapter has presented a detailed analysis of the propaganda of the National Socialist state. The author does not claim that this is a complete examination of all themes exploited by the Reichsministerium für Propaganda in Nazi publications since that is a subject worthy of a separate monograph, but the findings and conclusions advanced in this brief chapter suffice for a detailed analysis of similarities and differences between Russian terrorist, Nazi and Islamic terrorist propaganda that will follow later in this work. The analysis of Nazi propaganda has convincingly addressed one of the main arguments advanced by this study, namely, that propaganda is oftentimes believed by its users to be a miracle weapon, the disadvantages of which are rarely fully realized by propagandists. A reason for this overconfidence in its effectiveness is the complete focus of the author of a piece on getting a particular message across to an audience perceived as friendly or potentially friendly, which is why the propaganda frequently is of inferior quality. There is another possible explanation for the multiple weaknesses of the official Nazi propaganda. The regime must have been aware of the fact that some readers pay more attention and apply critical thinking to what they read, whereas others, perhaps even the majority, are much less inclined to do so. It is highly likely that the propaganda produced for the German and non-German public assumed that most readers belong in the second category. Certain propagandistic methods applied by the Nazis, such as obvious and unfounded generalization, exaggeration and plainly untrue statements, point in this direction.

Despite these defects, National Socialist writers and journalists must have been quite confident that many readers would accept their argumentation or lack thereof. The key to convincing readers to accept a flawed message was to cloak it in emotive language, which, it was obviously believed, would reduce the risk of serious analysis on the part of the German public. As a result, propagandists resorted to psychological terrorism by warning of the barbaric treatment Germans could expect from the 'Asian hordes' in the case of a Soviet victory. In concert with this effort, the state applied increasing physical repression as a deterrent in order to maintain order and prevent defeatist sentiments from spreading. However, a major problem that National Socialist propagandists were facing was reality-based developments on the ground, which often contradicted conclusions and arguments presented in Nazi publications. As the prospects of a Nazi victory in the Second World War became bleaker and rumors began to spread across the Reich, emotive language increasingly began to fail to cover up the precarious situation in the country.

Notes

1 Hans Gracht, *Alljuda als Kriegstreiber* (Berlin: Theodor Fritsch Verlag, 1939), p. 13; Jeffrey Herf, *The Jewish Enemy: Nazi Propaganda during World War II and the Holocaust* (Cambridge, MA: The Belknap Press of Harvard University Press, 2006), p. 64; *Völkischer Beobachter*, 25 February 1943, 'Proklamation des Führers zur Gruendungsfeier der NSDAP in Muenchen' [The Führer's Proclamation at the founding anniversary of the NSDAP in Munich].
2 National Archives and Records Administration (NARA), Record Group (RG) 230, M2108, Roll 3. SS Reichsführer Himmler to all party comrades in the field, October 1, 1944. Read and destroy immediately! Gracht, *Alljuda*, pp. 5 and 8; *Völkischer Beobachter*, 8 August 1943, 'Unser Weg'.
3 *Völkischer Beobachter*, Berlin Edition (all references to this newspaper are to the Berlin edition if not otherwise indicated), 22 March 1943, 'Keine Gnade für Rundfunkverbrecher' [No Mercy for Radio Criminals].
4 NARA, RG 230 M2108, Roll 3, SS Reichsführer Himmler to all party comrades in the field, 1 October 1944 [Read and destroy immediately!].
5 Reichsorganisationsleiter Dr. Robert Ley, 'Die Entwicklung der Parteiorganisation' [Development of the Party Organization], *Völkischer Beobachter*, 24 February 1943.
6 Wilhelm Weiss, 'Die Lehre von 1918' [The Lesson of 1918], *Völkischer Beobachter*, 1 August 1943.
7 Gracht, *Alljuda*, p. 5.
8 Ibid., p. 8.
9 *Völkischer Beobachter*, 3 August 1943, 'Man sollte es niemals vergessen!' [One should never forget it!].
10 Ibid.
11 Clayton D. Laurie, 'Goebbel's Iowan: Frederick W. Kaltenbach and Nazi Short-Wave Radio Broadcassts to America, 1939–1945', *The Annals of Iowa*, Vol. 53, No. 3 (Summer 1994), p. 220, accessed 10 July 2017, http://ir.uiowa.edu/annals-of-iowa/vol53/iss3/3.
12 NARA, RG 242, T81, Roll 36, 'American Views', *News from Germany*, Special Edition No. 2, July 1940, p. 1, Transcript of broadcast by Frederick Wilhelm Kaltenbach.
13 Ibid., p. 2; *Völkischer Beobachter*, 13/14 June 1943, 'Vorposten des Reichs' [Outposts of the Reich]; Herf, *The Jewish Enemy*, pp. 54, 90. The Nazis argued that they were forced to invade Czechoslovakia in March 1939 and the Soviet Union in June 1941, since these countries were allegedly controlled by Jews.
14 NARA, RG 242, T81, Roll 36, 'American Views', *News from Germany*, Special Edition No. 2, July 1940, p. 1.
15 Ibid., p. 5.
16 The importance Nazis attributed to myths and symbols is reflected in the description of Hitler's end. The regime reported, following the Führer's suicide on 30 April 1945, that 'the Fuehrer had died leading a band of followers in a final effort to turn back the 'Jewish Bolshevik influx into the sacred European heartland', Jay W. Baird, *The Mythical World of Nazi War Propaganda, 1939–1945* (Minneapolis:

University of Minnesota Press, 1974), p. 11. It is obvious that the Führer could not go down in history as a suicide, which is why Nazi propaganda again had to rewrite history. Suicide did, however, not represent an ignominious end to Hitler himself, who had made up his mind to exit history this way as early as mid-1943, if Germany lost the war, Ian Kershaw, *The End: The Defiance and Destruction of Hitler's Germany, 1939–1945* (New York, NY: Penguin Group, 2011), p. 118.

17 *Völkischer Beobachter*, 25 February 1943, 'Proklamation des Fuehrers zur Gruendungsfeier der NSDAP in Muenchen' [The Führer's Proclamation at the Founding Anniversary of the German National Socialist Workers Party in Munich].
18 Ibid.
19 Ibid.
20 Ibid., 9 October 1943, 'Der Führer: Von unserem Willen hängt der deutsche Sieg ab' [The Führer: German victory contingent upon our will].
21 Ian Kershaw states in his *The End* that desertions became an increasing problem with the approaching collapse in the east, Kershaw, *The End*, p. 120. Nearly 10,000 soldiers had been executed by the end of 1944, end note 95, p. 431.
22 *Völkischer Beobachter*, 9 October 1943, 'Unsere Rüstung immer besser und stärker' [Our Arms Continuously Better and More Powerful].
23 Ibid., 14 March 1943, 'Finstere Judashände am Werk'.
24 Ibid.
25 NARA, RG 242, T81, Roll 24. Propaganda-Abteilung Belgien an Carstensen, Reichsministerium für Propaganda, March 30, 1942. Meldung Nr. 26001. Wochenbericht [Weekly report No. 26001].
26 Ibid.
27 Ibid.
28 NARA, RG 242, T81, Roll 24, Propaganda-Abteilung Belgien an Carstensen, Reichsministerium für Propaganda, 9 June 1942. Meldung Nr. 26003[Report No. 26003]. Secret.
29 NARA, RG 242, T81, Roll 24, Propaganda-Abteilung Belgien an Carstensen, Reichsministerium für Propaganda, n.d. (possibly June 1942). Title: 'Vorschläge für die Fortsetzung der Arbeitereinsatz-Propaganda' [Proposals for the continuation of labor recruitment propaganda].
30 Ibid.
31 NARA, RG 242, T81, Roll 24, Propaganda-Abteilung, Krakau, Reichsministerium für Propaganda, 25 January 1942. Meldung Nr. 20002. Wochenbericht [Weekly report No. 20002].
32 Kershaw, *The End*, pp. 102 and 111.
33 Ibid., Kershaw calls such measures 'terroristic repression', Kershaw, *The End*, pp. 208 and 209. The Nazi regime refused to allow early evacuation from East Prussia, fearing that it would lead to complete chaos and convince other Germans to cease fighting, Kershaw, *The End*, p. 111.
34 Weiss, 'Die Hypotek von 1918' [The Burden of 1918], *Völkischer Beobachter*, 26 February 1943.
35 Wilhelm Weiss, 'Die Lehre von 1918' [The Lesson of 1918], *Völkischer Beobachter*, 1 August 1943.
36 Dr. W. Koppen, 'Unser Weg' [Our Way], *Völkischer Beobachter*, 8 August 1943. This, in turn, will guarantee a happier future.
37 *Völkischer Beobachter*, 6 August 1943, 'Ansturm der Sowjets ohne Rücksicht auf Verluste' [Soviet Onslaught with No Reagard for Losses].
38 Ibid.
39 NARA, RG 230, M2108, roll 2. 'Der Jäger der Südfront. Nachrichtenblatt unserer Division' [Rifleman of the Southern Front. Our division newspaper], 26 March 1945.

40 NARA, RG 230 M2108, Roll 3. SS Reichsführer Himmler to all party comrades in the field, 1 October 1944. Read and destroy immediately!
41 *Völkischer Beobachter*, 22 March 1943, 'Keine Gnade fuer Rundfunkverbrecher' [No Mercy for Radio Criminals].
42 NARA, RG 230 M2108, Roll 3. SS Reichsführer Himmler to all Party comrades in the field, 1 October 1944. Read and destroy immediately!
43 Herf, *The Jewish Enemy*, p. 89.
44 Ibid., p. 90.
45 Kershaw, *The End*, p. 116. A quote from Baldur von Schirach, the leader of the Hitlerjugend, from before the Nazi attack on the Soviet Union reflects the apocalyptic official party line: 'And even if heaven, hell, and the world/were to be allied against us/we would hold our heads high/and fight until our last man fell wounded', Baldur von Schirach, 'Die Fahne ist mehr als der Tod', Schulungsdienst der Hitlerjugend, Issue 6, March 1941, quoted in Baird, *The Mythical World of Nazi War Propaganda*, p. 8.
46 NARA, RG 230, M2108, Roll 3. SS Reichsführer Himmler to all Party comrades in the field, 1 October 1944. Read and destroy immediately!
47 NARA, RG 230, M2108, Roll 2, NSDAP 'Ausbildungsleitung Buschkrieg' [Training management, bush war], October 1944.
48 Ibid.

Bibliography

Baird, Jay W. *The Mythical World of Nazi War Propaganda, 1939–1945*. Minneapolis: University of Minnesota Press, 1974.

Gracht, Hans. *Alljuda als Kriegstreiber*. Berlin: Theodor Fritsch Verlag, 1939.

Herf, Jeffrey. *The Jewish Enemy: Nazi propaganda during World War II and the Holocaust*. Cambridge, MA: The Belknap Press of Harvard University Press, 2006.

Kershaw, Ian. *The End: The Defiance and Destruction of Hitler's Germany, 1944–1945*. New York: Penguin Group, 2011.

Koeppen, Werner 'Unser Weg' [Our Way]. *Völkischer Beobachter*, 8 August 1943.

Laurie, Clayton D. 'Goebbel's Iowan: Frederick W. Kaltenbach and Nazi Short-Wave Radio Broadcasts to America, 1939–1945'. *The Annals of Iowa*, Vol. 53, No. 3 (Summer 1994), pp. 219–45. Accessed 10 July 2017. https://core.ac.uk/download/pdf/61080746.pdf

Ley, Reichsorganisationsleiter Robert. 'Die Entwicklung der Parteiorganisation' [Development of the Party Organization]. *Völkischer Beobachter*, 24 February 1943.

National Archives and Records Administration (NARA, USA). Record Group (RG) 230, M2108, Roll 3.

Völkischer Beobachter (Berlin), Newspaper published by the German National Socialist Workers' Party.

Weiss, Wilhelm. 'Die Hypotek von 1918' [The Burden of 1918]. *Völkischer Beobachter*, 26 February 1943.

Weiss, Wilhelm. 'Die Lehre von 1918' [The Lesson of 1918]. *Völkischer Beobachter*, 1 August 1943.

6 Interpretations of jihad

Introduction

Jihad, perceived by Islamic mujahidun as a struggle in the path of Allah (jihad fi sabil Allah), occupies a central position in the ideology of Islamic militants. The many different extremist and non-extremist interpretations of and justifications for jihad deserve their separate chapters since they illustrate the great diversity within Islam. Furthermore, a detailed discussion of the concept of jihad from different perspectives is required in order to fully understand and be able to assess the arguments of the extremists and the counterarguments advanced by Muslim scholars who disagree with jihadis. This chapter briefly examines classical sources on jihad, particularly the writings of Ibn Taymiyya, which have inspired some Muslims to embrace extremist interpretations of their religion, in addition to the writings on jihad of modern Islamic militants, such as Sayyid Qutb, Muhammad ʿAbd al-Salam Farag, Abu Musʿab al-Suri, Abu Yahya al-Libi and Abu Bakr Naji.

It is not surprising that jihadist groups resorting to extreme violence attract more attention than attempts by traditional Islamic scholars to refute arguments advanced by organizations such as Daʿish (ISIS). The anti-extremist discourse is rarely referred to in Western media, but is quite active in Arab newspapers and on Arabic-language Internet websites. Some attempts to counteract extremist interpretations to the effect that the latter have nothing to do with Islam are too superficial to be convincing since the jihadists are Muslims, albeit with clear ulterior motives, whereas others, exposing weaknesses in extremist positions by analyzing the classical sources on which these positions are based, are generally more convincing. Some Western scholars have also challenged arguments of militant groups by providing evidence from Ibn Taymiyyaʿs works which appears to refute interpretations advanced by radical scholars who have embraced extremism, contending that the classical scholars who serve as the inspiration for modern extremists are in reality much more flexible than the rigid positions adopted by the militants. Like previous chapters in this volume, this chapter reveals that the greatest weakness of the extremists, an Achilles heel of many propagandists for that matter, is their tendency to be selective with

DOI: 10.4324/9781003260943-7

respect to the sources on which they base their arguments. Another issue discussed in this chapter is definitions of the term terrorism. The absence of a single universally accepted definition of this phenomenon complicates any discussion of jihad and arguments in defense of extremist interpretations of Islam. A brief comparison between a few Western definitions of terrorism and Islamic definitions will shed light on what constitutes 'legitimate' violence according to sources representative of different societies. Such a discussion is particularly called for when analyzing so-called suicide bombings or martyrdom operations as such bombings are called by jihadis.

Definitions

Historically, the term jihad has been rendered into Western languages as 'holy war'. More recently, however, journalists and scholars have abandoned the Western term in favor of the Arabic word jihad, which is derived from a verb meaning to strive. The qualifier 'holy' adds a religious dimension to the term, evidence that non-Muslims appear to accept that jihad is different from other kinds of warfare, a view on which non-Muslims and Muslims are in agreement.[1] That Muslims – both moderate and extremist – distinguish between jihad and regular war[2] can be deduced from the fact that the Arabic word '*harb*' (war) is not used to describe jihadi operations. One source states that 'He who fights with the sole objective that the word of Allah should become supreme is a mujahid in the cause of the Lord'.[3] The quote explains why Muslims do not use the word *harb* to describe this kind of struggle. History, as we shall see below, though, seems to provide evidence to the contrary with respect to the presumably lofty motives of mujahidun – past and present. In order to further clarify the religious nature of jihad, it is frequently used in combination with the phrase 'fi sabil Allah' (in the path of Allah). Three pairs of opposites are of particular interest in this context – defensive and offensive jihad, *fardh kifaya* (collective duty) and *fardh 'ain* (individual duty) and *jihad akbar* (greater jihad, against one's lower self) and *jihad asghar* (lesser jihad, military operations in the path of Allah).

Each of the three sets of opposites has caused much controversy among mainstream Muslims and jihadists in particular. The concept of defensive jihad is the kind of fighting the early Muslims engaged in following the hijra (migration) to Medina, when they were attacked by the Meccans.[4] Whatever the mujahidun's motivations might be, there should be no illusions about the nature of fighting, as one modern jihadi ideologue states, emphasizing the brutality and barbarity involved in vanquishing the enemy, who has to be massacred.[5] Jihad is seen by modern jihadis as a panacea for all problems of Muslim societies and the abandonment of which is even seen as a main reason for the present weakness of Islamic power.[6] Sayyid Qutb, an Egyptian jihadi ideologue executed by President Gamal 'Abd al-Nasir in 1966, calls those exclusively advocating defensive jihad defeatists. He argues that offensive jihad is necessary since a major objective of Islam is to remove all obstacles to allowing the religion to reach every human being on earth who then decides, without pressure, whether to convert.[7] Qutb's argument is partly based upon the Quran, which states unambiguously that there is no compulsion in religion.[8] With respect to the necessity of offensive jihad, however, one could argue that the Internet has made the concept of offensive jihad obsolete because it grants much of the world unimpeded access to the Quran online, though that was not the situation in 1964, when Qutb's book was published. Jihadi ideologues would remain unperturbed by this presumably weighty argument, still making their case by contending that the *jahili* (originally a term used to describe the pre-Islamic era's ignorance of the true religion, now used by jihadists to describe any non-jihadi society) system of institutions engage in anti-Islamic propaganda, and their unjust societies are founded on the concept of man lording it over other men, a system condemned by Islam and recognized as the exclusive prerogative of Allah. Therefore, as long as this un-Islamic system exists, there is a need for offensive jihad, a corollary of which is that offensive jihad is a more or less permanent condition.[9]

Much is at stake for moderate Islamic scholars who are engaged in an existential struggle with their militant critics. The disregard of the latter for the traditional role of the former as the sole interpreters of the Quran and the shari'a threatens to marginalize moderate 'ulama.[10] The moderates are sometimes fighting an uphill battle to win the hearts and minds of the young and restless generation to whom the message of activists appears more appealing in the face of unemployment, corruption, oppression and Western intervention in the Islamic world. The jihadi argument that a main purpose of their struggle in the path of Allah is to address the problem of man's usurpation of the divine prerogative to rule over man[11] appears to be substantiated by the Quran, which states that peace will prevail 'when the religion is entirely Allah's'.[12] If not contextually analyzed, this quote could be construed to imply that offensive jihad will continue until all of mankind has converted to Islam. The moderate camp highlights another Quranic *aya* (verse) which seems to validate their position that there is no compulsion in religion.[13] As we have seen above, the militants argue that through offensive jihad they merely establish the right conditions for individuals to accept or reject Islam, thereby doing non-Muslims a great favor by offering them an opportunity to embrace the true religion. The moderates' answer to this is that 'Islam does not enjoin upon Muslims to disseminate their religion by force of arms, because Islam believes that a creed cannot be imposed [upon an individual.]'.[14] Both camps appear to have found suitable quotes from the Quran to bolster their respective position.

Regarding the cases laid out in the previous paragraph, it could be argued that the moderates have found a stronger proof since there is an element of coercion before the militants allow people to make up their minds about conversion, namely, the invasion of countries as a precondition for granting complete freedom. A generous interpretation is that the occupation will last until everyone converts to Islam. The most plausible implication, though, is that the occupying force will remain irrespective of the population's willingness to embrace Islam since the jihadists would want to prevent the possibility of reverting to old 'falsehoods'. According to this view, the early Arab conquests in the seventh century cannot be considered an imperialist enterprise since the purpose was to establish the rule of God. Most likely, there were mujahidun, for whom this purpose outweighed other considerations, but they indubitably constituted a minority. The evidence which supports this assumption is found in the Quran and the hadith, which contain numerous references to *ghanima*, spoils. According to these references, Islam accepts distribution of booty acquired from vanquished tribes and peoples who resisted Muslim invasions. The Prophet himself presided, at least on one occasion, according to a hadith in *Sahih Muslim*, over this distribution.[15] Each mujahid could expect his share in this booty, an incentive which without doubt must have served to attract fighters and prompt them to exert themselves on the battlefield.

The two concepts of *jihad asghar* (the lesser jihad, which involves physical fighting) and *jihad akbar* (the struggle against the lower self) are as divisive among jihadis and moderates as the notions of defensive and offensive jihad discussed above. The Dar al-Ifta'al-Misriyya lists numerous examples of hadith in support of its argument of the existence in Islam of the concept of a greater jihad, concluding that 'the claim that the concept of jihad in Islam is exclusively limited to war and fighting contradicts reality. This claim is an expedient, which those who spread lies and extremist views exploit due to their misunderstanding of Islam'.[16] In an analysis of Islamic extremism, the same institution goes as far as to contend that the greater jihad, that is, the struggle against the lower self must precede the lesser jihad.[17] In the case of defensive jihad, or jihad asghar, Dar al-Ifta' scholars point out that a consensus must first be reached and allies sought among Muslim countries to act against the hostile occupying power, simultaneously considering the legality of such action according to Islamic and international law. The reference to international law is quite problematic from a militant perspective since that would imply equal status of divine and man-made law, an idea rejected by jihadis. Furthermore, the seeking of support of all Muslim countries appears to imply that a Muslim country cannot turn to a non-Muslim country for assistance, which makes the U.S.-led international coalition to eject Saddam Husain's troops from Kuwait in 1991 highly problematic. Obviously, the international coalition played into the hands of the militants, who would base their opposition to the coalition on a Quranic *aya* advising believers not to take unbelievers for friends.[18]

As we have seen in the previous discussion, the two concepts of jihad asghar and jihad akbar represent two extremes, fueled by passages in the Quran, which are exploited by proponents of one or the other camp to promote their position. One Quranic *sura* (chapter) draws a clear distinction between jihad asghar and jihad akbar without using these terms, stating unambiguously that the former takes precedence over the latter.[19] Furthermore, from the context, it is obvious that this particular Quran passage does not regard charitable work, which could be considered part of jihad akbar, as constituting jihad in the path of Allah. These *ayat* seem to strengthen the case of modern jihadis. However, as so often, the Quran provides other *ayat* which suggest that peace and tolerance should be the natural state of affairs. Sura 109:6 states 'You have your way [lit. faith], and I have my way [lit. faith]', a declaration which undermines the case of the jihadis. As a result, one critic of jihad asghar and the attempts of jihadis to portray jihad as an activity which exclusively includes fighting juxtaposes a quietist interpretation of jihad with the aforementioned extremist one. Based upon Quranic passages advocating peace and tolerance, the critic makes the case that extremist interpretations abase the Quran and insult Islam, 'a religion in which there is no and cannot be any violence or coercion',[20] explaining extremism as a result of later generations of activist clerics and politicians who exploit religion for expansionist purposes.

Despite the diametrically opposite stances taken by proponents of jihad asghar and jihad akbar, militants have realized that jihad is not all about fighting on battlefields. The written word and videos posted to the Internet are often as powerful as bombs used against the enemy, and the former are weapons without which it is difficult for the militants to wage an armed struggle. One jihadi source available on the Internet discusses the important role of mass media for the struggle in the path of Allah, outlining a specific strategy for media warfare. The author, Abu Bakr Naji, argues that a plan for media warfare is of particular importance since the media constitute a conduit which can be used for effective communication to the public of the militants' ideology. The author's advice for jihadi journalists and ideologues is that it is crucial sometimes to tell the truth regarding mistakes since such instances can be exploited to deflect enemy propaganda and establish an image of jihadi credibility in the minds of the public. Furthermore, clever use of the media will lead to new recruits – both civilian and military – joining jihadi ranks. Naji underscores the importance of targeting the military, particularly the lower ranks, who are generally dissatisfied with their work conditions. The desired result is to induce them to join the jihadis, or at least withdraw their support from the government. Naji also draws attention to mistakes which jihadis cannot afford to make, namely, killing Muslims, acknowledging the golden opportunity such acts offer enemy propagandists to criticize jihadi movements. Another piece of advice highlighted is that there is no point in amassing explosives without using them. Liberal use is encouraged for propaganda reasons. If a huge explosion is caused, the enemy cannot ignore reporting it and the damages caused.[21] Jihadi ideologues have thus realized the value of non-combat aspects to jihad, but whether this realization has granted them an advantage over the enemy is another issue, which is analyzed in detail in Chapters 9 and 10.

As to the non-military aspects of jihad, it seems that there is no hard evidence either in the Quran or hadith of the option of a spiritual, non-violent jihad. Some *ayat* could be interpreted as holding out the possibility of jihad as a non-violent activity, but there are no hadith which state that jihad is meant as a spiritual effort. The concept of jihad as a spiritual exercise appears to have been promoted particularly by Sufis. Both Abu Hamid Muhammad Ibn Muhammad al-Ghazzali and Muhyi al-Din Ibn al-'Arabi have discussed the greater jihad in their works. According to David Cook, these examples do not indicate that the prevailing view on jihad in early Islam was that it was not an effort based on violence. He argues that jihad entailed fighting human enemies and not the devil.[22] Cook's conclusion thus to a certain extent confirms the jihadi argument.

The last two opposites in the context of jihad, *fardh kifayya* (collective duty) and *fardh 'ain* (individual duty), figure prominently in the war of words between traditional/moderate 'ulama' and jihadi ideologues, due to the legitimacy which these terms bestow upon the respective camp. Moderates have to emphasize the former duty because it guarantees them and the ruling regime a decisive role in declaring jihad. On the other hand, jihadis in order to remain relevant have to wrest control of the interpretation of Islam from the traditional/moderate 'ulama and prove that their version of Islam is the true, original and unadulterated word of Allah. Abu 'Isa Muhammad ibn 'Isā ibn Sawrah ibn Shaddād al-Tirmidhi, compiler of one of the six canonical hadith collections, states that only the imam can issue an order for single combat against the enemy, contradicting the claim of jihadis that jihad is *fardh 'ain* (an individual duty, meaning that individuals can by themselves decide to engage in jihad against an enemy).[23] Al-Tirmidhi's ban on jihad as an individual duty is echoed by the Dar al-Ifta' al-Misriyya in a comment which states that 'the organization of jihad is the responsibility of the rulers and politicians', stressing that 'No single group or person may initiate jihad on their own...'.[24] However, the aforementioned institution allows for jihad as an individual obligation 'in countries where Muslim sanctuaries are attacked ... If they are unable to repel the enemy, jihad becomes an individual duty upon Muslims in neighboring countries'.[25] In the same comment on jihad, the Dar al-Ifta' also points out that 'The majority of Muslim scholars prohibited performing jihad for sons without the prior permission of their Muslim parents, because taking care of one's parents is an individual obligation, whereas performing jihad is a collective one'.[26] Generally speaking, traditional/moderate 'ulama do thus not completely reject the concept of *fardh 'ain*, but they accept it in very limited circumstances, and only as a result of an order issued by a ruler.

Jihadi ideologues generally prioritize the individual obligation to engage in jihad over the collective duty. The Egyptian jihadi Muhammad 'Abd al-Salam Farag (who was not an *'alim*, Islamic scholar) argued that modern 'Muslim' regimes have been established by unbelievers, a conclusion he drew from a Quranic *aya*: 'Those who do not rule by what Allah has revealed are unbelievers'.[27] They therefore have to be fought until Allah's laws have been reinstated by the jihadis. Modern rulers are, according to Farag, apostates from Islam who have been brought up on the ideas of imperialism as well as 'crusaderism', communism or Zionism. The only Islamic attribute they possess is their name.[28] Farag has made a case based upon the general claim that the rulers of Muslim countries are not Muslims, implying that they thus have to be fought. His argumentation is based on somewhat shaky ground since Ibn Taymiyya, a major inspiration for jihadi ideology, stated clearly that the Mongols, whom he accused of being unbelievers, since they did not rule by the shariʿa but by the Mongol tribal law, *yasa*, should not be fought. The reason which Ibn Taymiyya gave was that the majority population in the part of Syria that they occupied was Muslim and could practice their religion without restrictions.[29]

Modern Islamic militants have realized that jihad is not only about physical fighting, so in a sense they agree with the moderates. The former's emphasis on the importance of the war of words reflects this realization. Abu Bakr Naji proposes a multi-pronged media strategy. First, jihadi propaganda needs to target the Muslim masses to encourage as large a number as possible to join the jihad, provide positive support and adopt a negative attitude to those who do not join the jihadi effort. Second, jihadi propaganda also needs to target the lower ranks of the enemy's soldiers and persuade them to join the mujahidun. Third, Naji understands the importance of credible propaganda, so in order to instill trust in target groups he recommends that jihadis sometimes acknowledge mistakes.[30] Fourth, he warns against killing Muslims living under a regime of unbelievers since such an approach will expose the jihadis to negative media coverage. According to Naji, the Algerian GIA (Groupe Islamique Armée) was an example of such ignorant behavior. In this context, he stresses the importance for mujahidun of being in strict compliance with the shariʿa with respect to military operations. At the same time, excessive destruction of buildings and installations is something that jihadis should not shy away from; nothing causes as extensive a media coverage and strikes as much fear in the enemy as a good explosion.[31]

Abu Musʿab al-Suri, another jihadi strategist and ideologue, also provides insights into militant views on propaganda and the role of media in jihad. Judging by their language militants are generally quite upset about the anti-jihadi propaganda of 'heretics' and scholars working for Muslim rulers. The propaganda of these groups is clearly perceived as a serious threat to their cause. Al-Suri confirms this conclusion, stating that the moderates are guilty of presenting 'a distorted form of Islam adjusted to American standards'[32] Furthermore, he is quite disturbed by the propaganda of some of these scholars, who exceed the [moral] boundaries by attacking the duty of jihad and the principle of resistance. They even go as far as to claim that 'the ... mujahidun are not martyrs and will not enter Paradise!!...'.[33] The exclamation points indicate that al-Suri finds the latter statement particularly egregious. One can understand why since such powerful anti-jihadi propaganda has the potential seriously to damage recruitment to the militant cause. Despite this hostile attitude, al-Suri recommends that the activities of these groups be countered not by weapons but by arguments and evidence from Islamic law. By countering this propaganda, the jihadis imply that they are performing an important act of altruism since they prevent people from ending up in Hell. Interestingly enough, al-Suri states that armed force should be used only against invaders and leading apostates. As to the soldiers of the leaders, weapons should be used only in self-defense.[34] Al-Suri holds out this olive branch since he realizes that jihadis cannot alienate soldiers and expect them to join the jihad at the same time.

Jihadi propaganda targets both jihadis and the enemy. The title of al-Suri's book, *Da'wat al-muqawama al-Islamiyya al-'alamiyya* (Call for a Global Islamic Resistance), has a clear message for the mujahidun as well as their enemies. The author wishes to instill in the jihadis that they are part of something more than a cell or a group, namely, an important worldwide movement. His advice to jihadis to attribute their operations to one single movement reflects familiarity with how psychological warfare is waged. Al-Suri wants to create the impression in the mind of the enemy that the latter is fighting a powerful unified organization which has a global reach, implying that he risks to be attacked anywhere.[35] The author inculcates in the jihadis the importance of not surrendering and fighting until martyrdom.[36] From a mujahid perspective, this makes sense since the quickest way to enter heaven is to die on the battlefield. A second way to insure that the fighters are not just prepared, but actually *want* to die, is to emphasize that their participation in the global jihad is a covenant with Allah.[37] Most likely, many mujahidun do not want to violate such an agreement and disappoint Allah. An advantage of this strategy is that it also instills fear in the enemy, who does not necessarily wish to die. A disadvantage, of course, is the constant demand for new recruits because of the high 'turnover' of the old ones being blown to pieces. If the demand cannot be met, the impression will be that the jihad is in decline, which is something the leaders would want to avoid. In summary, the psychological warfare of militant ideologues reveals that they are aware of the potential benefits of propaganda.

During the spectacular early successes of Da'ish particularly, it seems that mujahidun propaganda had the desired effect on the enemy. As a result, Western governments and intelligence agencies publicly expressed doubts about the prospects of winning the war against terror. A State Department memo of the Obama administration argued in 2015 that the West-led coalition to defeat Da'ish is losing the propaganda war against the terrorist organization. This administration had already conceded before the memo's conclusions that Da'ish is more adept at spreading its message than the alliance is at convincingly countering the terrorist discourse.[38] A French intelligence officer has partly echoed the American view, stressing that there are two reasons, in particular, why it is so difficult to counter Da'ish's psychological warfare. First, the Islamic State disseminates most of its foreign propaganda in English, a language widely understood among young people in target countries. Second, the group uses thousands of social media accounts to reach its global audience. Third, IS propagandists also use 'Hollywood-style videos to promote a militant message presented in a form especially directed at young potential recruits'.[39] An Al-Jazeera article concurred in the assessment that Da'ish was being very successful in its media efforts, explaining that these successes are a result of the organization's spectacular brutality and willingness to do what other jihadi groups will not do, a fact which attracts media attention.[40] Finally, an internationally renowned Norwegian terrorism expert went as far as calling the war against terror a complete fiasco in 2016 since the jihadi movement's military strength, its ideological appeal, recruitment base and financing sources are still intact and have considerably increased in several areas.[41] Despite these strengths, however, the detailed analysis of Da'ish propaganda in subsequent chapters reveals that its media products are replete with weaknesses, sometimes unintentional and at other times intentional.

Ibn Taymiyya

Taqi al-Din Abu'l-'Abbas Ahmad Ibn 'Abd al-Halim Ibn 'Abd al-Salam Ibn Taymiyya al-Harrani al-Hanbali was born in 1263 CE at Harran, whence he fled to Damascus with his family in 1268 when the Mongols occupied his hometown. His father was an 'alim (Islamic scholar) and Ibn Taymiyya himself became an 'alim at the very early age of 19. His criticism of Sufism and what he perceived as innovations (*bid'a*) repeatedly landed him in prison, where he eventually died in 1328 CE.[42] In Ibn Taymiyya's times, the memory of the waning days of the Crusades was still fresh in people's minds. The fall of Acre, in Crusader hands until 1291 CE, effectively marked the end of Crusader presence in the Middle East. Furthermore, the Mongol invasions of Muslim lands had caused utter destruction, particularly in Baghdad, sacked in 1258 CE. The Mongol presence was very tangible in one of Ibn Taymiyya's most famous fatawa (fatwas) and clearly influenced his views on the defense and purity of Islam. One can also assume that his negative impression of Christianity[43] must have partly been influenced by the Crusades. When assessing his works, this hostile environment should thus be taken into account.

Despite the context of a hostile geopolitical medieval environment, or perhaps because of it, the scholarly community is at variance over Ibn Taymiyya's legacy. Jihadi ideologues seem to constitute a fairly homogeneous group, however, expressing approval of his works. Conversely, some scholars, such as DeLong-Bas, have adopted quite a critical position on the medieval 'alim, pointing out that his 'calls to jihad over any fraction of Islamic law stand in marked contrast to al-Wahhab's *Kitab al-Tawhid*'.[44] DeLong-Bas also stresses Ibn Taymiyya's literalist approach, at the expense of historical context, to certain important texts on which he relies for his argumentation.[45] Another scholar confirms this impression of Ibn Taymiyya as a rigid and inflexible interpreter of Islam, stating that according to Ibn Taymiyya an Islamic ruler had two major responsibilities – to uphold Islamic law and defend Muslim lands against external aggression. If a ruler failed in either of these respects, he had forfeited his right to rule since he could not be considered a Muslim.[46] The first condition seems reasonable, but to conclude that a ruler is not a Muslim, if he loses a war, strikes one as a harsh judgment. Furthermore, Ibn Taymiyya was no opponent to the use of coercion, which he believed was a necessary and useful means to an end. It is true that he detested killing, but he found violent enforcement of Islamic law preferable to non-Muslim oppression of Muslims.[47]

One of Ibn Taymiyya's most controversial fatawa is the one regarding the city of Mardin under Mongol occupation. An Egyptian government institution has argued that there is much confusion surrounding Ibn Taymiyya's works because many extremist ideologues have misinterpreted them, a result, presumably, of failure to consult qualified Islamic scholars. In his fatwa, Ibn Taymiyya states that the city cannot be considered part of *Dar al-Islam* (Abode of Islam), where Islamic law is observed. Likewise, it cannot be considered part of *dar al-harb* (abode of war), whose population is made up of *kuffar* (unbelievers). It belongs in a third category, 'where Muslims are treated according to their merit and non-Muslims [lit. "those outside Islamic law"] in accordance with theirs'.[48] The criticism expressed above refers to the fact that the misinterpretation of one single word has had very unfortunate consequences leading to much blood being spilt, Muslim and non-Muslim alike. Based on the one extant copy of Ibn Taymiyya's manuscript *Al-Fatawa al-kubra* No. 2757, available in the holdings of the Al-Asad Library in Damascus, the Dar al-Ifta' has concluded that the confusion is in regard to the verb 'yu'amalu', 'is treated'. Ibn Taymiyya's student, Ibn Muflih, has confirmed in his *Al-Adab al-Shar'iyya*, Vol. 1, p. 212 that the correct reading 'is treated'. Conversely, jihadis have traditionally insisted that the passage reads 'yuqatalu', meaning, 'is fought against',[49] which in their mind gives them the right to target any non-Muslim or, for that matter, Muslim who is considered an unbeliever or apostate by the extremists. The Dar al-Ifta''s explanation reveals that an extremist misinterpretation has greatly contributed to Ibn Taymiyya's reputation as an extremist Islamic scholar.

In spite of taking a harsh stance on certain issues, Ibn Taymiyya at times also evinces leniency, flexibility and forgiveness. One example is when he was offered the opportunity to have his enemies executed, but forgave them instead.[50] Another example is that he in one of his works lists numerous passages from the Quran which discuss Allah's loving and forgiving nature.[51] It is highly unlikely that Ibn Taymiyya would have paid so much attention to these qualities, had he agreed with the brutal methods of some jihadi groups such as the GIA or Da'ish. He insists that the salaf's (the early generations of Muslims) understanding of Islam was superior to that of subsequent generations. Unlike jihadists, however, he draws the conclusion that Muslims therefore should not expect their rulers to be paragons of virtue, implying that they should not be declared unbelievers or overthrown,[52] which is the goal of jihadis.[53] Interestingly enough, Ibn Taymiyya refers to a hadith which states that 'Allah will talk to each person directly without a mediator between them'.[54] The 'alim's reference to this hadith seems to suggest that Ibn Taymiyya was not opposed to believers drawing their own conclusions regarding the meaning of Quranic *ayat*. Furthermore, he did not automatically sanction violence to fight oppression, but recommended patience in its stead.[55] He also adopted a flexible stance on whether a Muslim had to leave his country if it was not ruled by Islam, arguing that the true emigrant was one who flees sin.[56] The message is clear – in the end it is the believer's conviction that matters. Again, many jihadis tend to disagree since they emphasize strict outward compliance with Islamic law.[57]

The argument above that the early Muslims' interpretation of Islam is superior to that of later generations may hold true for some Muslims, but this generalization ignores the fact that the understanding of different individuals is far from always identical and at the same level. Furthermore, Ibn Taymiyya disregards the fact that, every believer, including the salaf, interpreted/interprets the Quran. Jihadis may argue that the salaf were experts on their own society, but it is problematic to claim that they were experts on all future societies as well. If one assumes that Allah is a perfect being, one would most likely accept that the word of the Supreme Being does not change over time. However, immutability does not exclude flexibility. A characteristic of an eternal principle, it could be argued, is that it applies to any phenomenon, situation or condition anytime, anywhere. Some things in human society have undergone profound change over the course of 14 centuries. Now, if the immutable and eternal principle, that is, Islam, does not apply exactly the same way to modern society as it did 14 centuries ago to salafi society, which is what the jihadists want, then there are two possible problems. Either the principle is not eternal and immutable, or it is the people who implement it who constitute the problem. Since the Supreme Being is assumed to be infallible, the answer is obvious. By insisting on a rigid implementation of Islam, the jihadi ideologues fail to realize that they actually undermine the argument of immutability of the eternal principle. One could argue that what makes a principle eternal is that it is flexible enough to apply to any changed condition without causing serious discord, division or suffering in society. A case in point is the Islamic State's reintroduction of slavery, an act which seriously undermines Islam's status as eternal principle, and which for this reason will not be accepted by Muslims who apply critical thinking to jihadi arguments. Ibn Taymiyya's Mardin Fatwa is an example of a religious pronouncement by an 'alim who has understood that immutability does not exclude flexibility.

If a Muslim understands the relationship between immutability and flexibility, he/she will most likely realize that a similar relationship exists between the outward (*zahir*) aspects of Islam and the inner (*batin*) spirit of the law. A case in point is Muslims who live above the Arctic Circle. They obviously have to adjust their religion to a reality which differs fundamentally from life in the Arabian dessert. If jihadists insists that there is only one way to struggle in the cause of Allah, then the corollary will be that Islam should be confined to its original geographic location, that is, the Arabian Peninsula, which is a problematic consequence of a rigid position since it contradicts their militant objective of world domination, exposing an untenable argument. Furthermore, a compelling reason for Islam's status as a world religion with a presence in most countries today is Islam's ability to adopt a flexible approach to its relations with non-Arab cultures, societies and traditions. Without this flexibility, Islam would have remained a local phenomenon confined to the Arabian Peninsula. Also, Islam's Holy Book contains many *ayat* in which God commands the Prophet to follow the path of forgiveness and mercy: 'We have sent you as a mercy for all the worlds'.[58] 'Keep to forgiveness (O Muhammad), and enjoin kindness, and turn away from the ignorant'.[59] 'Good and evil are not alike. Repel evil with what is better. Then, he, between whom and you there was hatred, will become as though he was a bosom friend'.[60] Jihadists would make a much stronger case, were they consistently to emulate God's word as expressed in the above examples. Muhammad himself also evinced flexibility in matters pertaining to old traditions. Instead of razing the Ka'ba to the ground due to the idols that the pagan shrine housed, which would have been the preferred course of action of Da'ish, had it existed 14 centuries ago, the Prophet opted for a very pragmatic solution – he cleared the shrine of the idols and retained the structure as a holy place.[61] This act has completely escaped the attention of jihadist hardliners who argue that all similar structures must be destroyed.

Conclusion

This chapter has demonstrated that Muslims are at variance regarding the definition of jihad. Not surprisingly, militants tend to emphasize the violent aspects of jihad, while, many traditionalist/moderate 'ulama juxtapose this narrative with one which underscores that a peaceful and spiritual jihad is much better suited for a modern world which differs in profound ways from seventh-century Arabia. The moderates therefore lay emphasis on concepts such as *jihad akbar* and defensive jihad, the former of which some scholars argue was a notion introduced by later generations of Muslims under Sufi influence. Militants generally do not distinguish between defensive and offensive jihad and consistently argue that there is only one way to wage jihad, the offensive way. Furthermore, the position of many jihadi ideologues is that jihad is an eternal struggle to spread Allah's word worldwide by force of arms. Another issue which has created division in Islam is whether the collective or individual duty should be given precedence. Traditionalists and moderates have generally argued that the former is the rule because jihad can only be declared by an imam. On the other hand, militants insist that jihad is an individual duty, a position which enables them to bypass a decision made by religious or temporal authorities and launch jihad whenever and wherever they wish.

Both extremists and moderates as well as Western scholars concur that jihad differs from regular warfare because of the religious aspect of the struggle in the path of Allah. The traditional rendition of the term jihad in Western languages as 'holy war' underscores that the *impression* among non-Muslims concurred with that of Muslims that religion was the most important aspect of jihad. The qualifier 'holy' confirms that scholars and others in the West have accepted for a long time that jihad is a unique kind of warfare clearly distinct from other types of armed conflict.

Last but not the least, this chapter has examined the concept of immutability of Allah's word, upon which both jihadis and moderates are agreed, and the different conclusions the two camps draw from this conviction. The argument of the former is that Islam can only be applied the way it was applied by the companions of the Prophet Muhammad. The result is that the jihadi interpretation of immutability leads to rigidity. Conversely, the moderates contend that immutability does not exclude flexibility, which is evidenced by the history of Islam. Islam would not have gained the status of a world religion had Muslims followed the former path. The process of expansion involved a fair amount of adaptability and flexibility in the encounter with foreign nations and cultures. Islamic history thus reveals that the religion has spread because of its emphasis on the spirit over the letter of Allah's law. The moderates' realization that immutability does not exclude flexibility places a very powerful weapon at their disposal in the ongoing struggle to counter jihadi attempts to seize control of the Islamic discourse. Using this weapon in combination with exploiting weaknesses in jihadi, propaganda and additional tools will ensure that the overwhelming majority of Muslims continue to reject extremism.

Notes

1 The introduction to the English translation of Sahih Muslim, book 19 on jihad states that jihad has many aspects, one of which is fighting. Generally speaking, according to the translator's introduction, jihad 'is the name given to an all-round struggle which a Muslim should launch against evil…'. Muslim Ibn al-Hajjaj al-Naisaburi, Sahih Muslim, Book 19, *The Book of Jihad and Expedition* (Kitab al-Jihad wa'l-Siyar), accessed 5 August 2015, http://www.iium.edu.my/deed/hadith/muslim/019_smt.html. All further references to Muslim's works pertain to Book 19.
2 One example is Sayyid Qutb in *Ma'alim fi'l-tariq* [Milestones], SIME ePublishing Services (distributor), p. 31, accessed 21 July 2018, http://majallah.org/2017/01/qutbs-milestone.html. Another example is the Pakistani jihadi ideologue Abu 'Ala al-Mawdudi, who also confirms that jihad differs from other types of warfare since it constitutes a call for worship of God alone, referred to in David Cook, *Understanding Jihad* (Oakland: University of California Press, 2015, second edition), p. 100.

3 Muslim, *Sahih Muslim*. The quote is echoed by Abu Bakr Naji, who warns that only the mujahid of pure motivation, that is, who fights for non-temporal reasons, will be fully rewarded by Allah, Abu Bakr Naji, *Idarat al-Tawahhush* [Management of Savagery] (Markaz al-Dirasat wa'l-Buhuth al-Islamiyya), p. 49.
4 Muslim, *Sahih Muslim*; Khanzhan Kurbanov, 'Koran i Islamskii ekstremizm', [The Quran and Islamic Extremism], 6 April 2015, *Islam Review*, accessed 13 December, 2016, http://islamreview.ru/est-mnenie/koran-i-islamskij-ekstremizm/. The twentieth-century Shaikh Abu Zahra confirmed that 'jihad is permitted only to remove aggression and religious persecution against Muslims', an opinion which supports the concept of defensive jihad, 'Launching Offensive Attacks: The Unfounded Base for Extremists', *Dar al-Ifta' al-Misriyya*, accessed 5 August 2015, http://www.dar-alifta.org/Foreign?Viewrticle.aspx?ID=678&CategoryID=5.
5 Naji, *Idarat al-Tawahhush*, pp. 31–32, accessed 10 March 2016, https://pietervanostayen.files.wordpress.com/2015/02/idarat_al_tawahhush_-abu_bakr_naji.pdf. The website appears to be defunct.
6 Muhammad 'Abd al-Salam Farag, *Al-Faridha al-gha'iba* [The Neglected Duty] (Amman, n.p., n.d.), pp. 38–39, referred to in Cook, *Understanding Jihad* (Oakland: University of California Press, 2015, second edition), p. 110; 'Abdullah 'Azzam, 'Martyrs: The Building Blocks of Nations', in Cook, ed., *Understanding Jihad*, p. 129.
7 Qutb, *Ma'alim*, pp. 31, 33.
8 The Quran, 2:256.
9 Qutb, *Ma'alim*, p. 35.
10 This fear is reflected in the criticism of a leading Saudi Islamic scholar to the effect that terrorists do not consult traditional Islamic scholars, Salih Ibn Fawzan al-Fawzan, 'Al-Muntahiruna b'ism al-jihad ittiba' li'l-shaitan', *Okaz* (Saudi newspaper), 23 April 2009, accessed 20 July 2018, https://www.okaz.com.sa/article/257811/.
11 Cook, *Understanding Jihad*, p. 100.
12 *The Quran*, 8:39.
13 Ibid., 2:256.
14 'Shaikh al-Azhar yudha'u mafhum i'lan al-jihad', *Masrawy News*, 14 May 2015, accessed 9 September 2015, http://www.masrawy.com/News/News_Egypt/details/2015/5/14/580241/.
15 Muslim, *Sahih Muslim*, Book 19, No. 4340, No. 4364, No. 4392.
16 Dar al-Ifta'al-Misriyya, 'Hukm al-Jihad fi'l-Islam', accessed 5 August 2015, http://www.dar-alifta.org/AR/ViewFatwa.aspx?ID=3751.
17 Dar al-Ifta'al-Misriyya, 'Recruiting European Muslims in QSIS: What Kind of God they are Fighting for', accessed 5 August 2015, http://www.dar-alifta.org/Foreign/View/Article.aspx?ID=575&CategoryID=5.
18 *The Quran*, 3:28, in Abu Yahya al-Libi, *Al-Mu'allim fi Hukm al-Jasus al-Muslim* (Markaz al-Fajr li'l-I'lam, 2009), pp. 27–28, accessed 15 July 2017, http://fas.org/irp/world/para/libi.pdf.
19 The Quran, 'Surat Tawba', 19–21.
20 Kurbanov, 'Koran i Islamskii ekstremizm'.
21 Naji, *Idarat al-Tawahhush*, pp. 21, 26, 30, 41.
22 Cook, *Understanding Jihad*, pp. 35, 38.
23 al-Tirmidhi, *Al-Munhiyat*, pp. 246, 253–254, in Cook, *Understanding Jihad*, p. 22.
24 'Recruiting European Muslims in QSIS: What Kind of God Are They Fighting For?', accessed 5 August 2015, http://www.dar-alifta.org/Foreign/ViewArticle.aspx?ID=575&CategoryID=5.

25 Ibid.
26 Ibid.
27 The Quran, 'Ma'ida': 44.
28 Muhammad 'Abd al-Salam Farag, 'Al-Jihad al-Faridha al-Gha'iba', *Markaz al-Kalema al-Masihiyy*, accessed 30 July 2015, http://alkalema.net/algehad.htm.
29 Yahya Michot, trans. and ed., *Muslims under Non-Muslim Rule* (Oxford: Interface Publications, 2006), xvii, 4.
30 Naji, *Idarat al-Tawahhush*, p. 19.
31 Ibid., pp. 26, 28, 30.
32 Abu Mus'ab al-Suri ('Umar 'Abd al-Hakim), *Da'wat al-muqawama al-Islamiyya al-'alamiyya*, p. 1388, accessed 1 April 2017, https://ia800303.us.archive.org/25/items/Dawaaah/DAWH.pdf.
33 Ibid.
34 Ibid., p. 1389.
35 Ibid., pp. 1397, 1413.
36 Ibid., p. 1386.
37 Ibid., p. 1404.
38 Mark Mazzetti and Michael R. Gordon, 'ISIS Is Winning the Social Media War, US Concludes', *The New York Times*, 12 June 2015, accessed 27 July 2018, https://www.nytimes.com/2015/06/13/world/middleeast/isis-is-winning-message-war-us-concludes.html.
39 Hervé Brusini, 'Pourquoi la propaganda de l'Etat islamique est-elle si difficile à contrer?' 22 May 2015, *FranceTV Info*, accessed 29 May 2015, http://www.francetvinfo.fr/monde/proche-orient/offensive-jihadiste-en-irak/pourquoi-la-propagande-de-l-etat-islamique-est-elle-si-difficile-a-contrer_911483.html.
40 Musa al-Gharbi, *Al-Jazeera America*, 23 February 2015, accessed 20 July 2018, https://www.vredessite.nl/andernieuws/2015/week10/02-23-isil-jordan-propaganda.html.
41 Brynjar Lia, 'Fanatismens Seier? Jihadismens frammarsj i den arabiske verdenen', *Babylon, Nordisk Tidskrift for Midtøstenstudier*, Nr. 2 (2016), accessed 25 June 2018, https://www.journals.uio.no/index.php/babylon/article.view/4345/3813.
42 Ibn Taymiyya, *'Aqidat al-Wasitiyya*, trans. by Assas Nimer Busool, accessed 21 August 2015, http://www.salafipublications.com/sps/sp.cfm?subsecID=AQD04&articleID=AQD04003.
43 Yossef Rapoport and Shahab Ahmed, eds., *Ibn Taymiyya and His Times* (Karachi: Oxford University Press, 2010), p. 14.
44 DeLong-Bas, *Wahhabi Islam*, p. 250.
45 Ibid., p. 254.
46 Peters, *Jihad*, pp. 7–8, referred to in DeLong-Bas, *Wahhabi Islam*, p. 248.
47 Ibid., p. 49, referred to in DeLong-Bas, *Wahhabi Islam*, p. 250.
48 Ibn Taymiyya, *Al-Fatawa al-Kubra*, Vol. 3, p. 533, (Dar al-Kutub al-'Ilmiyya), quoted in Dar al-Ifta' al-Misriyya, 'Fatwa Ahl Mardin', accessed 8 May 2015, http://www.dar-alifta.org/AR/ViewFatwa.aspx?ID=3757. This comment in Arabic on Ibn Taymiyya's fatwa is no longer available under the above Internet address. 'Abdullah 'Azzam, Osama Bin Laden's mentor, disagreed with Ibn Taymiyya's fatwa, contending that if the shari'a is not the supreme law in a country, then that country is part of *dar al-harb* (the abode of war), Michot, *Muslims*, p. 38.
49 Ibn Taymiyya, *Al-Fatawa al-Kubra*, Vol. 3, p. 533, http://www.dar-alifta.org/AR/ViewFatwa.aspx?ID=3757. This comment in Arabic on Ibn Taymiyya's fatwa is no longer available under the above Internet address.
50 Ibn Taymiyya, 'Aqeedatul-Waasitiyyah', *Ahl-e Hadith*, accessed 5 August 2018, https://ahlehadith.files.wordpress.com/2010/07/aqeedatul-waasitiyyah.pdf.
51 Ibid.
52 Rapoport and Ahmed, *Ibn Taymiyya*, p. 14.

53 *Dabiq*, Issue 11 (Aug., Sept., 2015), pp. 4, 7; *Inspire* (Winter 2010), pp. 14–15.
54 Ibn Taymiyya, 'Aqeedatul-Waasitiyyah'. He has not provided the number of the hadith.
55 Ibn Taymiyya, *Al-Istiqama*, i, p. 32, referred to in Yahya Michot, trans. and ed., *Muslims under Non-Muslim Rule* (Oxford: Interface Publications, 2006), p. xvii.
56 Michot, *Muslims*, p. 12. Da'ish's position on *hijra* contradicts that of Ibn Taymiyya, arguing that it is incumbent upon a Muslim to emigrate to Dar al-Islam from dar al-kufr, *Dabiq*, Issue 10 (Jun., Jul., 2015), pp. 47–48.
57 *Dabiq*, Issue 11 (Aug., Sept., 2015), pp. 13, 17; Issue 10 (Jun., Jul., 2015), pp. 51, 67.
58 The Quran 21:107.
59 Ibid., 7:199.
60 Ibid., 41:34.
61 Sahih al-Bukhari, Hadith 2.671, *Alim*, accessed 22 July 2019, http://www.alim.org/library/hadith/SHB/671/2.

Bibliography

Brusini, Hervé. 'Pourquoi la propaganda de l'Etat islamique est-elle si difficile à contrer?' [Why Is the Propaganda of the Islamic State So Difficult to Counter?] 22 May 2015, *FranceTV Info*. Accessed 29 May 2015. http://www.francetvinfo.fr/monde/proche-orient/offensive-jihadiste-en-irak/pourquoi-la-propagande-de-l-etat-islamique-est-elle-si-difficile-a-contrer_911483.html.
al-Bukhari, Muhammad ibn Isma'il. *Sahih al-Bukhari*. Hadith 2.671, *Alim*. Accessed 22 July 2019. http://www.alim.org/library/hadith/SHB/671/2.
Cook, David. *Understanding Jihad*. Oakland: University of California Press, 2015; second edition.
Dabiq.
Dar al-Ifta' al-Misriyya.
DeLong-Bas, Natana J. *Wahhabi Islam: From Revival and Reform to Global Jihad*. New York: Oxford University Press, 2004.
Farag, Muhammad 'Abd al-Salam. 'Al-Jihad al-Faridha al-Gha'iba'. [The Neglected Duty]. *Markaz al-Kalema al-Masihiyy*. Accessed 30 July 2015. http://al-kalema.net/algehad.htm.
al-Fawzan, Salih Ibn Fawzan. 'Al-Muntahiruna b'ism al-jihad ittiba' li'l-shaitan' [Those who Commit Suicide in the Name of Jihad Follow Satan]. *Okaz*, 23 April 2009. Accessed 20 July 2018. https://www.okaz.com.sa/article/257811/.
al-Gharbi, Musa. *Al-Jazeera America*, 23 February 2015. Accessed 20 July 2018. https://www.vredessite.nl/andernieuws/2015/week10/02-23-isil-jordan-propaganda.html.
Kurbanov, Khanzhan. 'Koran i Islamskii ekstremizm' [The Quran and Islamic Extremism]. *Islam Review*,6 April 2015. Accessed 13 December, 2016. http://islamreview.ru/est-mnenie/koran-i-islamskij-ekstremizm/.
Lia, Brynjar. 'Fanatismens Seier? Jihadismens frammarsj i den arabiske verdenen' [Victory of Fanaticism? Jihadism's Advance in the Arab World]. *Babylon, Nordisk Tidskrift for Midtøstenstudier*, Nr. 2 (2016), pp. 60–85. Accessed 25 June 2018. https://www.journals.uio.no/index.php/babylon/article.view/4345/3813.
al-Libi, Abu Yahya. *Al-Mu'allim fi Hukm al-Jasus al-Muslim* [Guidance on the Ruling of the Muslim Spy]. Markaz al-Fajr li'l-I'lam, 2009. Accessed 15 July 2017. http://fas.org/irp/world/para/libi.pdf.

Mazzetti, Mark and Michael R. Gordon. 'ISIS Is Winning the Social Media War, US Concludes'. *The New York Times*, 12 June 2015. Accessed 27 July 2018. https://www.nytimes.com/2015/06/13/world/middleeast/isis-is-winning-message-war-us-concludes.html.

Michot, Yahya, trans. and ed. *Muslims under Non-Muslim Rule*. Oxford: Interface Publications, 2006.

al-Naisaburi, Muslim Ibn al-Hajjaj. Sahih Muslim, Book 19, *The Book of Jihad and Expedition*. Kitab al-Jihad wa'l-Siyar. Accessed 5 August 2015. http://www.iium.edu.my/deed/hadith/muslim/019_smt.html.

Naji, Abu Bakr. *Idarat al-Tawahhush* [Management of Savagery]. Markaz al-Dirasat wa'l-Buhuth al-Islamiyya. Abu Bakr Naji. Accessed 10 March 2016. https://pietervanostayen.files.wordpress.com/2015/02/idarat_al_tawahhush_-abu_bakr_naji.pdf. The website appears to be defunct.

The Quran.

Qutb, Sayyid. *Ma'alim fi'l-tariq* [Milestones]. SIME ePublishing Services (Distributor). Accessed 21 July 2018. http://majallah.org/2017/01/qutbs-milestone.html.

Rapoport, Yossef and Shahab Ahmed, eds. *Ibn Taymiyya and His Times*. Karachi: Oxford University Press, 2010.

al-Suri, Abu Mus'ab ('Umar 'Abd al-Hakim). *Da'wat al-muqawama al-Islamiyya al-'alamiyya* [Call of Islamic World Resistance]. Accessed 1 April 2017. https://ia800303.us.archive.org/25/items/Dawaaah/DAWH.pdf.

Taymiyya, Ibn. 'Aqeedatul-Waasitiyyah' [The Wasit Creed]. *Ahl-e Hadith*. Accessed 5 August 2018. https://ahlehadith.files.wordpress.com/2010/07/aqeedatul-waasitiyyah.pdf.

Taymiyya, Ibn. *'Aqidat al-Wasitiyya*. Translated by Assas Nimer Busool. Accessed 21 August 2015. http://www.salafipublications.com/sps/sp.cfm?subsecID=AQD04&articleID=AQD04003.

7 Rules of jihad

Introduction

The second chapter on jihad focuses on rules of engagement of and justifications for offensive jihad. Despite the savage brutality with which some terrorist organizations wage jihad, extremist groups appear to acknowledge that mujahidun must comply with certain restrictions which regulate how this struggle 'in the path of God' can be waged. Militants thus agree with their Muslim and Western critics that rules of engagement of jihad exist. Where they differ, however, is the interpretation of those rules. The former generally adopt positions promoting a very rigid and oftentimes even brutal implementation of recommendations made by classical 'ulama, frequently disregarding the historical context in which such recommendations were made. Disagreements do not merely exist between extremists and moderates but also among the former themselves. This is a clear weakness since such division oftentimes prevents cooperation between terrorist groups and coordination of military operations against the enemy. Needless to say, awareness of such lack of unity is of great value to counterterrorism officials, who can exploit it to their advantage. Another conclusion which can be drawn from the existence of disagreements among militant groups is that it suggests that counterterrorism agencies should perhaps consider developing different strategies for different organizations in lieu of a one-fits-all approach, perhaps involving some kind of contact with the somewhat less extreme groups. An example of a particularly vicious implementation of jihadi rules of engagement – albeit a unique one it has to be emphasized – is the defunct Algerian Groupe Islamique Armée (GIA), discussed in Chapter 8.

Another issue examined in this chapter is the motivations behind military operations 'in the path of God'. Classical sources such as the Quran and hadith frequently contradict modern extremist interpretations of rules of jihad and justifications for a literalist and selective interpretation of verses in the Quran without consideration of the historical context. In addition, modern mainstream Islamic and Western scholars are quite critical of the arguments advanced by extremist ideologues. This chapter briefly examines these debates and the arguments advanced by both sides in support of their position

DOI: 10.4324/9781003260943-8

on rules of engagement and motivations behind jihad. A serious problem for moderate interpretations of rules of jihad is the many contradictions in the Quran, with statements at times calling for mercy and on other occasions for strict and even brutal implementation of Islamic law against transgressors and all kinds of 'unbelievers'. The latter statements offer opportunities for extremists to make a case for what oftentimes amounts to a merciless implementation of Islamic law. The former statements, however, often enable moderate 'ulama who consider the historical context and the overall context of a sura to make a stronger case.

Rules of engagement

Jihad is governed by many rules, some of which are emphasized and contested differently by different militant groups. Mustafa Setmarian, a famous jihadi ideologue and strategist better known as Abu Mus'ab al-Suri, conveys a very clear and simple message to Muslims and non-Muslims alike:

> There will be no salvation for the umma, unless we follow the principle of hanging the last unbeliever of the last [Christian] priest by the intestines. The only weapon we have with which to face the modern machinery of the enemy is jihad and the love of death. The spirit is enriched by the love of death ... Mutilated bodies, skeletons, terrorism ... words so beautiful![1]

Another of his instructions regarding how to wage jihad reads: 'Terrorism is a duty; murder is a rule. All Muslim youths should become terrorists'.[2] It appears that Sitmarian's interpretation of the rules of conduct of jihad is focused on the concept of death, which he sees as the only solution for the enemy. Against the backdrop of the above extremist statements, it therefore comes as a surprise to learn that he found the Algerian terrorist organization GIA so extreme in its ideology and actions that the organization deserved his condemnation. Thus, notwithstanding his own bloodthirsty remarks, he censured the GIA for

> daring to publish fatwas which authorized the murder of wives and sons of those who worked for government institutions, thereby intensifying the confrontation with the civil militias, which had no relationship whatsoever with the government, adopting a *takfiri* [excommunicative] attitude in its public declarations and maintaining other stupid positions.[3]

In his book *Sumario de mi Experiencia en la Yihad Argelina (1988–1996)*, he also stated that the group's propaganda reflected 'ignorance, criminal principles, fanaticism, and supporting the murder of innocents'.[4] Setmarian's criticism of some jihadis' disregard for what he perceived as inviolable rules for the conduct of jihad reveals that extremist groups oftentimes find it difficult to get along and also that an individual who appears to be an ultra-extremist ideologue could actually turn out to be much less extreme than another individual or group.

In his major work, *Daʿwat al-muqawama al-Islamiyya al-ʿalamiyya*, Abu Musʿab al-Suri (Setmarian) strikes what seems to be a more conciliatory note toward the enemy than his statement above. He draws a clear distinction between Middle Eastern Christians and 'imperialist' Christians of the West. Accordingly, it is allowed to target missionary institutions, but not the churches of local Christians, and Middle Eastern Christian monks.[5] Interestingly enough, al-Suri advises mujahidun to avoid targeting places of worship, 'irrespective of religious affiliation, Christian, Jewish or other'[6] in the United States and Western countries allied with the US. It is unclear if al-Suri actually includes in this protected status religions traditionally labeled 'polytheistic' by Muslims. Furthermore, civilian citizens, including non-Muslims, of countries which are not party to the conflict [between Islam and the West] must not be harmed 'in order to preserve the reputation of the resistance [movement] in different circles of public opinion'.[7] Al-Suri also advocates a general ban on targeting women and children when they are separated from men, most likely for the same reason as the previous ban. His acceptance of the use of weapons of mass destruction,[8] however, appears to contradict his concern for civilian casualties. He adopts a moderate position in order to preserve the unity of Muslims and, most likely, guarantee a permanent access to manpower for the resistance movement, when he rejects excommunication of Muslims. For al-Suri it is sufficient to pronounce the *shahada* (profession of faith) to be considered a Muslim. Compared to the position adopted by the GIA and Daʿish, as discussed in subsequent chapters, this must be regarded as a moderate stance.

As discussed above, some jihadi ideologues take positions on various issues that are sometimes extremist and sometimes less so. An additional example is Sayyid Qutb's position on slavery. He argues that Islam accepted slavery because it was common practice at the time to enslave prisoners of war and that Islam therefore had to 'adopt a similar ... practice'.[9] Qutb also indicated that the practice would eventually be discontinued. This interpretation of the reason for the existence of slavery in Islam caused outrage in at least one ʿalim, who called Qutb's words dangerous and stressed that he was not an Islamic scholar, further complaining that such statements would only offer the enemies of Islam an argument against the religion, adding that slavery had existed in other revealed religions before Islam and that it would 'continue so long as Jihaad in the path of Allaah exists'.[10] Most likely, the ʿalim's reaction was based upon the conviction that Islam is Allah's immutable word. If gaining widespread acceptance, Qutb's statement would set a dangerous precedent since it would open the door to human manipulation of Allah's word, undermine the authority of the ʿulama and perhaps even make their services redundant, if all and sundry were allowed to question or reject religious scholars' traditional interpretation of Islam. This explains

140 *Rules of jihad*

the emphasis of the fact that Qutb was not an Islamic scholar. Despite the 'alim's rejection of Qutb's statement, it nevertheless deserves serious attention since it suggests that the latter realized that Islam had to be flexible on certain issues and deal in different ways with different time periods.

An issue on which Qutb was not at all flexible, however, is the true nature of jihad. He insists that jihad is not a temporary, but an eternal struggle, since falsehood and truth cannot exist side by side.[11] Qutb arrives at this conclusion after quoting a number of *ayat*, the last of which reads: 'And fight all the polytheists as they all fight you'.[12] Qutb contends, based upon Ibn Qayyim's interpretation, that this *aya* means that Allah commands Muslims to fight all polytheists without exception. This is a problematic position since Qutb interprets it to mean that Muslims *must* wage jihad against all *mushrikun* (polytheists). This is clear from Qutb's argumentation, which takes the reader through three phases – restraint, permission to fight if fought against and, finally, waging jihad even when not attacked. This is not an accurate reading of the *aya*, which merely says that Muslims should fight polytheists the same way as the latter fight Muslims. The *aya* does not include a blanket authorization to launch a jihad against all *mushrikun* without provocation. Furthermore, seventh-century Muslims were most likely not aware of the existence of any polytheists outside the Arabian Peninsula, so how would they fight them? Moreover, Qutb attempts to strengthen his case by resorting to contextual analysis. The problem is that this approach strengthens the case of 'ulama and other scholars who argue that Allah's commandment to the Muslims to fight all *mushrikun* is time-specific, the first third of the seventh century and geographically specific as well – the Arabian Peninsula – which completely undermines his argument that jihad is an eternal effort on the part of the Muslims.

It is possible that Qutb sensed that his argumentation led in a direction opposite to the one he desired, which could explain why he includes a rhetorical and emotive argument to the effect that it is difficult to imagine someone hearing Allah's word and following the developments of the Islamic jihad still believe that jihad is a temporary effort exclusively limited to the defense of the borders. It is clear that Qutb has used this rhetorical and emotive device to prevent the reader from thinking critically out of respect for Allah and His Messenger. Furthermore, Qutb's purpose is to make the reader think that (s)he lacks the intellectual ability to grasp such an obvious truth, should (s)he disagree with the author.[13] From Qutb's perspective, he has thus made his case despite the weak initial argumentation. In the last paragraph of the chapter on jihad, however, Qutb makes a surprising statement regarding what he believes is a right granted by Allah to any Islamic community anywhere in the world to seize political power in that society and establish [Allah's] rule.[14] Qutb seems oblivious to the strong possibility that Muslims wherever they do not constitute the majority will be regarded as a potential Trojan horse. By drawing attention to this issue, he has done Muslims, particularly those Muslims who disagree with him, a great disfavor, since such a call for treason will most likely increase surveillance of his co-religionists with possible restrictions imposed on their civil liberties as a result. As we will see in the chapters on Daʿish propaganda and ideology, though, he is far from the only ideologue inciting Muslims to violent action in the name of Allah.

Abu Bakr Naji, best known as author of *Idarat al-Tawahhush* (Management of Savagery), dispels any doubts about the nature of jihad and the rules of the struggle in the path of Allah. He rejects the notion of peaceful jihad, underscoring that the struggle on the battlefield ennobles a mujahid because it offers him opportunities to perform altruistic deeds, overcoming baser instincts such as selfishness.[15] Naji states the following regarding the jihad against the enemy: '...we are facing the people of the cross and the apostates who assist them and their army. There is nothing which prevents us from spilling their blood. On the contrary, we regard this as one of the foremost duties...'.[16] The permission to treat the people of the cross in this way is, according to Naji, granted on religious grounds – they do not pray and they do not pay *zakat* (alms tax). One could of course argue that many Christians pray, but in Naji's mind, that is immaterial. What matters is that they are not Muslims. When it comes to shedding Muslim blood, however, he finds no excuse for this. As a justification for the violent jihad of today, he argues that massacres are necessary because, like the situation after the death of the Prophet during the Ridda Wars [when some Arab tribes refused to recognize the legitimacy of the first Caliph Abu Bakr and therefore were considered apostates], some people must be massacred as a consequence of their status as apostates.[17] Having said that, Naji warns jihadis against going beyond the pale of the shariʿa. In a similar vein, he also states, without being very specific, that the violence against the enemy will be reduced, if he is reasonable and recognizes the truth. He also evinces flexibility in a discussion of the possible presence of Muslims at a target. His advice to the mujahidun is to attack oil installations when no workers are there in order to exclude the possibility of the accidental killing of Muslims. Naji seems to be unaware of the realities of shift work. His preference is, however, to attack pipelines where there are no people or tankers operated by unbelievers (i.e., non-Muslims).[18] The discussion of the rules of jihad, as interpreted by al-Suri, Qutb and Naji, has revealed that all three of these ideologues at times take very extreme positions and at others somewhat more flexible. This sets them apart from jihadi groups such as the Islamic State and GIA as demonstrated in subsequent chapters of this study.

Muhammad ʿAbd al-Salam Farag emphasizes the violent aspect of jihad. He argues that

> Jihad in the path of Allah, despite its extreme importance for the future of this religion, has been neglected and ignored by the ʿulama of our time in spite of the fact that they know it is the only way to restore and raise up the lofty edifice of Islam anew.[19]

Therefore, it is every Muslim's duty to exert his utmost efforts to restore the Caliphate. In this context, Farag underscores the importance of distinguishing between the near enemy and the enemy afar. He states that the struggle against the former takes precedence over the latter. The corollary of this is therefore that

> It is our obligation to concentrate on our Islamic issue, which is to establish Allah's law first in our country and make Allah's word rule. There is no doubt that the primary arena for jihad is the extermination of the unbelieving leaders and their replacement with a completely Islamic regime. This is where it begins.[20]

The reason why the leaders have to be eliminated, according to Farag, is that they are all apostates. Farag references a hadith found in al-Bukhari and Muslim (without providing the exact number of the hadith): 'He who fights to establish the rule of Allah's word, he [fights] in the path of Allah'.[21] Farag concludes that 'Fighting in Islam is [in order] to establish the word of Allah on earth, offensively as well as defensively. Islam was spread by the sword'.[22] Farag seems to ignore the main criticism that some non-Muslims hold against Islam, namely that it was spread by the sword, thereby undermining the efforts of mainstream Muslims to argue the opposite. Also, it is clear from Farag's further argumentation that he believes that overthrowing the unbelieving leaders of Muslim countries is a more realistic enterprise than launching a global jihad against all enemies at the same time.

Traditional and moderate Islamic authorities have generally taken a less extreme view of how jihad should be waged. Many hadith refer to the rules of conduct of jihad. At times, the instructions in these hadith are contradictory. Thus, according to one hadith, the Messenger Muhammad encouraged Muslims to fight against those who disbelieve in Allah. However, prior to fighting the *mushrikun* (polytheists), the Muslim army has to invite them to accept Islam. If they refuse, they should be attacked. If they do, they should be encouraged to migrate to a designated area in order to have all privileges and obligations of Muslims. Should the polytheists refuse to accept Islam, they would have to pay the *jizya* (poll tax), and if they refused, the Muslim army had to fight them. However, if they accepted to pay the *jizya*, they would be offered protection.[23] It is obvious that the context is that of the seventh century, when conquerors abounded not just in the Arabian Peninsula, but everywhere else in the world. What distinguishes moderates and extremists from one another, though, is the fact that the former accept that Islam must adopt flexibility, without changing its basic principles, since the world has changed fundamentally in 14 centuries. On the other hand, jihadis see in seventh-century Arabia an ideal Islamic society which must be emulated by modern man to reestablish the original true religion. Furthermore, jihadis could certainly argue that coercion with respect to the *jizya* is not an injustice since even modern states force their citizens to pay tax.

Another hadith seems to contradict the message conveyed in the previous one, advising that Muslims 'should not desire an encounter with the enemy', but should be firm when encountering him. This hadith obviously appears to lend support to the concept of defensive jihad.[24]

Other hadith, though contradictory as well, give us interesting insights into the personality of the Prophet Muhammad and his military leadership. According to one hadith, the Prophet ordered the killing of a man who had maligned Allah and himself.[25] This suggests that Muhammad perceived such critics to be more dangerous than many of his other enemies, as confirmed by the following example. There are also examples when the Prophet displayed surprising restraint regarding the treatment of enemies. It is reported that a tribe had stolen a number of his camels. They were pursued by a Muslim archer who eventually captured them and refused to provide water to the thirsty. When the group was brought to Muhammad, their captor asked him to send soldiers to punish the tribe, but Muhammad told him that they had already been deprived of some of their property and ordered their release.[26] On another occasion, a group of *mushrikun* who had spoken ill of the Messenger of Allah had been captured and brought to Muhammad. One would have expected their fate to be sealed, considering Muhammad's decision in the first hadith, but he forgave the men and ordered them released instead.[27] The final example is even more astonishing, since it seems to contradict the concept of jihad. A woman had demanded that Muhammad kill the polytheists of Mecca following the conquest of the city. The rationale was that their conversion to Islam could not be trusted since it was a result of their defeat. The Prophet replied: 'God is sufficient (against the mischief of the polytheists) and He will be kind to us'.[28] The hadith seems to suggest that there is no need to fight enemies because Allah will deal with them and protect the Muslims, obviously a conclusion that calls the whole concept of violent jihad into question.[29]

Unlike the message of extremist groups, numerous suras in the Quran speak of moderation and restraint. In Surat al-Nisa' and Surat al-Ma'ida, Allah tells the People of the Book, that is, Jews and Christians, not to go to extremes in their religion.[30] Technically speaking, this warning is directed at non-Muslims, but since Muslims belong to the People of the Book, Allah's message is for them as well.[31] One *aya* (verse) of Surat al-Anfal reads: 'But if they incline to peace, you [Prophet] must also incline towards it, and put your trust in God. He is the All Hearing, the All Knowing'.[32] This *aya* reveals that jihad should not be waged for the sake of fighting, but that negotiations should be initiated, if the enemy wants peace. One could interpret the *aya* as preferring peace to hostilities, or at least as expressing moderation and restraint, if circumstances allow. The Egyptian government institution Dar al-Ifta' al-Misriyya declares that Islam is based on mercy. This interpretation of the religion is in line with the emphasis on moderation in the above suras. The institution's message regarding the terrorist acts of Da'ish and other extremist groups is that they 'go against the natural disposition of

144 *Rules of jihad*

human beings'[33] and that such acts are caused by 'perverted mentalities that should be fought with all means possible to save humanity from those heinous acts'.[34] What is of particular interest in these two quotes is the absence of reference to Islam. Instead, the Dar al-Ifta' emphasizes humanity as a whole and that human beings have a shared destiny irrespective of religious affiliation, a truly extraordinary statement, which militants would reject off hand. The Dar al-Ifta' echoes several modern ideas in its promotion of moderation. The institution mentions human, animal and environmental rights, portraying these rights as important aspects of Islam, arguing that respect for Allah also entails respect for His creation. Furthermore, in its criticism of the Islamic State, the Dar al-Ifta' points out that 'Muslims were the first to introduce rules of warfare engagement'.[35] Detailed rules were enforced by Caliph Abu Bakr to the effect that old men, women and children must not be killed, hermits oppressed or fruit-bearing trees cut down.[36] These rules all demonstrate moderation and it is worth mentioning that they predate the Geneva Conventions by more than 1,300 years.

Even suras with violent content, such as Surat al-Tawba, stress moderation. It instructs Muslims to live in peace with the mushrikun (polytheists) with whom they have signed treaties which have not been violated by the former. Even when the polytheists violate a treaty, there will be a grace period of four months before Muslims take counter measures. Following this period, however, Muslims are ordered by Allah to 'kill the polytheists wherever you find them'.[37] But if they convert to Islam, they shall be spared and released. The *aya* ends with the reminder: 'Allah is Most Forgiving, Most Merciful'. The renowned ninth-century Islamic scholar and historian Abu Ja'far Muḥammad ibn Jarir al-Ṭabari interprets this *aya* as evidence that Allah has not asked Muslims randomly to kill *mushrikun*.[38] In the context of serious sins, the Quran frequently reminds Muslims of Allah's moderation and mercy. Such examples can be viewed as contradictions, offering extremists an opportunity to ignore the message of moderation. An alternative interpretation of such contradictions in the Quran is that they actually provide Muslims options – violence and rigidity, or flexibility and moderation. Representatives of the former approach are the Algerian GIA and the Islamic State, whereas the moderate approach is reflected in statements and comments of many official Islamic institutions such as the Dar al-Ifta' al-Misriyya. Surat al-Tawba is an excellent example of a sura which can be construed by extremists as permission to kill all polytheists. The sura discusses two kinds of relationships: it ensures peace for mushrikun with whom Muslims have concluded a treaty and violent jihad with polytheists who have violated their treaty. However, the sura says nothing about *mushrikun* who do not have a treaty with the Muslims and do not attack their religion. Many jihadis lump these polytheists together with those who have violated a treaty, making killing them a lawful act. This is the position of the Islamic State magazine *Rumiyah*, which argues 'Allah has ordered the killing of all mushrikin - whether military or civilian -...'[39] The *aya* clearly does not provide such an option regarding polytheists who do not have a treaty with the Muslims. The fact that they are not even mentioned considerably undermines the extremist argument.

For the mujahidun, the incentives held out for those participating in the struggle in the path of Allah made each battle a win-win situation. If they were victorious, they would receive a share of the *ghanima* (spoils); if they were killed, they would go to Paradise, considered the highest reward; and, finally, if they were defeated, but survived, they would have another opportunity to gain wealth or end up in Paradise in the next battle. It should be pointed out that the lot of a vanquished enemy was probably the same anywhere in the world in the seventh century. This fact seems to exonerate the conduct of early Muslim armies, but for their argument that jihad is unlike regular warfare. The practice of *ghanima* and slavery effectively undermines this claim.[40] This circumstance did not prevent Algerian GIA fighters in the 1990s and has not prevented Daʿish fighters in the twenty-first century from arguing that they were/are in full compliance with Islamic rules of conduct of jihad, when they resorted/resort to distributing booty and turning kidnapped women into sex slaves. A Dagestani scholar partly confirms the existence of strong worldly motivations among jihadis, particularly during the early Arab invasion of Dagestan, when the invaders perpetrated massacres of those who resisted and sold survivors into slavery. The scholar points out that these Muslim 'hawks' were subsequently followed by peaceful preachers and scholars. Interestingly enough, he compares the Muslim 'hawks' to American and European 'hawks', 'who export democracy on the wings of bombers'.[41] Dagestan is a part of the Russian Federation, which explains why the scholar 'forgot' to add the Soviet Union/Russia to the list of armies which have not lived up to their ideals.

Martyrdom operations and merits in Paradise

A serious analysis of the concept of jihad must by necessity include a discussion of what Western media call suicide attacks, and also of the merits of participating in jihad in the path of Allah. Generally speaking, jihadis regard what Western media call suicide attacks as martyrdom (*istishhadi*) operations. Traditional and moderate Islamic scholars tend to agree with the Western terminology.[42] The concept of *istishhad* is based upon the idea that the jihadi performs a sacrifice in the path of Allah[43] and in defense of the umma. Islam condemns suicide, and there is no question of suicide being legalized by extremist ideologues. From their perspective, strapping an explosives belt on to one's body is a sacrificial operation, reflective of a true Muslim's worship of Allah and an altruistic act carried out for the benefit of the Islamic community.[44] Mainstream ʿulama argue that *istishhad* by means of blowing oneself to pieces constitutes suicide. Their condemnation of martyrdom by explosives is based upon Surat al-Nisaʾ, 4:29, much of which deals with relations between men and women. *Aya* 29 ends with the words 'And do

146 *Rules of jihad*

not kill yourselves, for Allah is Merciful towards you'.[45] The following *aya* reads 'Whoever does that, out of hostility and wrongdoing, We will cast him into a Fire...'.[46] Another sura referred to is Surat al-Baqara, 2:195, which states 'And spend in the cause of Allah, and do not throw yourselves with your own hands into ruin, and be charitable. Allah loves the charitable'.[47] A leading Saudi 'alim, Salih Ibn Fawzan al-Fawzan, resorts to even more striking language in order to deter potential candidates for self-destruction from committing this sin, stating unequivocally that mujahidun who commit suicide in the path of Allah 'are fighting for the sake of Satan'.[48] Opponents to *istishhadi* missions can thus base their arguments on clear Quranic evidence in support of their position.

An obviously controversial aspect of martyrdom[49] is the presumptive merit accrued in Paradise from such action. Martyrs can expect a number of rewards in the afterlife. Ibn Taymiyya, an 'alim often referred to by jihadi ideologues, confirms that the mujahid 'will be in extreme bliss in both this worldly life and in the afterlife...'.[50] He also states that death in the path of Allah is the most virtuous of deaths, that martyrs are guaranteed entry into Paradise, and that a martyr can intercede for 70 of his family members.[51] This seems to contradict al-Wahhab's argument that no one but Allah can intercede for a Muslim.[52] Furthermore, the Quran states that, unlike Muslims on earth, martyrs in Paradise can enjoy alcoholic beverages without getting intoxicated. However, no explanation is provided why this sin on earth becomes acceptable in Paradise. A third incentive offered to residents in Paradise is the houris with swelling breasts (kawa'ib) that mujahidun can take to wives.[53] The posthumous prestige in society that accompanies the status of martyr[54] is, of course, another aspect of martyrdom that attracts certain individuals to the *istishhadi* cause, as is the 'fifteen minutes of fame' guaranteed when a mujahid's last video interview is posted to the Internet. An interesting theory argues that the mujahid's self-sacrifice in Allah's honor is derived from the account of Abraham's aborted sacrifice of Isaac after he heard a voice telling him to desist and the Muslim *'Id al-adhha* (Feast of Immolation) when Muslims sacrifice a lamb or goat.[55] If Abraham's aborted sacrifice of Isaac serves as jihadis' excuse for *istishhadi* attacks, they have missed a crucial point of the story, namely, that the sacrifice was not completed as a result of divine intervention. This is a convincing indication that such a 'sacrifice' is not acceptable.

The merits of dying a martyr discussed above raise legitimate questions regarding the motivation behind *istishhadi* operations, such as to what extent it reflects a spiritual or a temporal quest. The jihadi discourse frequently tends to emphasize the former. The Islamic State's magazine *Rumiyah* ran an article about a purported mujahid who had contemplated the question of a justification of an *istishhadi* mission which he was wishing to carry out. In anticipation of Allah's question, why he had blown himself to pieces, the mujahid had found an answer which, in his mind, made complete sense: 'I did this for You, my Lord'.[56] If true, this story is evidence that at least one mujahid thought that he would execute a martyrdom mission not for selfish reasons. It is possible that he had additional reasons as well, but the *Rumiyah* article does not suggest that possibility. Conversely, the sensual descriptions of Paradise[57] above indicate that there is ample opportunity for other motivations, as does a reference in the Al-Qaʻida's magazine *Inspire* to a sura promising that martyrs will be rewarded with absolution of their sins and admission to the beautiful gardens and mansions in Paradise.[58] Furthermore, another sura discusses punishment for not heeding Allah's warnings and rewards for the righteous. The Quranic chapter describes life in Paradise as an existence in which the inhabitants are happily busy, spouses leisurely recline in shades on couches and have all the fruits and anything else they can wish for.[59] This description of a life full of worldly activities is completed with one word – 'peace' – a possible indication of an ongoing life of absence of conflict, or an existence eventually crowned with a perfect state of mind, a spiritual dimension. The description is obviously meant to appeal to people who eke out an existence in an arid location under very Spartan conditions, but the *aya* also possibly holds out the promise of a higher form of existence, less focused on the senses and physical needs of the believers.

Al-Wahhab

Muhammad Ibn ʻAbd al-Wahhab's biography has already been discussed in Chapter 1. In this chapter, we will briefly focus on his views on jihad, and to what extent, his interpretation of Islam concurs with that of Ibn Taymiyya and that of modern jihadi ideologues.

Al-Wahhab adopted many positions which differ from those of Ibn Taymiyya and modern jihadi ideologues. One scholar writes that al-Wahhab did not in his writings discuss martyrdom and rewards in Paradise in the context of jihad because he did not want religion to be exploited for 'self-aggrandizement'.[60] This seems to suggest that he would have disapproved of the pre-martyrdom videos posted to the Internet and the articles in online jihadi magazines praising mujahidun carrying out *istishhadi* operations (suicide missions).[61] Furthermore, al-Wahhab did not interpret the violent verses in the Quran as general justification for war against unbelievers, instead, making a point of preserving life once war had broken out.[62] Also, Surat al-Tawba was not interpreted by al-Wahhab as a general justification for fighting all *mushrikun* (polytheists) and killing them.[63] Conversely, in *Rumiyah*, Islamic State ideologues argue that this sura is a general obligation to kill the *mushrikun*, though women and children are exempt, if they have not fought Islam.[64] Al-Wahhab's concern for the preservation of life and refusal to interpret Surat al-Tawba as permission to kill all polytheists is a convincing indication that he would not have approved of Daʻish's burning Muslim prisoners alive. The Islamic State defends its actions by reference to Surat al-Nisaʼ which states 'Indeed, those who disbelieve in Quranic verses - We will drive them into a fire'.[65]

148 *Rules of jihad*

This is Allah speaking, and nowhere is there any indication that the Supreme Being has delegated to any humans the right to send disbelievers into Hellfire or any other fire. It is clear from the sura that this is the prerogative of Allah. Therefore, when jihadis burn their prisoners, they are guilty of usurpation of Allah's authority, which is tantamount to *shirk*, the serious crime of elevating someone, namely, themselves, to the same status as Allah. The accusations that jihadis hurl against evil 'scholars' to the effect that they 'alter and distort the law'[66] thus apply to the jihadis' own actions. Finally, al-Wahhab does not see eye to eye with Ibn Taymiyya, arguing that reason and *ijtihad* (independent reasoning) should be the foremost guiding principles for Muslims, not necessarily the writings of the salaf (early Muslims).[67]

Based upon the fact that al-Wahhab and modern jihadi ideologues sometimes are at variance over the interpretation of Quranic verses, the question arises: Why do jihadis often refer to al-Wahhab in support of their extremist version of Islam? A major reason could be his focus on the concept of *tawhid*, oneness of God, which fits perfectly into the extremist discourse. If the jihadis appear wholeheartedly to embrace *tawhid* and promote this idea, it makes it more difficult to reject their extremist positions since this is a concept accepted by all Muslims. One can therefore suspect that Islamic militants exploit al-Wahhab's status as champion of *tawhid* to impute his status and legitimacy to their own extremist interpretation of Islam. Two other issues are also exploited by the jihadis in order to gain legitimacy as representatives of true Islam. First, by embracing Ibn Taymiyya, extremists establish a link to a period when Islam was under attack by Christianity, which allows them to argue that modern Muslims are experiencing a similar situation today. Second, the West's historical record of imperialism and support for Zionism in the twentieth century enables jihadi ideologues to shape an anti-West discourse, the origins of which go back all the way to the medieval Crusades, thereby 'revealing' the existence of a deep-rooted hostility of Western countries and implying that this is a distinguishing feature in the Western/Christian character. This strategy, that is, 'acquiring' Ibn Taymiyya and al-Wahhab, appears to work to a certain extent, particularly if the reader is not prepared or equipped to subject jihadi arguments to critical analysis.

Conclusion

As can be expected, traditional and extremist views on rules of and justifications and motivations for jihad differ considerably. Both approaches to jihad recognize the existence of rules but interpret these very differently. One reason for these differences is seemingly contradictory statements in the Quran, the existence of which allows traditionalists/moderates and extremists to build cases in support of their respective arguments. Not surprisingly, both sides evince selectivity with respect to verses in the Quran to bolster their case. Generally speaking, however, this chapter suggests that moderate 'ulama are more inclined to consider the historical context, the overall context of a sura, and other factors such as peaceful coexistence with the rest of the world, whereas extremist interpretations place much more emphasis on a 'literalist' approach to the Quran, arguing that God's word is immutable and that there is no room for human agency in the form of interpretation when assessing whether a Muslim is in compliance with Islamic law. This debate, which attracts much attention in Middle East media, is the object of discussion to a much lesser extent in Western media, in which extremist acts and arguments draw a much larger audience. Furthermore, another issue which figures even less prominently in Western, and Middle East media as well for that matter, is contradicting views within extremist ranks on rules of engagement. For obvious reasons, interest in both these debates has the potential of being of great benefit to agencies which make efforts to reduce the possibility of extremist violence. Also, the fact that the authority of traditionalist 'ulama is being challenged by extremists will guarantee continuous efforts of the former to counter militant arguments, thereby contributing to the international efforts to reduce the appeal of extremist propaganda.

The incentives for participating in classical jihad were several. A share in *ghanima*, or spoils, was one. The appeal that this prospect exerted to mujahidun should not be underestimated despite the official emphasis on the spiritual motivation for participation in jihad. Participation in jihad also offered an opportunity to acquire slaves, a practice that Da'ish engaged in during the apex of its power in Syria and Iraq. Concurrently, the spiritual motivation, that is, disseminating Allah's word, is certainly a reason for some mujahidun to join jihad since death on the battlefield automatically guaranties a right to reside in Paradise and enjoy all its benefits. A second incentive of death in the path of God is the belief that the martyr acquires the right to intercede on behalf of one's living relatives. The wish for martyrdom is obviously a strength in a fighting army, provided the mujahid can send as many enemies as possible to Hell.

A final observation which appears to have been overlooked by Islamic and Western scholars alike is that the many contradictions in the Quran constitute an opportunity in disguise. Generally speaking, the contradictions that can be found in the Quran can be confusing and exploited by detractors of Islam to argue that they undermine Allah's message to mankind. However, an alternative interpretation of the Holy Book's contradictory statements can be used to the benefit of moderate Muslims and the detriment of extremist interpretations by advancing the argument that these contradictions can actually serve to assist Muslims in interpreting the Quran since they can be explained by changing circumstances, thus encouraging the reader to adopt *ijtihad*, reasoning, when reading the Holy Book.

Notes

1 Óscar Pérez Ventura, 'Mustafa Setmarian, el Ideólogo de la Yihad Moderna', *Instituto Español de Estudios Estratégicos, Documentos Marco*, 24 March 2014, p. 8, accessed 30 July 2017, http://www.ieee.es/Galerias/fichero/docs_marco/2014/DIEEEM05-2014_Mustafa_Setmarian_IdeologoYihadModerna_OPVentura.pdf. (My translation.)

150 *Rules of jihad*

2   Ibid., p. 12.
3   Ibid., p. 21. (My translation.)
4   Ibid.
5   Al-Suri, *Da'wat al-muqawama al-Islamiyya al-'alamiyya*, p. 1381.
6   Ibid., p. 1390.
7   Ibid.
8   Ibid., p. 1400.
9   'The Heresies of Sayyid Qutb in Light of the Statements of the Ulamaa (Part 2)', *SalafiPublications.com*, accessed 5 August 2015, http://www.spubs.com/sps/sp.cfm?subsecID=NDV01&articleID=NDV010010&articlePages=3.
10 Ibid.
11 Qutb, *Ma'alim*, p. 35.
12 The Quran, 9:36.
13 Hitler resorts to a similar emotive device in his *Mein Kampf*; see Adolf Hitler, *Mein Kampf* (Munich: Zentralverlag der NSDAP, Frz. Eher Nachf., G.m.b.H., 1943 (first published 1925, Vol. 1 and 1927, Vol. 2), p. 311, accessed 9 August 2017, https://ia802302.us.archive.org/18/items/Mein-Kampf2/HitlerAdolf-Mein Kampf-Band1Und2855.Auflage1943818S..pdf.
14 Qutb, *Ma'alim*, p. 41.
15 Naji, *Idarat al-Tawahhush*, (Markaz al-Dirasat wa'l-Buhuth al-Islamiyya), p. 59, accessed 1 May 2016, https://pietervanostayen.files.wordpress.com/2015/02/idarat_al_tawahhush_-abu_bakr_naji.pdf.
16 Ibid., p. 31. (My translation.)
17 Ibid., p. 32.
18 Ibid., p. 43.
19 Farag, 'Al-Jihad: Al-Faridha al-gha'iba', *Markaz al-Kalema al-masihiyy*, accessed 30 July 2015, http://alkalema.net/algehad.htm. (My translation.)
20 Ibid.
21 Ibid.
22 Ibid.
23 Muslim Ibn al-Hajjaj al-Naisaburi, *Sahih Muslim*, Book 19, No. 4294, accessed 1 August 2019, http://www.iium.edu.my/deed/hadith/muslim/019_sm t.html.
24 Ibid., No. 4313.
25 Ibid., 4436.
26 Ibid., 4449.
27 Ibid., 4450.
28 Ibid., 4453.
29 Jihadists could argue that the hadith (tradition) is weak or has been manipulated, but this would undermine their own arguments regarding jihad since they often refer to collections of hadith, when they cannot find suitable suras (chapters in the Quran) to support their position. Generally, many historians are cautious about using hadith as historical evidence of what the Prophet Muhammad might or might not have said. Even if that is a valid position since the hadith were compiled and recorded long after the death of Muhammad and actual quotes therefore should be treated with caution by the historian, one could argue that the hadith are of interest to the researcher because, if they are not accurate, they could still reflect contemporary views, at least those of the compiler who decided to include them in the collection.
30 The Quran, 'Surat Al-Nisa'', 4:171, and 'Surat Al-Ma'ida', 5:77.
31 'Ali Ibn Yahya al-Haddadi, *Al-Ghuluww wa muzahirhu fi'l-hayat al-mu'asira* [Extremism and Its Manifestations in Contemporary Life], 'The Forbiddance and Danger of Extremism', *Abdurrahman.Org*, accessed 17 May 2017, https://abdurrahman.org/terrorism-extremism/.

Rules of jihad 151

32 The Quran, 8:61.
33 *Dar al-Ifta' al-Misriyya*, 'Recruiting European Muslims in QSIS: What Kind of God Are They Fighting for?' accessed 5 August 2015, http://www.dar-alifta.org/Foreign/ViewArticle.aspx?ID=575&CategoryID=5.
34 Ibid.
35 Ibid.
36 Ibid.
37 The Quran, 9:5. For other suras which emphasize mercy and moderation, see *The Quran*, 4:149 and 24:22.
38 *Dar al-Ifta' al-Misriyya*, 'The Fighting verses in the Quran: Are They a Hotbed for Extremism?' accessed 5 August 2015, http://www.dar-alifta.org?Foreign?ViewArticle.aspx?ID=578&CategoryID=5.
39 *Rumiyah* [Islamic State Magazine], Issue 5, January–February 2016, p. 6.
40 The Prophet Muhammad owned at least one slave according to a hadith in Muslim, *Sahih Muslim*, Book 19, No. 4450. The hadith provides no information about how the Prophet came into possession of the slave or how he was treated.
41 Kurbanov, 'Koran i Islamskii ekstremizm'.
42 See *Abdurrahman.org*, accessed 6 August 2018, https://abdurrahman.org/category/islam/suicide-bombings/; *Isuu*, https://www.scribd.com/document/3989813/Martyrdom-in-Islam-Versus-Suicide-Bombing; *Isuu*, https://issuu.com/themonthlytruthforce/docs/martrydomvssuicidebombing; *Abdurrahman.org*, https://abdurrahman.org/2015/07/23/how-can-you-be-a-martyr-if-you-are-in-the-hell-fire/.
43 Ivan Strenski, 'Sacrifice, Gift and the Social Logic of Muslim "Human Bombers"', *Library of Social Science*, accessed 24 May 2016, https://www.libraryofsocialscience.com/essays/strenski-sacrifice.html; *Rumiyah*, Issue 5, p. 8.
44 *Inspire*, Issue 15 (Spring 2016), p. 5.
45 The Quran, 4:29.
46 Ibid., 4:30.
47 Ibid., 2:195.
48 Salih Ibn Fawzan al-Fawzan, 'Al-Muntahiruna b'ism al-jihad ittiba' li'l-shaitan', *Okaz* (Saudi Newspaper), accessed 20 July 2018, https://www.okaz.com.sa/article/257811/.
49 *Istishhadi* operations are called *intihar* (suicide) operations by those who oppose them.
50 Ibn Taymiyya, *Majmu' al-Fatawa*, Vol. 28/353, accessed 25 May 2018, https://muwahhidmedia.files.wordpress.com/2013/09/translated-fatawa-ibn-taymiyya-on-jihad1.pdf. This text is no longer available from the website.
51 Ibn Taymiyya, 'Fataawa Sheikh ul Islam ibn Taymiyyah on Jihad', *Muwahhid Media*, accessed 24 February 2016, http://muwahhidmedia.files.wordpress.com/2013/09/translated-fataw-ibn-taymiyya-on-jihad.pdf.
52 David Commins, *The Wahhabi Mission and Saudi Arabia* (London: I.B. Tauris, 2006), p. 15, accessed 24 January 2018, http://asrdiplomacy.ir/wp-content/uploads/2017/03/The-Wahhabi-Mission-and-Saudi-Arabia-Book-1.pdf.
53 The Quran, 56:19, 78:33.
54 Strenski, 'Sacrifice'.
55 Ibid.
56 *Rumiyah*, Issue 3 (Nov., 2016), p. 15.
57 Cook, *Understanding Jihad*, p. 28. Cook also states that 'wearing gold and silk… are a major feature of the pleasures in store for the blessed'.
58 The Quran, 61:10–13, quoted in *Inspire* (Winter 2010), p. 26.
59 The Quran, 36:55–57.
60 Natana J. DeLong-Bas, *Wahhabi Islam: From Revival and Reform to Global Jihad* (New York: Oxford University Press, 2004), p. 255.

152 Rules of jihad

61 *Rumiyah*, Issue 5 (Jan., 2017), p. 8.
62 DeLong-Bas, *Wahhabi Islam*, p. 234.
63 Ibid., p. 238.
64 *Rumiyah*, Issue 5 (Jan., 2017), p. 6.
65 Ibid., p. 18.
66 Ibid., p. 27.
67 Rapoport and Ahmed, *Ibn Taymiyya*, p. 10.

Bibliography

Abdurrahman.org.
Commins, David. *The Wahhabi Mission and Saudi Arabia*. London: I.B. Tauris, 2006. Accessed 24 January 2018. http://asrdiplomacy.ir/wp-content/uploads/2017/03/The-Wahhabi-Mission-and-Saudi-Arabia-Book-1.pdf.
Dar al-Ifta' al-Misriyya.
DeLong-Bas, Natana J. *Wahhabi Islam: From Revival and Reform to Global Jihad*. New York: Oxford University Press, 2004.
Farag, Muhammad 'Abd al-Salam. 'Al-Jihad al-Faridha al-Gha'iba' [The Neglected Duty]. *Markaz al-Kalema al-Masihiyy*. Accessed 30 July 2015. http://alkalema.net/algehad.htm.
al-Fawzan, Salih Ibn Fawzan. 'Al-Muntahiruna b'ism al-jihad ittiba' li'l-shaitan' [Those Who Commit Suicide in the Name of jihad Follow Satan]. *Okaz*, 23 April 2009, Accessed 20 July 2018. https://www.okaz.com.sa/article/257811/.
al-Haddadi, 'Ali Ibn Yahya. *Al-Ghuluww wa muzahirhu fi'l-hayat al-mu'asira* [Extremism and Its Manifestations in Contemporary Life], 'The Forbiddance and Danger of Extremism' [English Translation], *Abdurrahman.Org*. Accessed 17 May 2017. https://abdurrahmanorg.files.wordpress.com/2014/10/the-forbiddance-of-extremism-ali-ibn-yahya-al-haddadi-authentic-translations-com.pdf.
Hitler, Adolf, *Mein Kampf* [My Struggle]. Munich: Zentralverlag der NSDAP, Frz. Eher Nachf., G.m.b.H., 1943 (first published 1925, Vol. 1 and 1927, Vol. 2).
Inspire.
Kurbanov, Khanzhan. 'Koran i Islamskii ekstremizm' [The Quran and Islamic Extremism]. *Islam Review*, accessed 6 April 2015, http://islamreview.ru/est-mnenie/koran-i-islamskij-ekstremizm/.
al-Naisaburi, Muslim Ibn al-Hajjaj. Sahih Muslim, Book 19, *The Book of Jihad and Expedition* Kitab al-Jihad wa'l-Siyar. Accessed 1 August 2019. http://www.iium.edu.my/deed/hadith/muslim/019_sm t.html.
Naji, Abu Bakr. *Idarat al-Tawahhush* [Management of Savagery]. N.p: Markaz al-Dirasat wa'l-Buhuth al-Islamiyya, n.d. Accessed 1 May 2016. https://pietervanostayen.files.wordpress.com/2015/02/idarat_al_tawahhush_-abu_bakr_naji.pdf. The website appears to be defunct.
Pérez Ventura, Óscar. 'Mustafa Setmarian, el Ideólogo de la Yihad Moderna' [Mustafa Setmarian: Ideologue of Modern Jihad]. *Instituto Español de Estudios Estratégicos, Documentos Marco*, accessed 24 March 2014. Accessed 30 July 2017. http://www.ieee.es/Galerias/fichero/docs_marco/2014/DIEEEM05-2014_Mustafa_Setmarian_IdeologoYihadModerna_OPVentura.pdf.
The Quran.
Qutb, Sayyid. *Ma'alim fi'l-tariq* [Milestones]. SIME ePublishing Services (Distributor). Accessed 22 May 2016. http://majallah.org/2017/01/qutbs-milestone.html. This website appears to be defunct.

Rapoport, Yossef and Shahab Ahmed, eds. *Ibn Taymiyya and His Times*. Karachi: Oxford University Press, 2010.

Rumiyah.

SalafiPublications.com. 'The Heresies of Sayyid Qutb in Light of the Statements of the Ulamaa (Part 2)'. Accessed 15 September 2019. http://www.spubs.com/sps/sp.cfm?subsecID=NDV01&articleID=NDV010010&articlePages=3.

Strenski, Ivan. 'Sacrifice, Gift and the Social Logic of Muslim "Human Bombers"'. *Library of Social Science*. Accessed 24 May 2016. https://www.libraryofsocialscience.com/essays/strenski-sacrifice.html.

al-Suri, Abu Mus'ab ('Umar 'Abd al-Hakim). *Da'wat al-muqawama al-Islamiyya al-'alamiyya* [Call of Islamic World Resistance]. Accessed 13 October 2019. https://ia800303.us.archive.org/25/items/Dawaaah/DAWH.pdf.

Taymiyya, Ibn. 'Fataawa Sheikh ul Islam ibn Taymiyyah on Jihad'. *Muwahhid Media*. Accessed 24 February 2016. http://muwahhidmedia.files.wordpress.com/2013/09/translated-fataw-ibn-taymiyya-on-jihad.pdf.

Taymiyya, Ibn. *Majmu' al-Fatawa* [Collected Fatwas]. Vol. 28/353. Accessed 25 May 2018. https://muwahhidmedia.files.wordpress.com/2013/09/translated-fatawa-ibn-taymiyya-on-jihad1.pdf.

8 Precursors to the Islamic State

In the 1990s and first decade of the twenty-first century, Al-Qaʿida maintained close ties with the Algerian Groupe Islamique Armée (GIA, or Al-Jamaʿa al-Islamiyya al-Musallaha in Arabic) and the group operating in Iraq under Musʿab al-Zarqawi's leadership, following the American occupation. Al-Zarqawi's group would later adopt the name Al-Qaʿida in Mesopotamia and then the Islamic State (IS or Al-Dawla al-Islamiyya fi al-ʿIraq). Both groups would, following initial close ties with Al-Qaʿida, become estranged from this organization because of differences in methodology. Despite sharing the same end goal – the eventual establishing of an Islamic caliphate and revival of the religion of the early Muslims (the Salaf) – the Al-Qaʿida leadership severed relations with the GIA and criticized Al-Qaʿida in Mesopotamia when they adopted an ideology and methods which were too extreme for Osama Bin Laden and his inner circle. This chapter examines the ideology and methodology of the GIA, Al-Qaʿida (as reflected in the organization's online magazine, *Inspire*), and the origins of the Islamic State, al-Zarqawi's organization Al-Qaʿida in Mesopotamia.

GIA history

Algeria is no stranger to terrorism, a widespread phenomenon both in the war of liberation 1954–1962 and in the jihadi insurgency of the 1990s, following the military coup against the FIS (Front Islamique du Salut), the victor in the 1992 elections. During the war of independence, the Front de Liberation Nationale (FLN) had resorted to terrorism to eject the French from Algeria. In response to this formidable challenge, the French foreign intelligence service, the Service de Documentation Extérieure et de Contre-Espionage, or SDECE, had set up an unofficial organization codenamed the Red Hand to target Algerian FLN fighters. The Red Hand represented an instrument of state terror since its purpose was to instill terror in FLN ranks in order to paralyze the independence movement. The French state-sponsored terrorist organization operated not only in Algeria but also in West Germany, targeting arms traders to whom the Algerian insurgents had turned for weapons. Another group being targeted by the French were Algerians living in West

Germany. The ruthless policies pursued by the French state in the war of independence were not very successful. They failed to prevent FLN access to weapons since the latter turned to the Soviet Union instead for its military hardware. Shortly prior to the French exodus from Algeria, French settlers formed the Organisation de l'Armée Secret (OAS), a terrorist organization engaging in terrorism both in Algeria and France. The unleashing of a war without rules, however, did not have the desired effect for the French, who had hoped to stop the recruitment of young fighters to the FLN. On the contrary, the harsh measures to which the state and French vigilante organizations resorted had the opposite effect – more Algerians joined the freedom fighters.[1] The uniquely barbarous acts of the Groupe Islamique Armée in the 1990s demonstrated that the Islamic terrorists had not learned the valuable lesson from the mistakes of the French state and vigilantes in the 1950s and 1960s.

The Afghanistan War 1979–1988 and deteriorating economic and social situation functioned as a catalyst for Algerian terrorism in the 1990s. The decline in oil prices in the 1980s, corruption, increasing foreign debt, youth unemployment and reduced welfare services and subsidies caused widespread discontent, particularly among the poor. The unpopularity of the government was clearly demonstrated in the elections of December 1991 when the FIS scored a great success, winning 231 of 430 seats in the Algerian parliament in the first round of the elections. The gains of the Islamists were perceived by the military as a threat to its control, a fear which prompted it to intervene and cancel the second round of parliamentary elections to prevent an Islamist victory, thereby exacerbating an already socially tense situation in the country. The ensuing armed conflict between the military and Islamic militants resulted in 50,000–100,000 fatalities. The rise of extremist Islamic factions was facilitated by the authorities' incarceration of moderate leaders.[2] Another contributing factor was the departure from Pakistan at the end of 1993 of approximately 1,500 Algerian mujahidun returning to their homeland. The large number of battle-hardened veterans of the Afghan war contributed greatly to the spread of extremist interpretations of Islam in Algeria and the rapid rise of terrorism.[3] The GIA, which did not yet bear that name,[4] had, however, begun its activities two years earlier with an attack on an army base and a massacre known as 'the Guemar massacre', perpetrated in November 1991.[5] Later, close ties were established between the GIA and Al-Qa'ida as demonstrated by the former having a representative in the latter organization.

Many different parties, domestic and external, appear to have been involved in the emergence of Islamic terrorism in Algeria. According to former Algerian Prime Minister Redha Malek, at the end of 1980, 3,000–4,000 Algerian volunteers were dispatched to Afghanistan encouraged by Islamic leaders in their country to wage jihad against the Soviet forces. Most likely, some of these Arab 'Afghan' veterans were among the mujahidun who later returned to Algeria. Other factors and actors, such as funding from Saudi

Arabia and other Gulf countries, and support from the Pakistani Inter-Services Intelligence (ISI) and the CIA, contributed to the extreme violence which erupted in Algeria in the 1990s.[6] The presence in Afghanistan of Algerian 'Afghans' also was reflected in the first Algerian extremist Islamic organization, the Mouvement Islamique Armé (MIA), founded in 1982 by Mustafa Bouyali. The numbers mentioned above suggest that Algerians made up a substantial part of Arab 'Afghans' operating in Afghanistan, according to one source 20,000 *in toto*, most of whom had received training in camps in Peshawar.[7] Finally, the Algerian regime itself played an important role in causing domestic terrorism. A Moroccan source contends that this problem in Algeria was in part self-inflicted since Algerian security services dispatched young men from Algeria, Morocco and Tunisia to receive training in Pakistan and fight against the Soviets in Afghanistan.[8]

Militant Islamic organizations in Algeria suffered from division from the early 1990s. Some of these groups adopted so extremist positions that even Al-Qaʻida became critical of them.[9] One of the terrorist groups formed in 1994 was L'Armée islamique du salut (AIS, or Jaish islamiyy li'l-inqadh in Arabic). AIS was the armed wing of the FIS and continued operations until 1997, when it declared a unilateral ceasefire.[10] Divisions within the GIA in 1996 led to the emergence of new groups such as the Islamic League for the Daʻwa and Jihad (La Ligue Islamique pour la daawa et le djihad, LIDD). This organization split from the GIA, rejecting the latter's use of massacres as a weapon of jihad. Like the AIS, it later joined the ceasefire camp. Rejection of some of the GIA's brutal methods also produced another splinter group, the Salafist Group for Preaching and Combat (La Groupe salafiste pour la predication et le combat, GSPC, or Al-Jamaʻa al-Salafiyya li'l-Daʻwa wa'l-Qital in Arabic).[11] The GSPC formed in 1999, having denounced the GIA's massacres. It attracted a large number of members of the GIA, growing in numbers from 700 to 3,000 in two years, indicating strong opposition to the ruthless methods of the GIA.[12] The GSPC established close ties with Al-Qaʻida. Both organizations shared religious leaders, and their mujahidun had fought together in Afghanistan, Iraq and other places.[13] The great number of extremist organizations in Algeria in the 1990s reflects the deep divisions among mujahidun. Most of these groups were 'moderate' compared to the GIA despite the fact that they subscribed to terrorist ideologies and methods. The death toll, estimated at having exceeded 100,000[14] by the beginning of the twenty-first century, provides a clear indication that the term 'moderate' is quite relative.

Following the FIS success in the 1991 elections, the Algerian state took action in a number of different ways to curb the influence of the Islamists. Early in 1992, President Chadli Bendjedid resigned, whereupon the military declared a state of emergency in the country. In September, the regime dissolved all Islamic associations, justifying this measure with the accusation that the Islamic Salvation Front was using the associations as 'administrative bases'.[15] Two days later, the government issued Law 30-94, creating three special courts for prosecution of perpetrators of 'acts against the security of the state'.[16] Three years later, in November 1995, the military regime decided that terrorist organizations had caused enough resentment among the population to allow the government successfully to hold presidential elections. The expectation was that Algerians would demonstrate support for the government's anti-terrorism measures in the face of the violent excesses of extremist groups. This calculation proved correct, as evidenced by high voter turnout despite the boycott of Islamist parties and groups.[17] Extremist groups had threatened to turn polling stations into coffins and the GIA announced that it would kill anyone who dared to vote.[18] Before the elections, several opposition parties, including FIS, had signed the Sant'Egido Platform in Rome, also known as the National Contract, calling for negotiations with the military government and suspension of violence by both sides. The government rejected the contract, demanding that the FIS renounce violence before negotiations could begin.[19] This was not the last time the government would take a rigid stance regarding negotiations with the Islamist opposition or Islamic terrorists. In October 1997, an Iranian offer of mediation between the Algerian government and the GIA was rejected by the Algerians on the grounds that the proposal revealed that 'Iran maintained ties with the group [GIA] which massacred innocent [civilians] in Algeria'.[20] It seems that the government had nothing to lose, if it engaged in a dialogue with the opposition and the terrorists. Many observers would most likely argue that the GIA, having excommunicated all Algerians except its own members, would not take an offer of mediation seriously. This could, however, have been exploited by the government for propagandistic purposes, accusing the GIA of adopting a rigid position.

In its short history, the GIA stands out as a terrorist organization which surpassed most other extremist groups in its use of brutal violence, concurrently, however, demonstrating the weakness of such an approach to political power. This group was born out of violence, thrived on violence and eventually fell victim to its own violence. The GIA adopted its name at a meeting attended by a large number of Algerian militant groups in October 1992.[21] The group was essentially an urban organization, but it possessed several rural strongholds as well. Its members were predominantly unemployed city youth in their early twenties, many with a criminal record.[22] In July 1996, its most infamous leader, 'Antar Zouabri, assumed leadership of the organization in what can be described as a palace coup. At the time, the army was carrying out intensive operations against terrorist groups, as a result of which many commanders were absent from a meeting that had been called to appoint a successor to the previous leader, Jamal Zitouni, who had been killed by the AIS. The meeting was convened as part of a power struggle and attempts to control the distribution of booty among GIA commanders. One of them, 'Ali Hasan Abu al-Walid, had been appointed temporary emir by the GIA's majlis al-shura (consultative assembly). By appointing himself emir, Zouabri effectively undercut any bid on al-Walid's part to be appointed permanent leader of the organization. Zouabri's leadership of GIA lasted until his death in February 2002 at the hands of security forces.[23] He met his end with two of his lieutenants, holed up in a house in his hometown Boufarik, after a three-hour fire fight with a Swat team.[24] Zouabri's career as a terrorist was not accidental – his brother had been the leader of an earlier Islamic militant group.[25] At his death the GIA, according to an Algerian official, did not exceed 40 mujahidun in strength, obviously a far cry from the group's heyday if an accurate assessment.[26]

Ideology

The foundation of GIA's barbaric acts was its 'ideology'. The GIA and other extremist groups argued that the Islamic movement in Algeria, that is, the FIS, had failed because it had not been sufficiently persistent in pursuing jihad. This was a clear indication that the militants had found the true path and that their approach constituted the only resolution to the problem.[27] This exclusivist ideology could serve as justification for any act and atrocity perpetrated by the terrorists and facilitated their rapid descent into barbarity. One of the GIA's leaders, Zitouni, issued a fatwa which justified killing wives and children of anyone working for the Algerian state. For obvious reasons, Zitouni also targeted journalists and intellectuals[28] since they could articulate criticism of terrorist methodology and had access to a large audience through media outlets, which could, from a terrorist perspective, influence public opinion in undesired directions, making a strong case for rejecting the extremist path. Like earlier Islamic ideologues, such as Sayyid Qutb and Muhammad 'Abd al-Salam Farag, leader of Egyptian Islamic Jihad, leaders of the GIA and other Algerian extremist groups argued that it was the duty of every true believer to wage jihad against the *kafir* (infidel) state, that jihad was a continuous process and that despotic and *kafir* rulers must be killed. As if that were not enough, Zouabri went one step further, issuing a fatwa justifying the killing of any Algerian who did not join the GIA or who had any kind of dealings with the state. This fatwa was based on the concept of 'hijra wa takfir',[29] that is, the duty of true Muslims to emigrate from kafir territories to areas controlled by the GIA or risk being excommunicated and becoming legitimate targets of the mujahidun. Al-Zouabri's fatwa made no distinction between old and young, man and woman, or born and unborn Algerians. The fatwa made a 'fetus in the mother's womb' a legitimate target as well.

The extreme positions adopted by the GIA were counterproductive since they resulted in increasing division in the extremist camp. Abu Hamza, a former imam of a London mosque and currently serving a life sentence in a US maximum security prison, is quite critical of the GIA's positions, denouncing their ideology as extremist. It is worth mentioning that Abu Hamza himself is no moderate Muslim. He condemns the group's excommunication of the whole Algerian population, including other jihadis who denounce democracy as kufr (unbelief). Abu Hamza states that the blanket takfir (excommunication) of Muslims also labeled true mujahidun as kuffar (unbelievers). The GIA's religious pronouncement led the group to declare that fighting 'mujahid apostates' took precedence over waging jihad against Christians and Jews. According to Abu Hamza, the fact that GIA mujahidun take Muslim women as war booty and violate them is clear evidence that these fighters disregard fundamental Islamic values. Their acts thus create division instead of unity in Muslim ranks.[30] An example previously referred to is the GSPC which split from GIA over methodological issues, establishing close ties with Al-Qa'ida, eventually becoming an Al-Qa'ida franchise in 2007 under the name of Al-Qa'ida in the Islamic Maghrib. The organization's virulent anti-Western rhetoric dispels any illusions regarding a possible moderate stance. It skillfully exploits history for propagandistic purposes, calling young Muslims to avenge America's crimes against Muslims in Abu Ghuraib and Guantanamo and to 'erase colonial borders'.[31] The GSPC also pledged that 'We shall never live in peace until every last Muslim land is set free from the crusaders, the apostates, and the collaborators'.[32]

Methodology

While many Algerian terrorist organizations made efforts to diversify their targets, some placed restrictions on who could be targeted, whereas the GIA put all scruples aside, making their jihad quite simple, declaring that the whole Algerian population constituted legitimate targets.[33] Initially, the GIA had retreated to the mountains and avoided targeting innocent civilians. This strategy was, however, abandoned when the organization began to carry out massacres of villagers. Other frequent targets were military personnel, school teachers, foreigners, rival Muslim clerics, university professors, journalists, trade unionists, doctors and politicians. By 1995, more than 200 teachers and over 100 Muslim scholars and preachers had been killed at the hands of the GIA.[34] Some groups were not primarily targeted for murderous purposes, but for raising funds. Small merchants and entrepreneurs were forced to make 'donations'. Algerian communities in Europe and North America constituted another financial source, making voluntary contributions to the cause. A network exceeding 5,000 Algerian activists abroad guaranteed a steady flow of money and arms smuggled into Algeria, enabling the terrorists to continue their deadly activities. Armed robbery of banks also helped to fill terrorist coffers, as did money-laundering resulting from real estate investments.[35] As early as 1993, the militant group had ordered all foreigners to leave Algeria within one month. The terrorists proved that they meant business, when they kidnapped seven Trappist monks and killed them in 1996. GIA fighters also tried their hands at hijacking. In 1994, they seized an Air France airliner, intending to crash it into the Eiffel Tower in Paris. During a stopover in Marseilles, French police stormed the aircraft, killed the four hijackers and rescued all passengers. One reason the plan was not successful was that the explosives the terrorists had brought onboard the airplane did not detonate,[36] suggesting a lack of expertise in this important field. They were more successful at setting off bombs at subway stations in the French capital.

The GIA's extremist interpretation of Islam was meticulously implemented in the group's jihad against the Algerian government and people. The civilian population suffered particularly, as victims of extremist violence, most likely because of the ease with which civilians could be targeted. One example is an attack carried out on the outskirts of the capital Algiers, where 400 victims had their throats slit in one single night.[37] Another extremist raid on a village near the town of Bougara south of Algiers resulted in the death of 120 men, women and children. These atrocities were not of unique occurrence. In the first half of 1997, the death toll resulting from massacres amounted to 10–40 victims daily.[38] The death toll in six villages attacked by jihadists in 1997 exceeded 3,000, testifying to the extent of the ongoing slaughter in the country.[39] The GIA sometimes turned on other terrorist groups who had incurred their ire. One example is the family of a leader who had severed relations with the GIA and had to pay for his decision with the death of 31 family members in 1997.[40] The irony of this case was that the population in this region had resisted forming local anti-terrorist militias. Acts such as this one did certainly not endear the militants with the locals. Adding insult to injury, the GIA issued a statement in 1997, in which the group, incredibly enough, assumed responsibility for slaughtering, burning and kidnapping Algerians, proud to claim credit for acts for which the GIA 'feared' that the other groups would claim responsibility. However, not all attacks led to massacres. On one occasion, the GIA organized a jailbreak, freeing 900 prisoners in the town of Batna. This act had positive repercussions for the GIA in the form of increased recruitment.[41] Furthermore, the ease with which terrorist operations were carried out against soft targets in Algiers and other cities has led some to conclude that certain segments of the population must have been supportive and involved in these activities.[42] Eventually, however, the ruthless operations of the GIA alienated Algerians, causing the demise of the organization.

The Algerian military and the jihadi insurgents frequently adopted similar strategies and tactics in their war against one another. One such strategy was infiltration of enemy ranks. Government agents were quite active penetrating jihadi organizations. Such efforts led to infighting, killings and fragmentation of insurgent groups. As a result, many GIA mujahidun left the organization, fearing for their lives. Furthermore, in order to discredit the mujahidun, agents of the Algerian government circulated rumors that the GIA was a government organization.[43] A former high-ranking Algerian intelligence officer has confirmed that these rumors were partly true. Some smaller GIA groups were autonomous, others infiltrated and still others directly controlled by the security service, the Département du renseignement et sécurité (DRS).[44] It seems obvious that at least some groups must have acted independently since they targeted military personnel. One study argues that the ability to infiltrate the GIA was a consequence of the military's summary execution of suspects following terrorist attacks as a warning to potential jihadis. Such acts naturally created resentment among young men and prompted many to join the GIA. This may seem as a counterproductive policy, but it offered an opportunity to the security services to infiltrate jihadi groups.[45] Conversely, at times, security officers' dealings with terrorists had undesired consequences since some officers ended up joining the terrorists, with one officer even taking over leadership of one jihadi group.[46] Furthermore, many junior officers and conscripts were sympathetic to the militant cause, going so far as to provide arms and ammunition to the mujahidun, and even deserting to them.[47] Also, both sides resorted to various forms of coercion and threats to achieve their objectives. The military would oftentimes kidnap and torture family members of GIA fighters to put pressure on the latter to turn themselves in or accept to work for the government.[48] The GIA, for its part, would threaten to kill the female members of state functionaries' families in order to compel them not to cooperate with the authorities.[49]

Both sides were at times quite successful with regard to certain counter measures, sometimes competing in barbarity. An ingenious strategy of the Algerian government was to enable villagers to defend themselves by arming them.[50] It could, however, be argued that this was a somewhat risky strategy, if some villagers were sympathetic to the terrorist cause. Despite the potential risks, this strategy appears to have been quite successful since it made GIA recruitment in rural areas much more difficult.[51] The threat of assassination of high-ranking government officials at the hands of mujahidun seems to have been an effective GIA strategy. As a result of this threat, 'most senior civil servants had been forced to flee their villas on the hills above Algiers'.[52] They had relocated to a guarded community west of the capital and many commuted to work by helicopter, which made it difficult for the terrorists to target them. It is somewhat surprising that the terrorists did not possess arms which could shoot down helicopters. Like rumors with respect to the military controlling the GIA discussed above, the Algerian public also suspected that the military perpetrated massacres, adopting methods rivaling those of the terrorists. Needless to say, it is difficult to provide hard evidence in support of such allegations.[53] The fact that some massacres allegedly perpetrated by the GIA occurred in the vicinity of military camps without the military intervening to rescue civilians being slaughtered by the terrorists does indeed seem odd, to say the least, since the commotion in the villages would most certainly have been heard in the military camps.[54] In summary, it is possible that both parties to the Algerian conflict perpetrated massacres, however, with the difference being that the GIA openly admitted responsibility for atrocities, whereas the military did not. Furthermore, both the government and the Islamic militants can claim success, but during the conflict, it was limited to the army's control of territory in the day and the insurgents' control of the same territory at night.[55]

Prominent characteristics of the Algerian Islamic insurgence were the GIA's heinous treatment of women and the mujahidun's lifestyle, both of which strongly suggest that the driving force behind the Islamic insurgency was partly based on materialistic considerations and non-spiritual desires. In a fatwa issued in 1997, the GIA assumed responsibility for kidnapping, raping and enslaving women, arguing that such crimes constituted sacrifices 'for the cause of Allah and a sign of sincere worship'.[56] This practice was also adopted by Islamic State in Iraq and Syria (ISIS), as discussed in Chapter 10. It is possible that this was one of the reasons for excommunicating the entire Algerian population, an act which made it permissible to kidnap Muslim women and violate them since they were no longer 'true' Muslims. A case in point is that of a 14-year-old girl who was abducted by the GIA, gang-raped daily by the mujahidun, after which Antar Zouabri 'took a sword and cut her body in two'.[57] This is only part of an eyewitness account by another abductee who managed to escape, but I will spare the reader the remaining gruesome details of this case. The lifestyle of many mujahidun also suggests that their motivations were not purely religious.

> The [GIA] ran rackets, in which they extorted a "tax for the revolution" from all the inhabitants; with this money they could afford to dress in name-clothes and wear Reeboks, Nikes, or Filas. They also ate well ... Some of the goods were stolen from the houses of the people they killed.[58]

It is the sad reality that the above activities were carried out under the cover of 'religion'. Fortunately, for Algerians, only a tiny minority of society embraced this extremist ideology.

Algerian mujahidun did not pose an existential threat to the regime despite waging a ruthless jihad against the government. Islamic militants are estimated to have numbered 10,000–15,000[59] fighters, but were not united in one single organization. GIA fighters made up a minority of this total, perhaps 2,500 fighters.[60] The GIA contributed considerably to this disunity as a result of its brutal jihad, which was opposed by less radical jihadi groups. Furthermore, the GIA facilitated the military's counterterrorism measures by alienating a majority of Algerians with a fatwa which excommunicated the whole population. In 1997, when the FIS declared a unilateral ceasefire, the estimated combined strength of the GIA and the GSPC, which were not part of the ceasefire, constituted 5,000–7,000 militants.[61] It is worth mentioning that the GSPC had split from the GIA and that the two organizations did not coordinate their jihad against the government. By 2000, 4,200 militants had withdrawn from the Algerian jihad. A majority of these, 3,000, belonged to the AIS (the FIS' armed wing).[62] Despite the fact that the GIA was not officially dissolved, by Zouabri's death in 2002, the group's role in the Algerian jihad had been reduced to insignificance.[63] The GIA's fate suggests that its *takfir* (excommunication) of Algeria's population had raised an insurmountable obstacle to recruitment of new fighters.

Al-Qaʿida history

The origins of Al-Qaʿida go back to the 1980s war in Afghanistan, where Osama Bin Laden and ʿAbdullah Yusuf ʿAzzam created the so-called 'Services Bureau'. Sometime between 1982 and 1984, Osama Bin Laden and his mentor, ʿAbdullah Yusuf ʿAzzam, set up an organization in Peshawar, Pakistan, called Maktab al-Khidmat (Services Bureau). Their purpose was to transfer donations from charity organizations in Saudi Arabia, the Arabian Gulf countries and Western Europe to the mujahidun in Afghanistan.[64] One source states that the Arab mujahid presence in Afghanistan was very limited when the Maktab al-Khidmat was founded, totaling 13 fighters only, and that this presence had reached 5,000 fighters by the late 1980s.[65] Another source estimates that Al-Qaʿida's membership stood at 50–314 jihadis in the mid-1980s, a number constituting roughly 15 percent of Arab 'Afghans'.[66] Later, when volunteers with military skills joined the organization, it began primarily to focus on planning military operations. The majority of these volunteers had received their military training in the Egyptian and Syrian armed forces.[67] Fresh recruits received military training in several camps funded by Bin Laden, who in the 1990s encouraged many of these recruits to travel to Algeria to participate in the jihad there.[68] Through its camps in Pakistan, Al-Qaʿida established ties with fighters who would later fight for the GIA in Algeria and then split from this organization, ultimately swearing allegiance to Osama Bin Laden and Al-Qaʿida in 2007 and adopting the name Al-Qaʿida in the Islamic Maghreb (AQIM). Al-Qaʿida's success in creating alliances was also reflected in its support for Abu Musʿab al-Zarqawi's organization in Iraq, Al-Tawhid wa'l-Jihad. Al-Zarqawi's affiliation with Al-Qaʿida demonstrates the latter's role in the emergence of the Islamic State in Iraq. Despite the relatively small number of fighters under Bin Laden's command, their multinational background allowed the Al-Qaʿida leader to play a role outside the Afghan theatre. The ties to other extremist organizations provided Al-Qaʿida with strategic depth and influence in several regions of the Islamic world, but these links also turned out to be a weakness when both the GIA and the Islamic State caused division among jihadi groups by adopting much more extreme tactics than Bin Laden's organization. These drawbacks did, however, not prevent Al-Qaʿida from carrying out spectacular international attacks such as the bombing of the American embassies in Kenya and Tanzania in 1998 and the terrorist attacks in the United States in 2001.

Al-Qaʿida's ideology

Al-Qaʿida's leaders realized early on the important role media could play in enhancing the organization's international reach. Printed and, later, online magazines would prove quite helpful fora for the dissemination of Al-Qaʿida's ideology. The first attempt in this direction was the *Al-Jihad Magazine*, funded by Bin Laden and distributed among mujahidun in Pakistan and Afghanistan by Maktab al-Khidmat during the Soviet presence in Afghanistan.[69] Another Al-Qaʿida magazine, *Inspire*, published online by Al-Malahem Media, reflects the organization's jihad in the twenty-first century. This part of the present chapter briefly examines the ideology and methodology of Al-Qaʿida, particularly as reflected in issues of the organization's English-language mouthpiece *Inspire*.

Not surprisingly, *Inspire* and the writings of Al-Qaʿida's ideologues devote many pages to justifying the jihad against those perceived as the enemies of Islam. ʿAbdullah Yusuf ʿAzzam, Al-Qaʿida's al-Azhar-trained first ideologue, argued in a fatwa entitled *Defense of Muslim Lands* that it was a religious duty for Muslims to support the jihad against the Soviet forces in Afghanistan, concluding that this was both a *fardh kifaya* and *fardh ʿayn*, that is, a collective and individual duty. This fatwa reflected the majority view among Arab mujahidun fighting the Russians in the 1980s. Another Al-Qaʿida ideologue, Bin Laden's second in command and successor Aiman al-Zawahiri, disagreed, contending that the primary task of Arab 'Afghans' should be to overthrow corrupt Arab regimes.[70] One can interpret the existence of these conflicting ideas regarding jihad as a 'democratic' debate climate within Al-Qaʿida. However, ʿAzzam's death (not from natural causes) in 1989 suggests otherwise. Abu Yahya Al-Libi, a religious scholar and third prominent Al-Qaʿida ideologue, killed in an American attack in Pakistan in 2012, adopted a position similar to that of al-Zawahiri, arguing that defeating the 'near enemy' should be a priority. He did not distinguish between the West and corrupt Arab regimes since the latter were supported by the former. According to al-Libi, the nearest enemy should first be forced to accept the shariʿa, whereupon the next enemy should be eliminated in the same way, 'until all [enemies] have surrendered to Allah's rule'.[71] Al-Libi's view suggests that Al-Qaʿida's ultimate goal is world domination. This view contradicts the frequently repeated message to the West in *Inspire*: '[i]f we live in peace and safety, you too shall live in peace and harmony'.[72] The quote from *Inspire* appears to hold out an olive branch, contradicting the view that the Islamic world is engaged in an existential struggle with the West.

Irrespective of whether the message to the West is an apocalyptic scenario or a conditional olive branch, the justifications for the jihad are the same in both cases – long-standing grievances of the Islamic world with respect to the West's treatment of Muslims. Al-Libi states that Western countries have carried out aerial attacks against mujahidun and Muslim civilians.[73] These crimes led him to conclude that Muslims must fight Christians, Jews and Muslim apostates.[74] *Inspire* provides similar justifications for targeting the United States arguing that the US is guilty of terrorism and aggression against other peoples.[75] Another 'crime' of Washington is its policy of inciting sectarian wars in the Middle East and wishes to annihilate the

Sunnis.[76] This is, of course, not a very convincing argument since it could be contended that the totalitarian Sunni regime in Iraq led by Saddam Husain until his overthrow in 2003, bears much responsibility for the Shi'i majority's mistrust of the Sunnis. Ironically, the accusation that the United States made efforts to incite sectarian strife in the Middle East is much more convincing regarding the intentions of Abu Mus'ab al-Zarqawi, the founder of the organization which later became known as the Islamic State. Al-Zarqawi's objective was to cause a Sunni-Shi'i civil war in Iraq, which would presumably unite all Sunnis and enable them to regain their traditionally dominant position in the country.[77] Finally, like many extremist Muslims, al-Libi, in contravention of Islamic tradition, argued that jihad was equal in importance to the five pillars of Islam. The elevation of jihad to the status of a pillar of Islam certainly helped to attract new recruits to the cause of the mujahidun as demonstrated by the jihads in Afghanistan, Algeria and other areas of conflict.

Methodology

Al-Qa'ida's publications offer scholars and counterterrorism experts invaluable insights into the organization's approach to propaganda and its *modus operandi*. Some issues of *Inspire* are devoted to a particular theme such as planning and carrying out professional assassinations and train derailments. The online magazine thus serves as a do-it-yourself terrorist manual and very cost-effective means of outsourcing terrorist operations by inciting potential terrorists to action. The English-language magazine thus constitutes a cheap way to establish a global jihadi presence for Al-Qa'ida. Issue 15, for instance, contains very detailed instructions for locating targets and building parcel, door-trap and car bombs. Such instructions are called open source jihad (OSJ) by Al-Qa'ida and is one way to incite 'lone-jihadi' operations without first having to establish a network of fighters. From a terrorist perspective, this method offers certain advantages. First, it disseminates dangerous knowhow, placing deadly weapons in the hands of anyone attracted to terrorism. Second, should the would-be terrorist be exposed before the nefarious plan has been executed, the damage will be much less than if a whole group of individuals were involved.[78] The disadvantage of lone-jihadi operations is, of course, that it is difficult to plan and carry out more sophisticated attacks. Nevertheless, there is propaganda value of many small attacks as well. The main theme in *Inspire*, Issue 17, is derailments. The importance of this theme and the detailed instructions for executing attacks against the rail networks in Western countries are testified to by 30 pages Al-Qa'ida devotes to the issue.[79] The magazine takes pride in quoting Western sources which confirm that terrorists have been inspired by the bomb-making manuals.[80] Such statements in the western press obviously have a clear propaganda value, implying that Al-Qa'ida's jihad is successful.

Inspire goes to great lengths in its propaganda to convince the reader of the enemy's vulnerabilities and the power of Al-Qaʻida. The organization's ideologues argue that the foundation of America's position as a superpower is its economy. This realization leads one of Al-Qaʻida's sheikhs to state that '[t]he most important goal for us at this time is to strike the economy at the head of the Kuffr [sic] (America)...'.[81] This goal will be reached by targeting American CEOs, which will cause disruption in the economy. According to Al-Qaʻida's worldview, the strength of the mujahidun is that they occupy the moral high ground and have justice on their side. The implication is that their operations enjoy the support of Allah, an authority against whom no superpower stands a chance. This is evidenced by the 9/11 attacks in the United States. *Inspire*'s propagandists claim that Americans kill and exploit Muslims and corrupt their societies.[82] In their view, the result of the jihad against America is a foregone conclusion since the party which suffers injustice (Muslims) will eventually prevail over evil (America). Evidence of this truth is found in the case of the Prophet Muhammad, who achieved great success despite suffering 'much more serious hardships than the mujahidun of today'.[83] Another strength of Al-Qaʻida is the organization's 'egalitarianism', as evidenced by the fact that 'Usama suffered the same hardships as his men'.[84] The link to the Prophet Muhammad is a clear morale booster because of his astounding success against his enemies. Linking the jihad of modern mujahidun to that of the Prophet is of course a clever propagandistic approach, which can always be employed in the face of adversity.

Inspire provides 'compelling evidence' that Al-Qaʻida mujahidun are following the 'right' path and that Allah has granted them success in their undertaking. According to the reasoning of the magazine's ideologues, the American dream is actually a nightmare. This claim is substantiated by a photomontage which conveys a clear message to the American public – a photo depicting a framed picture of the collapse of the Twin Towers in New York with the title 'A Timeless Masterpiece', signed by Osama bin Laden, next to a box containing a toy aircraft, a car bomb and an axe, placed on 100-dollar bills and a terrorist manual.[85] Another example of the fact that the jihadis are following the 'right' path is the emphasis on the evil phenomenon of racism in American society. The implication is that American society is based on injustice and that Americans who are being discriminated against will be much better off as Muslims.[86] Al-Qaʻida's plan is to exploit America's Muslims as a fifth column in its jihad against the American government.[87] Muslims will presumably eventually prevail in their jihad against the West since their operations in the United States and other Western countries will 'cause widespread frustration among citizens in these countries with increasingly strict measures taken by the state to ensure security'.[88] The reader may recall that this is a belief similar to that of Russian nineteenth-century terrorists discussed earlier in this volume. Furthermore, the citizens' frustration will, according to Al-Qaʻida, in turn, lead to panic in the government. Also, the jihad against the West is consistently cloaked in religious language and depicted as a war on Islam.[89] This portrayal of the conflict is important since the implication is that the mujahidun will prevail, the reason being that Allah supports the followers of the true religion.

In the West, Al-Qaʿida's targeting of civilians is used against the mujahidun based upon the argument that this is a barbaric practice, to which the jihadis respond that there are no innocent civilians. *Inspire* contends that the ruler is responsible for the war against Islam. The corollary to this claim is that since in a democracy the people are the ruler, there are no innocent civilians. The citizens are responsible for the policies of the government they have elected. They pay taxes which are used to fund the war against Islam. An additional argument is that a tit for tat is a fair game.[90] Al-Qaʿida's argumentation is problematic since it is fraught with obvious flaws. The main reason for this conclusion is that *Inspire*'s ideologues confound democracy with dictatorship. Under the latter, one man (or woman or a small number of individuals) formulates policy. In the former, the majority formulates policy. However, in a democracy, not everyone agrees with the majority. Furthermore, a portion of the population abstains from voting. *Inspire*'s contention is thus simplistic and aimed for consumption by people who do not exercise critical thinking. Moreover, taxes are paid by Muslims who live in the West. Do they deserve to die as well? Also, not all Muslims who live in Western countries feel that they are being discriminated against (a common jihadi argument). If it were the case that all Muslims are being discriminated against in Western countries, there would most likely be a mass exodus to Islamic countries. A final weakness of the case *Inspire* attempts to make is that only a tiny minority of Western Muslims, as well as Muslims in Islamic countries for that matter, decide to make common cause with the terrorists, even though some Muslims might sympathize with some of the arguments advanced in jihadi magazines, particularly with respect to the Palestinian issue and American involvement in the Middle East.

As has been seen in previous chapters examining the propaganda of extremist organizations and parties, their attempts to convince the reader of the legitimacy of terrorism often inadvertently exposes weaknesses in their ideologies and operations despite occasional strengths. Al-Qaʿida is no exception in this respect. A surprise is that *Inspire* magazine at times analyzes weaknesses and strengths of executed terrorist operations, providing feedback to terrorists and valuable information to counterterrorism experts alike.[91] Al-Qaʿida propagandists occasionally publicize information about the organization's sophisticated operations as well. An *Inspire* article states that Al-Qaʿida originally had intended to use ten different aircraft for the 9/11 attacks, but that the planners had faced insurmountable coordination problems relative to the execution of this operation.[92] The reason for providing this information was probably to demonstrate both to the enemy and Al-Qaʿida sympathizers that the sky is the limit with regard to the organizations operations and that the world can expect new spectacular terrorist acts in the future. The *Inspire* ideologues' enthusiasm sometimes gets the best of them. An example is where the author of an article makes the clearly hyperbolic claim that most modern sciences are based on previous Muslim research. This statement completely ignores the great contributions to science by India, China and other great civilizations. The first claim leads to an even greater exaggeration, where the magazine declares that 'nothing can benefit humanity except the one true religion, history and facts are a testament to this fact'.[93] Adolf Hitler made a similar claim about Aryans being the origin of all human culture.[94] Like the Nazi claim, that of Al-Qaʿida is based upon an assertion which has not been proven by providing irrefutable evidence, a common phenomenon in propagandistic writings, which can be described as non-fact + non-fact = fact.

Inspire sometimes makes real efforts to provide information partly based on evidence and to make a convincing case for a particular point of view. An example of the former is a report on an American raid on Qaifa, a village in central Yemen controlled by Sunni mujahidun. The report argues that the raid was a massacre, where women and children were 'shot in cold blood'.[95] For good measure, the article adds that the American soldiers then unleashed their dogs on the dead bodies, 'a scene that shows how devoid they are of any humanity'.[96] The Americans allegedly also 'burned two children in the cradle'.[97] Furthermore, the *Inspire* report states that American forces are co-operating with the Houthis in order to drive out Sunni mujahidun from the area and allow the Shiʿi Houthis to establish control over it. The allegation that Americans wish to empower the Houthis is not convincing since it is Washington's policy to contain Iran's (a Houthi ally) influence in the region. Furthermore, it is clear from the context that the reference to dogs, who are considered 'unclean' animals by Muslims, facilitates the conclusion drawn regarding American 'inhumanity'. Strangely enough, the magazine article has not referred to a report published on a British website on 9 February 2017 (several months before the *Inspire* issue was published), stating that nine children and several women were killed in the attack, which seems to confirm parts of the *Inspire* report.[98] A possible reason is that the British report does not confirm the claim that American soldiers unleashed dogs on the bodies of the dead civilians, information that will increase hatred of Americans among Muslims, which was possibly deemed more important than referring to a Western publication in support of some of the information in the *Inspire* report. The British report was based on interviews with survivors five days after the attack and it seems unlikely that they would not mention such an important detail, had it indeed occurred. It is of course possible that the interviewers intentionally omitted to include this detail in their report, but the title of their report, 'Revealed: Nine Children Killed in Botched Yemeni Raid', appears to exclude this possibility. The *Inspire* editors most likely assume that their readers do not diversify their sources.

Not surprisingly, *Inspire* is quick to exploit in its propaganda Al-Qaʿida's successes on the battlefield and emphasize the organization's strengths. One example is the Qaifa raid discussed above. Al-Qaʿida regards the clash between the Americans and mujahidun as a clear victory for the latter because of the downing of an American helicopter and killing of a number of American soldiers.[99] According to the British report, an Osprey aircraft crashed and was not shot down by Al-Qaʿida fighters. The same source states that one US soldier, not several as claimed by *Inspire*, was killed. Somewhat surprisingly, Al-Qaʿida announced that it had lost 14 men in the American attack.[100] Despite the discrepancies, *Inspire* can claim that the American raid was a victory for Al-Qaʿida because of the many children who were killed. Furthermore, the Al-Qaʿida magazine makes a convincing case regarding an advantage which it has over the West, namely, that a failed terrorist attack is still a success because the enemy can expect more terrorist acts to follow. *Inspire* advances an even more compelling argument, demonstrating its strength, when it states that the mere threat of a terrorist act is effective, even if it is not carried out, since enemy authorities have to spend resources to prevent the threat from being carried out.[101] This is indubitably a valuable advantage a terrorist organization has over a state. It is worth drawing attention to the fact that counterterrorism agencies could make the same case, but the terrorist organization would nevertheless have the advantage of being the underdog in a war which is at least by some to a certain extent viewed as justified.

Al-Qaʿida in Mesopotamia

The dissemination of Al-Qaʿida's ideology and its ties with more extremist groups may have proven to be a strength at first glance, as a result of the increase in strategic depth which such ties and alliances offer, but this advantage sometimes comes at the price of division. The contentious relationship between the GIA and Al-Qaʿida has already been examined in the beginning of this chapter. Another case in point to which we need briefly to turn our attention is that of Ahmad Fadhil Nazzal al-Khalayla, better known under his *nome de guerre* Abu Musʿab al-Zarqawi. His involvement with Al-Qaʿida, like the case of the GIA, was not without complications. Al-Zarqawi built an organization which later became the Islamic State in Iraq and Greater Syria (Al-dawla al-Islamiyya fiʾl-ʿIraq waʾl-Sham). This organization became a serious challenger to Al-Qaʿida's authority among mujahidun.

Al-Zarqawi had a criminal past and was a heavy drinker, but had a life-changing experience when his mother enrolled him in courses in a mosque in Amman, where he embraced Salafism. Having served time for drug possession and sexual assault, al-Zarqawi decided to have a career change. He attended training camps in Afghanistan after which he returned to Jordan in 1992. Sentenced to 15 years in prison for possession of an arsenal of weapons, al-Zarqawi was released in 1999 in an amnesty together with his religious mentor Abu Muhammad al-Maqdisi.[102] Upon his release, al-Zarqawi returned to Afghanistan, where he was entrusted by Bin Laden with running a training camp, but he consistently refused to swear *bai'a* (allegiance) to the Al-Qa'ida leader. Interestingly enough, while in Afghanistan, al-Zarqawi was critical of Bin Laden's support for the Taliban for the movement's killing of Muslims.[103] This is ironic since once established in Iraq, al-Zarqawi had a change of heart and had no compunction of doing exactly the same himself. He left Afghanistan with 300 fighters for Iran and then Iraq when his camp was attacked by anti-Taliban forces. His experience in Afghanistan prepared al-Zarqawi for the next chapter of his life.

In Iraq, al-Zarqawi embarked on his true mission – wreaking havoc for 'the cause of Allah'. He first created an organization called Al-Tawhid wa'l-Jihad (Oneness of God and Jihad) in April 2003, which initially comprised 70 individuals. Following his *bai'a* to Bin Laden in October 2004, Bin Laden appointed him emir of Qa'idat al-Jihad fi Bilad al-Rafidain (Al-Qa'ida in the Land of Mesopotamia).[104] Al-Zarqawi's grand scheme was to cause a civil war in Iraq. To this aim, he organized safe houses where his torturers would remove the legs of victims and behead them.[105] The extent of the violence that al-Zarqawi unleashed on Iraqi society is testified to by an estimate that he was responsible for 42 percent of all suicide bombings in the country between 2003 and 2004.[106] However, when his totalitarian ideology and racketeering began to affect not just Shi'is but Sunni tribes as well, there was a backlash since it created an opportunity for the American occupation authorities to support Sahwa (Awakening) Councils among the tribes to fight al-Zarqawi.[107] The massacres of Shi'is in Iraq caused his former mentor al-Maqdisi to criticize al-Zarqawi for such excesses, pointing out that very few Americans were targeted. Many Jordanians had initially supported al-Zarqawi, but this support quickly eroded when he launched a terrorist attack in Amman which resulted in 60 fatalities, mostly Muslims.[108] Al-Zarqawi's activities in Iraq were also criticized by Aiman al-Zawahiri, Al-Qa'ida's second in command, who advised him in 2005 to stop killing Shi'is and focus on the Americans instead.[109] The advice fell upon deaf ears, however, as the violence in Iraq spiraled out of control.

Major reasons for al-Zarqawi's ability to wield so much influence in Iraq were the support he enjoyed from former officials and officers of the Saddam Husain regime, Bin Laden's financial support and funding originating from other sources. Al-Zarqawi evinced no interest in cooperation with Sunni factions which had Ba'th, Soviet or Muslim Brotherhood leanings.[110] However, he was not averse to allow former Ba'thists to join his organization. These former party officials assisted in carrying out terrorist acts and smuggling mujahidun into Iraq.[111] One scholar has argued that this amounted to full-scale cooperation with the Ba'thists as a result of a pledge by Iraq's former vice president, Izzat Ibrahim al-Duri, in 2004 to support al-Zarqawi's terrorist activities.[112] The €680,000 Al-Qa'ida in Mesopotamia received monthly from Bin Laden allowed the organization continuously to attract new recruits.[113] Other sources of revenue were the sale of stolen American weapons, ransom paid for hostages, the smuggling of oil and donations from Middle East 'charities'.[114] A US intelligence source has estimated that al-Zarqawi had between 800 and 1,200 fighters under his command. They constituted only a small percentage of the total number of mujahidun in Iraq, though, estimated to number 10,000–30,000 fighters.[115] Al-Zarqawi's solvency should have allowed him to exert much more influence than he actually did, but his unsurpassed talent of alienating potential allies and other jihadi groups worked to his detriment.[116]

Conclusion

This chapter has revealed that a militant organization's cooperation with more radical groups can appear as a good idea since it will oftentimes provide strategic depth and the ability to attack the enemy on different fronts and from different directions. Concurrently, however, such an initiative may come at a cost for the less extremist partner, as evidenced by Al-Qaʿida's ties with al-Zouabri's GIA in Algeria and al-Zarqawi's Al-Qaʿida in Mesopotamia. Extremely radical leaders, such as the two aforementioned, are very difficult to control, particularly when the leaders of the less extremist organization are not located in the immediate proximity to the ultra-radicals. However, Al-Qaʿida's ties with the GIA caused Bin Laden less embarrassment than those with al-Zarqawi's organization since in the former case the GSPC split from the GIA and eventually adopted the name Al-Qaʿida in the Islamic Maghrib. In the latter case, the Islamic State severed all ties with Al-Qaʿida, only to become the sworn enemy of its affiliate in Syria, the Jabhat al-Nusra. The brief examination of the GIA and Al-Qaʿida in Mesopotamia (the future Islamic State) has revealed striking similarities with respect to the methodology of both organizations and the violent history of al-Zouabri and al-Zarqawi. Both leaders shared an extremely violent personality, a criminal past and time served in prison. Their personality had a profound impact on their ruthless leadership style and ideology and the means they applied to achieve their objectives. All of these reflected a lack of will to compromise and complete intolerance toward interpretations of Islam which differed from their own. The brief analysis of the Al-Qaʿida mouthpiece *Inspire* has confirmed the argument made elsewhere in this study, namely, that publications are considered by totalitarian ideologies as one of the most powerful weapons in their arsenal. Concurrently, the hubris of such ideologies with respect to the effectiveness of the argumentations of their propagandists frequently make them oblivious to the obvious pitfalls inherent in the business of manipulation of information.

Notes

1 Andrew Silke, 'Fire of Iolaus', in Tore Bjorgo (ed.), *Root Causes of Terrorism: Myths, Reality and Ways Forward* (London: Routledge, 2005), p. 254, referred to in Thomas Riegler, 'The State as a Terrorist: France and the Red Hand',

Perspectives on Terrorism, accessed 18 November 2015, http://terrorismanalysts.com/pt/index.php/pot/article/view/229/html. The Algerian military's annulment of the elections results of December 1991 had a similar effect, prompting many young Algerians to join Islamic militant groups, *Human Rights Watch*, accessed 26 April 2018, https://www.hrw.org/legacy/reports/1997/algeria/Algeria-05.htm#P207_32016.

2 Ray Takeyh, 'Islamism in Algeria: A Struggle between Hope and Agony', *Council on Foreign Relations* (Summer 2003), accessed 24 December 2016, http://cfr.org/world/islamism-algeria-struggle-between-hope-agony/p7335; Jumhuriyya Misr al-'Arabiyya, [Arab Republic of Egypt], *Mafhum al-irhab wa asbab zuhurihi fi al-Jaza'ir* (Cairo: wizarat al-difa', 1998), p. 71. Another scholar puts the death toll at between 100,000 and 200,000, David B. Ottaway, 'Algeria: Bloody Past and Fractious Factions', 27 August 2015, *Wilson Center*, accessed 18 January 2017, https://www.wilsoncenter.org/article/algeria-bloody-past-and-fractious-factions. In 2005, President Abdelaziz Bouteflika stated that 150,000 people had been killed in the conflict. This is possibly an inflated number, Roman Hagelstein, 'Explaining the Violence Pattern of the Algerian Civil War', *HiCN Working Paper 43*, March 2008, *Households in Conflict Network*, University of Sussex, accessed 29 April 2018, http://www.hicn.org/wordpress/wp-content/uploads/2012/06/wp43.pdf.

3 Maria Losacco, 'Le nuove direttrici jihadiste nel mediterraneo: il pericolo di al Qā'ida in Maghreb', *Centro Militare di Studi Strategici*, Ricerca CeMiSS 2009 – R34, accessed 20 April 2018, www.difesa.it/SMD_/CASD/IM/CeMiSS/Pubblicazioni/Documents/99201_Le_nuove_pdf.pdf, p. 14. Kohlmann states that this exodus of Algerian mujahidun from Afghanistan and Pakistan had begun as early as 1987, and that between 1,000 and 1,500 fighters had returned to Algeria by 1993, Evan F. Kohlmann, 'Two Decades of Jihad in Algeria: the GIA, the GSPC, and Al-Qaida', May 2007, *The NEFA Foundation*, p. 2, *Multi Language Documents*, accessed 20 July 2019, https://vdocuments.site/2-decades-of-jihad-in-algeria.html.

4 Kohlmann, 'Two Decades of Jihad', p. 3.

5 Losacco, 'Le nuove direttrici jihadiste', p. 15.

6 Redha Malek, 'Islamist Terrorism in Algeria: An Experience to Ponder', in Walter Laqueur (ed.), *Voices of Terror: Manifestos, Writings and Manuals of Al Qaeda, Hamas, and Other Terrorists from around the World and throughout the Ages* (Naperville, IL: Sourcebooks, Inc., 2004), pp. 441–442.

7 Bahi Muhammad Ahmad, *Judhur al-Irhab fi al-Jaza'ir* (Rabat?: n.p., 2010), p. 105. Bouyali was killed in the Algiers casbah in 1987, David B. Ottaway, 'Algeria: Bloody Past and Factitious Factions', *Wilson Center*, accessed 18 January 2017, https://wilsoncenter.org/article/algeria-bloody-past-and-fractious-factions; Emile Gallet, 'Algeria: The menace of Islamic fundamentalism', 30 September 1992, *League for the Fifth International*, accessed 10 January 2018, http://www.fifthinternational.org/content/algeria-menace-islamic-fundamentalism.

8 Ahmad, *Judhur al-Irhab*, p. 104.

9 Kohlmann, 'Two Decades of Jihad', p. 3.

10 Salima Mellah, 'Les Massacres en Algérie, 1992-2004', Dossier No. 2, Mai 2004, *Comité Justice pour l'Algérie*, accessed 21 April 2018, http://www.algerie-tpp.org/tpp/pdf/dossier_2_massacres.pdf, p. 18. The GIA attempted unsuccessfully to derail the peace negotiations between the government and the AIS by massacring 700 civilians on the outskirts of the capital over the course of three nights, Sofiane Khatib, 'Spoiler Management during Algeria's Civil War: Explaining the Peace', *Stanford Journal of International Relations* (Winter 2005), accessed 18 January 2017, https://web.stanford.edu/group/sjir/6.1.06_khatib.html.

11 Canada, Immigration and Refugee Board of Canada, *Algeria: Interview with Jean-Michel Salgon, Specialist on Algerian Armed Groups*, 26 September 2000, accessed 24 December 2016, http://www.refworld.org/docid/3ae6ad543c.html; 'Abu Turab yakhlufu 'Antar al-Zuwabri fi qiyadat al-jama'a al-islamiyya al-musallaha fi al-Jaza'ir', *Al-Islam al-Yawm*, 14 May 2002, accessed 24 December 2016, http:www.islamtoday.net/nawafeth/artshow-13-960.htm.
12 Kohlmann, 'Two Decades of Jihad', pp. 12–13.
13 Ibid., p. 18.
14 M[ounir] (?) Boudjemaa, 'Terrorism in Algeria: Ten Years of Day-To-Day Genocide', in Walter Laqueur (ed.), *Voices of Terror: Manifestos, Writings and Manuals of Al Qaeda, Hamas, and Other Terrorists from around the World and throughout the Ages* (Naperville, IL: Sourcebooks, Inc., 2004), p. 447.
15 Jumhuriyya Misr al-'Arabiyya, *Mafhum al-irhab*, p. 57; Ahmad, *Judhur al-Irhab*, p. 100.
16 Jumhuriyya Misr al-'Arabiyya, *Mafhum al-irhab*, p. 57.
17 Malek, 'Islamist Terrorism', p. 444.
18 Peter Humi, 'Algerians Prepare for First Free Presidential Election', *CNN World News*, accessed 26 April 2018, http://www.cnn.com/WORLD/9511/algeria_election/index.html.
19 *Human Rights Watch*, accessed 26 April 2018, https://www.hrw.org/legacy/reports/1997/algeria/Algeria-05.htm#P207_32016; Lucy Dean, ed., *The Middle East and North Africa 2004* (London and New York: Europa Publications, 2004), p. 167, accessed 26 April 2018, https://books.google.com/books?id=pP315Mw3S9EC&pg=PA168&lpg=PA168&dq=voter+turnout+in+Algeria+november+1995&source=bl&ots=_6coh6lD-M&sig=mZgfw2y4JTzf7FrQIP1V042asbQ&hl=en&sa=X&ved=0ahUKEwiYqcK-J_9vaAhWBnoMKHVWYCeg4ChDoAQg1MAU#v=onepage&q=voter%20turnout%20in%20Algeria%20november%201995&f=false. Soon after the Sant'Egido Platform, the government issued the Rahma Law, an initiative promising full amnesty for mujahidun who were not guilty of blood crimes and reduced sentences for other fighters. Like the Sant'Egido Platform, this initiative failed because it was considered too lenient by regime hardliners, Khatib, 'Spoiler Management'.
20 Ahmad, *Judhur al-Irhab*, p. 114.
21 Abu Hamza al-Masri, *Khawarij and Jihad* (Birmingham: Maktaba al-Ansar, 2000), p. 67, Spring 2000, accessed 20 April 2018, https://www.kalamullah.com/Books/Khawarij%20and%20Jihaad.pdf.
22 Martin Stone, *The Agony of Algeria* (New York, NY: Columbia University Press, 1997), p. 185.
23 ''Antar al-Zouabri, 'dhabbah' jama'at GIA al-jazai'r' ['Antar al-Zouabri, the Butcher of Algeria's GIA], 10 May 2015, *Bawabat al-harika al-Islamiyya*, accessed 24 December 2016, http://islamist-movements.com/28316; Khatib, 'Spoiler Management'. Before the assassination of al-Zituoni, Zouabri set himself up as the leader of the Sky Battalion with the assistance of a former army officer, 'Ammari Saifi, who had left the army and joined the GIA. The latter was instrumental in enabling Zouabri to assume leadership of the GIA, establishing himself as the seventh leader of the organization, 'Abu Turab', *Al-Islam al-Yawm*.
24 Belkacem Kolli, 'Fin de Antar Zouabri, fin de GIA?' [The End of Antar Zouabri], 2 November 2002, *rfi* [Radio France Internationale], accessed 20 April 2018, http://www1.rfi.fr/actufr/articles/026/article_13958.asp; 'Ightiyal 'Antar al-Zuabri za'im al-jama'a al-Islamiyya al-musallaha fi al-Jaza'ir fi Masqat ra'sihi ba'da 6 sinawat min al-malahaqa wa suqut al-mi'at min al-dhahaya' [The

174 *Precursors to the Islamic State*

Killing of Antar al-Zuabri, Leader of the GIA in Algeria, in His Home Town, After Six Years of Pursuit and the Death of Hundreds of Victims], *Al-Sharq al-Awsat*, 10 February 2002, accessed 24 December 2016, http://archive.aawsat.com/details.asp?article=87425&issueno=8475.
25. Abu Hamza al-Misri, *Khawarij and Jihad*, p. 67.
26. 'Ightiyal Antar al-Zuabri', *Al-Sharq al-Awsat*, 10 February 2002.
27. Takeyh, 'Islamism in Algeria'.
28. 'Antar al-Zouabri', *Bawabat al-harika al-Islamiyya*.
29. Ibid.
30. Abu Hamza, *Khawarij and Jihad*, p. 65.
31. 'A Call to Battle from the Mujahideen of the GSPC to the Monotheists of the Islamic Maghreb', September 5, 2005, *Ansarnet*, in Kohlmann, *Two Decades of Jihad*, p. 20.
32. 'Al-Qaida's Committee in the Islamic Maghreb: The Battle of Badr in the Islamic Maghreb', 11 April 2007, http://alhesbah.org/v/showthread.php?t=121075, quoted in Kohlmann, *Two Decades of Jihad*, p. 23.
33. Abu Hamza, *Khawarij and Jihad*, p. 69.
34. Kohlmann, 'Two Decades of Jihad', p. 5; "Antar Zouabri', *Bawabat al-harika al-Islamiyya*; Malek, 'Islamist Terrorism', p. 444.
35. Takeyh, 'Islamism in Algeria'; Stone, *The Agony of Algeria*, p. 189; Jumhuriyya Misr al-'Arabiyya, [Arab Republic of Egypt], *Mafhum al-irhab*, pp. 449–450; Canada, Immigration and Refugee Board of Canada, *Algeria*.
36. Kohlmann, 'Two Decades of Jihad', pp. 4–6; Ottaway, 'Algeria'.
37. Malek, 'Islamist Terrorism', p. 444.
38. Mellah, 'Les massacres en Algérie', p. 20.
39. Boudjemaa, 'Terrorism in Algeria', p. 450.
40. Ibid., pp. 19–20.
41. Abu Hamza, *Khawarij and Jihad*, p. 69.
42. Jumhuriyya Misr al-'Arabiyya, *Mafhum al-irhab*, p. 58.
43. Abu Hamza al-Misri, *Khawarij and Jihad*, pp. 67–68; Immigration and Refugee Board of Canada, 'Algeria'. 'Abu Turab', *Al-Islam al-Yawm*. Martin Stone states that agents from the Algerian Sécurité Militaire infiltrated the GIA, Stone, *The Agony of Algeria*, p. 187.
44. Mohammed Samraoui, *Chronique des années de sang* (Paris: Denoël, 2003), pp. 95, 215, referred to in Neil Grant Landers, *Representing the Algerian Civil War: Literature, History, and the State* (Dissertation), accessed 29 April 2018, http://digitalassets.lib.berkeley.edu/etd/ucb/text/Landers_berkeley_0028E_13922.pdf, pp. 83–84.
45. Stone, *The Agony of Algeria*, p. 187.
46. Ahmad, *Judhur al-Irhab*, p. 104.
47. Stone, *The Agony of Algeria*, p. 194.
48. Abu Hamza al-Misri, *Khawarij and Jihad*, p. 68.
49. Stone, *The Agony of Algeria*, p. 193.
50. Abu Hamza al-Misri, *Khawarij and Jihad*, p. 68.
51. Kohlmann, 'Two Decades of Jihad', p. 68.
52. Stone, *The Agony of Algeria*, p. 192.
53. Immigration and Refugee Board of Canada, 'Algeria'; Ottaway states that security forces carried out extrajudicial killings of civilians, then laying the blame at the feet of the terrorist, Ottaway, 'Algeria'.
54. Abu Hamza al-Misri, *Khawarij and Jihad*, p. 70; Mellah, 'Les massacres en Algérie', p. 20.
55. Mellah, 'Les massacres en Algérie', p. 19.
56. Abu Hamza al-Masri, *Khawaarij and Jihad*, p. 69.

57 Nacéra Belloula, *Algérie, le massacre des innocents* (Paris: Fayard, 2000), pp. 117–120; quoted in Meredith Turshend, 'Algerian Women in the Liberation Struggle and the Civil War: From Active Participants to Passive Victims?' *Social Research*, Vol. 69, No. 3 (Fall 2002), p. 900.
58 Baya Gacemi, *Moi, Nadia, femme d'un émir du GIA* (Paris: Éditions du Seuil, 1998), pp. 133–134, in Turshend, 'Algerian Women', p. 901.
59 Stone, *The Agony of Algeria*, p. 189.
60 Ibid.
61 Takeyh, 'Islamism in Algeria'.
62 Immigration and Refugee Board of Canada, 'Algeria'.
63 Kohlmann, 'Two Decades of Jihad'.
64 Hisham al-Hashimi, *'Alam Da'ish: min al-nash'a ila i'lan al-khilafa* (London: Dar al-Hikma, 2015), p. 16. Djallil Lounnas states that this organization was founded in 1984, Djallil Lounnas, 'AQMI, une filiale d'Al-Qaïda ou organization Algérienne?' *Maghreb-Machrek*, No. 208, Été 2011, p. 40.
65 Peter Bergen, *The Osama Bin Laden I Know: An Oral History of al-Qaeda's Leader* (New York, NY: Free Press, 2006), p. 41.
66 Kim Cragin, 'Early History of Al-Qa'ida', *The Historical Journal*, Vol. 51, No. 4 (Dec., 2008), p. 1065.
67 al-Hashimi, *'Alam Da'ish*, p. 17.
68 Mohamed Mokeddem, *Les Afghans algériens: de la Djamaa à Al-Qaïda* (Algiers: ANEP, 2002), p. 59, in Lounnas, 'AQMI', p. 43.
69 Cragin, 'Early History of Al-Qa'ida', p. 1048.
70 Ibid., pp. 1051, 1057.
71 *International Institute for Counter-Terrorism*, 'Abu Yahya Al-Libi: Profile of an Al-Qaeda Leader' (Mar., 2012), pp. 11–12, accessed 10 April 2018, https://www.ict.org.il/UserFiles/Abu%20Yahya%20al-Libi.pdf.
72 Sheikh Khubaib as-Sudani, 'A Moment in the Life of Sheikh Usama', *Inspire*, Issue 15 (Spring 2016), p. 24, accessed 10 August 2017, https://azelin.files.wordpress.com/2016/05/inspire-magazine-15.pdf.
73 'Abu Yahya Al-Libi', p. 11.
74 Ibid., p. 12.
75 *Inspire*, Issue 15, p. 16.
76 Ibid., p. 4.
77 Michael Weiss and Hassan Hassan, *ISIS: Inside the Army of Terror* (New York, NY: Regan Arts, 2015), pp. 18, 29.
78 *Inspire*, Issue 15, p. 4.
79 Ibid., Issue 17, pp. 65–95.
80 Ibid., Issue 15, p. 13.
81 Abdulrahman bin Mohammad, 'Analyzing the Impact of Muslims Targeting the Qurayshi Economy', *Inspire*, Issue 15, p. 31. According to Bin Muhammad, American power and society represent kufr, that is, unbelief.
82 Sheikh Khubaib as-Sudani, 'A Moment in the Life of Sheikh', p. 22.
83 Ibid., p. 21.
84 Ibid.
85 *Inspire*, Issue 15, p. 41.
86 Ibid., Issue 16, p. 33.
87 Abd Allah Al-Murabit, 'A Message to Our Muslim Brothers in America', *Inspire*, Issue 16, p. 37.
88 *Inspire*, Issue 15, p. 43.
89 Ibid., p. 44.
90 Ibid., p. 45.
91 *Inspire*, Issue 16, pp. 7–8; Issue 17, p. 17.

176 *Precursors to the Islamic State*

92 Sheikh Khubeib As-Sudani, 'A Thousand Times Greater than USS-Cole [sic]', *Inspire*, Issue 16, p. 19.
93 Ibrahim bin Hassan Al-Asiri, 'The American Globalization is Falling', *Inspire*, Issue 16, p. 47.
94 See Chapter IV.
95 *Inspire*, Issue 17, p. 4.
96 Ibid.
97 Ibid., p. 5.
98 Namir Shabibi, Nasser al-Sane, Jack Serle, Jessica Purkiss, 'Revealed: Nine Children Killed in Botched Yemeni Raid', *The New Arab*, accessed 8 April 2018, https://www.alaraby.co.uk/english/indepth/2017/2/9/revealed-nine-children-killed-in-botched-us-yemen-raid.
99 *Inspire*, Issue 17, p. 5.
100 Shabibi et alie, 'Revealed'.
101 *Inspire*, Issue 17, pp. 11, 13.
102 Michael Weiss and Hassan Hassan, *ISIS: Inside the Army of Terror* (New York, NY: Regan Arts, 2015), pp. 2, 6, 8, 11; George Michael, 'The Legend and Legacy of Abu Musab al-Zarqawi', *Defense Studies*, Vol. 7, No. 3 (Sept., 2007), pp. 338–339.
103 Michael, 'The Legend', p. 340.
104 Hisham al-Hashimi, *'Alam Da'ish: min al-nash'a ila i'lan al-khilafa* (London: Dar al-Hikma, 2015), pp. 27–28; Weiss and Hassan, *ISIS*, pp. 34, 36; Michael, 'The Legend', p. 341.
105 Weiss and Hassan, *ISIS*, pp. 30, 34.
106 Ibid., p. 28.
107 Ibid., p. 43.
108 Michael, 'The Legend', p. 347.
109 Weiss and Hassan, *ISIS*, p. 58.
110 Al-Hashimi, *'Alam Da'ish*, p. 29.
111 Weiss and Hassan, *ISIS*, p. 27.
112 Michael, 'The Legend', p. 342.
113 Al-Hashimi, *'Alam Da'ish*, p. 28.
114 Weiss and Hassan, *ISIS*, p. 27.
115 Kevin Whitelaw, 'Blown Away', *US News and World Report*, June 19, 2006, p. 24, referred to in Michael, 'The Legend', p. 341. Al-Hashimi estimates that the mujahidun in Iraq numbered at least 10,000 fighters, al-Hashimi, *'Alam Da'ish*, p. 31.
116 Al-Hashimi states that al-Zarqawi made several attempts to usurp control of other jihadi groups, al-Hashimi, *'Alam Da'ish*, p. 29.

Bibliography

Ahmad, Bahi Muhammad. *Judhur al-Irhab fi al-Jaza'ir* [The Roots of Terrorism in Algeria]. Rabat?: n.p., 2010.
al-Asiri, Ibrahim bin Hassan. 'The American Globalization Is Falling'. *Inspire*, Issue 16 (Autumn 2016), pp. 40–41.
Bawabat al-harika al-Islamiyya.
Belloula, Nacéra. *Algérie, le massacre des innocents* [Algeria, Massacre of the Innocent]. Paris: Fayard, 2000.
Bergen, Peter. *The Osama Bin Laden I Know: An Oral History of al-Qaeda's Leader*. New York, NY: Free Press, 2006.
Bjorgo, Tore, ed. *Root Causes of Terrorism: Myths, Reality and Ways Forward*. London: Routledge, 2005.

Boudjemaa, M[ounir] (?). 'Terrorism in Algeria: Ten Years of Day-To-Day Genocide'. In Walter Laqueur, ed., *Voices of Terror: Manifestos, Writings and Manuals of Al Qaeda, Hamas, and Other Terrorists from around the World and throughout the Ages.* Naperville, IL: Sourcebooks, Inc., 2004, pp. 447–50.

Canada, Immigration and Refugee Board of Canada. *Algeria: Interview with Jean-Michel Salgon, specialist on Algerian armed groups,* 26 September 2000. Accessed 24 December 2016. http://www.refworld.org/docid/3ae6ad543c.html.

Cragin, Kim. 'Early History of Al-Qa'ida'. *The Historical Journal,* Vol. 51, No. 4 (December 2008), pp. 1047–67.

Dean, Lucy, ed. *The Middle East and North Africa 2004.* London and New York: Europa Publications, 2004. Accessed 10 May 2018. https://books.google.com/books?id=pP315Mw3S9EC&pg=PA168&lpg=PA168&dq=voter+turn-out+in+Algeria+november+1995&source=bl&ots=_6coh6lD-M&sig=mZgf-w2y4JTzf7FrQIP1V042asbQ&hl=en&sa=X&ved=0ahUKEwiYqcKJ_9vaAhW-BnoMKHVWYCeg4ChDoAQg1MAU#v=onepage&q=voter%20turnout%20in%20Algeria%20november%201995&f=false.

Gacemi, Baya. *Moi, Nadia, femme d'un émir du GIA* I, [Nadia, Woman of an Emir of the GIA]. Paris: Éditions du Seuil, 1998.

Hagelstein, Roman. 'Explaining the Violence Pattern of the Algerian Civil War', *HiCN Working Paper 43* (March 2008), *Households in Conflict Network,* University of Sussex. Accessed 29 April 2018. http://www.hicn.org/wordpress/wp-content/uploads/2012/06/wp43.pdf.

al-Hashimi, Hisham. *'Alam da'ish: min al-nash'a ila i'lan al-khilafa* [The World of Da'ish: from the Rise to the Proclamation of the Caliphate]. London: Dar Al-hikma Publishing and Distribution, 2015.

Humi, Peter. 'Algerians Prepare for First Free Presidential Election'. *CNN World News,* 15 November 1995. Accessed 26 April 2018. http://www.cnn.com/WORLD/9511/algeria_election/index.html.

Human Rights Watch.

International Institute for Counter-Terrorism.

Al-Islam al-Yaum.

Jumhuriyya Misr al-'Arabiyya, [Arab Republic of Egypt]. *Mafhum al-irhab wa as-bab zuhurihi fi al-Jaza'ir* [The Concept of Terrorism and the Reasons of Its Appearance in Algeria]. Cairo: wizarat al-difa', 1998.

Khatib, Sofiane. 'Spoiler Management during Algeria's Civil War: Explaining the Peace'. *Stanford Journal of International Relations* (Winter 2005). Accessed 18 January 2017. https://web.stanford.edu/group/sjir/6.1.06_khatib.html.

Kohlmann, Evan F. 'Two Decades of Jihad in Algeria: the GIA, the GSPC, and Al-Qaida'. May 2007, *The NEFA Foundation,* p. 2, *Multi Language Documents.* Accessed 20 July 2019. https://vdocuments.site/2-decades-of-jihad-in-algeria.html.

Kolli, Belkacem. 'Fin de Antar Zouabri, fin de GIA?' [The End of Antar Zouabri, the End of the GIA?] 2 November 2002. *rfi* [Radio France Internationale]. Accessed 20 April 2018. http://www1.rfi.fr/actufr/articles/026/article_13958.asp.

Landers, Neil Grant. *Representing the Algerian Civil War: Literature, History, and the State* (Dissertation), pp. 83–84. Accessed 29 April 2018. http://digitalassets.lib.berkeley.edu/etd/ucb/text/Landers_berkeley_0028E_13922.pdf.

Losacco, Maria. 'Le nuove direttrici jihadiste nel mediterraneo: il pericolo di al Qā'ida in Maghreb' [New Jihadi directives in the Mediterranean region: the danger of Al-Qaida in the Maghreb]. *Centro Militare di Studi Strategici,* Ricerca

CeMiSS 2009 – R3. Accessed 20 April 2018. www.difesa.it/SMD_/CASD/IM/CeMISS/Pubblicazioni/Documents/99201_Le_nuove_pdf.pdf.
Lounnas, Djallil. 'AQMI, une filiale d'Al-Qaïda ou organization Algérienne?' [Al-Qaida in the Islamic Maghreb: An Al-Qaida Affiliate, or an Algerian Organization?] *Maghreb-Machrek*, No. 208, Été [Summer] 2011, pp. 37–57.
Malek, Redha. 'Islamist Terrorism in Algeria: An Experience to Ponder'. In Walter Laqueur, ed., *Voices of Terror: Manifestos, Writings and Manuals of Al Qaeda, Hamas, and Other Terrorists from around the World and throughout the Ages*. Naperville, IL: Sourcebooks, Inc., 2004, pp. 439–46.
al-Masri, Abu Hamza. *Khawarij and Jihad*. Birmingham: Maktaba al-Ansar, 2000. Accessed 20 April 2018. https://www.kalamullah.com/Books/Khawarij%20and%20Jihaad.pdf.
Mellah, Salima. 'Les Massacres en Algérie, 1992-2004' [The Massacres in Algeria, 1992-2004]. Dossier No. 2, Mai 2004. *Comité Justice pour l'Algérie*. Accessed 21 April 2018. http://www.algerie-tpp.org/tpp/pdf/dossier_2_massacres.pdf.
Michael, George. 'The Legend and Legacy of Abu Musab al-Zarqawi'. *Defense Studies*, Vol. 7, No. 3 (September 2007), pp. 338–57.
Mohammad, Abdulrahman bin. 'Analyzing the Impact of Muslims Targeting the Qurayshi Economy'. *Inspire*, Issue 15 (Spring 2016), pp. 26–31.
Mokeddem, Mohamed. *Les Afghans algériens: de la Djamaa à Al-Qaïda* [The Algerian 'Afghans': From the GIA to Al-Qa'ida]. Algiers: ANEP, 2002.
al-Murabit, Abd Allah. 'A Message to Our Muslim Brothers in America'. *Inspire*, Issue 16 (Autumn 2016), pp. 36–37.
Ottaway, David B. 'Algeria: Bloody Past and Fractious Factions'.27 August 2015. *Wilson Center*, Accessed 18 January 2017. https://www.wilsoncenter.org/article/algeria-bloody-past-and-fractious-factions.
Riegler, Thomas. 'The State as a Terrorist: France and the Red Hand'. *Perspectives on Terrorism*, pp. 22–33 Accessed 23 November 20019. http://terrorismanalysts.com/pt/index.php/pot/article/view/229/html.
Samraoui, Mohammed. *Chronique des années de sang*. Paris: Denoël, 2003.
Shabibi, Namir, Nasser al-Sane, Jack Serle, and Jessica Purkiss. 'Revealed: Nine Children Killed in Botched Yemeni Raid'. *The New Arab*. Accessed 8 April 2018. https://www.alaraby.co.uk/english/indepth/2017/2/9/revealed-nine-children-killed-in-botched-us-yemen-raid.
Al-Sharq al-Awsat, Saudi newspaper.
Silke, Andrew. 'Fire of Iolaus'. In Tore Bjorgo, ed., *Root Causes of Terrorism; Myths, Reality and Ways Forward*. London: Routledge, 2005, pp. 241–55.
Stone, Martin. *The Agony of Algeria*. New York, NY: Columbia University Press, 1997.
As-Sudani, Sheikh Khubaib. 'A Moment in the Life of Sheikh Usama'. *Inspire*, Issue 15 (Spring 2016), pp. 20–24. Accessed 10 August 2017. https://azelin.files.wordpress.com/2016/05/inspire-magazine-15.pdf.
Takeyh, Ray. 'Islamism in Algeria: A Struggle between Hope and Agony'. *Council on Foreign Relations* (Summer 2003). Accessed 24 December 2016. http://cfr.org/world/islamism-algeria-struggle-between-hope-agony/p7335.
Turshend, Meredith. 'Algerian Women in the Liberation Struggle and the Civil War: From Active Participants to Passive Victims?' *Social Research*, Vol. 69, No. 3 (Fall 2002), pp. 889–911.
Whitelaw, Kevin. 'Blown Away'. *US News and World Report*, 19 June 2006.

9 Islamic State media production and Islam

Introduction

The present analysis argues that Islamic State propaganda suffers from a number of weaknesses. If Muslims choose not to subject extremist argumentation to scrutiny, it raises a serious obstacle to efforts made to counter Islamic extremist ideology. The key to successful counterterrorism and national security is thus to design a method to induce a will to analyze propaganda. This chapter analyzes the IS approach to propaganda, why it has adopted certain methods, their strengths and weaknesses and proposes a method for countering the 'Caliphate's' extremist version of Islam.

All governments use propaganda[1] in one form or another in order to influence their citizens. The extensive use of ideological propaganda in authoritarian and totalitarian[2] systems – a phenomenon that particularly permeates these societies – suggests that, unlike in democratic societies, it is perceived as closely linked to regime survival and a tool which will allow for the system to exist in perpetuity. Despite the historical record which clearly does not substantiate such an assumption, dictatorships, not surprisingly, appear to spend precious little time reflecting on their own mortality. Generally speaking, the higher the degree of coercion in a society, the more intensive the efforts to legitimize the regime and conceal its true nature by resorting to propaganda. Chapter 5 on Nazi propaganda has confirmed this argument and so will the discussion of Daʻish propaganda in this chapter.

The German Nazi Party clearly realized in the 1920s the importance of propaganda for the realization of the party's objectives.[3] This chapter argues, however, that the panacea that ideological propaganda is viewed as by totalitarian leaders is in reality a double-edged sword. One of its major functions is to conceal or justify flaws in the prevailing system of government or convince citizens of the non-existence of such flaws, or even the necessity of these flaws despite their negative effects on society. Concurrently, the critical-minded citizen understands that propaganda actually constitutes a weakness since it is frequently utilized with the intention of perpetuating a negative situation instead of addressing it. Justifying obvious flaws in a system without alleviating these flaws or eliminating them is a policy that will not convince critical citizens. This chapter focuses on the IS use of printed and visual propaganda in its publications, analyzing the strengths and weaknesses of the argumentation adopted to convince the reader and viewer of the irrefutability of the IS extremist interpretation of Islam. The analysis presented here substantiates the argument advanced above, revealing that propaganda is indeed a double-edged sword, which constitutes a clear danger both to the audience and the author. The research presented in this chapter focuses on the dangers and pitfalls that IS propaganda poses and perhaps unwittingly creates for the totalitarian ideology of the IS. Concomitantly, a clear understanding of the IS ideological propaganda will considerably increase the ability of governments and Islamic institutions effectively to counter the extremist discourse.

In his *Propaganda: The Formation of Men's Attitudes*, Jacques Ellul argues that '[i]neffective propaganda is no propaganda'.[4] Furthermore, the author contends that propaganda constitutes a danger to the audience as well as to the propagandist since false promises tend to turn against him.[5] Conversely, the present chapter advances the argument that effectiveness and potential danger are determined by the audience, depending on to what extent the reader or viewer is inclined to analyze the message. Like anything perceived through our senses, propaganda is interpreted differently as a result of our upbringing, education, social standing, personal experiences, etc. This circumstance makes the effects of propaganda difficult to predict. Furthermore, manipulated information often has additional weaknesses as a result of mistakes made by its authors. One could argue, therefore, that 'effective' propaganda that is accepted by a significant part of the population could at the same time be 'ineffective' because there will always be individuals who discern its weaknesses. A corollary of the aforementioned is that uncritical thinking on the part of the audience or the readership turns flawed propaganda into effective propaganda. Unlike Ellul, the present author advances the argument that even propaganda devoid of false promises and intentional inaccuracies could constitute a double-edged sword and pose a danger to the propagandist who has overlooked or disregarded inconsistencies in the argumentation.

Ellul also contends that propaganda is instrumental in attempts at creating a new type of man,[6] an argument which appears to apply to Communists, Nazis and Fascists, but perhaps less so to Daʻish.[7] The 'Caliphate' believes that its propaganda will *return* all Muslims to a true Islamic condition, a conviction which seems to contradict Ellul's argument. What IS propagandists fail to realize, however, is that this is actually a new creation since it is most likely not particularly appealing, if not impossible, for modern man to be like seventh-century man because the world has changed in fundamental ways in 1400 years. From an Islamic perspective, it could therefore be argued that the IS project is tantamount to *bid'a* (innovation), which is denounced by Islamic extremists, including IS ideologues.[8] ^Like Nazi Germany, where the main text upon which the propaganda was based,

Mein Kampf was available to all citizens; in the IS, the Quran, which is of course not a propagandistic text and can therefore be used to counter and undermine IS propaganda, is available to all citizens to substantiate or refute Daʻish propaganda. *Mein Kampf* was for obvious reasons not conducive to exposing Nazi propaganda since it was itself Nazi propaganda and therefore reinforced the regime's message to Germans. In summary, what seems to set Daʻish apart from Nazism, Fascism and Communism does not hold up to scrutiny. Also, with regard to propaganda effectiveness, a comparison between Nazi Germany and the IS yields the conclusion that the former regime was in a stronger position to achieve its objectives as a result of its sources.

In their *Propaganda and Persuasion*, Garth Jowett and Victoria O'Donnell define propaganda as 'a form of communication that attempts to achieve a response that furthers the desired intent of the propagandist'[9] and argue that the propagandist in order to achieve success 'has to gather a great deal of information about the intended audience'.[10] This chapter corroborates the applicability of Jowett and O'Donnell's definition of propaganda to IS communication with its audience, but the second contention is more problematic. The IS operates in an Islamic context, which it manipulates to justify its extremist interpretation of Islam. This common frame of reference makes the reaction of the audience more predictable than in certain other cases of propaganda where the population is more diverse, particularly, since the source that 'Caliphate' ideologues draw upon, the Quran, is beyond criticism, a position upon which Muslims are agreed. This fact to a certain extent facilitates the task of IS propagandists. Furthermore, what seems like a convincing argument in a non-Islamic context does not necessarily carry the same weight among Muslims who embrace extremist ideas: '[T]he one who benefits from the audience's response, if the response is the desired one, is the propagandist and not necessarily the audience'.[11] Daʻish would certainly reject this argument, contending that the 'Caliphate' promotes the common Islamic good by inducing the audience to follow the 'path of God', a course of action from which both the audience and the propagandist presumably benefit temporally, spiritually and in the hereafter without exception. Furthermore, IS propagandists would contend that those who do not benefit are individuals who do not follow the path of God and, by definition, will find themselves in a highly unpleasant environment in the afterlife.

It has already been pointed out above that appearances are deceptive. White propaganda refers to a message that appears to be correct and with an identifiable source.[12] This premise becomes problematic in the context of IS propaganda, the credibility of which is on the surface convincing since the source, typically the Quran or the hadith (prophetic traditions), is impeccable. Furthermore, the accuracy of the message can easily be verified, if the receiver consults the Quran or the hadith for the specific passage referred to in the message. In order to convince the audience that the purpose of Daʻish propaganda is not to reap any benefit for the IS at the expense of the audience, the

'Caliphate' will typically lay out a smokescreen in the form of an additional quotation from a sacred source, aimed at dispelling any doubts on the part of the reader, viewer or listener. An appropriate Quranic quotation would be 'And I did not create the jinn and mankind except to worship Me. I do not want from them any provision, nor do I want them to feed Me'.[13] The implication is that whatever action the IS takes, it is not for its own selfish benefit, but for the benefit of all who work for the cause of God. The present chapter will reveal that this is quite a stretch. At first glance, however, the reference above may come across as a rather efficient attempt to mask the 'Caliphate's' manipulation, that is, its extremist interpretation, of an impeccable source. What oftentimes seems to be non-manipulated and legitimate information will, upon closer scrutiny, turn out to be propaganda concealed under layers of quotations from the Quran and the hadith.

To a certain degree, findings of scholars who have studied Nazi propaganda can be applied to IS communication with its audience as well. David Dennis, a scholar who has studied the cultural sources of Nazi propaganda, has advanced the argument that, in order to achieve their objectives and strengthen the confidence of the German people, the Nazis strove to 'invok[e] great works of Western culture in the name of [their] ideals'.[14] The National Socialist strategy is a clear precedent to the IS approach to propaganda. Whereas the Nazi Party worked hard to achieve its objectives by appropriating great Western cultural personalities, the IS focuses on appropriating the Quran, the hadith and prominent Islamic scholars such as Ibn Taymiyya as justification for its extremist interpretation of Islam,[15] which is part of the argument advanced in this chapter. Furthermore, Dennis argues that 'Nazi leaders regarded their movement as the culmination of Western culture',[16] a claim mirrored in the contention of the IS that it is the truest reflection of God's law since the early Islamic Caliphate and that it therefore is a duty to emigrate to the 'Caliphate'.[17] The Nazis' purpose in exploiting the legacy of cultural heroes was to convince the German population of their legitimacy.[18] This is reminiscent of Da'ish's approach to the Quran, prophetic traditions and leading Islamic scholars constantly referred to in their propaganda. The approach to propaganda adopted in this work, however, differs somewhat from that of Dennis by its focus on the weaknesses of the ideological aspects of IS propaganda.

Another author who took great interest in propaganda was Adolf Hitler, who in his *Mein Kampf* discusses certain ideas and approaches which are somewhat similar to those of the IS. Hitler argues that '[e]very attempt to fight a worldview (Weltanschauung) with instruments of power will eventually fail, so long as the struggle does not take the form of an attack for a new spiritual attitude (eine neue geistige Einstellung)'.[19] Hitler's argument simultaneously corresponds with and differs from the philosophy of the IS. The difference is that Hitler wants to replace the competing worldview with a new spiritual one, whereas the 'Caliphate' wants to restore the true and unadulterated Islam of the past. The similarity is the uncompromising attitude with respect to how to achieve the objective.[20] Interestingly, and perhaps somewhat surprisingly, another commonality between Hitler and the IS is that Hitler thought he was 'acting in the cause of the Creator',[21] which is exactly what Daʻish argues that the IS is doing.[22]

This brief introduction to the use of propaganda in totalitarian systems of government will inform our critical examination of the IS use of propaganda, highlighting its strengths and weaknesses. A detailed analysis of a regime's manipulation of information is a particularly effective approach to understanding the official mind of a specific society. One reason for this is that the researcher is in a unique and fortunate position of not being impeded by the absence of information in a text. This is explained by the argument that what a document does not say is at least as revealing about the mindset of its author as what it states explicitly. This assumption will be substantiated in the following analysis of the IS language, references to historical events and selection of topics and issues for discussion in its publications. A regime's propaganda reveals much about the way it wishes to be perceived by its own citizens and its view on the outside world. The research for this chapter has primarily drawn upon the 'Caliphate's' online magazine *Dabiq*. The 'Caliphate', proclaimed by the 'Caliph' Abu Bakr al-Baghdadi, is a totalitarian 'state', the goal of which is eventual worldwide domination in the name of God.[23] This objective is viewed as an inevitability by contributors to *Dabiq*, an assumption which carefully avoids a detailed discussion except for a few references to the Quran, to the effect that God is with the mujahidun, not necessarily a convincing argument.

Like many other Islamic extremist organizations such as Boko Haram, the Taliban and Al-Qaʻida, the IS makes frequent reference to God and the Quran in its attempt to create a perception that its rule is sanctioned by the ultimate authority. Based upon the conviction that God is on its side, presumably confirmed by its successes, the IS appears oblivious to potentially negative aspects of propaganda, as indicated above. The claim to divine legitimacy is tantamount to putting all one's eggs in one basket, as it were. It is a contention that makes the IS vulnerable instead of invincible since an impeccable track record is required to sustain the 'Caliphate's' allure to potential followers. It is a corollary of Daʻish's claim that its detractors will jump at any adversity suffered by the organization, no matter how insignificant, and exploit it to undermine the IS legitimacy, by contending that the 'Caliphate' does not enjoy divine support. If there are too many instances of 'lack of divine intervention' in support of Daʻish, it will give some of those attracted to its extremist ideology food for thought, and its leaders will find it increasingly difficult to explain away such adversity.

Media production

The *Al-Hayat Media Center*, the 'Caliphate's' unofficial ministry of propaganda, plays a crucial role in the IS domestic and external public relations.

Its central position in the 'caliphal' system of government is reflected in its multifaceted operations. The center ran the *Al-Bayan* radio station during the apex of IS power. It broadcasted in Arabic, English, French, Russian and Kurdish, ensuring the 'Caliphate' an international reach.[24] Another aspect of the center's international focus was *Al-Hayat's* video production unit, which produced videos, available from its website and subtitled in English, French, Russian, Turkish, German and Uyghur, revealing the importance of these languages to reach the IS international audience.[25] Many of these videos focused on IS military operations and executions of enemies.[26] The intention was, of course, to create the impression among potential recruits that the 'Caliphate' was successful and among enemies that the IS was invincible. Another purpose was to instill terror in their enemies that swift 'justice' awaited them if captured by the 'Caliphate's' mujahidun. The many brutal videos posted to the Internet were part and parcel of the IS psychological warfare. The purpose was twofold – to instill fear in the enemy; and to demonstrate steadfastness and consistency with regard to policy, that is, to create the impression that the IS would not be influenced by any outside criticism.[27] The third aspect of IS propaganda was its defunct online magazine *Dabiq*, which is the main focus of this chapter. This brief discussion indicates the importance that Da'ish attributed to the virtual or psychological battlefield, a fact which warrants a serious approach to this aspect of jihad. The virtual battlefield has been studied to a much lesser extent than the military/terrorist operations of the IS despite the former's importance as a necessary complement to the latter, an argument which will be substantiated by the present critical examination of the 'Caliphate's' propaganda.

Photos made up a substantial part of every issue of the IS online magazine *Dabiq*, revealing the 'Caliphate's' belief in the saying that a picture is worth a thousand words. A recurring theme was an apocalyptic battle that will take place in Dabiq, Syria, between the powers of darkness (the Crusaders and their allies) and Islam and end with the victory of the latter. One of the photos that reflect this theme shows two American soldiers supporting a wounded colleague in front of a burning structure. The adjacent text says 'Until it burns the Crusader armies in Dabiq'.[28] Based upon a prophecy attributed to the Prophet Muhammad, Da'ish leaders firmly believe that a series of apocalyptic battles will occur in Damascus, Jerusalem and Constantinople. These battles are called *Al-Malhama al-kubra* (the great battle) and will be fought against the Crusaders (the West) north of Aleppo, Syria.[29] In a text published in Italian, the 'Caliphate' explains that it is convinced that the 'coalition of almost eighty nations, as stated in the hadith [Prophetic traditions] that are fighting the Muslims will be defeated at Dabiq'.[30] Not surprisingly, the theme was frequently used in IS propaganda and intended for all who sympathize with the IS, particularly mujahidun, since it 'ensures' an Islamic victory, a powerful message as long as IS fighters were successful on the battlefield. It would, however, be difficult to explain the prophecy if the 'Caliphate' met with a series of defeats. Like the picture mentioned above, other photos represent power as well, for instance, mujahidun armed with assault rifles[31] and celebrating fighters on flatbed trucks, captured tanks and other military equipment driving through cities with the raised black tawhid (oneness of God) banner.[32] Photos such as the ones discussed above greatly reinforce the message of IS invincibility and the inevitability of a 'Caliphate' victory over its enemies. The combination of Islamic prophecies, enemy soldiers depicted in humiliating situations and IS use of enemy equipment is a persuasive message so long as Da'ish is successful and its (potential) followers do not scrutinize the propaganda.

Hijra

A central concept in IS propaganda is *hijra* (emigration), the idea that Muslims should live in IS and the implication of which is that Muslims should emigrate to the 'Caliphate'. Da'ish substantiates this argument by introducing the concept of a '[w]orld divided into two camps' – *dar al-Islam* (abode of Islam) and *dar al-harb* (abode of war). The former refers to an area where Islam and peace rule and the latter to the rest of the world. The 'Amir al-Mu'minin (commander of the believers), Caliph' al-Baghdadi is quoted as saying

> Therefore, rush O Muslims to your state. Yes, it is your state. Rush because Syria is not for the Syrians, and Iraq is not for the Iraqis. The earth is Allah's. "Indeed, the earth belongs to Allah. He causes to inherit it whom He wills of His servants. And the [best] outcome is for the righteous".[33]

The 'Caliph's' statement above that the 'Caliphate' is a state for all Muslims is a clear indication that it is not a nation-state, that there is no room for nationalism and that national borders are not recognized. The advantage of this approach is that al-Baghdadi can address a global audience of Muslims, a strategy which will presumably increase the chances of people actually emigrating to the IS. Furthermore, the quotation within the IS leader's quote is from the Quranic sura Al-A'raf. The reference to this particular sura is a clever way to underscore the importance of *hijra* and the division of the world since Al-A'raf signifies the partition between Paradise and Hell.[34] The implication here is obvious – if there is a paradise on earth, it is the IS, and if there is a hell, it is *dar al-harb*. It is difficult to be more explicit about the importance of emigration to the 'Caliphate', but in order to completely dispel any remaining doubts al-Baghdadi adds 'hijra to the land of Islam is obligatory'.[35]

As if the above arguments are not sufficient, the *Dabiq* propagandists clarify in another issue of the magazine that for those who are negligent in fulfilling the duty of hijra, 'their refuge is Hell',[36] referring to a Quranic sura in support of this position. This brief quotation from a Quranic verse appears to confirm the IS position that emigration to *dar al-Islam* is incumbent upon Muslims and is also reflected in al-Baghdadi's call on '[Islamic] scholars, fuqaha' (experts in Islamic jurisprudence) ... and judges ... people with military, administrative, and service expertise, and medical doctors, and engineers...'[37] to join the 'Caliphate'. This point is further impressed upon the readers of *Dabiq* when the 'Caliph' refers to hijra as *wajib 'ayni* (individual obligation).[38] The discussion of al-Baghdadi's call on Muslims to emigrate to the 'Caliphate' and the great lengths to which he and IS ideologues go to depict emigration as a duty suggest a number of things. First, the brief quotation from the Quranic sura, warning Muslims who do not emigrate to the IS, is problematic for what it has omitted. The quotation is taken out of context since the part of the verse not quoted is a discussion between angels and Muslims on Judgment Day who in their lifetime preferred to reside in *dar al-harb* instead of emigrating to *dar al-Islam* despite the fact that they could not practice Islam freely. There is no reference in the verse to Muslims who live in non-Islamic countries where they enjoy civil rights and are able to practice their religion more or less without restrictions, which is the situation of most Muslims in the West today. In this instance, IS propagandists have forged a double-edged sword as a result of manipulating the Quran to suit their own agenda, an argument which can be substantiated if the reader refers to the specific Quranic verse. An additional potential weakness is that the reader might find IS arguments convincing so long as the 'Caliphate' can claim successes, but be less inclined to emigrate with a family when IS mujahidun encounter adversity.

The IS emphasis on hijra as a duty and its call on professionals such as Islamic scholars, experts in jurisprudence, judges, Muslims with military, administrative and service experience, and medical doctors and engineers to emigrate is of great interest to the student of the 'Caliphate' since it enables scholars to draw a number of plausible conclusions about the domestic situation in the IS. This is information which the 'Caliphate' for obvious reasons is not inclined to share with the reader of *Dabiq*. First, a general call to hijra suggests that Da'ish needs to increase its population in order to expand its tax basis. This is becoming a growing concern with the loss of territory and intensification of anti-Da'ish airstrikes,[39] particularly against oil installations vital for the IS ability to maintain an administration, pay its fighters and offer professionals attractive salaries. Second, the call to hijra is quite possibly an indication that the 'Caliphate's' armed forces are overstretched and in dire need of fresh volunteers to increase the number of mujahidun and replace fallen fighters. Third, the call for medical doctors is an indication that a shortage of professionals exists and that this situation makes it difficult to treat the many casualties from military operations and to provide healthcare to the civilian population, a service which helps to make IS propaganda credible. Fourth, media professionals and engineers are needed to enable the 'Caliphate' to expand its psychological warfare and reach new audiences and readers with media products in more languages.

Finally, the need for Islamic scholars and experts in jurisprudence is somewhat surprising since there must be a large number available locally in Iraq and Syria. Possible explanations are that Islamic scholars and legal experts have fled, been eliminated or refused to cooperate. If confirmed, these reasons would be quite embarrassing to the 'Caliphate' on account of its 'true' Islamic character. The conclusion one can draw from the above analysis is that what is said and what is omitted in IS propaganda constitute invaluable sources for scholars.

Noah and 'free choice'

'Caliphate' propagandists describe their society in very reassuring terms in order to attract *muhajirun* (emigrants). A six-pronged approach is used to persuade Muslims to perform hijra to the 'Caliphate': (1) reference to Moses in a quotation from the Quran, 'And I hastened to You, my Lord, that You be pleased'.[40] This sura, Ta Ha, discusses the flight of Moses and the Israelites from Egypt to receive God's law and the Promised Land and seems, therefore, to be an appropriate Quranic quotation. (2) The 'Caliphate' provides homes for all muhajirun'.[41] In another issue, *Dabiq* states: 'Do not worry about money or accommodation ... There are plenty of homes and resources to cover you and your family'.[42] (3) Emigrants can make a crucial contribution 'towards the liberation of Makkah, Madinah and Al-Quds' (Jerusalem).[43] (4) Such a contribution will lead to a positive outcome for all *muhajirun* (emigrants) on Judgment Day. (5) As if to put extra weight behind its recommendation for hijra, the IS has added a warning as well, 'It's either the Islamic State or the flood'.[44] The 'flood' refers to the flood mentioned in the Bible, and the implication is that only those who emigrate to the 'Caliphate' will escape disaster. This warning with a picture of an ark in stormy waters adorns the cover of the second issue of *Dabiq*.[45] The approach discussed in this paragraph appears to work in favor of the 'Caliphate', but IS propagandists most likely have overreached when they believe to have discovered a hidden message in the story of Noah (Nuh in Arabic) which can be exploited for their political agenda – to prove the fallacy of democracy and 'free choice'.

The IS argument is that there was no alternative to and no 'free choice' regarding Noah's warning to the people to mend their ways and observe God's law.[46] God's word and 'true' religion do not entail any options. The conclusions the author of the *Dabiq* article wants the reader to draw are that (1) democracy and 'free choice' will lead mankind into the abyss of unbelief and away from 'true' religion; (2) the totalitarian system that the 'Caliphate' has imposed on its population and which aims at establishing global rule is the only way to salvation; (3) it is God's will. The argument about the fallacy of free choice is problematic since it is weaker than the other points discussed in the previous paragraph. In his avidity to build a solid argument, the author has overreached, most likely hoping that the weak foundation upon which the conclusion from the story of Noah rests will go unnoticed and unchallenged by the reader. There is a substantial intellectual void between the Biblical story and the presumed corollary that the author posits. To Muslims, Noah was a prophet who was entitled to convey God's word to man, guaranteeing, as a consequence of his status as a prophet, that the message that he shared with mankind was God's unadulterated word. The IS claim that its interpretation of Islam is the only way to salvation is founded on a risky premise, namely that the audience will overlook the obvious fact that the 'Caliph' Abu Bakr al-Baghdadi is not a prophet and focus on the prophethood of Noah instead.

It is a grave sin, certainly punishable by death in IS-controlled territory, to question the Prophet Muhammed's status as the last prophet. As a result, the contention that the IS is the only way to salvation for mankind is weaker than Noah's warning to the people since neither al-Baghdadi nor any other living Muslim can convincingly argue that God has revealed this truth to him or her. In addition to being tantamount to blasphemy, as pointed out above, a claim to divine revelation in modern times would also open up a Pandora's box for the authority of the 'Caliph', for the simple reason that any Muslim who so wishes could claim to be the recipient of divine wisdom. This is a prospect which could seriously undermine the totalitarian system of government in the IS. The reader can therefore conclude that it was a mistake by Daʻish ideologues to engage in a discussion about free choice since it creates confusion regarding the Prophet's and the 'Caliph's' status.

The 'Caliphate' will most likely dismiss the above analysis as sophistry or anti-Islamic propaganda aimed at leading devout Muslims astray, but it remains a fact that the method of selective reference to sacred sources in defense of IS positions has clearly revealed the dangers involved in adopting such an approach despite the undisputed authority of the Quran. This authority is being manipulated by proponents of extreme interpretations of Islam to justify their positions. The IS exploitation of a text which is accepted by Muslims as sacred and beyond criticism does, however, not automatically confer the same status on the positions held by those who attempt to use the sacred text to their own advantage. The 'Caliphate's' manipulation of the story of Noah confirms the basic argument of this chapter that a totalitarian regime is vulnerable because of its own propaganda. This conclusion confirms that the danger of human error, ignorance or manipulation is real when it comes to interpreting the Quran. Daʻish leaders argue that such a possibility does not apply to them because the 'Caliphate' is the true embodiment of God's word and law. This position creates a conundrum for IS ideologues as a consequence of their rejection of human agency and involvement with regard to understanding God's word. In response to this rejection, the critical reader might argue that human beings form the prism which refracts God's light when it reaches their senses. In view of human involvement with sacred texts, the 'Caliphate's' insistence on a monopoly on what is true Islam is problematic. The sense of exceptionalism and divine mission pushes the IS to enter the labyrinth of propaganda, which at times turns out to be an enemy in disguise.

Another problem with respect to the IS claim that its interpretation of Islam is the only correct one and that there is no alternative to the 'Caliphate', as discussed above in the context of the story of Noah, is that most Muslims appear to agree that the IS in its present incarnation is not the solution to the problems of the Islamic world. The circumstantial evidence that strongly suggests this conclusion, without having all Muslims respond to an opinion poll, is the fact that a clear minority of Muslims has been convinced by the 'Caliphate's' propaganda that it is their obligation to emigrate to the IS and contribute to its struggle 'in the path of God', that is, jihad. A third weakness of the IS position is the linkage between Noah and the relatively modern concept of democracy (even if democracy is traced back to the ancient Greek, the story of Noah predates them), of which Noah was not aware. IS propagandists fail satisfactorily to explain the connection between Noah and democracy, most likely in hopes that this stratagem, that is, introducing a new concept (parliamentary democracy) of which Noah could not have been aware, will go unnoticed by the reader. This is an approach that frequently informs the argumentation of IS authors who contribute articles to the 'Caliphate's' publications in their attempts to justify extremist interpretations of Islam.[47] Finally, the author guides readers in the right direction, in case they have not yet drawn the correct conclusion, by providing the missing piece of the puzzle:

> So until we return to the correct state of Islamic affairs, it's upon us all to work together to eradicate the principle of "free choice", and not to deceive the people in an attempt to seek their pleasure, neither by calling to "free choice" directly, nor by alluding to it indirectly.[48]

It is clear from the *Dabiq* contributor's article that the 'Caliphate', for obvious reasons, views 'free choice' as a major threat to the leader's authority.

In summary, the 'Caliphate' appears to have made a strong case with respect to hijra by addressing both spiritual and temporal aspects of life with solid arguments. One could, of course, have doubts whether a battlefield is the best place for children to grow up, but such a disadvantage can be offset by the argument that it should be every parent's loftiest goal to allow their children to defend the IS and go to paradise. The faint of heart might also argue that there is no guarantee that the 'Caliphate' will survive for long, in which case hijra would be a wasted effort. The IS will, most likely, respond to this legitimate doubt by contending that God has enjoined that mankind observe the law. Since Daʻish is the best expression of God's law, it will survive. Based upon the above discussion of the IS arguments in favor of hijra,[49] one can conclude that IS propagandists have almost accomplished the task of convincing the reader since four of the above points seem effectively to dispel potential doubts. From the perspective of the critical reader, however, the reference to Noah has weakened the IS case against 'free choice'.

Bai'a

A prominent concept, in addition to hijra, in IS propaganda is *bai'a* (swearing allegiance). The symbolism of this procedure is powerful, which explains why *Dabiq* is replete with photos of tribal leaders and representatives giving *bai'a* to the IS.[50] The propaganda value of this ceremony cannot be overestimated since this public display of loyalty contributes to creating the impression that people rally around the cause of God, meaning the 'Caliphate'. In societies where Islamic tradition and tribal values still play a role, photos of *bai'a* events exude power, authority and loyalty; the more such photos, the better propaganda. Photos of people giving *bai'a*, if taken in a geographic variety of places, create the impression that the 'Caliphate' enjoys worldwide support, which is, of course, one goal of its propaganda.[51] In the IS, tribes and citizens give *bai'a* to God and Islam and, by extension, to the 'Caliph' instead of to a constitution, which the IS would dismiss as a 'manmade' document, not sanctioned by God. Furthermore, there is another important aspect to *bai'a*, namely that it constitutes a sort of bonding; participants in these events become a part of a global Islamic brotherhood with a bright future as promised by the IS. This must indubitably be a powerful experience (if voluntary) in a chaotic world where Islam is being perceived as a religion under siege. However, a problem arises, if tribes do not continue to give *bai'a*. The great propaganda value of *bai'a* is also reflected in *Dabiq's* emphatic call to Muslims to organize pledges of allegiance and '[p]ublicize them as much as possible'.[52] The reasons for this public display of allegiance to the IS are that it demonstrates Muslims' loyalty to the *umma* (religious community), and it also instills terror in the hearts of the *kuffar* (unbelievers).[53]

Global Islamization

'The mission of the Islamic State is neither local nor regional, but rather global'.[54] With statements such as the aforementioned, it becomes a priority of IS propaganda in a detailed and consistent fashion to enumerate victories and territorial expansion. This, without doubt, serves as a significant morale booster, as it instills in IS fighters the idea that they are part of a great cause, from which they will gain significant benefit in the hereafter. With this statement, the 'Caliphate' makes a long-term commitment to Islamize the world, implying that the jihad will continue for a long time. This is a statement which could actually serve the IS cause and offer an opportunity to explain away adversities as bumps in the road toward establishing global Islamic rule. In another passage, *Dabiq* has quoted the founder of the Islamic Shafi'i legal school, al-Shafi': 'One's authority will not be consolidated except after overcoming tribulation'.[55] This quotation could be used by the IS to explain setbacks in its struggle for the cause of God as a temporary phenomenon. It comes with an implied caveat, however, namely that the setbacks come initially only and not after authority has already been established. This interpretation is further strengthened by the implied timeline. The quotation does not refer to global authority, so the IS obviously cannot contend that al-Shafiʿ is referring to continuous 'tribulations' until authority has been established at some very distant point in the future. Had the Islamic legal scholar referred to such a case, the IS could use it to explain away any setback that occurs on the road to Islamic world domination, the 'Caliphate's' final objective.

Benefits of life in the 'Caliphate'

Part of IS propaganda emphasizes the benefits of living in the 'Caliphate', the list of which is quite long according to *Dabiq*. The magazine draws the reader's attention to the millions of dollars that the IS pumps into services that are important to the Muslims.[56] This is a rather vague statement and therefore suitable for propaganda purposes. Concurrently, however, it could have negative consequences since it would be difficult to explain why these investments have decreased or even ceased altogether, were such a situation to occur. Furthermore, the 'Caliphate's' propagandists stress the security and stability enjoyed by areas under its control. Again, it would be difficult to sustain this narrative, if the number of airstrikes were to increase drastically, or a successful ground war offensive against Daʿish were to be launched, which was the case in 2017. Another benefit that citizens of the IS enjoy is that it '[e]nsur[es] the availability of food products and commodities in the market, particularly bread'.[57] This is an indication that the IS, like many governments in the Middle East, fears the possibility of bread riots, should the supply be disrupted or bread be subject to price hikes. It is a common policy in the Middle East pursued by many states to subsidize the price on bread in order to assuage discontent with authoritarian regimes. The safety of life in Daʿish is emphasized by referring to the reduced crime rate, following the IS takeover.[58] A possible explanation for reduced crime is the totalitarian nature of the state and the draconian interpretation and implementation of the shariʿa (Islamic law). Many students of the Middle East would, however, most likely give little credence to the claim that crime rates are lower than previously, arguing that the crimes perpetrated and documented by the 'Caliphate' itself are not included in the statistics, which is why it compares favorably to the pre-IS period.

Dabiq also lists other positive aspects of IS rule. The 'Caliphate' requests that the community provide names of orphans, widows and the needy so that *zakat* (charitable tax intended for the poor) can be distributed among the less affluent members of society. This activity presents excellent photo opportunities as reflected in photos of mujahidun patting orphans on the head and distributing food to those in need.[59] Another example of policies that benefit the population is the reduction in the price of gasoline and its distribution for free among the poor in Nineveh Province, Iraq.[60] The *Dabiq* article in question does not explain why the poor need gasoline. The regime also demands that weapons acquired from the al-Asad regime or the Free Syrian Army (FSA) be turned in to the authorities.[61] This order suggests that the IS does not trust its citizens, except for the mujahidun and members of the *hisba* (Islamic police), to carry arms, which, in turn, is an indication that at least a part of the population has not been swayed by IS propaganda to support the 'Caliphate'. Finally, the list of positive policies put in place by the Islamic regime is completed with an admonition to those bearing arms against the IS that they repent before they are captured, the purpose of which is to demonstrate the 'magnanimous' and 'lenient' policies of the IS against transgressors.[62] Unfortunately, for the IS, the numerous grisly photos of the fate of IS 'enemies' tend to detract from the rosy image that Da'ish attempts to paint of life in the 'Caliphate'.[63]

The IS also prides itself on its 'extensive healthcare' with a detailed list of services that it provides.[64] *Dabiq* reports that the Da'ish has opened medical colleges in Al-Raqqa and Mosul, offering three-year programs open both to male and female students. The magazine stresses the Islamic nature of the education provided by emphasizing that female students are taught by female staff. The curriculum raises questions, however, since these medical colleges graduate 'doctors' after three years who are trained in surgery among other things. The teaching staff are 'degree holders', but *Dabiq* does not specify what degrees they hold. The fact that the 'Caliphate' was proclaimed as recently as July 2014 raises additional questions. The critical reader probably wishes to know whether these degrees can be considered legitimately Islamic since they have most likely been conferred by 'apostate' Arab regimes or by 'Crusader' medical institutions. Another issue that *Dabiq* does not address is the origin of the medical equipment and the medication prescribed to patients. It would be embarrassing to admit that they are most likely of 'Crusader' or 'apostate' origin. Education is provided free of charge and the medical program appears to attract students from outside the 'Caliphate', who make up 50 percent of the student body. This article ends with the encouraging words: 'The Islamic State offers everything that you need to live and work here, so what are you waiting for?'[65] The fact that Da'ish has opened two medical colleges suggests that medical professionals are in great demand and that many IS fighters are in need of surgery since such skills are emphasized in the program.[66] The length of the training program, however, indicates that the 'Caliphate' will for the foreseeable future have to recruit doctors from other parts of the world.

Global Islamic solidarity

A common aspect of IS propaganda is the 'Caliphate's' use of 'enemy' sources that confirm Da'ish claims. References in Western sources to the fact that IS mujahidun have their own state and command a multi-ethnic army are quickly exploited by *Dabiq*, presumably for the propaganda value of such statements since they confirm IS successes.[67] The observant reader will, however, recognize the obvious contradiction between this positive information and the much more frequent negative material relating to Western powers. If the reader gets accustomed to denunciations of the West, (s)he might find a positive reference less convincing or even suspicious. In IS calculations, the gains of occasionally asking the reader to trust the judgment of the enemy obviously outweigh the possible disadvantages of giving the enemy credit for certain positive conclusions. The discussion in this paragraph of contradictions in IS propaganda allows the analyst to draw a number of conclusions. Western sources, despite their enemy status, will be utilized by *Dabiq* so long as they play into the hands of the IS.[68] It is important for the 'Caliphate' to demonstrate to *Dabiq's* readers that the IS is being taken seriously by the enemy, that it is a real state and not just a group, and therefore that it poses a serious threat to Western interests and instills fear in Americans and Europeans. Without question, this serves as a morale booster for actual mujahidun and also contributes to recruitment efforts. The reason for *Dabiq's* highlighting the Western source's reference to the IS multi-ethnic army is, most likely, that the 'Caliphate' wants the reader to believe that it enjoys worldwide support for its ideology, that mujahidun flock to its battlefields from all nations and that it is not a national movement limited in its scope. Furthermore, this 'support' implies that Western and non-Islamic power is gradually collapsing, and the IS is indeed paving the way for the global domination of Islam. The example discussed in this paragraph demonstrates that IS propagandists know how to exploit enemy sources to their own advantage in 'Caliphate' propaganda and to calculate the cost of a potentially negative impact.

The idea of a worldwide community without borders and national distinctions analyzed above is a recurring theme in *Dabiq*. This reveals a clear understanding on the part of the *Al-Hayat Media Center* of the value of contrasting the alienation that some Muslims experience in non-Muslim and Muslim societies alike with the true Islamic life that they can lead in a state where God's law rules. On the occasion of the proclamation of the 'Caliphate' Amir al-Mu'minin [the commander of the faithful], al-Baghdadi addressed the world's Muslims as follows:

> O Muslims everywhere.... Raise your head high, for today - by Allah's grace - you have a state and khilafah [caliphate], which will return your dignity, might, rights, and leadership. It is a state where the Arab and non-Arab, the white man and black man, the easterner and westerner are all brothers ... Allah brought their hearts together, and thus, they became brothers by His grace, loving each other for the sake of Allah, standing in a single trench, defending and guarding each other, and sacrificing themselves for one another'.[69]

This is indeed a powerful message to Muslims who are not wont to analyze the statements of the IS. One has to give al-Baghdadi due credit for these astoundingly ingenious lines. They are extremely effective in several different ways, if taken out of the historical context and left without further analysis and comment, which is, of course, the speaker's intention. Al-Baghdadi's address is quite clearly intended as an emotional appeal to all Muslims to rally around the 'khilafa' (Caliphate) and not as a philosophical discourse that encourages reflection on the part of followers and believers. The proclamation instills hope and a sense of empowerment. It reestablishes a link to the glorious Islamic past and creates a sense of belonging for Muslims who experience alienation in their life. Last but not the least, this is, presumably a golden opportunity to right the many wrongs and address historical grievances, resulting from Western intrusion. This is a state where there is no room for economic or social discrimination, racism or nationalism.

Visual propaganda

Dabiq photographs have briefly been discussed above, but the subject deserves more attention since visual propaganda is at least as important in *Dabiq* as the written word, an impression to which testifies the fact that most pages in the magazine have at least one photograph. The diversity of themes conveyed by these photos is impressive. One such theme is the enemy's crimes perpetrated against civilians. Many photos and much statistics show the results of Syrian regime and coalition airstrikes against IS targets, emphasizing the number of civilian fatalities and casualties, including women and children. Furthermore, the civilian nature of the targets, such as markets, is frequently stressed.[70] However, it is quickly pointed out that swift retaliation can be expected for those who attack the 'Caliphate', particularly the 'Nusairis' (the Syrian Alawi minority regime) and the 'Safawis' (the Shi'i-dominated government in Iraq).[71] The term 'Safawi', used in reference to the Shi'i government in Baghdad, was deliberately chosen to establish the regime's link to a 'foreign' enemy state, Iran, thereby implying the 'illegitimacy' of Iraqi governments since the US-led invasion of the country and the overthrow of Saddam Husain. The term Safawi has serious negative connotations in the Sunni world since the Safavids were an originally Sunni Sufi brotherhood later turned Shi'i that converted the Sunni majority population of Persia to Shi'ism by the sword in 1501, making Twelver (Ithna 'Ashari) Shi'ism the official religion of the Safavid Empire. It can thus be concluded, for the reason stated above, that photographs showing IS retaliation are found in greater number in *Dabiq* because they convey power, which most likely satisfies the IS self-image better than gaining a reputation as the underdog. This is a natural reaction by a totalitarian regime since it is part of its nature to display power either to reassure or deter its citizens.

Another crucial aspect of IS 'power projection' is photos that show recently conquered territories. These photos are deemed important for the IS propaganda effort because they convey two messages: (1) the IS is an unstoppable force and (2) the 'Caliphate's' end goal, world domination, is inevitable and gradually being realized. Enemy military equipment is another favorite motif of IS photographers. Armored personnel carriers (APCs), tanks and other Western- or Russian-manufactured military equipment captured from the Iraqi and Syrian government forces are frequently displayed on the pages of *Dabiq*.[72] A third, albeit less frequently displayed, aspect of IS power is forgiveness. An example of the 'softer side' of the 'Caliphate', which radically departs from the unforgiving and harsh image that it enjoys, this power should not be underestimated. It holds out hope for the 'apostates' who have taken up arms against the IS and whom a gruesome fate awaits, if they fall into the hands of IS mujahidun. This offer is extended on one condition, however, that the 'guilty' party repents before being captured, which probably means that only enemy deserters or defectors who manage to get through to IS-occupied territory are pardoned. *Dabiq* refers to 'the many instances of repentance by the apostate members of the Iraqi government and its forces'.[73] This is one of the few contexts when forgiveness is emphasized by the IS, accompanied by an appropriate Quranic quote: 'And Allah turns in forgiveness to whom He wills; and Allah is knowing and wise'.[74] As a reminder for those who do not fully appreciate the magnanimity of the IS, the *Al-Hayat Media Center* has a subtle message for those enemies who are hesitant about repenting and joining the IS – a great number of grisly photos in *Dabiq* showing dead enemy soldiers and fighters[75] and Western hostages, enemy soldiers and adulterers facing a firing squad, an executioner's sword or knife or an excited rock-throwing crowd.[76] The message could not be clearer – seize the opportunity when God offers one or suffer the consequences.

Photos are also utilized to demonize the enemy, interspersed with graphic descriptions, as if the visual propaganda were not sufficient to convey the message. Many photos show both enemy and IS civilian casualties. Furthermore, in order to reinforce the visual impact of photos, *Dabiq* propagandists also resort to very graphic verbal descriptions of IS operations, such as '...he used to detonate explosive devices against the crusader patrols [in Iraq] ... to turn them into severed body fragments mixed with their vehicles' wreckage'.[77] The purpose is, of course, to convey to the readership how helpless and vulnerable their enemies are despite their superior technology. Also, enemy war crimes such as the Syrian government's use of barrel bombs[78] and photos with accompanying clarifications such as 'Sunnis murdered by the Safawis [the Shi'i-dominated government in Baghdad]'[79] are highlighted in *Dabiq*. The visual sources are intended to fan Sunni hatred of Shi'is in Iraq and Alawis in Syria and to prevent Sunni cooperation with the Iraqi and Syrian governments. This is most likely an effective IS strategy since few Sunnis would remain indifferent to such photos.

Conclusion

Important purposes of black and gray propaganda are to conceal, excuse or even argue that some flaws are necessary in a particular system of government. Daʿish has, throughout its existence, evinced a blind faith in the effectiveness of propaganda as evidenced in its publications. An exaggerated belief in the advantages of propaganda oftentimes comes at a price, however, since manipulation of information is in reality a double-edged sword. The danger which the sword poses to its wielder is commensurate with the critical thinking skills of the reader or observer – the more developed the skills, the greater risk to the propagandist. Conversely, an uncritical readership is an ideal audience since it plays directly into the hands of extremist propagandists by turning flawed propaganda into the opposite. With this in mind, the examination of IS propaganda in this chapter has enabled the present author to draw a number of conclusions. First, the IS has a certain advantage over non-Islamic groups and societies employing propaganda, owing to the fact that it exploits a sacred text which is acknowledged by Muslims as God's word. The implications are that the Quran is beyond human criticism, and that, traditionally, only a limited group of professionals, namely, the ʿulama, have been engaged in interpreting the divine message. Outside of this group, some Muslims who are not accustomed to interpreting the Quran are less likely to discover the weaknesses of IS propaganda. Second, the milieu in which the 'Caliphate' operates is less diverse than many other societies where greater religious, political and philosophical diversity and lesser authority of religion and traditional social norms pose a greater challenge to the propagandist. This situation, to a certain degree, facilitates the IS task of manipulating its audience, by allowing the group to use distorted and misrepresented 'Quranic' language to underpin its extremist message. Third, like the Nazi Party before it which made consistent efforts to appropriate great European cultural, scientific and political personalities, the IS employs the same approach to Islamic scholars and religious personalities to win hearts and minds, an effort the intention of which is to induce the reader to conclude that 'Caliphate' leaders' extremist interpretation of the Quran is legitimate and based on tradition.

Notes

1 The term propaganda is here used to characterize a sustained effort to convince an audience of the veracity of a particular point of view achieved by manipulation of and selectivity regarding information and sources.
2 Totalitarian is here used to describe a state the regime of which strives to establish far-reaching control of many aspects of human activity.
3 Alfred Rosenberg, 'Beethoven', *Völkischer Beobachter*, 26 March 1927, quoted in David B. Dennis, *Inhumanities: Nazi Interpretations of Western Culture* (Cambridge: Cambridge University Press, 2012), p. 1.
4 Jacques Ellul, *Propaganda: The Formation of Men's Attitudes* (New York: Alfred A. Knopf, 1965), p. x.

Islamic State media production and Islam 197

5. Ibid., pp. xvi, 22.
6. Ibid., p. xvi.
7. The names IS, 'Caliphate' and Da'ish are used interchangeably for stylistic reasons throughout the chapter to refer to the territories formerly and presently controlled by this organization.
8. *Dabiq*, Issue 8, (March/April 2015), *Al-Hayat Media Center*, p. 39; David Cook, *Understanding Jihad* (Oakland: University of California Press, 2015, second edition), pp. 76, 77, 245.
9. Garth S. Jowett and Victoria O'Donnell. *Propaganda and Persuasion* (Thousand Oaks, CA: SAGE Publications, Inc., 1999), p. 1.
10. Ibid., p. 9.
11. Ibid.
12. Ibid., p. 12.
13. The Qur'an: *Arabic Text with Corresponding English Meanings*, edited by Saheeh International (Jeddah: Abul-Qasim Publishing House, 1997), 51:56–57.
14. David B. Dennis, *Inhumanities*, p. 2.
15. *Dabiq*, Issue 10 (Jun., Jul., 2015), pp. 8–9.
16. Dennis, *Inhumanities*, p. 2.
17. *Dabiq*, Issue 1 (Jun., Jul., 2014), p. 10.
18. Dennis, *Inhumanities*, pp. 2, 457.
19. Adolf Hitler, *Mein Kampf* (Munich: Fritz Eher Nachfolger, 1943), p. 189.
20. *Dabiq*, Issue 2 (Jun., Jul., 2014), p. 3; Hitler, *Mein Kampf*, p. 507.
21. Hitler, *Mein Kampf*, p. 70.
22. *Dabiq*, Issue 1 (Jun., Jul., 2014), p. 27.
23. Ibid., p. 13. A further indication of the 'Caliphate's' global ambitions is a map of the world on the reverse of its five-dinar gold coin, *ISSUU*, 'Lo Stato Islamico, una realtà che ti vorrebbe comunicare', p. 48. Accessed 3 January 2016. http://issuu.com/031041/docs/lo_stato_islamico_una_realt_che_.
24. *Dabiq*, Issue 9 (May., Jun., 2015), p. 65.
25. Ibid., p. 43; Issue 10 (Jun., Jul., 2015), p. 77.
26. Ibid., Issue 2 (Jun., Jul., 2014), pp. 33–34; Issue 9 (May, Jun., 2015), pp. 33, 78.
27. Sven Johannesen, 'Islamisk Stat', September 2014, *Faktalink*, accessed 6 June 2015, http://www.faktalink.dk/titelliste/islamis-stat/hele-faktalinket-om-islamisk-stat.
28. *Dabiq*, Issue 1 (Jun., Jul., 2014), p. 3.
29. Ibid., Issue 3 (Jul., Aug., 2014), pp. 9, 15.
30. 'Lo Stato Islamico' *ISSUU*, p. 60.
31. *Dabiq*, Issue 1 (Jun., Jul., 2014), p. 5.
32. Ibid., pp. 6–10; 'Lo Stato Islamico', *ISSUU*, p. 52.
33. *Dabiq*, Issue 1 (Jun., Jul., 2014), p. 10.
34. The Qur'an, 7, n. 326, p. 194.
35. *Dabiq*, Issue 1 (Jun., Jul., 2014), p. 10.
36. The Qur'an, 4:97; *Dabiq*, Issue 10 (Jul., Aug., 2015), p. 48.
37. *Dabiq*, Issue 1 (Jun., Jul., 2014), p. 11; Issue 3 (Jul., Aug., 2014), p. 26.
38. Ibid., Issue 1 (Jun., Jul., 2014), p. 11.
39. Hamza Hendawi, 'Islamic State's Double Standard Sow Growing Disillusion', *Associated Press*, 18 January 2016. Accessed 18 January 2016, http://www.msn.com/en-us/news/world/islamic-states-double-standards-sow-growing-disillusion/ar-BBonCK1?li=BBnb7Kz&ocid=U219DHP.
40. The Qur'an, 20:84; *Dabiq*, Issue 2 (Jun., Jul., 2014), p. 3.
41. *Dabiq*, Issue 2 (Jun., Jul., 2014), p. 3.
42. Ibid., Issue 3 (Jul., Aug., 2014), p. 33.
43. Ibid., Issue 2 (Jun., Jul., 2014), p. 3.

198 *Islamic State media production and Islam*

44 Ibid., p. 1.
45 Ibid.
46 Ibid., pp. 5–6, 9.
47 Ibid., p. 1.
48 Ibid., p. 11.
49 (1) Reference to Moses in a quotation from the Quran. (2) The 'Caliphate provides homes for all muhajirun'. (3) Emigrants can make a crucial contribution 'toward the liberation of Makkah, Madinah, and Al-Quds' (Jerusalem). (4) Such a contribution will lead to a positive outcome for all muhajirun (emigrants) on Judgment Day. (5) 'It's either the Islamic State or the flood'.
50 *Dabiq*, Issue 1 (Jun., Jul., 2014), p. 12.
51 *Dabiq*, Issue 5 (Oct., Nov., 2014), p. 24; Issue 8 (Mar., Apr., 2015), pp. 14–15.
52 Ibid., Issue 2 (Jun., Jul., 2014), p. 3.
53 Ibid.
54 Ibid., Issue 1 (Jun., Jul., 2014), p. 13; Issue 2 (Jun., Jul., 2014), pp. 39–42.
55 Ibid., Issue 1 (Jun. Jul., 2014), p. 40.
56 Ibid., p. 13.
57 Ibid. See also *Dabiq*, Issue 2 (Jun., Jul., 2014), p. 35 and 'Lo Stato Islamico', *ISSUU*, p. 27.
58 Ibid.
59 Ibid., Issue 2 (Jun., Jul., 2014), p. 38; 'Lo Stato Islamico', *ISSUU*, p. 25.
60 'Lo Stato Islamico', *ISSUU*, p. 25.
61 *Dabiq*, Issue 2 (Jun., Jul., 2014), p. 38.
62 Ibid., Issue 1 (Jun., Jul., 2014), p. 14.
63 Ibid., Issue 7 (Jan., Feb., 2015), pp. 5, 8, 66.
64 Ibid., Issue 9 (May, Jun., 2015), pp. 25–26.
65 Ibid., p. 26.
66 Ibid.
67 Ibid., Issue 1 (Jun., Jul., 2014), p. 33; Douglas A. Ollivant and Brian Fishman, 'State of Jihad: The Reality of the Islamic State in Iraq and Syria', *War on the Rocks*, 21 May 2014. Accessed 22 December 2015, http://warontherocks.com/2014/05/state-of-jihad-the-reality-of-the-islamic-state-in-iraq-and-syria/.
68 See Chapter 5 for the same approach used by the *Völkischer Beobachter*.
69 *Dabiq*, Issue 1 (Jun., Jul., 2014), p. 7.
70 Ibid., pp. 42–43.
71 Ibid., pp. 44–45.
72 Ibid., pp. 44, 46–47.
73 Ibid., pp. 48–49.
74 The Qur'an, 9:15; *Dabiq*, Issue 1 (Jun., Jul., 2014), p. 49.
75 *Dabiq*, Issue 1 (Jun., Jul., 2014), p. 15; Issue 3 (Jul., Aug., 2014), p. 18.
76 Ibid., Issue 3 (Jul., Aug., 2014), pp. 4, 12–13, 21.
77 Ibid., Issue 9 (May, Jun., 2015), p. 40.
78 Ibid., p. 36.
79 Ibid., Issue 1 (Jun., Jul., 2014), p. 16.

Bibliography

Associated Press.
Cook, David. *Understanding Jihad*. Oakland: University of California Press, 2015; second edition.
Dabiq.
Dennis, David B. *Inhumanities: Nazi Interpretations of Western Culture*. Cambridge: Cambridge University Press, 2012.

Ellul, Jacques. *Propaganda: The Formation of Men's Attitudes*. New York: Alfred A. Knopf, 1965.

Hendawi, Hamza. 'Islamic State's Double Standards Sow Growing Disillusion'. *Associated Press*, 18 January 2016. Accessed 18 January 2016. http://www.msn.com/en-us/news/world/islamic-states-double-standards-sow-growing-disillusion/ar-BBonCK1?li=BBnb7Kz&ocid=U219DHP.

Hitler, Adolf. *Mein Kampf* [My Struggle]. Munich: Zentralverlag der NSDAP, Frz. Eher Nachf., G.m.b.H., 1943 (first published 1925, Vol. 1 and 1927, Vol. 2).

ISSUU. 'Lo Stato Islamico, una realtà che ti vorrebbe comunicare' [The Islamic State, a Reality that you would like to Communicate]. Accessed 3 January 2016. http://issuu.com/031041/docs/lo_stato_islamico_una_realt_che_.

Johannesen, Sven. 'Islamisk Stat' [The Islamic State]. September 2014. *Faktalink*. Accessed 6 June 2015. http://www.faktalink.dk/titelliste/islamis-stat/hele-faktalinket-om-islamisk-stat.

Jowett, Garth S. and Victoria O'Donnell. *Propaganda and Persuasion*. Thousand Oaks, CA: SAGE Publications, Inc., 1999.

Ollivant, Douglas A. and Brian Fishman. 'State of Jihad: The Reality of the Islamic State in Iraq and Syria'. *War on the Rocks*, 21 May 2014. Accessed 22 December 2015. http://warontherocks.com/2014/05/state-of-jihad-the-reality-of-the-islamic-state-in-iraq-and-syria/.

The Quran.

Rosenberg, Alfred. 'Beethoven'. *Völkischer Beobachter*, 26 March 1927.

Völkischer Beobachter, newspaper published by the German National Socialist Workers' Party.

10 Islamic State legitimacy and perception of the enemy

Introduction

This chapter continues the analysis of IS propaganda in the preceding chapter, focusing on additional important aspects of the IS approach to manipulation of information. Whereas the previous chapter examined IS media production and exploitation of Islam for Da'ish propaganda, the present chapter focuses on legitimacy and those who are perceived as the enemies of Islam. The pitfalls of an over-confidence in propaganda as an unequaled instrument for concealing the negative aspects and weaknesses of a totalitarian ideology are assessed as they relate to, inter alia, regime legitimacy, criticism of rival groups, democracy and emotive argumentation. Like the previous chapter, this chapter clearly reveals the double-edged nature and limitations of the 'Caliphate's' efforts to attract new recruits to its jihad against the West and its attempts to appeal to mainstream Muslims for support.

Legitimacy

Totalitarian regimes are obsessed with the issue of legitimacy and the 'Caliphate' is no exception. History has provided ample evidence of the importance of the issue to such regimes, Nazism in Germany, Fascism in Italy and Stalinism in the Soviet Union, to name a few. The IS will most likely reject any suggestions of similarities between the 'Caliphate' and the aforementioned regimes, but the creation of myths and the cults of personality are aspects of propaganda that these systems do have in common. In the case of the IS, the cult of personality is less pronounced than in the other systems of government since the 'Caliph' does not figure as prominently in the visual limelight as Mussolini, Hitler and Stalin did. The cult of personality is expressed more subtly in the 'Caliphate', but the leader's presence is clearly felt in the many references to him and his speeches in *Dabiq*. One such example is

> ...we can see that The Islamic State is the entity that most emulates the millah [religion] of Ibrahim [Abraham] with regards to imamah

DOI: 10.4324/9781003260943-11

[Islamic leadership] in the areas where it exists. It has carried out the command of Allah...in the best possible manner...All this, after Allah had granted the imam of The Islamic State the blessing of performing hijra and fighting jihad in His cause, on top of already having been characterized by his noble lineage, sound intellect, and a prestigious level of knowledge and religious practice.[1]

This quotation from *Dabiq* is a clear indication of the connection between legitimacy, cult of personality and propaganda as argued above.

The purpose of the passage quoted above is to establish an irrefutable argument which substantiates the legitimacy of the IS. A clever approach has been devised to achieve this objective. The author of the *Dabiq* article initially builds his case by claiming that the IS better than any other society on earth emulates true Islam. The next step is to trace true Islam not just back to the Prophet Muhammad, but all the way back to Abraham (Ibrahim in Arabic), who according to God was the earliest paragon of the Islamic religion[2] and who is accorded the status of prophet by the Quran.[3] A problem is that Jews claim him as their patriarch and that this was done long before Islam was revealed to Muhammad. This constitutes a problem only to the critical non-Muslim reader, however, since Muslims believe that the Prophet Muhammad was God's instrument to convey Islam to mankind and that God's word cannot be disputed. Having thus demonstrated, by reference to the Quran ('And who would turn away from the religion of Ibrahim except one who makes a fool of himself')[4] an indissoluble link between the IS and true Islam, the article's author has established a foundation to build on for subsequent evidence. The evidence presented so far thus works very well in an Islamic context.

The critical reader will most likely not be satisfied with the evidence presented above in support of the argument regarding the legitimacy of the 'Caliphate'. (S)he will demand more tangible evidence, which will, from a scholarly perspective, be nearly impossible to provide unless the scholar takes God's word, conveyed through a human being, the Prophet Muhammad, as hard evidence in the case. A problematic statement in the quotation above with respect to the IS's legitimacy is the claim that the 'Caliphate' better than any other society implements and reflects true Islam. This is a weak link in the chain of evidence presented by *Dabiq*, to the extent that many Muslims will not be convinced by this claim. The fact that a clear minority of Muslims has emigrated to the IS constitutes circumstantial evidence of the validity of this conclusion. Aware of this problem, the author resorts to diversionary tactics. In order to turn the reader's attention away from this weakness in the argument, the author introduces a claim which will convince the readership that the IS is indeed the only representative of true Islam on this earth. This is achieved by referring to al-Baghdadi's purportedly impeccable and irrefutable religious credentials – his waging jihad for the cause of God, his 'noble lineage' and his position as an Islamic scholar, an *'alim*.

The *Dabiq* argument 'All this, after Allah had granted the imam of the IS the blessing of performing hijra and fighting jihad in His cause' implies that al-Baghdadi enjoys the support of God, since the latter has 'granted the imam the blessing...'.[5] With this implication, the author establishes a link (a tenuous one, to be sure, from the perspective of the critical reader) between al-Baghdadi and God, implying divine sanction, or even divine intervention in support of the 'Caliph'. From the extremist perspective, this is a convincing argument since the IS contends that performing hijra to the land of Islam, that is, the 'Caliphate' and waging jihad constitute religious duties which a true believer cannot shirk. With this contention, the author has significantly strengthened his case. The reason is that the 'Caliphate' convincingly can advance the argument that it is the only state which fulfills this crucial Islamic duty. This appears to be the strongest link in the chain of evidence presented to the reader. Once this has been achieved, the author, quite realistically, expects his audience to deduce that the IS is more Islamic than other 'Islamic states'. Therefore, performing hijra to the 'Caliphate' and assisting it in its jihad is an Islamic duty as well.

The 'noble lineage' refers to the fact that many Muslims claim descent from the Prophet Muhammad's family, an assertion which is difficult to substantiate or refute. Despite the difficulty to verify it, the claim confers high social and religious status on the person who is believed to be a descendant of the Prophet Muhammad. This status entitles an individual to wear a black turban, the one worn by al-Baghdadi prior to his death, and to bear the honorific title of Sayyid. Modern science could, however, potentially cause problems for the multitude of claimants to 'prophetic' descent, if DNA testing could be applied instead of relying on stories handed down from one generation to another regarding genealogy. There would most likely be some resistance on the part of the claimants to 'prophetic' descent due to a potentially embarrassing outcome, if it were established that many claims are spurious. Another possible negative consequence of DNA testing could be that all or a very large number of claims are found to be genuine, which would lead to the social status of 'sayyidhood' being significantly devalued. These possible disadvantages of DNA testing thus lead the critical reader to conclude that the likelihood of such a procedure is fairly slight. In the light of the aforementioned, al-Baghdadi's claim to 'prophetic' ancestry must therefore be considered an asset, which will stand him in good stead, since it is difficult to refute by providing hard evidence to the contrary.

Al-Baghdadi's last asset, his scholarly credentials, seems to hold up to scrutiny since he indeed holds a doctoral degree in Islamic sciences earned from the Islamic University of Baghdad.[6] Based upon this information and al-Baghdadi's participation in jihad against the Americans, following the invasion of Iraq in 2003, IS propagandists argue that he possesses all required qualifications to occupy his position as 'caliph', all in accordance with the conditions prescribed by the shari'a.[7]

The way IS ideologues have constructed the above argument reveals that they do not assume that all Muslims will accept their argument without subjecting it to some critical analysis. It is worth mentioning in this context that, most likely, only religious scholars, particularly those who disagree with the IS extremist interpretation of Islam, will adopt a serious analytical approach to the 'Caliphate's' claims to legitimacy and leadership and they will naturally look for evidence to refute these claims. Based upon this assumption, one can conclude that most Muslims who join the IS have found at least some parts of the argument discussed above convincing for one reason or another. This leads the scholar to conclude that this must also have been the author's assumption and that he has successfully made a case, which was the original intention and which demonstrates that IS propaganda works to a certain extent, if the reader does not undertake to conduct serious analysis and research with respect to the argument under discussion. This goes to show that propaganda does not need to be perfect in order to convince an audience, a conclusion which is bad news for Islamic scholars opposed to extremist interpretations of their religion and counterterrorism officials since it makes their work more difficult.

Concurrently, there is good news as well, namely that the above analysis of the arguments advanced by the 'Caliphate' in support of its legitimacy offers a crucial insight into the propaganda methods utilized by Daʻish ideologues. This insight allows the scholar to conclude that a key to any success that the IS might have in its propaganda war against its enemies is the 'Caliphate's' blending of extremist arguments which do not appeal to a majority of Muslims with mainstream arguments which many more Muslims will accept. In other words, even if IS propagandists do not convince millions of Muslims actively to join their cause, there is a possibility that many Muslims will not fight the IS because they find some of its arguments reasonable. Now, the *'alim* (religious scholar) and the intelligence officer alike might ask why this is good news since it appears to work in favor of Islamic extremists. The answer is that understanding how the IS constructs its propaganda will guide both experts in their efforts to counter the IS discourse.

Problems of 'true' Islam

A key goal of the IS and other Islamic extremists is to reinstate the 'unadulterated' Islam of the Salaf (early generations of Muslims). This reinstatement will occur through a revival of the central Islamic tenet of *tawhid* (oneness of God) '...in matters ignored or abandoned by "Islamic" parties in our times...'.[8] Furthermore, the 'Caliphate' contends that, in order to be successful, the revival of *tawhid* needs to be accompanied by the realization on the part of the *jama'a* (Islamic community) that it needs to 'use the absent obligation of jihad as its fundamental means for change, implementing Allah's will'.[9] To justify this position, the IS quotes a passage from the Quran: 'And fight them until there is no fitnah and [until] the religion, all of it, is for

Allah'.[10] At first glance, the 'Caliphate's' position appears to be based on a solid foundation since *Dabiq* refers to a Quranic verse in support of the argument. The reader of the Quranic passage quoted in the magazine will, however, note that the quotation does not explain what form the fighting should take. It is, however, clear from the specific *sura* (Quranic chapter) as a whole that Muslims need to resist the hostility of the unbelievers (*kafirun*) with arms until the latter embrace Islam. This appears to support the goal of the IS to establish global domination of Islam since anyone who opposes its extremist interpretation of Islam can be labeled a *kafir* (unbeliever). The Quranic chapter as a whole also appears to sanction the legitimacy of jihad in order to achieve the IS goal.

The attentive reader will, however, note that the 'Caliphate' in its zeal to convince hesitant Muslims has completely ignored the historical context. This approach to the Quranic text is understandable since the quotation has to fit into *Dabiq's* argumentation. An historical analysis of the *sura* could potentially undermine the argument under discussion, which is why the IS ideologues have avoided such an approach. In defense of their treatment of the Quranic text, they will most likely contend that an historical approach is tantamount to irreverence since it would imply doubt of God's word. The author of the present volume strongly rejects this criticism since no disrespect for Islam or any other religion is intended in this study. The point is that the Quran was not written in the twenty-first century but a very long time ago, a fact which is crucial to the analysis of the 'Caliphate's' arguments. As a result of IS selectivity with respect to its argumentation, the latter suffers from a number of weaknesses. (1) The *sura* discusses the situation in the Arabian Peninsula in the Prophet Muhammad's lifetime. (2) The Al-Anfal *sura* refers to the Quraish tribe only. This is the Prophet Muhammad's own tribe, the majority of which opposed him before the Muslims vanquished Mecca. (3) The *sura* discusses treatment of Arab unbelievers exclusively. (4) The *sura* clearly states that those who subject Muslims to persecution have to be fought. (5) It does not sanction war against those who do not fight Muslims. (6) Finally, the majority of non-Muslim Arabs in the Prophet's lifetime were polytheists. They constituted the target of Muslims since they subjected the latter to persecution. (7) Based upon the complete text of the Al-Anfal *sura*, the critical reader will draw the conclusion that the 'Caliphate's' interpretation of the Quranic chapter is quite a stretch and actually completely misleading without the historical context.

The importance of contextual analysis is further illustrated by the fact that the Al-Anfal *sura* does not discuss jihad against all non-Muslims in order to establish global domination of Islam. In fact, the context clearly imposes geographic, ethnic and temporal limits on jihad. The target is Arab non-Muslims who subject Muslims in the Arabian Peninsula to persecution in the Prophet's lifetime, that is, the first and second decade of Anno Hegirae (the 620s and 630s of the Common Era). In order to execute God's will, the IS's mujahidun would have to travel back in time to a distant past instead of waging war against Muslims who disagree with them and the world's non-Muslim majority population. This particular example reveals numerous weaknesses in IS propaganda, and a simplistic and quite selective, albeit understandable, approach to sources, when it comes to convincing Muslims of their duty to join the 'Caliphate'.

Emotive argumentation

Like Chapters 5 and 9 of this study, the present chapter contends that propaganda is a double-edged sword, which is why the IS frequently resorts to emotive argumentation, that is, argumentation intended to elicit an emotional reaction in the reader, when other types of arguments may fall short of producing the desired effect. One example of this approach is the publication in *Dabiq* of a number of photos of IS mujahidun who have carried out terrorist attacks in Europe with an adjacent caption saying: 'Join the caravan of Islamic State knights in the lands of the crusaders',[11] a clear message to sympathizers in Christian countries to emulate IS 'knights' and carry out terrorist acts. The reference to knights is interesting since it, like the Arabic word *'faris'*, carries romantic connotations. The *faris*/knight is a mounted hero whose moral rectitude is infused with religious fervor. This depiction of IS mujahidun as romantic heroes embodying religious ideals is reflected in some *Dabiq* photos showing mounted mujahidun armed with swords.[12] The concept that the *Al-Hayat Media Center* team wishes potential followers to embrace is that the mujahidun who kill Crusaders (Christians) are not criminals, but pious Muslims who fight for justice and for God. Furthermore, the photos of sword-wielding mujahidun on horses galloping across the desert establish a link to a bygone era of early Muslims fighting for their religion. These photos are meant to legitimize the 'Caliphate's' violent jihad, the message being that those who join them will be just as heroic as the mujahidun of the early days of Islam. By underscoring the 'romantic' aspects of jihad, the IS hopes to attract a certain type of individual susceptible to such propaganda.

The *Dabiq* quotation above is a powerful and effective message which quite possibly will facilitate recruitment efforts. Its propaganda strives to establish a link to the early days of Islam when Muslims were persecuted. This is an approach that plays on the emotions of some modern Muslims who will easily identify with the plight of early Muslims partly based upon history, perceived grievances and their own experience as outsiders. With the reference to knights, IS propagandists reveal their media acumen by casting their net as widely as possible in their proselytizing campaigns. The example above is an obvious effort to appeal to Muslims in Western/Christian societies who feel alienated or simply bored and are looking for an 'adventurous' or 'meaningful' mission in life. The target audience this time is individuals who might not be inclined to subject IS arguments to scrutiny before embracing the 'Caliphate's' ideology. These individuals constitute a very dangerous category of IS followers due to their lack of interest in reason and analysis of the IS ideology. Another example of the 'romantic' approach to recruitment is highlighting the life of certain 'martyrs', mujahidun killed in action, on the pages of *Dabiq*.[13] The possibility of gaining '15 minutes of fame' (half a page or a page in *Dabiq*) and a laudatory epitaph could attract individuals who wish to leave some kind of legacy or simply enjoy a brief moment of previously not experienced recognition or attention. Some IS propaganda is clearly directed at a young audience. An example is a video in which a former German rapper engaged in a snowball fight says 'You can live here and enjoy yourself; I invite you to [join the] jihad'.[14] This is an attempt to show a younger generation that life in the 'Caliphate' does not exclude having fun. The danger of these messages is that, if not skillfully countered, IS propaganda that 'romanticizes' life as a mujahid will find a loyal audience.

Democracy, nationalism and socialism

The vast majority of articles in *Dabiq* are contributed by men, a conclusion substantiated by the fact that the magazine highlights articles contributed by women under the heading 'From Our Sisters'. Articles penned by women are thus considered unusual or special, or it would not be necessary to stress the author's gender. One such article will be analyzed here. Not surprisingly, it follows the IS ideological line, condemning, inter alia, nationalism, democracy and socialism. All of these are ideas which purportedly were not conveyed to man by God, which is why they are '*kufri*' (infidel) goals. To illustrate how serious a fallacy they are, the author has issued a stark warning that they lead straight to Hell in the Hereafter.[15] The warning is presumably substantiated by reference to a Quranic verse – 'And He [God] shares not His legislation with anyone'.[16] 'Hukm', the Arabic word here rendered into English as 'legislation', also means 'rule'. It is quite possible that the author has selected a translation of the Quran which fits the purpose of her article – to condemn democracy. Legislation is one of the most important tasks that a parliament has. Furthermore, the parliament as an institution is a reflection of a democratic system of government. Therefore, when God rejects the idea of sharing legislative power with anyone, the implication is that the Lord rejects democracy. This appears to be evidence in support of the author's dismissal of a democratic system of government. However, upon further examination, the author's blanket rejection of nationalism, democracy and socialism is problematic.

According to both Sunni and Shi'i interpretations of Islam, democratic elements were part of the early days of the religion.[17] One example is Abu Bakr, the first successor to the Prophet Muhammad, who was actually elected caliph in the Saqifa[18] after what might be described as a process somewhat similar to democratic elections, including a public, albeit tumultuous, debate.[19] Four candidates emerged during this debate. Sunni and Shi'i 'ulama alike more or less agree upon what happened in the Saqifa, but interpret this event in radically different ways. The accounts of the events at the Saqifa are quite problematic for Salafists and Islamic extremists. Their argument that Muslims need to return to the 'true' Islam of the early generations of believers appeals to some Muslims, though they might not necessarily agree with IS means of attaining this goal. The 'Caliphate's' condemnation of 'modern' phenomena such as democracy, however, to a certain extent contradicts the history of early Islam, which is the ideal that Da'ish holds up to Muslims. The corollary of the IS's argument is that its ideologues have to condemn the way the first caliph was elected as well. Sunni Salafists could, of course, contend that Abu Bakr was anointed as the Prophet's successor by Muhammad himself, but there is really no hard evidence to substantiate this argument. Furthermore, it is contradicted by Shi'i 'ulama. What happened in the Saqifa, however, is described both in Sunni and Shi'i sources, although they disagree about the interpretation. These accounts confirm the democratic process, which gives the historian more material to work with than the case is if only Sunni or Shi'i sources are considered. What makes the accounts of the events at the Saqifa useful to the researcher is the fact that Shi'i religious scholars do not deny what happened but condemn the event as usurpation of 'Ali's mandate to succeed the Prophet as caliph.[20]

Another problematic statement in the article under discussion is its condemnation of nationalism. Again, there are similarities between extreme nationalism and Islamic extremism despite the 'secular' nature of the former and 'religious' nature of the latter. The critical reader will not be deceived by superficial labels used to distinguish between ideologies which do have certain concepts in common. One example is the elevation of one's own group, nation, ideology or religion above all other groups, nations, ideologies or religions, with the concomitant discrimination against and intolerance displayed toward outsiders, dissidents and minorities.[21] The superficial difference between an extreme secular ideology and a radical minority interpretation of a religion cannot obfuscate the clear similarities between the two. The strength of the IS propaganda, namely that IS extremism is enjoined by God, whereas extreme nationalism was invented by man, is at the same time its greatest weakness since it is possible to establish a number of similarities between the two ideologies as noted above. The question that arises in the mind of the reader is 'Why are the consequences of something of divine origin and something of human origin so similar?' The premise of the IS argument is what is of divine origin is by definition different from what originates in the human mind, a fact which makes replacing God's law with human law an unpardonable transgression.[22] The question is dangerous since the answer could be regarded as an example of *shirk*, elevating the non-divine to divine status, something that is anathema to every true Muslim, which explains the emphasis on *tawhid* (oneness of God) in IS ideology. A critical analysis of this particular example of the 'Caliphate's' propaganda has convincingly demonstrated the validity of the argument advanced by the present author that propaganda is perceived as a formidable weapon by totalitarian leaders, whereas it, in reality, frequently constitutes a double-edged sword which, at times, has dire consequences for the credibility and legitimacy of systems built on extreme coercion.

Finally, the author's condemnation of socialism reflects her unfamiliarity with certain similarities between socialism and Islam. Both embrace the concepts of social justice, compassion for – or in socialism at least an interest in improving the economic situation of – the downtrodden and redistribution of wealth. It can be argued, therefore, that the duty of Muslims to transfer some of their wealth to the less fortunate in society entails all three aforementioned concepts. The significance of this duty is reflected in the fact that *zakat* (charitable tax) constitutes one of the five pillars of Islam. It is obvious from the Quran that God cares for the poor, orphans and widows.[23] A general rejection of socialism is thus problematic without identifying exactly what aspects of this ideology contradict Islam.

Criticism of rival jihadist groups

Much space in *Dabiq* is devoted to criticism of rival groups and Muslims who fight the IS. Muslims who capture territory from it and replace 'the law of Allah with the law of man'[24] become *kuffar* (unbelievers), that is, forfeit their status as Muslims. An example of a group that the 'Caliphate' has condemned is the Islamic Front, which fought the al-Asad regime in Syria. The Islamic Front's sin consisted of its 'commitment to respect ALL religious sects in Syria...',[25] a position which the IS found anti-Islamic. Another favorite target of IS ideologues was the Jawlani Front;[26] judging by the frequent denunciations of this group, it was the foremost challenger to the authority of the 'Caliphate'. It is interesting to note that, despite the rejection of Western culture and most things Western, the IS on certain occasions resorts to Western culture to get its message across. Using two Arabic words, '*nifaq*' and '*riya*', both of which translate as hypocrisy, to describe the speech of a Jabhat al-Nusra leader, the *Dabiq* contributor denouncing one of the group's leaders finally finds the English word that best describes the leader's speech – 'idiocy'. Incidentally, one of the Jabhat al-Nusra leader's claims that aroused the 'Caliphate's' ire was that he was 'the man most wanted by America'.[27] Incredibly enough, this title gave rise to dispute among mujahidun belonging to rival groups and vying for this honorific title.

Dabiq, in order to build a stronger case against other jihadi groups in the Islamic world, emphasizes the differences between the 'Caliphate' and its rivals. The magazine therefore reports that '[w]hen the parties of deviance in ar-Raqqah plotted against the muhajirun [emigrants] and ansar [supporters]...the [IS] muwwahid mujahidun expelled them...'.[28] The IS argument is that they are the only true Muslims because they

> enforced prayer, collected the zakat...executed the *hudud* [Islamic legal punishment], judged in their courts by what Allah revealed, returned the rights of the oppressed, fought the *kuffar* and apostates, and enforced the *jizyah* [poll tax] upon Ahlul-Kitab [Jews, Christians, and Zoroastrians].[29]

Al-Qaʿida, a competing group, is accused of cooperation with the enemy, as a result of which it is 'no longer pos[ing] a threat toward the safety and security of the crusader homeland'.[30] Furthermore, Al-Qaʿida in Yemen allegedly passed control to a civilian council after the capture of the city Al-Mukalla.[31] By acting this way, Al-Qaʿida is, from an IS perspective, guilty of replacing God's law with manmade law and therefore disqualified from representing true Islam. Equally serious is the accusation that Al-Qaʿida 'refrain[s] from the strict application of Shariʿah, when faced with local resistance'.[32] Interestingly enough, IS ideologues hold Osama Bin Laden in high esteem, but denounce his successor Aiman al-Zawahiri, who allegedly opposes 'the policies of the mujahid Shaykh Usama Ibn Ladin'.[33] The Taliban does not fare better in IS propaganda and is grouped together with al-Zawahiri, both accused of 'submit[ting] fearfully to American policies'.[34]

It is obvious from *Dabiq* articles that the 'Caliphate' leaders do not wish to criticize Bin Laden's legacy. After all, he is the mujahid who took responsibility for the 9/11 attacks in the United States, something that the IS has not been able to replicate. By separating Bin Laden from his successor, al-Zawahiri, however, Daʿish propagandists weaken their case since they accuse the Taliban and al-Zawahiri of refusing to fight the Americans out of fear. This is a problematic accusation since it passes over in silence the close ties between Osama Bin Laden and the Taliban, an inconsistency which is difficult for the 'Caliphate' to address, but which *Dabiq* attempts to conceal by taunting al-Zawahiri, calling him 'a leader with no real authority'.[35] This does not, however, strengthen the IS's case because of its propagandists' attempt to conceal one inconsistency by diverting the reader's attention with a second inconsistency. If al-Zawahiri were 'a leader with no real authority', *Dabiq* would not target him with so much criticism. The condemnation of rival terrorist groups suggests that Daʿish regards them as a serious threat to the uncontested leadership which it strives for. The denigration and outmaneuvering of competitors is part and parcel of IS efforts to create a global and united jihadi front under its leadership.

Relations with Islamic sects and other religions

The 'Caliphate's' relations with other religions and Islamic sects are extremely contentious. The IS proudly publicizes attacks on churches and other houses of worship, including Shi'i mosques and Sufi shrines.[36] This is in line with the Da'ish objective of 'making the religion of Allah triumphant over all other religions, and...continu[ing] to fight the people of deviation and misguidance until we die trying to make the religion triumphant'.[37] The statement is undoubtedly intended to demonstrate the single-mindedness and unwavering commitment of the mujahidun to their religion, namely to fight until death for the cause of Allah. The quotation reflects the IS ideologues' rejection of 'free choice', as discussed above, and their argument that there is no alternative to 'true' Islam, just as falsehood is no real alternative to truth. There is no direct reference to physical violence or war in the quotation under discussion, but in light of the 'Caliphate's' aggressive operations against other religions and what it perceives as un-Islamic symbols,[38] such as the removal of crosses from churches, destruction of Sufi tombs and the murder of Yazidi men and sexual enslavement of Yazidi women, violence and coercion are integral parts of IS policies toward religious minorities or majorities as in the case of the Shi'is of Iraq. Based on this record, there can be little doubt that the IS interprets the word 'fight' in a physical sense. It is possible that some Muslims who do not make an effort to analyze the message that the 'Caliphate' sends to all believers actually find the above quotation appealing. Its exclusive focus on a temporal approach to religion is, however, problematic since there is no mention of the spiritual aspects of Islam.

As a consequence of the IS policy toward other religions and Islamic sects, 'Caliphate' ideologues argue that Da'ish is on a mission to destroy *shirk* (polytheism). This argument serves as a justification for IS mujahidun destroying or removing crosses from churches and belfries.[39] A photo of an IS mujahid destroying a cross on a belfry in Mosul explains this act with the following text: 'Destroying a symbol of *shirk* in the city of Mosul'.[40] According to this text, Christianity is considered *shirk* by the IS. This view is difficult to reconcile with the traditional *dhimmi* (protected) status of Christians residing in IS. A possible justification for the IS act is the Christian concept of Trinity and the Christian argument that Jesus is God's son, which could be interpreted by 'Caliphate' ideologues as *shirk*. This interpretation is, however, problematic since there is no evidence that Christians *equate* Jesus with God (which would undoubtedly be tantamount to *shirk*), a fact which undermines the IS argument. Furthermore, the cross in and of itself is not a symbol of *shirk* either, for the same reason as arguing that Jesus is God's son is not *shirk*, namely that the cross is not equated with God.

The importance of removing certain anti-Islamic symbols is also evident in IS references to history. The removal of border markers delineating the Iraqi-Syrian border was hailed as a great achievement by the IS[41] and a giant step toward re-establishing a borderless 'Caliphate' and eliminating the Western legacy in the Middle East in the form of artificial borders and states created by the Europeans, following the Great War. This valuable photo opportunity was also exploited to emphasize the difference between the 'Caliphate' and its rivals, the Taliban, who have only proclaimed an emirate confined within the borders of Afghanistan.[42] For the first time since the demise of the Ottoman Caliphate in 1924, a supranational 'caliphate' has been established. This symbolic event helps create an emotional link with the original Islamic community of the seventh century. Furthermore, the presence of the 'Caliphate's' official spokesman, Abu Muhammad al-'Adnani underscores the symbolic importance of this event and a photo in *Lo Stato Islamico*[43] depicting the removal of border markers sends a clear message to all Muslims, namely, that the Western order imposed on the Islamic world is quickly unraveling. Also, in the context of this initiative, the IS proudly announced that the 'Caliphate' was larger than many modern states, at the same time evoking the legacy of the great Umayyad and Abbasid Caliphates.[44] The comparison with these empires is somewhat problematic because quite a few caliphs were not exactly paragons of Islamic piety and some mere figureheads controlled by mercenary armies. This is definitely not the image of itself that the IS wants to convey to the world and the comparison is therefore somewhat unfortunate since it detracts from the positive effect already created with the initial two parts of the publicity stunt discussed above. Generally speaking, however, *Dabiq* propagandists clearly recognized the value of this event, which is why they seized the opportunity to exploit it. This is an excellent example of a situation in which *Dabiq* excels in media acumen.

In view of IS hatred of the West, the 'Caliphate's' use of '*kufri*' (infidel) know-how, equipment and resources is difficult to reconcile with the 'purist' Islamic arguments of the 'Caliphate'. If Allah is almighty and, as Da'ish contends, supports their campaign and insures their success, why rely on non-Islamic means to achieve their Islamic goals? In IS parlance, this could be labeled as tantamount to disbelief. Likewise, one could argue that the Prophet relied on God, the Islamic community and the skills of the Muslims when fighting the polytheists in Mecca and elsewhere in the Arabian Peninsula. Utilizing *kufri* resources and know-how could therefore be interpreted as not relying on God but unbelievers in establishing God's religion on earth. Since IS propaganda vehemently rejects any cooperation whatsoever with its enemies, this is, in the mind of the critical reader, a problematic approach, as it could be interpreted as 'impure' and non-Islamic. The 'Caliphate' could, with somewhat greater success, argue that improvised explosive devices and suicide vests are legitimate weapons since they themselves actually manufacture them, though they did not invent these weapons, but those that they criticize did, which remains problematic from a 'purist' Islamic perspective.

The IS publicizes the 'crimes' of the enemy, concurrently passing over in silence its own crimes. *Dabiq* provides a long list of reasons for the 'Caliphate's' policy of killing Americans: (1) US support for anti-IS forces in Iraq; (2) US support for anti-IS forces in Syria; (3) the US has killed women, children and the elderly, and American soldiers have allegedly executed families and raped women in Iraq; (4) the 'Caliphate's' offer of exchanging James Foley for Muslim prisoners was 'arrogantly ignored'; (5) a failed US rescue attempt in Al-Raqqa (the IS capital); (6) the IS warning to the United States after American airstrikes began that it would execute James Foley was ignored; and (7) US support for Israel.[45] Foley's alleged crime was that he had been 'documenting the wars [in Afghanistan and Iraq] through the crusaders' eyes'.[46] The ultimate responsibility for Foley's execution, however, according to Daʻish, rests with President Obama, who 'refused to release our Muslim brothers and sisters from their prisons'.[47] This long list of alleged American crimes may to some look convincing at first glance. Its weakness is, however, what it does not contain, namely the 'Caliphate's' own crimes, statistics which, if it made the list, would undermine the IS argument of being a safe haven for the world's Muslims. There are strong indications that the primary target is not US and other Western citizens, but other Muslims, and the 'Caliphate's' mujahidun have killed many more Muslims and non-Westerners than Americans and Europeans.[48] A possible conclusion on the part of the critical reader is that the Muslims and non-Westerners who have been killed in great numbers must have been guilty of greater crimes than Americans and other Westerners. For obvious reasons, this issue has not been clearly addressed in IS publications – it would not be conducive to creating a positive image for the 'Caliphate', if Muslims were its main target. The IS response to such accusations would, most likely, be that those killed are not real Muslims but 'apostates' since the majority disagrees with Daʻish's official line.

Fears and psychological warfare

Despite its preoccupation with the 'Caliphate's' invincibility, a consequence of 'divine' support, *Dabiq* unintentionally gives the reader clues as to what the IS fears. These fears are revealed by the efforts to respond to enemy propaganda. The type of enemy propaganda discussed in *Dabiq* also tells the readership what kind of information manipulation Daʻish leaders believe works. The 'Caliphate' clearly does not want people (at least not Muslims in the Middle East) to believe that IS mujahidun 'love killing and slaughter and that they kill people on suspicions'.[49] The enemy propaganda 'even claimed that they would cut off the fingers of those who smoked'.[50] So, how does the IS counter such propaganda? For instance, by recounting 'touching' events: 'Once a Muslim woman came out to us with her children and requested us to kill her and not to take her as a slave!'[51] The IS mujahidun gave her bread and aid and 'clarified things to her'. She returned after a few days and had this to say: 'By Allah, I did not see anything but good from them and what they have brought forth for the people of the [Palestinian Yarmouk] camp [in Damascus] within days hasn't been provided to us by factions over years!'[52] This shows the reader what kind of counter-propaganda the IS thinks works. Furthermore, as a result of their focus on IS 'good deeds', *Dabiq* propagandists, most likely inadvertently, provide an important piece of information to students of the organization, namely the impression among some Muslim women that they will be enslaved by IS mujahidun. One can conclude from the story that the woman is a Sunni Muslim since she would have been referred to as an apostate had she been a Shi'i Muslim. In summary, IS counterpropaganda reveals what Da'ish does not want Muslims to believe, obviously a weakness which can be exploited by 'Caliphate' critics.

The 'Caliphate's ideologues clearly recognize that propaganda is a type of warfare in which success is as important as on the battlefield. This recognition enables them to discern the weaknesses of the enemy.[53] The IS has realized that the enemy's manipulation of information can be studied and presumably exploited against the enemy himself in the war of words between the 'Caliphate', the West and everyone else whom Da'ish considers an adversary. An example of this realization, which the IS appears to have put to better use than its American foe, is the phrase to 'degrade and defeat', which was frequently repeated by US officials during operations against the 'Caliphate'. *Dabiq* understood the irony of using the same language as its American adversary: 'The result...will see the [international] crusader coalition - in America's words - degraded and ultimately defeated'.[54] Using the American expression in the 'Caliphate's' own propaganda context added a dimension to the original expression by taunting the US-led coalition. This subtlety was certainly not lost on Muslims who sympathize with the IS or are critical of American foreign policy.

Billboards were a more traditional form of propaganda commonly used in cities and towns in the IS to influence its citizens to embrace the official line. The demonization of the enemy constituted a prominent theme in such street advertisement. One example is a billboard with the following text: 'Al-hamla al-salibiyya 'ala'l-Islam', which translates as 'the crusader campaign against Islam'.[55] To make the message even more powerful and convincing, the artist had written the words inside a noose of a blood-drenched rope. In its propaganda, the 'Caliphate' sees the world in black and white only. Its propaganda shows, with no doubt left in the mind of the reader or observer, that it believes it is involved in an existential and apocalyptic struggle and therefore it can afford no fence sitters. There is a good chance that some Muslims will be affected by this type of propaganda.

Clash of religions

A problem for Western powers is that nineteenth- and twentieth-century history provides ample evidence to substantiate some IS claims, but it weakens the case the 'Caliphate' is attempting to make to cloak this evidence in religious language, though the religious focus is understandable, since it is viewed as more effective propaganda by Da'ish leaders. The purpose is to allow the emotions aroused by the propaganda to exclude the possibility of embarrassing questions on the part of the target group such as 'why does the "Caliphate" kill Muslims?' *Dabiq*, as has been discussed above, is full of photos of dead Muslims. The 'Caliphate's' ideologues have 'resolved' this problem by redefining Islam in accordance with their black-and-white worldview. Those who do not agree with their interpretation of Islam in every aspect are not considered 'true' Muslims and should therefore, for their own good, be coerced to follow the 'correct' path enjoined by God. This is, however, a problematic position since it leaves an overwhelming majority of believers outside the religious 'pale' of the IS.

Nevertheless, IS propagandists believe that they can 'convert' hesitant Muslims to their cause because some of their less violent goals most likely appeal to certain Muslims who might be persuaded to join Daʻish and fill non-military positions. Despite the ubiquitous presence of domestic and global 'Caliphate' propaganda, most Muslims outside the IS, and, at least part of the population in the IS itself, have not embraced its extremist ideology. This is an easily substantiated claim for the simple reason that relatively few Muslims emulate the behavior of IS zealots, or Daʻish would have tens of millions of mujahidun under its command.[56]

Another factor that is problematic when shaping the conflict with the West in religious terms is that recent conflicts between Western countries and countries in the Middle East have not been religious conflicts, but conflicts with Middle Eastern dictators, who were not exactly paragons of Islamic piety, such as Saddam Husain and Muʻammar al-Qadhdhafi. Another example of a non-religious conflict is the Suez War of 1956, the rationale for which was to reestablish Western financial control over and military presence in Egypt. Furthermore, the Egyptian president at the time, Gamal Abd al-Nasir, was an Arab socialist and nationalist whom France, Great Britain and Israel attempted to unseat. Also, he had a record of incarcerating members of the Muslim Brotherhood. Some Muslims will quite possibly argue that the American invasion of Afghanistan in 2001 was tantamount to a war against Islam since the Afghan regime at the time was Islamic. Also, the Taliban did not attack the United States, a fact which appears to strengthen the 'clash-of-religions' argument. However, Western apologists will contend that the US-led coalition waged war against an individual, Osama Bin Laden, and his extremist ideology and not against Islam. It can thus be concluded that there is ample evidence that contradicts the IS's discourse of anti-Islamic conflicts with the West. Despite the availability of such evidence, 'Caliphate' propagandists are convinced that playing the 'Islamic card' is an effective approach since it exploits Muslim emotions and loyalties, thereby reaching a global Islamic community instead of a more limited audience, susceptible to 'secular' arguments.

Domestic dissent

The argument that part of the 'Caliphate's' population had not been completely won over to the IS's ideology appears to be confirmed by messages on certain billboards in IS-controlled areas. One billboard depicts a mujahid standing guard with aircraft flying behind him. The text says 'sanantasiru raghma 'ala al-tahaluf al-'alamiyy', that is, 'we will triumph despite the worldwide alliance'.[57] It is obvious from this message that the IS is under pressure, that coalition airstrikes have somewhat of a demoralizing effect and that some citizens doubt the benefits of certain IS policies. Therefore, Da'ish deems it prudent to preempt defeatism and boost morale with such slogans. Another photo in the IS publication displays an old advertisement for tobacco being removed and replaced, and a new message posted to a billboard saying "tadkhin samm qatil", that is, 'smoking is a deadly poison'.[58] This message suggests that some citizens find it difficult to discard old habits even at the risk of being punished for non-compliance. Other billboards and murals carry special messages for women such as 'sirru jamaliki iltizamuki bishar'i llahi, hijabuki al-shar'i', that is, 'The secret of your beauty is your obligation [to follow] God's law, your law-prescribed hijab'.[59] Other similar messages are 'ihtishami sirru jamali', which translates as 'my modesty is the secret of my beauty',[60] and 'al-hijab faridha, ka al-salat', that is 'like prayer, [wearing] the hijab is a duty'.[61] The above messages suggest that not all women in the 'Caliphate' observed the correct dress code and that some other citizens found it hard to accept Da'ish's version of the shari'a. IS ideologues therefore had to remind them of their duties.

Reports of coup attempts and division within the IS suggest that not all leaders and fighters believed in or agreed with official propaganda. According to an Arabic-language newspaper, a group of leading IS officials conspired in the summer of 2015 to remove al-Baghdadi from power by planting improvised explosive devices on a rural road south of the IS capital Al-Raqqa that al-Baghdadi would be traveling on sometime between 10 and 13 June 2015. The conspirators were, however, betrayed, as a result of which 13 leaders were executed. Some of these leaders were members of the General Military Council. The botched coup attempt was reportedly a result of serious disagreement over military operations and the targeting of jihadist groups opposed to the 'Caliphate'. Furthermore, according to the newspaper, some IS officials had questioned al-Baghdadi's qualifications to lead the IS, arguing that Syrians were more entitled to the 'Caliphate' than Iraqis.[62] Another report, published on a Russian-language website two months after the first one, claimed that 18 field commanders out of a total of 122 mujahidun accused of attempting to topple al-Baghdadi were executed in Mosul on 31 August 2015. The coup would have been carried out on the previous day, but was betrayed by arrested mujahidun.[63] The above conspiracies indubitably constituted a serious concern for the IS leadership, even if they did not indicate disagreement over ideology.

If correct, the reports referred to above reveal crucial information about sentiments in leading IS circles. The two different dates and geographic locations of the conspiracies are clear indications that these are two separate events and not conflicting accounts of one incident. This information is important since it reveals the existence of sharp tensions within the IS. This impression is strengthened by the proximity in time between the two events. The fact that the IS leadership publicized the first incident by displaying the heads of the executed conspirators[64] also provides important information because it tells the reader that the 'Caliphate' took the attempt seriously and that the fate of those involved in the first conspiracy did not deter other leaders and fighters from planning a second attempt to remove al-Baghdadi from power. Also, the information that some IS leaders questioned the 'Caliph's' military strategy and the legitimacy of his rule partly because of his Iraqi origin testify to the existence of nationalist sentiments in IS ranks. This circumstance contradicts the official discourse, which emphasizes unity and rejects distinctions based on nationality, revealing that nationalism, despite the constant reference to Islam, is a factor that students of multiethnic Islamic terrorist organizations need to devote attention to. Furthermore, the first source reported that the executed leaders were from the Maghreb, Syria, Yemen and Kuwait in addition to a Chechen and a Kurd. This information is important since it suggests that the opposition to al-Baghdadi's rule was not exclusively nationalist, but at the same time transnational. Also, the fact that nationalism appears to have figured as a factor in the criticism of al-Baghdadi demonstrates that the religious qualifications of the 'Caliph', touted by IS propagandists, as discussed earlier in this chapter, are not considered an exclusive criterion for whether an individual is qualified to occupy the highest position in the IS. A final observation regarding the first conspiracy is that there is no reference to Iraqi conspirators, which could indicate that Iraqis constituted al-Baghdadi's primary power base. The second incident reported is a possible confirmation of this assumption since more people were executed in Mosul, which would have less serious consequences for the 'Caliph' in an area where he enjoys strong local Iraqi support and therefore could run a lesser risk when eliminating opponents than in a region where Iraqis are not in the majority.

Conclusion

The IS went to great lengths to convince Muslims of its exclusive right to speak for the umma (Islamic community). This claim reveals that IS leaders realized that legitimacy is a crucial and contested issue, which deserves their full attention. In order to dispel any doubts regarding legitimacy issues, the 'Caliphate' made consistent efforts convincingly to establish that its interpretation of the Quran is in complete accord with the true and original word of God and the early generations' practice of Islam. The preferred method of doing this is to exploit short Quranic passages which appear to confirm IS positions if taken out of context, but not necessarily so if the whole context of a sura is considered. A second approach to establishing legitimacy adopted by the IS is to emphasize the 'Caliph's' religious qualifications which make him fit for the leadership role. A third method employed by IS propagandists to convince Muslims of the 'Caliphate's' legitimacy is to heap praise on the work of the selfless 'caliphal' administration and the mujahidun.

Daʿish leaders clearly understood the value of emotive argumentation, symbolic acts and counterpropaganda, all of which constitute integral parts of the IS discourse. 'Logical' argumentation at times needs to be complemented by words which produce an emotional response on the part of the audience. The purpose is to reach and enthuse Muslims who might not be convinced by 'logic' or simply do not possess the patience or skills to analyze IS propaganda. The chapters devoted to Nazi manipulation of information in this study attest to how effective an approach this can be when combined with other forms of suasion. Another part of the 'Caliphate's' propaganda efforts focuses on symbols and symbolic acts. The IS deemed it beneficial to its cause to remove or destroy Christian, Shiʿi and Sufi symbols, tombs and shrines. The reasoning behind this intolerance was to extirpate anything in IS-controlled territory which could be perceived as a challenge or an alternative to the 'Caliphate's' authority. If a symbol was removed or destroyed, it suggested total control, which is the impression that Daʿish wished to create. Furthermore, such an initiative could be touted as an act of devotion in line with the official policy of purifying Dar al-Islam (territory controlled by Islam) of non-Islamic influences. The act of removing Christian symbols has a political aspect to it as well. In Daʿish propaganda, the Christian faith is linked to 'Crusader' efforts to establish military, economic and cultural control over Dar al-Islam. In this context, the public removal of past symbols of European imperialism assumes connotations, the value of which can hardly be overestimated: the 'Caliphate' has been proclaimed in order to eliminate the humiliating past and restore the glory and power of Islam. A similar argument in reference to the 'humiliation' of 1918 was advanced in National Socialist propaganda.

IS leaders are firm believers in the effectiveness of counterpropaganda and brutal suppression of any dissent. The extremely negative news coverage in Western media of the oppressive IS treatment of Muslims and non-Muslims alike made counterpropaganda a crucial operation to 'rectify' the poor image of the 'Caliphate' and prevent Muslims in the West from embracing this image. Sometimes, this form of propaganda was used to taunt US efforts to fight Daʿish by ridiculing American threats and using American slogans. As for dissent, it existed despite the very serious consequences of disobeying IS's strict rules for social activity. Interestingly enough, dissent existed both at the grassroots and the highest level in the 'Caliphate' hierarchy. Reports of summary executions of commanders who had disagreed with al-Baghdadi regarding the conduct of military operations and even conspired to remove him from power constitute evidence that his authority, despite efforts of official propaganda, was not uncontested.

The examination in the previous and present chapter of IS propaganda has revealed its strengths and weaknesses. One problem with propaganda in a totalitarian system is to verify the extent of its effectiveness. It is in the nature of the system that opinion polls are quite possibly not reliable since respondents will face serious consequences if they express dissent to the official line. As a consequence, dictators do not know what their citizens really think, a fact which could undermine official propaganda. It could be argued that a dictator is not interested in what his citizens believe, as a corollary of his coercive power, and that the only thing of interest to him is to what degree 'subjects' comply with policies. This attitude, it has been argued in the present chapter, reflects the double-edged-ness of the sword of propaganda. From this, one can draw the conclusion that totalitarian systems prioritize form over content, which potentially reduces the effectiveness of propaganda as a tool to insure compliance. The IS, despite its condemnation of *dunya* (concepts and phenomena reflective of the temporal world) and promotion of spiritual values as a reflection of God's law, constituted a not necessarily realized conundrum for IS propagandists since the 'Caliphate' in reality undermined its own propaganda with its contradictory overwhelming focus on form at the expense of content. The critical examination of propaganda in the 'Caliphate' has substantiated this argument. This and the previous chapter have used historical, contextual, linguistic, rhetorical and logical analysis to explain the strengths and weaknesses of IS propaganda. The latter constitute a serious challenge to Da'ish's legitimacy and authority, a fact which can be exploited by Muslims and non-Muslims who oppose the totalitarian ideology of the IS.

Notes

1 *Dabiq*, Issue 1 (Jun., Jul., 2014), p. 27.
2 The Qur'an, 3:67.
3 Ibid., 4:125, 163.
4 Ibid., 2:130; *Dabiq*, Issue 1, p. 27.
5 *Dabiq*, Issue 1, p. 27.
6 Hisham al-Hashimi, *'Alam da'ish: min al-nash'a ila i'lan al-khilafa* [The World of Da'ish: From Rise to Proclamation of the Caliphate] (London: Dar Alhikma Publishing and Distribution, 2015), p. 283.
7 'Lo Stato Islamico, una realtà che ti vorrebbe comunicare', p. 54, *ISSU*. Accessed 3 January 2016. http://issuu.com/031041/docs/lo_stato_islamico_una_realt_che_.
8 *Dabiq*, Issue 1, p. 35.
9 Ibid.
10 The Qur'an, 8:39; *Dabiq*, Issue 1, p. 35. The term *fitna* has several different meanings in Arabic – unbelief, enticement and civil strife.
11 *Dabiq*, Issue 10 (Jul., 2015), p. 5.
12 Ibid., pp. 26, 29.
13 Ibid., pp. 40–41.
14 'Hier hat man Spass', *Focus*, 14 January 2015. Accessed 3 January 2016, http://www.focus.de/politik/ausland/islamischer-staat/wir-kommen-wie-der-islamische-staat-das-netz-zum-virtuellen-schlachtfeld-macht_id_4404223.html.
15 *Dabiq*, No. 10, p. 42.
16 The Qur'an, 18:26; *Dabiq*, Issue 10, p. 43.
17 Answering-Ansar.org, *Saqifa: The Debacle of Islamic Government*. Accessed 29 January 2016. https://goaloflife.files.wordpress.com/2011/08/saqifa.pdf.

Islamic State legitimacy 219

18 An assembly hall in Medina.
19 Wilferd Madelung, *The Succession to Muhammad: A Study of the Early Caliphate* (Cambridge, UK: Cambridge University Press, 1997), p. 31.
20 Ibid., p. 141.
21 See Adolf Hitler, *Mein Kampf* (Munich: Fritz Eher Nachfolger, 1943) and *Dabiq*, Issue 1–10.
22 *Dabiq*, Issue 10, pp. 50, 53.
23 The Qur'an, 2:83.
24 *Dabiq*, Issue 10, pp. 50, 53.
25 Ibid., Issue 2 (Jun., Jul., 2014), p. 25.
26 The Al-Qa'ida affiliate in Syria Jabhat al-Nusra, later renamed Hay'at Tahrir al-Sham.
27 *Dabiq*, Issue 2, p. 25.
28 Ibid., No. 10, p. 51. *Dabiq* has resorted to powerful symbolical language in its criticism of other mujahidun. The terms *'muhajirun'* and *'ansar'* refer to the first Muslims who emigrated from Mecca to Medina and converts in Medina who supported the Prophet Muhammad. The inference is that modern emigrants to and supporters of the Islamic State play a role similar in importance to that of early Muslims in defending Islam. The term *'muwahhid'* signifies those who emphasize the oneness of God. The "Caliphate" here draws a clear distinction between its supporters and those of other groups, who are presumably not true *muwahhidun*, since they disagree with IS ideology.
29 Ibid. *Hudud* are the boundaries for human behavior determined by God. This term is used for crimes against God, *inter alia*, theft, illicit sexual relations, imbibing intoxicants and apostasy. Some *hudud* crimes carry the death penalty, *Oxford Islamic Studies Online*. Accessed 25 January 2016. http://www.oxfordislamicstudies.com/article/opr/t125/e757. On an additional note, it is not surprising that the IS emphasizes the importance of *hudud*. *Hadd* (the singular form of *hudud*) also signifies the cutting edge of a knife or sword, which are the tools preferred by the IS when carrying out the death penalty.
30 *Dabiq*, Issue 10, p. 51.
31 Ibid., p. 67.
32 Ibid.
33 Ibid.
34 Ibid.
35 Ibid., p. 74.
36 Ibid., Issue 2, pp. 14–17; Issue 9 (May, Jun., 2015), p. 41.
37 Ibid., Issue 2, p. 11.
38 Ibid., Issue 2, pp. 14–17; Issue 9, p. 41.
39 Ibid., Issue 10, p. 59.
40 Ibid.
41 Ibid. Issue 1, p. 13.
42 Antonio Elorza, 'La fuerza del Islam', *El Pais*, 10 June 2015, accessed 25 June 2015, http://elpais.com/elpais/2015/06/08/opinion/1433780384_967380.html.
43 'Lo Stato Islamico', 55, *ISSUU*, accessed 3 January 2016, http://issuu.com/031041/docs/lo_stato_islamico_una_realt_che_.
44 *Dabiq*, Issue 1, p. 40.
45 Ibid., Issue 3 (Jul., Aug., 2014), pp. 3–4.
46 Ibid., p. 37.
47 Ibid.
48 'Paris attacks: Isis responsible for more Muslim deaths than westerners', *The Independent*, 17 November 2015, accessed 24 January 2016. http://www.independent.co.uk/news/world/europe/paris-attacks-isis-responsible-for-more-muslim-victims-than-western-deaths-a6737326.html; Dean Obeidallah, 'Who's Killing

Muslims?' *CNN*, 15 January 2015, accessed 24 January 2016, http://www.cnn.com/2015/01/15/opinion/obeidallah-al-qaeda-hypocrisy/.
49 *Dabiq*, Issue 9, p. 70.
50 Ibid.
51 Ibid.
52 Ibid.
53 Ibid.
54 Ibid., Issue 10, p. 34.
55 'Lo Stato Islamico', *ISSUU*, p. 38.
56 According to US intelligence estimates, most of the more than 10,000 mujahidun who traveled to Syria in 2015 joined the IS, 'Inside the Surreal World of the Islamic State's Propaganda Machine', *The Washington Post*, 20 November 2015, accessed 3 January 2016, https://washingtonpost.com/world/national-security/inside-the-islamic-states-propaganda.
57 'Lo Stato Islamico', *ISSUU*, p. 37.
58 Ibid., pp. 16, 35.
59 Ibid., p. 36.
60 Ibid.
61 Ibid.
62 *Al-'Arabi al-Jadid*. 'Muhawalatu inqilabi 'ala al-baghdadi tantahi bi tasfiyati 13 qiyadan li-da'ish'. 2 July 2015, Accessed 2 February 2016. http://www.alaraby.co.uk/politics/2015/7/2/%D9%85%D8%AD%D8%A7%D9%88%D9%84%D8%A9-%D8%A7%D9%86%D9%82%D9%84%D8%A7%D8%A8-%D8%B9%D9%84%D9%89-%D8%A7%D9%84%D8%A8%D8%BA%D8%AF%D8%A7%D8%AF%D9%8A-%D8%AA%D9%86%D8%AA%D9%87%D9%8A-%D8%A8%D8%AA%D8%B5%D9%81%D9%8A%D8%A9-13-%D9%82%D9%8A%D8%A7%D8%AF%D9%8A%D8%A7-%D9%84%D9%80-%D8%AF%D8%A7%D8%B9%D8%B4.
63 '*Razbrod i raskol v Islamskom gosudarstve*', *Politus.ru*, 8 September 2015, accessed 7 January 2016, http://politus.ru/v-mire/981-razbrod-i-raskol-v-islamskom-gosudarstve.html. Also, see the following Czech article, '*Rozkol v Islámském státě*', *NWOO.ORG*, accessed 7 January 2016, http://www.nwoo.org/2015/09/10/rozkol-v-islamskem-state/.
64 *Al-'Arabi al-Jadid*. 'Muhawalatu inqilabi 'ala al-baghdadi tantahi bi tasfiyati 13 qiyadan li-da'ish'.

Bibliography

Answering-Ansar.org.
Al-'Arabi al-Jadid. 2 July 2015. 'Muhawalatu inqilabi 'ala al-baghdadi tantahi bi tasfiyati 13 qiyadan li-da'ish' [Coup attempt against al-Baghdadi ends with execution of 13 Da'ish leaders]. http://www.alaraby.co.uk/politics/2015/7/2/%D9%85%D8%AD%D8%A7%D9%88%D9%84%D8%A9-%D8%A7%D9%86%D9%82%D9%84%D8%A7%D8%A8-%D8%B9%D9%84%D9%89-%D8%A7%D9%84%D8%A8%D8%BA%D8%AF%D8%A7%D8%AF%D9%8A-%D8%AA%D9%86%D8%AA%D9%87%D9%8A-%D8%A8%D8%AA%D8%B5%D9%81%D9%8A%D8%A9-13-%D9%82%D9%8A%D8%A7%D8%AF%D9%8A%D8%A7-%D9%84%D9%80-%D8%AF%D8%A7%D8%B9%D8%B4.
Dabiq.
El Pais (Madrid).
Elorza, Antonio. 'La fuerza del Islam' [The Power of Islam], *El Pais*, 10 June 2015. Accessed 25 June 2015. http://elpais.com/elpais/2015/06/08/opinion/1433780384_967380.html.

Focus (Berlin).

al-Hashimi, Hisham. *'Alam da'ish: min al-nash'a ila i'lan al-khilafa* [The World of Da'ish: From the Rise to the Proclamation of the Caliphate]. London: Dar Al-hikma Publishing and Distribution, 2015.

Hitler, Adolf. *Mein Kampf* [My Struggle]. Munich: Zentralverlag der NSDAP, Frz. Eher Nachf., G.m.b.H., 1943 (first published 1925, Vol. 1 and 1927, Vol. 2).

The Independent (Online).

ISSUU. 'Lo Stato Islamico, una realtà che ti vorrebbe comunicare' [The Islamic State, a Reality That You Would Like To Communicate]. Accessed 3 January 2016. http://issuu.com/031041/docs/lo_stato_islamico_una_realt_che_.

Madelung, Wilferd. *The Succession to Muhammad: A Study of the Early Caliphate.* Cambridge: Cambridge University Press, 1997.

NWOO.ORG. 'Rozkol v Islámském státě'. Accessed 7 January 2016. http://www.nwoo.org/2015/09/10/rozkol-v-islamskem-state/.

Obeidallah, Dean. 'Who's Killing Muslims?' *CNN,* 15 January 2015. Accessed 24 January 2016. http://www.cnn.com/2015/01/15/opinion/obeidallah-al-qaeda-hypocrisy/.

Politus.ru. 8 September 2015. 'Razbrod i raskol v Islamskom gosudarstve' [Disorder and Division in the Islamic State]. Accessed 7 January 2016. http://politus.ru/v-mire/981-razbrod-i-raskol-v-islamskom-gosudarstve.html.

The Qur'an.

The Washington Post (Washington, DC).

11 The eleven fears of Islamic terrorist organizations

An overwhelming majority of works on terrorism are geared toward examining the actions of terrorist individuals and organizations, and the consequences of the fear that their violent acts instill in targeted governments and civilian populations. Much less attention has been devoted to the fears of terrorists themselves despite the fact that such fears exist and are obvious from the works of terrorist ideologues. Most human beings experience fear in certain situations, be these actual or reflected upon as possibilities. The critical reader will perhaps object that this is a very general claim that has not been substantiated by evidence. The response to this criticism is, however, very simple: Any person can ask herself or himself what they fear and most likely find at least one fear. Trepidation can focus on the safety of oneself, loved ones, uncertainty about a country's future in times of war, environmental and natural disasters or even the possibility of the extinction of all life or the death of the planet itself. It is clear from the writings examined in this volume that Islamic extremists focus their attention on God and human beings and do not engage in philosophical speculation about other aspects of life or our cosmic environment. This very limited focus reduces existence to a trichotomy of belief, unbelief and violent struggle to ensure that the actions enjoined upon humans by God will be enforced without exception. This outlook simplifies life to a great extent for those who are not willing to discern nuances, alternatives, exceptions or anomalies, thereby creating a refuge from the 'evils' which otherwise complicate life. Since the apprehensions of non-extremists are reduced by Islamic extremists to one fear only – the fear of God – it could be argued that the militants have rationalized away the above examples of anxiety by contending that human beings should have one concern only to avoid turning death into an unpleasant experience as a consequence of opposition to God's will. By contrast, the mujahid fearful of God can expect ample rewards in the hereafter.[1]

With a mindset such as the one described above, the mujahid may seem like a formidable antagonist, an enemy without an Achilles' heel, impervious to any feeling of fear, but fortunately for those who oppose terrorism extremists do experience fear, albeit a type of fear the nature of which differs from that experienced by ordinary people. Terrorists are human beings and

Fears of Islamic terrorist organizations 223

have their own fears, which at times surface in their own writings. It goes without saying, however, that generally no effort is made to expose these apprehensions to the enemy. This is evidenced by the fact that extremist writings and propaganda emphasize that Islamic terrorists have one fear only – God, which is a powerful cover for any individual anxiety they may experience. Individual and collective fears of Islamic extremists and their organizations deserve the unswerving attention of their potential victims since familiarity with these vulnerabilities will help researchers and analysts determine the mindset of rank and file extremists and their leaders. Furthermore, conversance with extremist thinking and fears will facilitate formulation and adoption of effective policies to counter Islamic extremism in the Middle East and elsewhere. Therefore, this chapter will examine individual and collective fears of Islamic terrorists and their organizations, focusing on the following aspects of such fears: (1) espionage and infiltration; (2) internal division; (3) loss of popular support; (4) fear of democracy; (5) fear of adversity; (6) enemy propaganda; (7) challenges from other extremist groups; (8) loss of revenue; (9) exposure of ideology and methodology as illegitimate; (10) de-radicalization and self de-radicalization. The eleventh fear differs from the other fears since it is a fear to which mujahidun frequently refer and of which they pride themselves – the fear of God. Unlike other things which keep terrorists awake at night, this fear is perceived as a strength, in part, because it strengthens an organization's legitimacy. The importance of the enumerated fears is obvious since any one of them could pose a serious problem to an extremist organization and, in some cases, perhaps even spell the demise of such an entity. The examination in this chapter of the above fears will chiefly be based on primary sources, particularly extremist publications, since such magazines, books and newspapers constitute a treasure trove for the researcher.

Espionage and infiltration

The first fear that will be subjected to scrutiny is espionage/infiltration. One reason for an emphasis on this fear is the publication in 2009 of Abu Yahya al-Libi's (Hasan Qa'id) *Al-Mu'allim fi hukm al-jasus al-muslim* [Guidance on the Ruling of the Muslim Spy]. Al-Libi's book-length effort exhaustively to examine the internal threat of espionage activities targeting extremist organizations is a clear indication of how seriously militant organizations take the possibility of infiltration of agents working for domestic and foreign enemies. The following quote from the work provides the researcher with a wealth of information:

> [This book is dedicated] to those who have died and departed to [meet] their Lord; to those among our superior leaders and their pious soldiers who have been unwavering in their achievement. [This book is dedicated] to the mother whose heart has been torn out in bereavement

[over the loss of a child], to the spouse whose heart has been broken by widowhood, to those whose eyes have become sore from crying over being orphaned, to the captives in the prisons of unjust tyrants, to those who have been harmed by the meanness of spies and the baseness of the soldiers of Satan.[2]

Al-Libi has chosen evocative language instantaneously to capture the reader's attention. His purpose is to provoke empathy with the victims of unjust acts. The reader is induced to experience, on a personal level, the suffering at the hands of the enemy. This approach to the subject speaks volumes of how it is perceived by the author and the organization to which he belongs. Having ensured the reader's attention, the second objective is to convince the reader that spies are the root of all the suffering described in the passage. The third objective is to alert the readership to the danger of agents operating in their midst and how morally corrupt it is to cooperate with the enemy, a claim the validity of which is enhanced by his purported association with Satan. Al-Libi finishes his argument with an appropriate Quranic quote to the effect that the victims were all mistreated for no other reason than their belief in Allah. The purpose of the reference to religious persecution is, of course, to induce all Muslims to circle the wagons and join the struggle against oppression of the umma (Muslim community).

The benefits to the foe of using spies against the Islamic umma are confirmed by al-Libi, when he states that they constitute the frontline troops of the enemy in the 'furious Crusader campaign'[3] of America and her allies against Muslims. These spies kidnap mujahidun leaders and provide crucial intelligence on mujahidun movements to the enemy's air force. The phrase 'they have spread all over the lands like locusts'[4] indicates that the enemy has been very successful in recruiting Muslim spies and causing great harm to the Islamic fighters. The admission by al-Libi of enemy successes and the detailed information that he provides regarding the results of enemy operations renders this information highly credible since it cannot be dismissed as propaganda. The admission thus, for obvious reasons, constitutes crucial intelligence for the forces that fight Islamic extremism. Furthermore, it is also al-Libi's assessment that the enemy's dependence on spies is even greater than on his army and 'the most destructive weapon that the enemy has used'[5] against the Muslims. Such candor regarding extremist vulnerabilities and enemy successes is indeed astounding and invaluable to those whose task it is to counter extremism. It is possible that radical Islamic ideologues believe that occasional admissions of this nature will prompt those sympathetic to the militant cause to make even greater efforts to prevent enemy infiltration and espionage.

The Algerian state was an 'enemy' who realized the great value of having its agents infiltrate extremist groups. One scholar has concluded that 'The evidence for systematic, even excessive infiltration of militant organizations by the [Algerian] regime, however, is strong and pervasive'.[6] The Algerian

Fears of Islamic terrorist organizations 225

Département du Renseignement et de la Sécurité's (DRS) penetration of extremist groups dates back to the 1980s. This is suggested by the fact that Usama Bin Ladin suspected that Algerian mujahidun who arrived in Pakistan to join the anti-Soviet fight were agents of the Algerian regime, which explains why few Algerian fighters participated in operations against the Soviets.[7] These suspicions also appear to have prompted Al-Qa'ida in 2005 to delay the merger with the GSPC (La Groupe salafiste pour la predication et le combat) since the organization could have been infiltrated by the Algerian security services (DRS or Da'irat al-isti'lam wa'l-Amn in Arabic).[8] As already discussed in detail in Chapter 8, the DRS was able to penetrate some GIA groups to the extent that these groups were actually controlled by the security service, a circumstance which raises questions about the responsibility for terrorist acts carried out by government-controlled militant groups.

Hamas is another example of an organization which has successfully been infiltrated. Israel has made extensive use of informants in Palestinian society and moles operating inside the organization. The estimate of Palestinian sources is that Israel over the course of three decades succeeded in recruiting over 20,000 Palestinians to provide information about Palestinian society and leaders of militant organizations.[9] Some Palestinian collaborators would agree to work for Shin Bet (the Israeli internal security agency) lured by monetary compensation, whereas others were tricked and blackmailed into doing so by Shin Bet agents posing as representatives of foreign companies. If the Palestinians were reluctant to collaborate with the Israeli intelligence agency, once they had realized for whom they were working, Shin Bet would go to great lengths 'persuading' them to collaborate by various coercive methods including threats to disseminate fake photos of the victim in compromising situations.[10] Israeli intelligence would go as far as ordering their Palestinian collaborators to recruit young men to terrorist cells controlled by the Israelis, inciting the 'terrorists' to attack Israeli targets as directed and have them killed before they could execute their mission. Palestinian sources claim that this was done in order to demonstrate to the Israeli public how effective their intelligence agencies are and to boost morale in the Israel Defense Force (IDF).[11]

Israel has also been very active recruiting informants in its northern neighbor Lebanon. However, Lebanese security services have been quite successful discovering spy rings controlled by the Israelis. The extent of the network of informers working for the Israelis is impressive. It testifies to the ability of Israeli intelligence agencies to recruit Lebanese from all walks of life and religious affiliations, some of whom have operated undetected for a long time.[12] One invaluable collaborator was the owner of an automobile dealership who supplied cars to Hizbullah. Each vehicle would have a GPS tracking device attached to it, which enabled the Israelis to locate homes, offices and arms depots of the organization. The long arm of Israeli intelligence reached into Syria as well, where the Israelis have a record of assassinations of Hizbullah and Hamas leaders.[13] The cases of Hamas and Hizbullah demonstrate the skills which Israeli intelligence agencies possess in recruiting collaborators in the Middle East. It is true that the target organizations and Lebanese agencies have been able to detect and put an end to the activities of many collaborators, but since infiltration of enemy ranks is an ongoing activity carried out by intelligence agencies, one can assume that such operations will continue despite disruptions. The unique value of human intelligence collected by informants on the ground offsets the high risk of detection involved in such operations.

Internal division

Internal division is a problem with which many terrorist organizations struggle. Disagreements about leadership, military tactics and ideological orientation are partly explained by the totalitarian nature of the organizations affected by division. Successful commanders who are close to action in the field do not always agree with leaders who issue orders and directives from a distance. It could also be that some commanders believe that they deserve to play an increased role in decision-making because of successes in the field. The possibility of such divisions is thus something with which leaders are preoccupied and for which they need to draw up contingency plans. Division reflects negatively on myths, and images deemed necessary to maintain discipline within an organization and an external perception of the monolithic nature of the leadership of an extremist organization. The swiftness and brutality which is frequently considered necessary to deal with opposition and dissent bears clear testimony to how strong this fear is on the part of totalitarian leaders, considering the high stakes in any power struggle. Reactions to 'rebellion' are therefore a result of apprehension with regard to a possible loss of authority of an individual leader or an organization as a whole. Should such a situation occur, it might have dire consequences for a radical group, not least from a propagandistic perspective, since it risks to detract from the credibility of a terrorist organization.

Part of the necessary myth created around extremist organizations is their claim to complete unity in all aspects of operations and policies for the simple reason that it is conducive to projecting an image of power, inevitability of goals and invincibility. In other words, doubt about these three factors is a very undesirable situation which extremists will go to great lengths to prevent from occurring. Despite efforts made by extremist organizations to maintain the image of complete unity, realities at times destroy myths and images. A case in point is the split which occurred in the GIA when a number of leading members of the organization formed the GSPC in 1998 as a result of opposition to the excessive brutality with which the GIA leadership waged jihad against the Algerian government and Algeria's population in general who had been excommunicated by the terrorist organization. Unlike the GIA, the GSPC pledged not to attack civilians. The above argument that disunity is a constant fear of terrorist leaders was further confirmed when the GSPC leader was replaced by a more radical one in 2003.[14] Another example of serious dissent are reports of coup attempts within Da'ish and attempts to assassinate its leader al-Baghdadi as discussed in Chapter 7 under the heading Domestic dissent. These attempts were betrayed by arrested co-conspirators and led to the summary execution of large numbers of leading Da'ish members and fighters.[15] The fact that these reports were published in both the Arabic-language[16] and international press must be of great concern for the Da'ish leadership, though it could be argued that this terrorist organization which prides itself on savage actions might actually view such reports with approval since they demonstrate what happens to those who oppose 'God's will'. However, if that were the case, the organization's mouthpieces would have discussed these conspiracies in detail, which did not happen. One can therefore conclude that these events were not publicized by the IS because they were deemed to damage the image of unity, crucial to the organization's authority. The evidence presented above confirms that extremist leaders fear internal division.

Loss of popular support

Popular support in one form or another – taxes, recruitment, donations, information, etc. – is crucial to the effective performance of a militant group. The possibility of the loss of such support is therefore one of the fears which terrorist organizations experience. A perfunctory glance at the GIA's engagement with the Algerian public may seem to contradict the argument that extremist groups fear the loss of popular support. In 1996, the GIA leader 'Antar Zouabri took the unique step of excommunicating the whole Algerian population.[17] His resorting to *takfir* (excommunication) seems to indicate that losing popular support was not a possibility which he feared. Zouabri explained this drastic act with the accusation that the Algerian people did not support the group's jihad against the regime, a position which made Algerians *kuffar* (unbelievers) and therefore legal targets in the jihad against the authorities. It can be argued that, if the context is put to scrutiny, the GIA fatwa does not support the assumption that the group did not fear the loss of popular support. The fatwa was the result of Algerians having *already* withdrawn or failed to demonstrate their support for the GIA and does therefore not indicate that Zouabri did not fear losing their assistance in the jihad. This was already a *fait accompli*, and the purpose of the *takfir* was to frighten the population into resuming or demonstrating their support for the jihad. The very fact that Zouabri excommunicated Algerians is strong circumstantial evidence of the importance of popular assistance and therefore of the presence in his mind of the fear of not being able to draw upon this support for the group's jihad.

Critics who are not convinced of the validity of the above argumentation might advance the counterargument that a terrorist group is not necessarily in need of popular support, if all its needs are met by foreign sources. This is a valid argument which deserves consideration. However, even if a group receives all the support it believes it needs from foreign sources, it still needs the local population at least to take a neutral stance in a conflict with a regime. Such a stance is a minimum requirement for a potentially successful jihad against a 'kafir' regime since it will actually serve as a positive environment for jihad. If the terrorist group does not need to fear popular 'disloyalty', it can devote its full attention to the struggle, without having to consider the possibility of popular informers providing to the authorities information about the whereabouts of its fighters. However, if such a popular position is not forthcoming, it could be exploited by regime propaganda to the effect that the terrorists are not freedom fighters but have sold the country out to nefarious foreign interests. Furthermore, it is worth mentioning that the counterargument advanced here does not reflect the Algerian realities at the time since Zouabri's fatwa explicitly states that the Algerian people has *failed* to support the jihad against the Algerian regime.[18] It is obvious from the fatwa that Zouabri has not taken a neutral position of Algerians into consideration since his argument is based upon the lack of active support by Algerians for the jihad. A similar situation occurred a decade later, in 2006, when Algerians were withdrawing their support for the GSPC. By then, the extremist insurgency had reached a point where most Islamists abandoned the GSPC's militancy for a more accomodationist approach, accepting the government's offer of amnesty in exchange for abandoning militancy.[19]

Fear of democracy

The fear and hatred of democracy is obvious from jihadi propaganda since it offers an appealing alternative to the totalitarian ideology of extremist groups. Democracy is therefore denounced as a form of unbelief which usurps God's authority and 'legislative prerogative'. The IS rejection of democracy is based on a Quranic *aya*: 'And He [God] shares not His legislation with anyone'.[20] The IS argues that, since God is the sole legislator, the concepts of democracy and 'free choice' are tantamount to *shirk* because they elevate human beings to the status of God.[21] From this follows the corollary that the 'Caliph's' authority cannot be questioned as a result of his position as God's representative, a claim which safeguards the former's totalitarian rule. To win over Muslims who might have lingering doubts about Da'ish's argument, a contributor to the magazine reminds the reader that nationalism, democracy and socialism lead straight to Hell in the hereafter.[22] By linking these three concepts to Hell, IS ideologues demonstrate their fear of these ideas and their hope that the reader is not sufficiently knowledgeable about political and Islamic history to realize that all three concepts are actually part of Islamic history.[23] The fact that the IS has to threaten its readers with hellfire reveals the magnitude of its fear of democracy. Like Da'ish, the GIA of Algeria demonstrated its deep fear of and insecurity about the core democratic concept of free speech by targeting journalists and intellectuals in the civil war of the 1990s.[24] The access of the latter to the audience which the GIA was attempting to persuade to adopt the extremist cause and their ability to expose the ideology of the terrorists made them the GIA's most formidable opponents in the country.

The two examples referred to above suggest that democracy is a lethal weapon in the fight against totalitarian ideologies because it can be turned into an intellectual nightmare for extremists. At the same time, however, democracy is a dangerous weapon in the wrong hands since it is used by terrorists to advance their agenda. Despite this weakness, civil liberties constitute a powerful means to counter extremist narratives. Democratic societies are in a strong position to emphasize that Muslim terrorists are guilty of *shirk* (polytheism). It could be argued that they are exercising and benefiting from the very freedoms which they have denounced as usurpation of God's power. Free speech in democratic societies is what enables them to act with very few restraints in ways which they are not able to act in terrorist-controlled territories. Furthermore, scholars and journalists in democratic societies need to draw attention to the deep fear which extremists experience when faced with having to engage with critical thinkers since they will not allow such a debate in their own territories. This is quite problematic from a logical perspective because they have turned human fear into an attribute of God. The militants argue that their goal is to establish a global society ruled by the law of God and that they have only one fear, namely, the fear of God. It contradicts reason, which incidentally is a legitimate method in Islamic discourse, for the simple reason that it implies that the Almighty fears humans, a conclusion which would make God highly anthropomorphic, which, in turn, could be considered *shirk* since such an argument would to a certain extent imply a lowering of the status of God to that of humans.

The discussion under the above heading has demonstrated what powerful instruments democracy places at the disposal of the independent mind to counter violent ideologies. A counterargument could, of course, be advanced that the arguments of a critical thinker will not reach the population of a totalitarian society since the government strives to restrict and control social and intellectual activity. That may be true to a certain extent, but the reader should bear in mind that total control is only an objective and not a complete reality. The reader is referred to the discussion of this subject in previous chapters of this study. Perhaps, more important than getting an alternative message through to the population of terrorist-controlled territories is the fact that extremist propaganda aims at luring new recruits to a particular geographic area to fulfill different functions and that these potential recruits live in 'Crusader-' or 'apostate-controlled' states. This implies that the main focus should be on preventing citizens from 'falling victim' to radicalization.

Fear of adversity

Adversity on the battlefield can have serious consequences for the morale of the mujahidun. It is therefore a matter about which the leadership of a terrorist organization is quite concerned. An analysis of Da'ish propaganda confirms this fear. A photo of a billboard in Da'ish-controlled territory shows a fighter on guard with enemy aircraft traversing the sky behind him. The text on the billboard promises that the IS will prevail and eventually triumph over the international alliance which is fighting the organization.[25] It can be concluded from the text that the bombings must have a negative effect on the morale of the population, which is why Da'ish propagandists find it necessary to prevent defeatist sentiments from spreading by promising eventual victory.[26] A report concerning a speech by the IS leader Abu Bakr al-Baghdadi concludes that it reflects weakness. After loss of territory in Iraq and Syria, al-Baghdadi broke his silence with a video address to the umma, calling for Muslims to contribute to the jihad. The analyst concludes that recent military failures have caused a fear that they will negatively affect the morale of the mujahidun, which has prompted al-Baghdadi to address the Muslim public.[27]

The IS claim to divine legitimacy has the potential of causing embarrassment. The reason is that it is hard to convincingly explain away a pattern of adversity on the battlefield. One failed operation might not cast doubt on the validity of the claim to divine legitimacy, but a series of failed initiatives or territorial losses cause problems from a propagandistic perspective. The failures could indicate that the organization does not enjoy divine support for its military strategy or tactics. An even more damaging conclusion would be that failure is a sign that Da'ish does not enjoy divine support for its ideology in general. The IS typically attempts to draw attention away from military failures and direct the public's focus to a prophecy which promises victory for the Muslims in an apocalyptic battle at Dabiq, Syria.[28] This is certainly a powerful argument since the source of the prophecy is a hadith, but, again, it is difficult to boost morale with a prophecy, no matter the source, if defeats occur with too great a frequency. The IS adopted a special method – in addition to the prophecy already mentioned – to deal with such a situation. Photos of mujahidun armed to the teeth frequently figured prominently in IS publications as part of a media strategy the intent of which was to project an image of power and divert Muslim attention away from negative news.[29] In order to boost morale and explain away adversity, the IS also used a quote from the founder of the Shafi'i legal school, al-Shafi': 'One's authority will not be consolidated except after overcoming tribulation'.[30] The implication is that the IS is bound to encounter setbacks, but these are of a temporary nature only. Furthermore, Da'ish propagandists could, of course, also refer to the initial difficulties the Prophet encountered in Mecca and the subsequent hijra to Medina, emphasizing that these difficulties were later overcome by resolute action on the part of the Muslim umma. However, it is hard to imagine that this approach will prove effective in the face of constant defeat.

Reduced recruitment appeal

Da'ish has made great efforts internationally to recruit professionals and mujahidun. The multilingual magazines *Dabiq and Rumiyah* testify to this global recruitment effort, ensuring that the IS's extremist message reaches as widespread an audience as possible. In its heyday, during the spectacular initial successes of Da'ish, the now defunct online magazine *Dabiq* made repeated calls for hijra (migration) to Da'ish-controlled territory. Performing hijra to the 'Caliphate' was a religious duty, according to IS propagandists. However, the calls for migration to the IS reveal that there were strong temporal reasons for encouraging Muslims to move to the 'holy land'. Al-Baghdadi called for Muslims with military and medical expertise, in particular, to join the IS,[31] reminding the faithful that this was incumbent upon true Muslims, a *wajib 'ayni* (individual obligation).[32] Da'ish's 'job ads' reveal that its leaders feared that the organization's manpower would be depleted as a result of military and terrorist operations and that there was an urgent need for medical professionals to attend to injured mujahidun and provide medical services to the population. Such a situation could, however, potentially negatively affect recruitment of mujahidun and reduce the appeal for Muslim families with non-military expertise to join the 'Caliphate'. Encouraging Muslims to settle in the IS could also reflect a fear that Da'ish would not be able to meet its obligations to the civilian population without expanding its tax base. A quote from *Dabiq* reveals the urgency of the matter and that IS leaders without a doubt feared the possibility of failure to attract mujahidun and settlers: 'The Islamic State offers everything that you need to live and work here, so what are you waiting for?'[33] It is no surprise that there is no reference to the hazards involved in joining the 'Caliphate' such as coalition bombings.

The IS did not publish any migration statistics on Muslims settling in the 'Caliphate', which makes it somewhat difficult to estimate the success of its propaganda. However, considering the fact that there are approximately 1.5 billion Muslims in the world, success would likely at least be counted in the millions. It is clear that migration to the IS has not reached such numbers since that many travelers would not go unnoticed by authorities in their countries of origin. The failure to attract masses of settlers must thus have been a source of serious concern for the IS leadership. Again, success is oftentimes measured in numbers, and no matter how skillful the propaganda, it is difficult to maintain a myth or claim without some kind of evidence, a problem that the Nazi regime grappled with as well. In addition to the developments discussed above, the spectacular decline in the fortunes of the 'Caliphate' must have considerably reduced the allure of this extremist entity. A serious problem for the IS and other terrorist organizations is that their appeal largely depends on success. When fortunes change, one can expect recruitment numbers to decrease, in particular, with regard to non-military settlers. The fear that defeat and failure will affect recruitment negatively is quite real, unless extremist ideologues succeed in redefining the notions of success and defeat.

Enemy propaganda

Despite strident rhetoric on the part of militant ideologues, enemy 'propaganda' is a phenomenon which they view as a serious threat. Al-Libi has confirmed this with a quote from Ibn Taymiyya's *Al-Sarim al-maslul* to the effect that the pen is a more dangerous weapon than the sword.[34] The implication is that extremist Muslims believe that enemy propaganda is dangerous because it works. With the quote from a medieval Islamic scholar, the Al-Qa'ida ideologue al-Libi has provided a clear hint to the 'enemy' as to how to deal with Islamic extremism, namely, that those who oppose it must focus on its propaganda. Another militant Muslim, the Al-Qa'ida ideologue Abu Mus'ab al-Suri, confirms the damage 'enemy' propaganda can cause among the faithful. He denounces scholars working for Muslim rulers, accusing them of distorting Islam and adjusting it to American standards.[35] His fear of moderate Islamic scholars is obvious since it is not sufficient to denounce them as moderates. Al-Suri uses what he believes is more effective propaganda by linking their Islamic scholarship to the American enemy, essentially making them traitors to the umma. Furthermore, al-Suri finds the argument of these scholars that the mujahidun are not martyrs and will not enter paradise when they die particularly dangerous for the extremist cause and worthy of condemnation.[36]

Challenges from other extremist groups

A serious problem for extremist organizations embracing totalitarian ideologies is if they refuse to cooperate with other extremists unless the latter swear allegiance to the former or completely embrace their tactics and agenda. An example of an organization which insists on *bai'a* (swearing allegiance) is the IS.[37] Such a position risks to draw a militant group into armed conflict with other terrorists, thus diverting from the jihadi cause precious resources – manpower, money and materil – which could instead be used against governments and other targets. A situation such as this would under normal conditions constitute a fear due to its obvious negative effects, but instead of inducing a rational fear, such a situation elicits blind hatred for those who disagree with a particular group's position or tactics. Such a development can be described as a negative emotion replacing another one, causing even more negative consequences. An illustrative example is the rivalry between the GIA and AIS, leading to the former's 1996 declaration of war on the AIS, the armed wing of the Algerian Islamic Salvation Front (FIS, al-Jabha al-Islamiyya li'l-Inqadh), a decision leading to the GIA's involvement in two wars simultaneously. Incredibly enough, the GIA prioritized the struggle with the AIS over the war against the Algerian government, a decision which would cost the GIA dearly, since the AIS succeeded in assassinating the GIA leader Jamal Zitouni.[38] His death had grave consequences for the latter organization as a result of the new leader's completely indiscriminate savagery. The GIA's downward spiral was further exacerbated by 'Antar Zouabri's (the new GIA leader) decision to take the GIA into a third war. This time around the organization did not limit itself to targeting a specific group, but excommunicated Algeria's whole population. This desperate move reflected the GIA's frustration with the organization's changing fortunes. Instead of dispassionately analyzing the reasons for the lack of progress on the battlefield, the best initiative Zouabri could think of was completely to alienate most Algerians.

From the 'enemy's' perspective, any rivalry between terrorist organizations is welcome news, and history seems to confirm that tension among militant organizations is not an infrequent phenomenon. In the 1990s, the GIA was subjected to embarrassing criticism not just by domestic rivals but also by terrorist organizations based in neighboring states such as the Egyptian Islamic Jihad (EIJ) headed by Aiman al-Zawahiri and the Libyan Islamic Fighting Group (LIFG). Both groups criticized the GIA for its excessive use of *takfir* (excommunication) and its targeting of Algerian civilians.[39] It comes as no surprise that such criticism is frequently met with a barrage of scathing counterpropaganda since the former could potentially be very damaging for recruitment and popular support for the inflexible groups who are inclined to cooperate with other groups only on their own terms. More examples of rivalries among terrorist groups are those between Al-Qa'ida and the Taliban on the one hand and Da'ish on the other hand. When a competing extremist organization disagrees about a certain aspect of the IS's jihad, the latter group will make every effort to create doubts about the former's motives by drawing attention to the rival's purported negligence in one respect or another. Concomitantly, Da'ish has accused Al-Qa'ida of cooperating with the enemy instead of fighting him.[40] Likewise, the IS has accused the Taliban of defeatism, surrendering to the Americans.[41] The strident propaganda directed against rivaling extremist groups testifies to the rigid extremists' fear of the ideological challenge such groups pose. Such propaganda facilitates the task of security services since it provides valuable intelligence regarding the morale and state of mind of the rigid militants.

Loss of revenue

Like any other organization, militant groups are dependent on a steady flow of revenue to realize their objectives and adopt different methods to raise funds. During the civil war in the 1990s, Algerian groups targeted merchants and entrepreneurs to extract 'donations' for the jihadi cause. Algerian expatriate communities contributed donations to the militants' cause as well. Thousands of Algerian activists abroad ensured a continuous flow of funds and arms to the insurgents at home. Bank robberies and money laundering were other ways to fund operations.[42] Extortion in the form of a tax levied on every citizen, in addition to the activities listed above, allowed the extremists to lead a comfortable and 'modern' life style, with some of their possessions and 'equipment' originating from their slaughtered victims.[43] Considering the heavy dependence on external sources of revenue for terrorist activities, the leaders must have feared that the flow of money could one day dry up. Furthermore, the materialistic life style of the mujahidun must have constituted a godsend for the Algerian regime since the evidence found in raids against terrorist hideouts could easily be exploited for propagandistic purposes in official media. In the twenty-first century, the IS adopted similar methods to fund its operations, including the levying of heavy taxes on the population, extortion, demanding ransom for kidnapped victims and raising funds abroad.[44] Unlike the Algerian terrorists, however, ISIS managed to seize Iraqi banks, Syrian and Iraqi oil wells and Iraqi antiquities, thus guaranteeing the organization access to unique resources to wage its jihad.[45] With the territory previously controlled by the 'Caliphate' recovered by the Iraqi government and Syrian regime and access to former sources of revenue denied, ISIS leaders must fear that the changed fortunes could lead to the complete marginalization of the IS. Radically diminished revenues have prevented Da'ish from sustaining an army of tens of thousands of mujahidun, a fact which has forced the extremists to focus on small-scale operations and rely more on lone-wolf attacks to remain relevant and divert attention from the catastrophic collapse of the 'Caliphate' as a state, a reality which is difficult to explain in IS propaganda.

Exposure of ideology and methodology as illegitimate

Legitimacy is a constant concern of extremist organizations in the Islamic world, as testified to by persistent propaganda efforts to convince Muslims that each group's interpretation of Islam is the only true and original religion. Militants correctly fear that loss of legitimacy will result in loss of material and moral support for their extremist agenda, a possibility which will, in turn, lead to marginalization and irrelevance, obviously a major concern of any terrorist group. This fear is reflected in extremist intolerance toward competing groups, the strident rhetoric with which propagandists denounce critics, and their attempts at finding excuses for failures and justifications for heinous acts, as has been discussed in several previous chapters of this volume. One such challenge has come from Abu Hamza, former imam of a London mosque. Interestingly, no stranger to extremist views himself, Abu Hamza denounced the GIA for its *takfir* of the entire Algerian population, branding the group's ideology 'extremist'.[46] Similar criticism was expressed by al-Maqdisi of al-Zarqawi's massacres of Shi'is in Iraq. Al-Maqdisi, al-Zarqawi's former mentor, pointed out that few Americans were targeted.[47] Al-Qa'ida's second in command, Aiman al-Zawahiri, also joined in this criticism, urging al-Zarqawi, leader of the forerunner to the IS, to focus on Americans instead of Shi'is.[48]

The IS has displayed clear sensitivities when targeted by 'enemies'. A *Dabiq* report reveals that Da'ish does not want Muslims to believe that IS mujahidun 'love killing and slaughter and that they kill people on suspicions'.[49] The IS's reaction shows that it does not have a problem with killing and slaughtering per se, but fears the impression that personal inclinations of the mujahidun play a role in these acts. It is important for IS leaders that the impression of arbitrariness is completely eliminated since such a view would contradict the organization's myth that it acts in accordance with God's law, in which there is no room for human passion. The corollary is that every person is guaranteed due [divine] legal process, which is, of course, a convenient way of justifying and avoiding responsibility for atrocities committed in the name of God.[50]

De-radicalization and self de-radicalization

The last two fears of extremist organizations to be discussed here are de-radicalization and self de-radicalization. The former refers to attempts by security and counterterrorism agencies eventually to reintegrate radicalized individuals into society after it has been determined that they no longer pose a threat to fellow citizens.[51] This is, of course, a result highly undesired by terrorist groups since it most certainly involves a debriefing process, during which the extremist provides valuable information about the ideology and methodology of a terrorist group. De-radicalization programs often include 'psychological therapies, counseling, religious instruction and activities aimed at promoting civic engagement'.[52] Self de-radicalization is another phenomenon which terrorist leaders fear. It is initiated by the individual himself/herself and not by counterterrorism agencies who attempt to de-radicalize a captive terrorist. Self de-radicalization occurs when an individual reexamines his/her commitment to a violent ideology and comes to the realization that the best course of action is to abandon the ideology in question.

The terrorist organization Al-Gama'a al-Islamiyya which was particularly active in Egypt in the 1990s is a good example of self de-radicalization. In 2002, several leading members of the group renounced violence, a declaration denounced by some leaders abroad. A year later, however, the group as a whole declared that it would not resort to violence in the future, following which the Egyptian government began to release incarcerated members of the group.[53] Self de-radicalization of a part or all members of a terrorist organization is most likely a worst case scenario for such a group. Even if it only pertains to some members, it negatively affects the credibility of the group, raising doubts about the commitment to the jihadi cause by the remaining members. It goes without saying that when successful, de-radicalization and self de-radicalization are highly desired by governments which fight terrorism, since these processes can be exploited for propagandistic purposes even when governments have a minimal involvement bringing about such developments.

Conclusion

An advantage many mujahidun have over their enemy is their attitude toward death. Dying on the battlefield is considered a reward and a goal for which the fighter should strive. The possibility of death in combat, therefore, does not constitute a fear of mujahidun, at least in theory. An army of soldiers with such fighting spirit might seem like an invincible force since its troops do not fear death. A leader might not fear for his personal safety, but he will no doubt fear the negative consequences of a succession struggle erupting, following his demise, a bid for power by a rival etcetera. The examination of fears of terrorist organizations in this chapter does not claim to be a complete survey of such concerns of militant Islamic groups, but it nevertheless provides insight into some weaknesses of radical Islamic organizations to which scholars and counter-terrorism experts have not paid sufficient attention. When considering the fears discussed in this chapter, an enemy who does not fear death will no longer appear invincible. Fortunately, for counterterrorism agencies, extremist propaganda oftentimes provides clues as to what constitutes a fear to terrorists, who, at times, unwittingly provide clues to their fears. A major purpose of terrorist groups is to instill fear in governments and citizens in order to force authorities to impose such severe restrictions on the lives of citizens that the latter – assisted by the terrorists – will cause the collapse of the government. This chapter has argued that if extremists can strike fear in the hearts of government officials and citizens, governments can adopt the same strategy in their war against terrorism. Militant Islamic groups strive to create a myth that they fear nothing except God. However, a careful examination of extremist propaganda reveals that like other human beings terrorists have their own fears, albeit different from those of the ordinary citizen. Thus, the analyst has to go beneath the diversionary tactics applied by extremists in their propaganda to expose their fears and act accordingly. In conclusion, this chapter has revealed that the fears of extremist Muslims are a direct consequence of their exclusivist ideology and the intolerance they display toward those who criticize their ideologies. Without these fears, Islamic militant groups would obviously be a much more formidable enemy, but as our analysis above has demonstrated, it is extremely difficult to overcome these fears because of the totalitarian nature of their ideologies.

Notes

1 See Chapter 9.
2 Abu Yahya al-Libi (Hasan Qa'id), 'Al-Mu'allim fi hukm al-jasus al-muslim' [Guidance on the Ruling of the Muslim Spy] (Markaz al-Fajr li'l-I'lam, 2009), p. 3, *Federation of American Scientists*, accessed 23 May 2018, https://fas.org/irp/world/para/libi.pdf.
3 Ibid., p. 8.
4 Ibid.
5 Ibid., p. 9.

6 Stephen Harmon, 'From GSPC to AQIM: The Evolution of an Algerian Islamist Terrorist Group into an Al-Qa'ida Affiliate and Its Implications for the Sahara-Sahel Region', *Concerned Africa Scholars*, Bulletin No. 85 (Spring 2010), p. 25, accessed 13 January 2017, https://citeseerx.ist.psu.edu/viewdoc/download?doi=10.1.1.461.7941&rep=rep1&type=pdf
7 Jean-Pierre Filiu, 'The Local and Global Jihad of Al-Qa'ida in the Islamic Maghrib', *Middle East Journal*, Vol. 63, No. 2 (Spring 2009), p. 214, in Harmon, 'From GSPC to AQIM', p. 25. The DRS's Arabic name is Da'irat al-Isti'lam wa'l-Amn.
8 Andrew McGregor, 'Military Rebellion and Islamism in Mauretania', *Terrorism Monitor*, Vol. 3, No. 4 (24 Feb., 2005) http://www.jamestown.org/single/?no_cache=1&tx_ttnew[tt_news]=27597, in Harmon, 'From GSPC to AQIM', p. 25.
9 Zaki Chehab, *Inside Hamas: The Untold Story of the Militant Islamic Movement* (New York, NY: Nation Books, 2007), p. 69.
10 Ibid., pp. 71–72.
11 Ibid., p. 77.
12 Nicholas Blanford, *Warriors of God: Inside Hezbollah's Thirty-Year Struggle against Israel* (New York, NY: Random House, 2011), p. 464.
13 Ibid., pp. 465–466.
14 Harmon, 'From GSPC to AQIM', accessed 13 January 2017, http://concernedafricascholars.org/docs/bulletin85harmon.pdf.
15 '*Razbrod i raskol v Islamskom gosudarstve*', *Politus.ru*, 8 September 2015, accessed 7 January 2016, http://politus.ru/v-mire/981-razbrod-i-raskol-v-islamskom-gosudarstve.html. Also, see the following Czech article, '*Rozkol v Islámském státě*', *NWOO.ORG*, accessed 7 January 2016, http://www.nwoo.org/2015/09/10/rozkol-v-islamskem-state/.
16 *Al-'Arabi al-Jadid*. 'Muhawalat inqilabi 'ala al-baghdadi tantahi bi tasfiyati 13 qiyadan li-da'ish', 2 July 2015, accessed February 2, 2016, http://www.alaraby.co.uk/politics/2015/7/2/%D9%85%D8%AD%D8%A7%D9%88%D9%84%D8%A9-%D8%A7%D9%86%D9%82%D9%84%D8%A7%D8%A8-%D8%B9%D9%84%D9%89-%D8%A7%D9%84%D8%A8%D8%BA%D8%AF%D8%A7%D8%AF%D9%8A-%D8%AA%D9%86%D8%AA%D9%87%D9%8A-%D8%A8%D8%AA%D8%B5%D9%81%D9%8A%D8%A9-13-%D9%82%D9%8A%D8%A7%D8%AF%D9%8A%D8%A7-%D9%84%D9%80-%D8%AF%D8%A7%D8%B9%D8%B4.
17 Harmon, 'From GSPC to AQIM', p. 14.
18 Ibid.
19 Ibid., p. 25.
20 The Qur'an, 18:26.
21 *Dabiq*, No. 2, p. 11.
22 Ibid., No. 10, pp. 42–43.
23 For a detailed discussion regarding this issue, refer to Chapter 6 and the heading 'Noah and "free choice"'.
24 ''Antar al-Zouabri, "dhabbah" jama'at GIA al-jaza'ir', *Bawabat al-harika al-Islamiyya*, accessed 24 December 2016, http://islamist-movements.com/28316.
25 'Lo Stato Islamico, una realtà che ti vorrebbe comunicare', p. 37, ISSUU, accessed 3 January 2016, http://issuu.com/031041/docs/lo_stato_islamico_una_realt_che_. IS fear of the negative impact of coalition airstrikes has also been confirmed by other sources, Hamza Hendawi, 'Islamic State's Double Standards Sow Growing Disillusion', *Associated Press*, 18 January 2016, accessed 18 January 2016, http://www.msn.com/en-us/news/world/islamic-states-double-standards-sow-growing-disillusion/ar-BBonCK1?li=BBnb7Kz&ocid=U219DHP.

238 *Fears of Islamic terrorist organizations*

26 Chapter 5 discusses how the National Socialist regime dealt with the same problem.
27 Linda Hinz, 'Entlarvende Botschaft des IS-Chefs: "Baghdadis Worte zeigen wie viel Angst er hat"', 29 December 2015, *FOCUS*, accessed 1 March 2016, http://www.focus.de/politik/ausland/islamischer-staat/entlarvendeaudio-botschaft-des-terrorfuersten-schwere-verluste-fuer-is-baghdadis-worte-zeigen-wie-viel-angst-er-hat_id_5178868.html.
28 'Lo Stato Islamico', p. 60.
29 *Dabiq* Issue 1 (Jul., 2014), p. 5.
30 Ibid., p. 40.
31 *Dabiq*, Issue. 1, p. 11; Issue 3 (Sept., 2014), p. 26.
32 *Dabiq*, Issue. 1, p. 11.
33 Ibid., Issue 9 (May 2015), p. 26.
34 Ibn Taymiyya, 'Al-Sarim al-maslul', 1/392, quoted in Abu Yahya al-Libi, *Al-Mu'allim fi hukm al-jasus al-muslim*, p. 41.
35 Al-Suri, *Da'wat al-muqawama al-Islamiyya al-'alamiyya*, p. 1388.
36 Ibid.
37 *Dabiq*, Issue 1, p. 12.
38 Harmon, 'From GSPC to AQIM', p. 14.
39 Ibid.
40 *Dabiq*, Issue 10 (Jul., 2015), p. 51.
41 Ibid.
42 Takeyh, 'Islamism in Algeria', in Stone, *The Agony of Algeria*, p. 189; Jumhuriyya Misr al-'Arabiyya, [Arab Republic of Egypt], *Mafhum al-irhab*, pp. 449–450; Canada, Immigration and Refugee Board of Canada, 'Algeria'.
43 Baya Gacemi, *Moi, Nadia, femme d'un émir du GIA* (Paris: Éditions du Seuil, 1998), pp. 133–134, referred to in Turshend, 'Algerian Women', p. 901.
44 Janine di Giovanni, Leah McGrath Goodman and Damien Sharkov, 'How Does ISIS Fund Its Reign of Terror?' *Newsweek*, 6 November 2014, accessed 30 December 2018, https://www.newsweek.com/2014/11/14/how-does-isis-fund-its-reign-terror-282607.html; Ana Swanson, 'How the Islamic State Makes Its Money', 18 November 2015, *The Washington Post*, accessed 29 December 2018, accessed 29 December 2018, https://www.washingtonpost.com/news/wonk/wp/2015/11/18/how-isis-makes-its-money/?noredirect=on&utm_term=.fde4f040dbad.
45 di Giovanni, McGrath Goodman and Sharkov, 'How Does ISIS Fund Its Reign of Terror?' *Newsweek*.
46 Abu Hamza, *Khawarij and Jihad* (Birmingham: Maktabah al-Ansar, 2000), p. 65.
47 Michael, 'The Legend', p. 347.
48 Weiss and Hassan, *ISIS*, p. 58.
49 *Dabiq*, Issue 9, p. 70.
50 Islamic and Western scholars' exposure of weaknesses in extremist arguments has been discussed in detail in several chapters in this volume, including Chapters 7–9.
51 One scholar defines the term as follows: '"*de*radicalization" should only be used to refer the methods and techniques used to undermine and reverse the completed radicalization process, thereby reducing the potential risk to society from terrorism', Lindsay Clutterbuck, PhD, 'Deradicalization Programs and Counterterrorism: A Perspective on the Challenges and Benefits', accessed 30 December 2018, https://www.mei.edu/sites/default/files/Clutterbuck.pdf.
52 John Horgan, 'Programs Offer Hope in Countering Terrorism', 4 February 2015, *LA Times*, accessed 31 December 2018, https://www.uml.edu/News/news-articles/2015/latimes-terrorism.aspx.

53 *The Investigative Project on Terrorism*, 'Gama'a al-Islamiyya (IG)', accessed 30 December 2018, https://www.investigativeproject.org/profile/128/gamaa-al-islamiyya-ig; *U.S. Department of State*, Chapter 8 – 'Foreign Terrorist Organizations', accessed 1 January 2019, https://www.state.gov/j/ct/rls/crt/2005/65275.htm.

Bibliography

Al-'Arabi al-Jadid. 2 July 2015. 'Muhawalatu inqilabi 'ala al-baghdadi tantahi bi tasfiyati 13 qiyadan li-da'ish' [Coup Attempt against al-Baghdadi Ends with Execution of 13 Da'ish Leaders]. Accessed 2 February 2016. http://www.alaraby.co.uk/politics/2015/7/2/%D9%85%D8%AD%D8%A7%D9%88%D9%84%D8%A9-%D8%A7%D9%86%D9%82%D9%84%D8%A7%D8%A8-%D8%B9%D9%84%D9%89-%D8%A7%D9%84%D8%A8%D8%BA%D8%AF%D8%A7%D8%AF%D9%8A-%D8%AA%D9%86%D8%AA%D9%87%D9%8A-%D8%A8%D8%AA%D8%B5%D9%81%D9%8A%D8%A9-13-%D9%82%D9%8A%D8%A7%D8%AF%D9%8A%D8%A7-%D9%84%D9%80-%D8%AF%D8%A7%D8%B9%D8%B4.

Bawabat al-harika al-Islamiyya. Accessed 24 December 2016. http://islamist-movements.com/28316.

Blanford, Nicholas. *Warriors of God: Inside Hezbollah's Thirty-Year Struggle against Israel*. New York, NY: Random House, 2011.

Canada, Immigration and Refugee Board of Canada. *Algeria: Interview with Jean-Michel Salgon, Specialist on Algerian Armed Groups*, 26 September 2000. http://www.refworld.org/docid/3ae6ad543c.html.

Chehab, Zaki. *Inside Hamas: The Untold Story of the Militant Islamic Movement*. New York, NY: Nation Books, 2007.

Clutterbuck, Lindsay. 'Deradicalization Programs and Counterterrorism: A Perspective on the Challenges and Benefits'. Accessed 30 December 2018. https://www.mei.edu/sites/default/files/Clutterbuck.pdf.

Dabiq.

di Giovanni, Janine, Leah McGrath Goodman and Damien Sharkov. 'How Does ISIS Fund Its Reign of Terror?' *Newsweek*, 6 November 2014. Accessed 30 December 2018. https://www.newsweek.com/2014/11/14/how-does-isis-fund-its-reign-terror-282607.html.

Filiu, Jean-Pierre. 'The Local and Global Jihad of Al-Qa'ida in the Islamic Maghrib'. *Middle East Journal*, Vol. 63, No. 2 (Spring 2009), pp. 213–26.

Gacemi, Baya. *Moi, Nadia, femme d'un émir du GIA*. Paris: Éditions du Seuil, 1998.

Hamza, Abu. *Khawarij and Jihad*. Birmingham: Maktabah al-Ansar, 2000.

Harmon, Stephen. 'From GSPC to AQIM: The Evolution of an Algerian Islamist Terrorist Group into an Al-Qa'ida Affiliate and Its Implications for the Sahara-Sahel Region'. *Concerned Africa Scholars*, Bulletin No. 85 (Spring 2010), pp. 12–29. Accessed 13 January 2017. https://citeseerx.ist.psu.edu/viewdoc/download?doi=10.1.1.461.7941&rep=rep1&type=pdf.

Hendawi, Hamza. 'Islamic State's Double Standards Sow Growing Disillusion'. *Associated Press*, 18 January 2016. Accessed 18 January 2016. http://www.msn.com/en-us/news/world/islamic-states-double-standards-sow-growing-disillusion/ar-BBonCK1?li=BBnb7Kz&ocid=U219DHP.

Hinz, Linda. 'Entlarvende Botschaft des IS-Chefs: "Baghdadis Worte zeigen wie viel Angst er hat"' [IS Chief's Revealing Message: al-Baghdadi's Words

Show the Extent of His Fear]. 29 December 2015, *FOCUS*. Accessed 1 March 2016. http://www.focus.de/politik/ausland/islamischer-staat/entlarvendeaudiobotschaft-des-terrorfuersten-schwere-verluste-fuer-is-baghdadis-worte-zeigen-wie-viel-angst-er-hat_id_5178868.html.

Horgan, John. 'Programs Offer Hope in Countering Terrorism'. 4 February 2015, *LA Times*. Accessed 31 December 2018. https://www.uml.edu/News/news-articles/2015/latimes-terrorism.aspx.

The Investigative Project on Terrorism. 'Gama'a al-Islamiyya (IG)'. Accessed 30 December 2018. https://www.investigativeproject.org/profile/128/gamaa-al-islamiyya-ig.

ISSUU. 'Lo Stato Islamico, una realtà che ti vorrebbe comunicare' [The Islamic State, a Reality That You Would Like to Communicate]. Accessed 3 January 2016. http://issuu.com/031041/docs/lo_stato_islamico_una_realt_che_.

Jumhuriyya Misr al-'Arabiyya, [Arab Republic of Egypt]. *Mafhum al-irhab wa asbab zuhurihi fi al-Jaza'ir* [The Concept of Terrorism and the Reasons of Its Appearance in Algeria]. Cairo: wizarat al-difa', 1998.

al-Libi, Abu Yahya. *Al-Mu'allim fi Hukm al-Jasus al-Muslim* [Guidance on the Ruling of the Muslim Spy]. Markaz al-Fajr li'l-I'lam, 2009. Accessed 23 May 2018. http://fas.org/irp/world/para/libi.pdf.

McGregor, Andrew. 'Military Rebellion and Islamism in Mauretania'. *Terrorism Monitor*, Vol. 3, No. 4 (24 February 2005) (no pagination). Accessed 13 January 2017. https://jamestown.org/program/military-rebellion-and-islamism-in-mauritania/

Michael, George. 'The Legend and Legacy of Abu Musab al-Zarqawi'. *Defense Studies*, Vol. 7, No. 3 (September 2007), pp. 338–57.

NWOO.ORG. 'Rozkol v Islámském státě' [Division in the Islamic State]. Accessed 7 January 2016. http://www.nwoo.org/2015/09/10/rozkol-v-islamskem-state/.

Politus.ru. 8 September 2015. 'Razbrod i raskol v Islamskom gosudarstve' [Disorder and Division in the Islamic State]. Accessed 7 January 2016. http://politus.ru/v-mire/981-razbrod-i-raskol-v-islamskom-gosudarstve.html.

The Qur'an.

al-Suri, Abu Mus'ab ('Umar 'Abd al-Hakim). *Da'wat al-muqawama al-Islamiyya al-'alamiyya* [Call of Islamic World Resistance]. Accessed 13 October 2019. https://ia800303.us.archive.org/25/items/Dawaaah/DAWH.pdf.

Swanson, Ana. 'How the Islamic State makes Its Money'. 18 November 2015, *The Washington Post*. Accessed 15 December 2018. https://www.washingtonpost.com/news/wonk/wp/2015/11/18/how-isis-makes-its-money/?noredirect=on&utm_term=.fde4f040dbad.

Takeyh, Ray. 'Islamism in Algeria: A Struggle between Hope and Agony'. Middle East Policy Vol. 10, No. 2 (May 2003), pp. 62–75. Accessed 10 September 2019. https://www.researchgate.net/publication/229678691_Islamism_in_Algeria_A_Struggle_Between_Hope_and_Agony

Turshend, Meredith. 'Algerian Women in the Liberation Struggle and the Civil War: From Active Participants to Passive Victims?' *Social Research*, Vol. 69, No. 3 (Fall 2002), pp. 889–911.

U.S. Department of State. Chapter 8- 'Foreign Terrorist Organizations'. Accessed 1 January 2019. https://www.state.gov/j/ct/rls/crt/2005/65275.htm.

The Washington Post (Washington, DC).

Weiss, Michael and Hassan Hassan. *ISIS: Inside the Army of Terror*. New York, NY: Regan Arts, 2015.

12 A comparative evolution of terrorism

This chapter discusses the evolution of terrorism over the course of centuries and to what extent modern terrorist movements represent continuity with respect to methodology and ideology. Furthermore, the chapter will seek an answer to the question why certain aspects of terrorism appear to have undergone little modification over the course of centuries despite rapid technological progress in modern societies. The previous analysis of different types of terrorism in different historical periods and societies will allow us to address the above questions. The focus of the discussion will be on six aspects of terrorism as examined in this volume: causes of terrorism, ideology, methodology, deception, state terrorism and propaganda.

Causes of terrorism

In any study of terrorism, a discussion of the causes of this phenomenon is key to understanding and countering militant extremism. Previous chapters in this volume have identified several similarities among violent movements, be they religious or non-religion-based or a blend of both. The Jewish Sicarii rose up against foreign Roman occupation and their own religious establishment for economic and religious reasons as a result of oppressive Roman taxation in addition to the mandatory tithe due to Jewish priests for the maintenance of the Temple in Jerusalem[1] and the cooperation of Jewish high priests with Roman officials.[2] The revolt against the rule of the high priests to a certain extent resembles the refusal of modern Islamic militants to accept mainstream Islamic religious scholars' monopoly on interpreting the Quran. This is reflected in the writings of Sayyid Qutb,[3] Abu Yahya al-Libi[4] and online magazines such as Al-Qaʻida's *Inspire*[5] and Daʻish's *Dabiq*[6] in the twenty-first century. Events in Iraq almost two millennia after Sicarii activities display certain similarities to the situation in Judah under Roman rule. The occupation of Iraq following the toppling of Saddam Husain in 2003 caused Abu Musʻab al-Zarqawi, leader of Al-Qaʻida in Iraq, to carry out terrorist operations against the foreign occupation forces. The Americans and British were, however, not the only enemies of al-Zarqawi, as demonstrated by numerous massacres of Iraq's Shiʻi majority population by

DOI: 10.4324/9781003260943-13

his organization.[7] Like the Sicarii, he turned against some of his own coreligionists, although Shi'is were not considered true Muslims by al-Zarqawi, whose objective was to reestablish traditional Sunni domination of Iraq.[8] A third similarity between the Sicarii and modern Islamic militants is the importance attributed to human agency in the context of God's will, 'jihad fi sabil Allah' (jihad in the path of Allah) or what was termed *herem* by ancient Jews. This term is mentioned in the Old Testament and sanctioned terrorism against outsiders (Canaanites) who were to be ejected from the Promised Land or destroyed if they remained there.[9] These two terms thus display a conceptual connection between ancient Jewish and modern Islamic terrorists, a fact which convincingly demonstrates the rationale for the long-term historical approach to the study of terrorism adopted in the present work.

Other examples of religious and secular causes of terrorism are the Medieval Nizari Isma'ilis (Assassins) and Russian terrorists of the nineteenth and early twentieth centuries. The case of the Nizaris evinces strong religious reasons for terrorism. They often suffered religious persecution in the Seljuq Empire carried out both by the ruler and Muslims who disagreed with their aggressive proselytizing. As a result of the latter, Nizaris therefore fell victim to the state terrorism of the Seljuqs[10] and popular anger.[11] Their response to this persecution was to resort to assassination of temporal and religious leaders who had caused their ire. Conversely, the terrorism unleashed by Russian militant opponents to the tsarist regime was exclusively secular in nature. The causes of the violence perpetrated against the regime were economic exploitation of workers, extreme poverty in rural areas and oppression against the political opposition.[12] The tsarist regime's obvious lack of interest in political reform led organizations such as Narodnaia Volia and the Party of Socialist Revolutionaries (PSR) to embrace the idea of 'propaganda of the deed', a concept that forceful action was needed to achieve change in Russia.[13] Despite the fact that the Russian terrorist organizations were not based on religious convictions, they nonetheless share, with earlier movements, economic exploitation and political oppression as causes of terrorism.

Ideology

The ideologies represented by the groups, organizations and states examined in this study have more in common than the factors which cause terrorism briefly discussed above. Two such aspects that many totalitarian ideologies and states share are intolerance and exclusivity. It should be pointed out, however, that the latter does not necessarily produce the former. Both aspects of totalitarian ideologies are present in all organizations and movements examined in this study from the ancient Sicarii to the Islamic State. The Muwahhidun (Wahhabis) are infamous for their intolerance toward Muslims who declined to accept their strict interpretation of Islam, their destruction of Shi'i shrines and massacres of Shi'is in southern Iraq in 1801 being a case in point.[14] However, it is worth mentioning that the followers of Muhammad Ibn ʿAbd al-Wahhab, the founder of the Muwahhid movement, appear to have adopted a more rigid position on compliance with the founder's recommendations to Muslims since al-Wahhab himself seems to have emphasized conversion based upon reasoning over resorting to violence to achieve the movement's objectives of returning all Muslims to the 'true' path of Allah.[15] The Nizaris (Assassins) also seem to have preferred a non-violent approach to conversion over conversion by the sword, the latter being a reaction to persecution to which they themselves were subjected.[16] Based upon the aforementioned, one can thus conclude that the Nizaris and al-Wahhab were not necessarily the first to resort to violence against Muslims who disagreed with them, but that the former could actually, at least at times, have been subjected to violence at the hands of the latter.

The element of exclusivity is present in all ideologies examined in this study from the Sicarii and Zealots to Daʿish. This contention is obvious from the discussions in previous chapters. One reason totalitarian and terrorist movements emphasize exclusivity is that it is conducive to consolidating claims to legitimacy. Based upon the aforementioned, the observation can be made that extremist groups believe that legitimacy can be achieved by establishing a clear distinction between adherents to a particular ideology and individuals who do not embrace the principles espoused by the ideologues of a terrorist group. In other words, anyone who disagrees has either gone astray or deserves to be labeled an enemy. An advantage of this approach from the perspective of the militants is that it diverts the attention of followers and potential proselytes away from weaknesses in the argumentation of ideological doctrines and propaganda, instead directing the focus on the enemy (individuals who disagree). This stratagem has good prospects of success, when critical thinking is not applied by the target audience. The reason is that an enemy is expected to possess a number of negative qualities, which increases the likelihood of acceptance of the message on the part of the followers. The validity of this conclusion is obvious from the analysis of the doctrines and propaganda presented in the chapters on nineteenth-century Russian terrorists, Nazis and the Islamic State.

In certain respects, interpretations of religion display significant similarities. Perhaps, somewhat surprisingly so, this is the case of the Sicarii and Zealots and some modern extremist Islamic organizations such as the GIA (Groupe Islamique Armée) and Daʿish. Oneness of God was emphasized by ancient Jewish militants[17] to the same extent as the IS's extremist interpretation of Islam justifies its terrorist acts against anyone who in their view is guilty of 'apostasy' or 'idolatry', a verdict which could, of course, be issued against any offender guilty of an act deemed serious enough by the extremists to deserve the ultimate punishment. *Exodus* is clear on the consequences of offering sacrifice 'to any other god than the LORD',[18] an offense punishable by death. This explains why ancient Jewish militants rejected recognition of the rule of the Roman emperor since such recognition would elevate him to the same level as God, in other words an act implying polytheism. Muhammad Ibn ʿAbd al-Wahhab places equal emphasis on the concept of tawhid (oneness of God) as the Jewish Zealots and Sicarii, as evidenced by the title of one of the books which he authored, *Kitab al-Tawhid* (The Book of Oneness of God).[19] The continued central role of this concept in modern extremist Islamic discourse is reflected in the Banner of Tawhid, the black banner carrying the confession of faith under which Daʿish and other Islamic militants wage jihad. In the 1990s, the GIA adopted an even more extreme position than *Exodus*, declaring all Algerians who did not join the group disbelievers deserving of death.[20] Daʿish has adopted a somewhat less extreme position, but has exacted similar punishment on captured Allawi (Shiʿi pro-regime) soldiers in Syria.[21]

In the discourse of secular terrorist organizations and states, 'the people' has replaced 'religion' as a term which presumably bestows legitimacy on any act executed by or policy pursued by a political elite. This is evidenced by names of Russian terrorist groups such as Narodnaia Volia and Narodnaia Rasprava, People's Will and People's Retribution, respectively, and the concept of Volk (nation, people) in Nazi discourse.[22] The Nazi slogan 'Ein Volk, ein Führer' (one nation, one leader) was the rationale for the totalitarian system imposed on Germany by the German National Socialist Workers Party (NSDAP). The concept of the Volk emphasized the differences of human 'races', arguing that the Aryan 'race' was the apex of human evolution and that this position had to be protected against genetic dilution through blending with 'lower races'.[23] The Nazi regime was prepared to rule in the name of the Volk, but had no intention of allowing its Aryan citizens a say in the political process, which would be determined by a limited inner circle of individuals deemed by the Nazi leadership best qualified for this task.[24] Incidentally, modern Islamic terrorists have adopted an approach similar to that of the Nazis concerning totalitarian rule, arguing that parliaments and democracy are institutions and concepts created by man and therefore illegitimate since they usurp the authority of God.[25] The argument advanced by Islamic extremists is that a totalitarian caliphate is the only institution sanctioned by God and that God's representative, that is, whoever happens to be their leader, is the Muslim best qualified to interpret God's word in a temporal and religious context. To the secular Russian and Nazi terrorists, the concept of the 'people' was invoked in a near mystic fashion, fulfilling the role of a higher power which supposedly granted them blanket permission to perpetrate any heinous act carried out in the name of the people.

Despite the many similarities between secular and religious extremist movements, they also display at least one important difference. The kind of society the Jewish Sicarii and Muslim Salafist militants strove/strive to establish differs radically from what Russian extremists viewed as the ideal future revolutionary society. The former aimed/aim for a *restoration* of their religion to its original unadulterated state as reflected in Jewish society before the Roman occupation and Islamic society of the earliest generations

A comparative evolution of terrorism 245

of Muslims. Such a position would have been completely alien to most Russian extremists, the objective of whom was to *build a new* society based on just principles. Some scholars might advance a counterargument to the effect that Russian *narodniki* (populists) advocated the creation of a society based on traditional values of Russia's majority peasant population. This may seem as a compelling argument, but it would more or less exclusively have pertained to the organization of rural society, not necessarily affecting the rest of Russian society as reflected in the program of the PSR, a party supported by Russian peasants.

Russian terrorists frequently adopted as brutal an approach to their enemies as Islamic and Jewish militants, but they appear generally not to have endorsed a totalitarian system of government in lieu of oppressive tsarist rule. A famous extremist pamphlet, the *Katekhizis Revoliutsionera*, states that it is the task of the revolutionary to destroy the civil order. It embraces a democratic process concerning the decision-making process, but it is not clear whether that would be part of a future revolutionary society.[26] The reluctance to discuss post-revolutionary society is not surprising since the pamphlet states without ambiguity that its objective is to destroy. One militant activist, the renowned Russian anarchist Mikhail Bakunin, envisioned a post-revolutionary society built on 'complete freedom and equality' for men and women.[27] This future society would, however, not be a parliamentary democracy since Bakunin had warned against 'the empty talk of parliamentarians', an indication that he did not see a point in having such an institution in society, at least not in situations which demanded quick decisions.[28] The terrorist organization Narodnaia Volia states unequivocally that it intends to transfer power to the Russian people, elect a constituent assembly in free elections, introduce universal suffrage, freedom of expression, assembly and the press and transfer ownership of the land to the people and control of factories to the workers.[29] Narodnaia Volia failed to overthrow the tsarist autocracy, so we do not know whether these militant Russian activists would have introduced genuine democracy in their country. However, the fact that they declared this to be their goal distinguishes some Russian terrorists from all the other similar organizations discussed in this volume, at least with regard to the new society which they envisioned in their writings.

Methodology

Methodology is another area in which scholars can observe a high degree of similarity among extremist groups over the course of centuries. Since the Sicarii emerged, almost 2,000 years ago, terrorists have been aware of the high propaganda value of their acts, and many groups have planned their operations accordingly in order to achieve the strongest possible impact on the enemy and public. Sicarii assassinations of victims in crowded areas[30] demonstrate a clear understanding of the power of propaganda, which is why terrorist organizations have always incorporated it into their operations. One reason the Sicarii and a millennium later the Nizaris relied to such a high degree on daggers must have been that there were not many other weapons available at the time, though poison was certainly a viable alternative. However, a plan relying on the use of the latter would probably require much more time-consuming preparation than an attack which could be executed much more swiftly with a dagger which could be concealed with ease. Another reason was most likely the propaganda value of the dagger as a weapon. When an assassin stabs a victim or slits his throat, this will oftentimes cause massive bloodletting. This graphic way of death naturally serves as a warning to enemies not to incur the ire of a terrorist organization. The ease with which a cold weapon can be concealed and the brutal way of killing a victim are certainly considerations which must have led the GIA in the 1990s and Palestinian terrorists and the Islamic State in the twenty-first century to revive the use of knives[31] despite great technological progress over two millennia which has brought forth many new sophisticated weapons.

Alfred Nobel's invention of dynamite in the 1860s ushered in an era where explosive devices became the preferred weapon among Russian and later terrorists alike. It could be argued that this weapon was a break with the past, but at the same time it represented continuity, if one considers the purpose of terrorist acts, since the use of bombs against human targets possessed propagandistic value when such acts were successful. One advantage of dynamite when it was first used for terrorist acts in the nineteenth century was that a militant did not have to be in close proximity to the intended target. Another reason why terrorists embraced dynamite must have been that a bomb, if sufficiently powerful, did not have to hit the target in order to achieve the desired effect, which made an explosive device superior to a fire arm. If a bullet does not hit the target, it results in a failed assassination attempt. However, the bombs used by Russian extremists were far from being the perfect weapon since they could go off prematurely, if not handled with extreme care, to which fact testify the many unintended explosions in hotel rooms and apartments with death or missing limbs as a result.[32]

A somewhat surprising similarity between Russian terrorists of the nineteenth century and Islamic terrorists is the perception of the former that their terrorist zeal was based on 'religious fanaticism', a belief which presumably made them invincible. This conviction was a result of the view that their suffering at the hands of the tsarist oppressors would eventually lead to the 'bliss of martyrdom and self-sacrifice'.[33] Scholars and others familiar with the discourse of Islamic terrorists will recognize the similar view on the mission which they have taken upon themselves to accomplish. Like mujahidun, many Russian terrorists expected to die, executing a terrorist act. Furthermore, some Russian terrorists defined their struggle against oppression in religious terms, emphasizing the resemblance between their struggle and the experience of early Christian martyrs. Both mujahidun and Russian militants thus expect that death will be the outcome of their struggle, but they view death as something desirable. Both attribute the highest value to death, but for different reasons: to the mujahid, death is a gift to God, the ultimate sacrifice 'in the cause of God', which guarantees entry into Paradise, whereas, to the Russian terrorist, death is a gift to the people. The sacrifice of the latter will not lead to Paradise, but to the liberation of the oppressed. Another similarity is the use of the terms martyrdom and sacrifice. The use of these terms testifies to the fact that Russian terrorists did not view death as suicide, which is exactly what Islamic terrorists argue as well.[34] A question which remains to be answered is how common the view discussed above was among nineteenth-century Russian terrorists. The critical reader will understand that it is difficult to answer this question. It is worth mentioning, however, that the above interpretation of the terrorist mission was discussed in an editorial of the newspaper *Zemlia i Volia*, a major underground revolutionary newspaper, a fact which allows us to conclude that the views expressed must have been supported by at least one prominent member of the editorial staff and quite possibly by other prominent members of the militant organization with the same name as well. It is difficult to conceive of the possibility that an ideological publication would publish an editorial expressing a view that was widely opposed by editors and readers.

The increase in literacy rates, students enrolled in technical and chemistry courses at institutions of higher learning and technological advancements led extremists to engage in innovative thinking in order to reduce the gap between themselves and their enemies in the asymmetric warfare being waged against governments. An example of this development is a late nineteenth-century Russian female terrorist's interest in developing a powerful rocket which could cause extensive damage if launched at the tsar's Winter Palace in St. Petersburg.[35] This extraordinary and futuristic idea testifies to the ability of terrorists to consider the use of weapons which did not yet exist. Another similar idea which Russian terrorists were considering in 1907, four years after the Wright brothers' first flight, was to bombard one of the tsar's palaces from the air.[36] Modern terrorists also display a similar ability of innovative thinking. One example is to use trucks as weapons by driving into crowds at high speed, killing and injuring scores of civilians. Motor vehicles are obviously not new inventions, but modern terrorists have thought of a very unusual way of using them to their advantage. Daʿish encourages its sympathizers in Western countries to buy, rent, carjack or 'borrow' trucks, listing 'ideal targets' (outdoor festivals, markets etcetera) for terrorist acts.[37] The aforementioned examples demonstrate innovative creativity on the part of terrorists and also constitute evidence of continuity over the last 125 years, showing that innovative methodology is not limited to twenty-first-century extremists.

A further aspect of methodology is the desire of some militant movements throughout history to control territory. The Sicarii withdrew to a desert stronghold near the Dead Sea from which they carried out attacks

248 *A comparative evolution of terrorism*

on surrounding towns and villages.[38] The Nizaris' takeover of numerous mountain fortresses in the Middle Ages reflect a similar wish.[39] These bases served as safe havens whence they could exert control over adjacent territory, come to the rescue of other nearby fortresses when these were attacked and project power and coordinate operations targeting individuals outside their own sphere of influence. The Muwahhidun of the eighteenth and nineteenth centuries established control over territory by allying with Ibn Saʻud, the leader of a small town in central Arabia.[40] This alliance ensured protection against the many enemies the Muwahhid religious leader Muhammad Ibn ʻAbd al-Wahhab made as a result of his efforts to convert Muslims to his interpretation of Islam and to extend Muwahhid influence to all corners of the Arabian Peninsula. Control of territory was thus crucial to the success of al-Wahhab's efforts to disseminate his ideas.[41] The Taliban in Afghanistan and the Islamic State in Iraq and Syria are recent examples of organizations which established control of large contiguous territories, albeit of ephemeral duration, partly as a result of their hostility toward the West, in consequence of which they had to fight an enemy who ejected them from most of the territory which they controlled.[42] It is possible that both organizations have realized that control of territory comes at the cost of certain vulnerabilities since such control has to be perpetuated lest recruitment be drastically reduced. Furthermore, territorial control also exposes a terrorist organization to aerial attacks. Historically, most terrorist groups have lacked the capacity or desire to establish control over large contiguous areas.[43]

Deception

Rulers, counterterrorism agencies and terrorists have always played a game of hide-and-seek, trying to outsmart one another in attempts to gain a decisive advantage over the adversary. The Nizaris, for instance, used conversion and deception, posing as Turkish soldiers, Sufis or Christian monks to approach their targets.[44] Seeking employment with a prominent government official was also a method which was adopted by the Nizaris to enable them to carry out assassinations.[45] In more recent times, similar approaches have been adopted by Russian terrorists and the Taliban. The Taliban has proven particularly adept at infiltrating the Afghan armed forces to attack foreign military personnel stationed in Afghanistan.[46] Furthermore, frequently, intelligence agencies and terrorists have been successful in placing their agents in enemy organizations. The Okhrana received invaluable intelligence from its agent, the leader of the PSRs' Combat Organization for five years and Russian terrorists achieved the same success by placing their agent in a position inside the Tret'e Otdelenie (the Okhrana's predecessor).[47]

The Algerian and Israeli governments have been equally successful as the Russian tsarist government in their efforts to infiltrate terrorist organizations. In the 1990s, the Algerian government was involved in a struggle against Islamic terrorists similar to that of the Russian government in the late nineteenth century and early twentieth century. The country's security services managed to infiltrate some terrorist groups and control others.[48] Ironically, the Algerian security services adopted methods as brutal as those the French had used three decades earlier against Algerian liberation fighters.[49] It is worth noting in this context that Algerian Islamic terrorist groups scored their own successes as evidenced by the support they enjoyed among security personnel in junior positions.[50] Like its Russian and Algerian equivalents, the Israeli domestic intelligence service, the Shin Bet, has an impressive track record with regard to infiltration of Palestinian society. Shin Bet operatives would pose as representatives of Western companies and dupe Palestinians into working for them until they revealed to the latter that they were actually working for Israeli intelligence. At this point, the Palestinians, faced with the threat of being exposed to their own, had no choice but to continue working for the Israelis since exposure would quite possibly lead to death at the hands of Palestinian organizations such as Hamas.[51]

A common method used both by terrorists and law enforcement agencies has been to circulate disinformation to mislead or discredit the enemy. The advantage of disinformation is that it can be used in different ways, depending on what the objective is of creating deception. It can be used successfully by terrorists to give subtle hints regarding the date or target of a future operation, when the purpose is to lead law enforcement and intelligence agencies in the wrong direction in order to reduce surveillance or protection of a target which a militant organization plans to attack.[52] Disinformation can also be used by security services to disseminate false information to the effect that a terrorist individual or a militant organization in reality works for a law enforcement agency. In such a case, the purpose is to cause damage to the reputation of the individual or group in question, cause doubt in the minds of potential recruits about the wisdom of joining an organization which is possibly infiltrated by enemy agents or sow division among terrorists.[53] Another way to disseminate disinformation is to claim responsibility for a terrorist act executed by someone else. The obvious intention of such a claim is to improve the standing of a group, an act which will presumably increase the appeal of joining the group. Another purpose could be to diminish the reputation of a successful organization which might pose a challenge to the authority of the group engaging in deception or to cause confusion in the minds of intelligence officials.

A further method aimed at lowering the guard of the enemy is to use women and children. Terrorist organizations and law enforcement agencies have both used women to infiltrate enemy organizations. This was a phenomenon particularly common in tsarist Russia. The tsarist Okhrana benefited greatly from a female informant whom they had succeeded in placing in the PSR's Combat Organization.[54] Militant groups in tsarist Russia often used women for non-lethal missions such as smuggling weapons and ammunition.[55] According to the Okhrana, children were also used by terrorists for similar tasks.[56] In the nineteenth and early twentieth century, Russian women frequently volunteered to execute terrorist acts such as throwing bombs and shooting at officials. When caught, these women were normally treated as harshly as their male colleagues.[57] Today it appears that most women who resort to such violence are found in the Islamic world. A majority of these women have gone on 'martyrdom' missions for the Nigerian terrorist organization Boko Haram. This group is also infamous for using girls to carry out such missions. Teenage girls or even pre-teens are kidnapped and after some time given a choice to become the wife of a Boko Haram fighter or to carry out a 'martyrdom' mission.[58] Based upon the above, one can conclude that terrorist organizations have for more than a century used women and children to facilitate their operations. However, this continuity reveals a couple of differences between Russian militants in the early part of that period and more recent terrorist organizations such as Boko Haram and the Islamic State. The former never used children to execute violent acts, whereas the latter two have brainwashed or threatened children to carry out terrorist acts.[59] Another difference between Russian and recent Islamic terrorism is that many women reached leading positions in Russian extremist organizations,[60] whereas that is unheard of in Boko Haram or the Islamic State, organizations which treat women as cannon fodder or even worse, particularly in the case of the latter organization.

State terrorism

One characteristic which sets state terrorism apart from the kind of terrorism practiced by groups and organizations is the great resources of a state which can be exploited for terrorist purposes against its own citizens and other states. The primary asset of the Nizari state in the Middle Ages was probably of psychological nature, namely the assassins who could be dispatched to exact revenge on rulers and high officials who had persecuted Nizari followers. The fact that a number of high-profile operations had been successful must have cemented the organization's reputation as a fearful opponent who could not be challenged without serious consequences for an attacker. A second source of Nizari power were the many mountain fortresses in remote areas[61] which made potential punitive action against them a dangerous and difficult operation. These two factors most likely made up for the lack of huge armies raised by the Nizaris. One can most certainly conclude that it was fear and inaccessibility which guaranteed the longevity (183 years) of the Nizari Isma'ilis. Conversely, the enormous military power of the Nazi state could not prevent the collapse within 12 years of the mighty 'thousand year' Third Reich. The Mongols were the superpower which put an end to Nizari power and the Nazis' weak strategic position between enemies in the West and East, diminishing resources, limited manpower, alienation of most of the world, costly strategic mistakes (the attack on the Soviet

Union), elimination of a part of its own population and ruthless aggression against other states were factors which contributed to their relatively quick demise. It can thus be concluded that resources, including manpower, in and of themselves do not necessarily constitute a guarantee for great power or the longevity of a state. What matters more is how these resources are used.

Like the Islamic State and unlike the Nizaris and the Muwahhid leader Muhammad Ibn ʻAbd al-Wahhab, Nazi Germany was a terrorist state which had few compunctions about how to implement brutal policies in Germany and occupied territories alike. Nizari terrorism generally targeted high-ranking officials,[62] whereas neither the Nazis nor Daʻish drew a distinction between civilians in high or low positions or legal concepts such as guilt and innocence for that matter. Nazi treatment of Jews and IS treatment of Yazidis confirm this claim.[63] A major difference between the medieval state and the two modern states was thus that the Nazis and the Islamic State practiced mass terrorism. The Third Reich and the Islamic State were totalitarian states led by dictators who believed that they were acting in the cause of a higher power and so did the Nizari state. The first leader of the Nizaris, Hasan-i Sabbah, believed that he was appointed by God for his mission.[64] The founder of the Muwahhid movement, Muhammad Ibn ʻAbd al-Wahhab, was as convinced as the other two Muslim leaders that his interpretation of Islam was the only correct one, but there is evidence that he preferred, at least initially, to use reasoning instead of brute force to convert Muslims who had 'gone astray'.[65] Reasoning and proselytizing were arts in which the Nizaris, like al-Wahhab, excelled. The former would oftentimes seize fortresses by first converting the garrison to Nizari Ismaʻilism.[66] One can only with great difficulty imagine that the Nazi regime or Daʻish would display such patience when confronting an enemy on the battlefield.

Two other examples of state terrorism, the Taliban and Daʻish, deserve attention as well. Both entities formerly controlled large contiguous territories. The Taliban state constituted the majority of Afghan provinces. Conversely, the Islamic State (Daʻish) spanned large parts of two countries – Iraq and Syria. The Taliban lost their state when they refused to extradite Osama Bin Laden to the United States and Daʻish appears to have met the same fate, losing all its territory in Iraq and Syria as a result of its war against the al-Asad regime, Russia, an international coalition and the Shiʻi-dominated government in Iraq. It can be argued that both the Taliban and the Islamic State pursued terrorist policies against their own population and anyone who happened to disagree with their extremist interpretation of Islam.[67] Interestingly enough, both organizations are at one another's throats in Afghanistan, vying for control in the war-torn country. As discussed earlier in this study, some groups embracing totalitarian ideologies find it difficult to cooperate with other groups unless those groups swear allegiance to them.[68] One recent reason for Daʻish's increased interest in Afghanistan could be its search for an alternative base which could be expanded to a new state in lieu of the one lost in Iraq and Syria. Conversely, the IS challenge to the

Taliban's authority could have contributed to the latter's interest in negotiations to achieve a departure of NATO troops from Afghanistan. A consequence of the recent Taliban takeover of Afghanistan is most likely that the regime will have to devote more attention to rivaling extremist groups in the country. Having said that, the Islamic State's war on Shiʻis most likely constitutes an insurmountable obstacle to rallying all Afghans behind their cause since the Taliban takes a somewhat more conciliatory position on relations with Shiʻis.[69]

A result of the Taliban and the Islamic State's loss of territory was the loss of crucial resources which enabled them to maintain functioning societies. However, despite this loss, drug trafficking continued to be an important source of income for both organizations.[70] Oil helped fill the coffers of the IS treasury while it controlled oil wells in Iraq and Syria, but as the organization began to lose territory it came to rely more on drug trafficking to keep its government running. The increasing reliance on drugs was also explained by a shrinking population and diminished tax revenues. The Taliban, despite its loss of a state in 2001, continued to be a wealthy organization as a result of trafficking in heroin. The trade in drugs thus goes to show that an organization which loses control of a state can remain relevant despite loss of revenue. Loss of territory could actually prove a blessing in disguise since hiding in the desert, mountain caves or among civilian populations makes tan organization less vulnerable to attack than controlling a government bureaucracy and infrastructure in a capital city. There is thus good reason to caution Western intelligence agencies and military commanders not to be too quick in announcing the demise of an extremist organization. It remains to be seen to what extent the Taliban can benefit from their renewed control of Afghanistan.

Propaganda

A characteristic that all terrorist organizations and states examined in this study share is the conviction that they can reap benefits from propaganda. The propaganda of the three earlier movements – the Sicarii, Nizaris and Muwahhidun – is clearly similar to the idea of 'propaganda by the deed' of later periods. A likely explanation why they emphasized this type of propaganda over the written word is lower literacy rates than in the twentieth and twenty-first centuries. Furthermore, oral reports of a terrorist event were most likely disseminated at a higher speed by word of mouth than in written form which would undoubtedly reach a more limited audience. Also, like in later periods, a terrorist act executed in a locale in the presence of a large number of people has high propagandistic value since it instills fear in the target audience. The assassinations carried out by the Sicarii and Nizaris and razing to the ground of saints' tombs or massacres perpetrated by the Muwahhidun would all have attracted the attention of the public and served as an unmistakable warning to dissenters. Executions of terrorists – public in earlier periods or behind prison walls in later periods – were most certainly deemed by rulers and counterterrorism authorities to have a similar propagandistic value, the purpose, of course, being to serve as a deterrent to continued terrorist acts and instill confidence in the public that the government deals with terrorists in an effective way. However, it is doubtful whether executions are an effective deterrent when terrorists are prepared, or even wish, to die for a 'higher cause'. It appears that neither terrorist acts nor executions of terrorists were effective in tsarist Russia. They did not prevent continued terrorism, and they did not lead to a general uprising and the overthrow of the tsar, which was the objective of the extremists.[71] Likewise, Nazi mass retaliation against villagers in occupied territories did not break partisan resistance.[72]

The increasing focus on written and other forms of propaganda than 'propaganda by the deed' over the course of the last 150 years suggests that terrorists firmly believe in its effectiveness. The detailed analysis of the propaganda of Russian terrorist organizations, the Nazis and the Islamic State in this work reveals an important difference between terrorist propaganda produced by states such as Nazi Germany and Da'ish, and that published by militant anti-regime groups such as Narodnaia Volia or the PSR operating in an authoritarian society. A crucial purpose of the former two was to 'protect' the people or religious community from 'alien' ideas by erecting an ideological firewall. A second function of this kind of propaganda is to proselytize abroad. This function is particularly obvious in Da'ish's online magazines *Dabiq* and *Rumiyah*, and Al-Qa'ida's *Inspire*, which encourage Muslims in the West to carry out terrorist acts against their fellow-countrymen.[73] By contrast, one purpose of the propaganda published by Russian terrorists was to reach the Russian population by penetrating the firewall of the tsarist government. Like the state terrorists of a later era, they also made serious efforts to convert expatriates and Western public opinion to their cause.[74] Furthermore, there is evidence in the writings of Russian terrorists that moral principles played a prominent role in justifying their actions. Some militants argued that an overemphasis on terror would only cause too much bloodletting in society and not be conducive to a final revolutionary victory. Others contended that restrictions should be imposed on who should be targeted, arguing that government officials should be their main focus. A third argument advanced by Russian terrorists was that blanket terrorism against a whole class of people such as capitalists or factory owners could not be justified since workers would suffer as well as a result of unemployment.[75]

Justifications of terrorism in Nazi and Islamic State propaganda are to a much lesser extent than those of Russian militants concerned with morality and compassion, two concepts which are almost completely absent in Nazi texts, at least in a positive sense, and much less prominent in Da'ish than in Russian terrorist propaganda. In the context of the Nazi ideological discourse, racism presumably obviates a discussion of morality and compassion since the latter two concepts constitute obstacles to the purification of the Aryan race through the elimination of all Jews.[76] The Islamic State's resolution to the question of what should be done about the 'enemies of Islam', 'Crusaders', Jews and 'polytheists' is quite similar to the Nazi concept of 'Endlösung' (final solution).[77] Both arguments defy logic since they are based on pseudoscience in the Nazi case and Quranic quotes almost invariably taken out of context and without a serious attempt to contextualize the quotes by Da'ish propagandists.[78] Almost nothing, perhaps with the exception of Sergei Nechaev's writings, is permeated with such hatred of the 'enemy' in the Russian terrorist discourse,[79] and it is difficult to imagine that Russian terrorist organizations examined in this study would create a society based upon such 'ideals' because the vast majority seems to have disagreed with Nechaev's views; otherwise, these ideas would have gained much more currency in the writings of the Narodnaia Volia and PSR. Some historians might argue that this conclusion is not based upon historical fact since the Red Terror in the Russian Civil War 1918–1921 and Josef Stalin's brutal policies resulting in the death of millions of Russians appear to suggest otherwise. This is a somewhat valid point, but a strong counterargument would be that, unlike the Narodnaia Volia and the PSR, the purpose of the Bolsheviks was to build a society based on the Marxist idea of the 'dictatorship of the proletariat'.[80] The two terrorist organizations, however, did not believe in the idea of a dictatorship, advocating a future society guaranteeing civil rights to all Russians.[81]

A final point that needs to be made in this chapter is the conclusion which can be drawn from the analysis of ideologies and propaganda in previous chapters of the present work, namely that propaganda in its various forms – a method of persuasion particularly exploited by the modern terrorist states examined in this volume – is far from being the miracle weapon which totalitarian states and organizations believe it is, a conclusion at which one can arrive by examining the great efforts made to benefit from it.[82] What the propagandas of Russian, Nazi and Da'ish ideologues have in common is the obvious flaws of the tsarist regime, the Weimar Republic and contemporary governments in the Islamic world. Poverty, unemployment and exploitation made it equally easy for militants to highlight the failures of their societies. Russian and IS terrorists had the additional advantage of being able to exploit the existence of oppressive regimes. The Nazi Party, prior to its assumption of power, did not have the luxury of being in a position to criticize the political oppression of democratic Weimar governments, which is certainly one reason why the NSDAP had to invent the simplistic narrative that all negative aspects of the German state could be blamed on German Jews and democracy, the latter of which presumably enabled the former to control 'true' Germans.[83] When it comes to addressing the flaws of contemporary society, however, both Nazis and the Islamic State were at a disadvantage since their recipe for building the ideal society was fraught with contradictions and the brutality and oppression of which they accused their 'enemies'. In both cases, their rule led to disaster and indescribable suffering. One of their major weaknesses was to make all citizens 'equal' by forcing them to adopt a single ideology thereby relinquishing their right to question decisions made by the Führer or 'Khalifa' (Caliph). By contrast, the advantage which Russian militants had over the Nazis and Da'ish was that they wished to make all Russians equal, not by forcing them to adopt a single ideology, but by unconditionally granting every citizen the right to be different if (s)he so wished, as discussed in the previous paragraph.

Previous analysis of terrorist propaganda in this study has revealed that manipulation of information is a double-edged sword. Nazi and IS propaganda, when analyzed, clearly demonstrates the great confidence both terrorist states placed in their ability to convert the public to their cause. A major weakness of this propaganda is the overconfidence of its authors in their ability to sway public opinion to their advantage based on this 'powerful' weapon. A meticulous analysis of the arguments advanced by the NSDAP and Da'ish reveals that their approach to manipulation of information, as a matter of fact, places a formidable counterterrorism tool in the hands of educational institutions, law enforcement and intelligence agencies. Instead of inspiring awe in the latter, the perceived 'media acumen' of Nazi and IS propagandists should not be allowed to blur the reality of weak argumentation as exposed in a detailed analysis of the methods of propaganda production adopted by both states.[84]

Conclusion

As argued throughout this work, the examination of different terrorist organizations and states in different time periods will greatly contribute to the understanding of totalitarian ideologies and the methodology adopted to implement these. The analysis in previous chapters has revealed that each terrorist organization may be unique in a limited number of aspects but similar to other militant groups in many more ways, irrespective of how many centuries might separate them. A comparative approach to different organizations, operating in different societies and time periods, will thus make terrorism a less unpredictable phenomenon, revealing a high degree of continuity over the course of time. Furthermore, in a comparative context, it is worth noting that what might constitute a unique characteristic in the present work should not be perceived as in all eternity limited to one single organization, but rather having the potential of being repeated in, or adopted by, a different group, in a different society, at a different time. The approach to the study of terrorism presented in this work thus demonstrates certain advantages over an approach more limited in scope, focusing on one group operating in the context of one particular religion, society or time period only.

Notes

1 Richard Horsley, 'The Sicarii: Ancient Jewish "Terrorists"', *The Journal of Religion*, Vol. 59, No. 4 (Oct., 1979), p. 446.
2 David M. Rhoads, *Israel in Revolution: 6-74 C.E.: A Political History Based on the Writings of Josephus* (Philadelphia: Fortress Press, 1976), pp. 98–99; Martin Hengel, *The Zealots: Investigations into the Jewish Freedom Movement in the Period from Herod I until 70 A.D.*, trans. David Smith (Edinburgh: T. & T. Clark, 1989), p. 352. Rhoads, *Israel in Revolution*, p. 106.
3 Sayyid Qutb, *Ma'alim fi'l-tariq*, SIME ePublishing Services (distributor), p. 35, accessed 21 July 2018, http://majallah.org/2017/01/qutbs-milestone.html.
4 'Abu Yahya Al-Libi: Profile of an Al-Qaeda Leader', March 2012, *International Institute for Counter-Terrorism*, pp. 11–12, accessed 10 April 2018, https://www.ict.org.il/UserFiles/Abu%20Yahya%20al-Libi.pdf; Michael Weiss and Hassan Hassan, *ISIS: Inside the Army of Terror* (New York, NY: Regan Arts, 2015), pp. 18, 29.
5 For an analysis of the contents of *Inspire*, see Chapter VIII in this volume.
6 For a detailed analysis of the contents of *Dabiq*, see Chapters 9 and 10 in this volume.
7 George Michael, 'The Legend and Legacy of Abu Musab al-Zarqawi', *Defense Studies*, Vol. 7, No. 3 (Sept., 2007), p. 347.
8 Weiss and Hassan, *ISIS*, pp. 18, 29.
9 David C. Rapoport, 'Fear and Trembling: Terrorism in Three Religious Traditions', *The American Political Science Review*, Vol. 78, No. 3 (Sept., 1984), p. 669.
10 Daftary, *The Ismailis*, pp. 362, 373; Hodgson, *The Secret Order*, p. 103.
11 Hodgson, *The Secret Order*, p. 93.
12 Adam B. Ulam, *Prophets and Conspirators: Prerevolutionary Russia* (New Brunswick and London: Transaction Publishers, 1998 (first published in 1977 by Viking Press), pp. 80, 91.
13 Many of the extreme ideas circulating in nineteenth-century Russian terrorist circles are summarized in a political pamphlet entitled *Katekhizis Revoliutsionera*, Sergei Gennadievich Nechaev, 'Katekhizis revoliutsionera', in Evgenia L. Rudnitskaia, ed., *Revoliutsionnii radikalizm v Rossii: deviatnadtsatii vek* (Moscow: Arkheograficheskii Tsentr, 1997), pp. 244–245.
14 Ondrej Beranek and Pavel Tupek, 'From Visiting Graves to Their Destruction: The Question of Ziyara through the Eyes of Salafis', Crown Paper 2, July 2009, *Crown Center for Middle East Studies*, p. 20, accessed 24 January 2018, https://www.brandeis.edu/crown/publications/cp/CP2.pdf; Sheikh-Dilthey, 'Dariyyah', p. 143; Kucukcan, 'Some Reflections', p. 64.
15 DeLong-Bas, *Wahhabi Islam*, pp. 17–18; Muhammad Ibn 'Abd al-Wahhab, *Kitab al-Jihad*, p. 379, in DeLong-Bas, *Wahhabi Islam*, p. 82.
16 See footnotes 10 and 11 above.
17 Martin Hengel, *The Zealots*, pp. 81, 306; Solomon Zeitlin, 'Masada and the Sicarii', *The Jewish Quarterly Review*, Vol. 55, No. 4 (Apr., 1965), p. 303.
18 The International Bible Society, 'Exodus 22 – New International Version', *Biblica*, accessed 17 May 2019, https://www.biblica.com/bible/niv/exodus/22/.
19 Muhammad Ibn Abdul Wahhab, *Kitab at-Tawheed Explained*, compiler and trans. Sameh Strauch (Al-Riyadh: International Islamic Publishing House, 2000).
20 ''Antar al-Zouabri, "dhabbah" jama'at GIA al-jaza'ir' 10 May 2015, *Bawabat al-harika al-Islamiyya*, accessed 24 December 2016, http://islamist-movements.com/28316.
21 Al-Hayat Media Center, *Rumiyah*, Issue 7 (Mar., 2017), p. 29.
22 See Chapter 4 for a detailed discussion of the Nazi concept of Volk.

23 NARA, Record Group (RG) 242, T81, Roll 22, Informationsdienst der Dienststelle des Beauftragten des Fuehrers fuer die gesamte geistliche und weltanschauliche Erziehung der NSDAP. Reichsleitung. Jahrgang 1935, Nr. 47. Ausgabetag: 2. August. Streng vertraulich! Nur fuer den Dienstgebrauch! Dr. Werner Huettig, Rassenpolitisches Amt der N.S.D.A.P. Rassisches Denken und praktische Politik.
24 Alfred Rosenberg, *Der Mythus des 20. Jahrhunderts: Eine Wertung der seelisch-geistigen Gestaltungskaempfe unserer Zeit* (Munich: Hoheneichen Verlag, 1939), pp. 546–547.
25 *Dabiq*, Issue 2 (Jun., Jul., 2014), pp. 5–6, 9.
26 Sergei Gennadievich Nechaev, 'Katekhizis revoliutsionera', in Evgenia L. Rudnitskaia, ed., *Revoliutsionnii radikalizm v Rossii: deviatnadtsatii vek* (Moscow: Arkheograficheskii Tsentr, 1997), pp. 244–245.
27 Philip Pomper, *Sergei Nechaev* (New Brunswick, NJ: Rutgers University Press, 1979), pp. 281–286; Randall Law, *Terrorism: A History* (Cambridge: Polity Press, 2013), p. 78.
28 Ibid.
29 'Program of the Executive Committee', *Narodnaia Volia* No. 3, 11 January 1880, in Rudnitskaia, *Revolutsionnii radikalizm*, pp. 417–419.
30 Richard Horsley, 'The Sicarii: Ancient Jewish "Terrorists"', pp. 436, 438.
31 Redha Malek, 'Islamist Terrorism in Algeria: An Experience to Ponder', in Walter Laqueur, ed., *Voices of Terror: Manifestos, Writings and Manuals of Al Qaeda, Hamas, and Other Terrorists from around the World and throughout the Ages* (Naperville: Sourcebooks, Inc., 2004), p. 444; Isabel Kershner, 'Israeli Dies as Palestinian Attackers Stage Assaults in Jerusalem', *New York Times*, 16 June 2017, accessed 20 May 2019, https://www.nytimes.com/2017/06/16/world/middleeast/israel-palestinians-attack-jerusalem.html; Al-Hayat Media Center, *Rumiyah*, Issue 4 (Dec., 2016), p. 8; *Inspire*, Issue 15 (Spring 2016), pp. 36–37.
32 From Arkady Harting, Head of Intelligence Section [Temporarily Visiting Geneva] to P. I. Rachkovskii, Paris, no date. Box 214, Reel 396, Okhrana Records; Boris V. Savinkov, *Vospominaniia terrorista*, *Lib.ru/Klassika*, accessed 7 September 2015, http://az.lib.ru/s/sawinkow_b_w/text_0010.shtml (first published in 1909), pp. 12, 81.
33 Editorial published in the newspaper *Zemlia i Volia*, No. 1, 25 October 1878, in Rudnitskaia, *Revoliutsionnii radikalizm*, p. 407.
34 Ivan Strenski, 'Sacrifice, Gift and the Social Logic of Muslim "Human Bombers"', *Library of Social Science*, accessed 22 May 2016, https://www.libraryofsocialscience.com/essays/strenski-sacrifice.html; *Rumiyah*, Issue 5, p. 8.
35 Oleg V. Budnitskii, *Terrorizm v rossiiskom osvoboditel'nom dvizhenii: Ideologiia, etika, psikhologiia (vtoraia polovina XIX-nachalo XX v.)* (Moscow: ROSSPEN, 2000), p. 35.
36 Savinkov, *Vospominania*, p. 111.
37 Al-Hayat Media Center, *Rumiyah*, Issue 9 (Apr., May, 2017), p. 56.
38 Solomon Zeitlin, 'Masada and the Sicarii', p. 303.
39 Shafique N. Virani, 'The Eagle Returns: Evidence of Continued Isma'ili Activity at Alamut and in the South Caspian Region Following the Mongol Conquests', *Journal of the American Oriental Society*, Vol. 123, No. 2 (Apr., Jun., 2003), p. 365.
40 Helmtraut Sheikh-Dilthey, 'Dariyyah: Das Herz Saudi-Arabiens', *Anthropos*, Vol. 84, No. 1/3 (1989), p. 142.
41 See Chapter I for a discussion of al-Wahhab's interpretation of Islam.
42 Unfortunately, the fact that the Taliban has reestablished control over Afghanistan 20 years after the emirate's ouster has demonstrated that a powerful enemy

can be vanquished with the right amount of perseverance, attrition and war fatigue. The National Socialists would have explained this phenomenon by reference to the *Wille* of the Volk, whereas Islamic extremists call it God's will.
43 For an historical approach to terrorism, see Gérard Chaliand and Arnaud Blin, eds., *The History of Terrorism From Antiquity to Al Qaeda* (Berkeley: University of California Press, 2007).
44 Daftary, *The Isma'ilis*, p. 376; Bernard Lewis, 'The Ismā'īlites and the Assassins', in Marshall W. Baldwin, ed., *A History of the Crusades* (Madison: University of Wisconsin Press, 1969, I, second edition), pp. 111, 125.
45 David C. Rapoport, 'Fear and Trembling', p. 666.
46 Kathy Gannon and Rahim Faiez, 'Taliban Infiltrate Afghan Army to Target Foreign Troops', *The Associated Press*, 18 June 2017, accessed 26 May 2019, https://www.militarytimes.com/news/your-military/2017/06/18/q-a-taliban-infiltrate-afghan-army-to-target-foreign-troops/.
47 Daly, *The Watchful State*, pp. 98–100; Pipes, *The Degaev Affair*, p. 56; Ulam, *Prophets and Conspirators*, pp. 306–307.
48 Mohammed Samraoui, *Chronique des années de sang*, 2003, pp. 95, 215, referred to in Neil Grant Landers, *Representing the Algerian Civil War: Literature, History, and the State* (Dissertation), accessed 29 April 2018, http://digitalassets.lib.berkeley.edu/etd/ucb/text/Landers_berkeley_0028E_13922.pdf, pp. 83–84.
49 David B. Ottaway, 'Algeria: Bloody Past and Fractious Factions', 27 August 2015, *Wilson Center*, accessed 18 January 2017, https://www.wilsoncenter.org/article/algeria-bloody-past-and-fractious-factions.
50 Martin Stone, *The Agony of Algeria* (New York, NY: Columbia University Press, 1997), p. 194.
51 Zaki Chehab, *Inside Hamas: The Untold Story of the Militant Islamic Movement* (New York, NY: Nation Books, 2007), p. 73.
52 From the Okhrana Office, Paris to the Department of the Police, No. 1205, 12 August 1913; From Okhrana Office, Paris to the Department of the Police, No. 1258, 17 August 1913.
53 Jonathan Daly, *Autocracy under Siege: Security Police and Opposition in Russia 1866–1905* (DeKalb: Northern Illinois University Press, 1998), p. 94; Richard Pipes, *The Degaev Affair: Terror and Treason in Tsarist Russia* (New Haven, CT: Yale University Press, 2003), p. 39.
54 Daly, *The Watchful State*, pp. 98–100.
55 Pavel Pavlovich Zavarzin, *Zhandarmy i Revoliutsionery: Vospominaniia* [Gendarmes and Revolutionaries: A Memoir] (Paris: Published by the author [izdanie avtora], 1930), pp. 117–119, 143–144, 148.
56 Ibid.
57 From Harting, Head of Intelligence Section to the Director of Department of the Police, 20 April 1906. Top Secret. Box 214, Reel 396, Okhrana Records.
58 Vladimir Hernandez and Stephanie Hagarty, 'Made-up to Look Beautiful. Sent Out to Die. The Young Women Sent into Crowds to Blow Themselves Up', *BBC*, accessed 28 May 2019, https://www.bbc.co.uk/news/resources/idt-sh/made_up_to_look_beautiful_sent_out_to_die.
59 Lizzie Dearden, 'Isis Is Using Far More Child Soldiers than the World Realised', *Independent*, 19 February 2016, accessed 28 May 2019, https://www.independent.co.uk/news/world/middle-east/isis-using-more-child-fighters-than-feared-as-suicide-bombers-and-soldiers-after-brainwashing-at-a6883626.html.
60 Amy Knight, 'Female Terrorists in the Russian Socialist Revolutionary Party', *The Russian Review*, Vol. 38, No. 2 (Apr., 1979), pp. 139, 144, 146; Vera Broido, *Apostles into Terrorists: Women and the Revolutionary Movement in the Russia of Alexander II* (New York, NY: Viking Press, 1977), p. 183.

61 Shafique N. Virani, 'The Eagle Returns', p. 365.
62 Daftary, *The Ismailis*, pp. 362, 373.
63 Alfred Rosenberg, 'Der Weltparasit', *Völkischer Beobachter*, 6 June 1943; Cathy Otten, 'Slaves of Isis: The Long Walk of the Yazidi Women', *The Guardian*, 25 July 2017, accessed 30 May 2019, https://www.theguardian.com/world/2017/jul/25/slaves-of-isis-the-long-walk-of-the-yazidi-women.
64 Adolf Hitler, *Mein Kampf* (Munich: Fritz Eher Nachfolger, 1943), 70; Al-Hayat Media Center, *Dabiq*, Issue 1 (Jun., Jul., 2014), p. 27; Daftary, *The Ismailis*, pp. 337, 369; Hodgson, *The Secret Order*, p. 59.
65 Husain Ibn Ghannam, *Tarikh Najd* [History of Najd], p. 477, referred to in David Commins, *The Wahhabi Mission and Saudi Arabia* (London: I.B. Tauris, 2006), accessed 24 January 2018, http://asrdiplomacy.ir/wp-content/uploads/2017/03/The-Wahhabi-Mission-and-Saudi-Arabia-Book-1.pdf, p. 25.
66 Hodgson, *The Secret Order*, p. 85.
67 Bruce A. Robinson, 'Religious Intolerance in Afghanistan', *Religious Tolerance*, 20 November 2001, accessed 29 May 2019, http://www.religioustolerance.org/rt_afgha.htm; Al-Hayat Media Center, *Dabiq*, Issue 3 (Jul., Aug., 2014), pp. 4, 12–13, 21.
68 See Chapters 7 and 8 in this volume.
69 Akhilesh Pillalamarri, 'Revealed: Why ISIS Hates the Taliban', *The Diplomat*, 29 January 2016, accessed 29 May 2019, https://thediplomat.com/2016/01/revealed-why-isis-hates-the-taliban/.
70 Colin P. Clarke, 'ISIS Is So Desperate It's Turning to the Drug Trade', *Fortune*, 24 July 2017, accessed 30 May 2019, http://fortune.com/2017/07/24/isis-mosul-defeated-news-territory-islamic-state-drugs/; Christopher Woody, 'Heroin Is Driving a Sinister Trend in Afghanistan', *Business Insider*, 30 October 2017, accessed 30 May 2019, https://www.businessinsider.com/taliban-control-of-heroin-drug-production-trafficking-in-afghanistan-2017-10.
71 Ulam, *Prophets and Conspirators*, p. 99; Chaliand and Blin, *The History of Terrorism*, p. 137; 'Program of Zemlia i Volia', May 1878, in Rudnitskaia, *Revoliutsionnii radikalizm*, p. 395; 'Podgotovitel'naia Rabota Partii' [Preparatory Work of the Party]. *Kalendar' Narodnoi Voli 1883-go goda'* [1883 Almanac of Narodnaia Volia], Geneva, 1883, in Rudnitskaia, *Revolutsionnii radikalizm*, p. 421.
72 United States Holocaust Memorial Museum, 'Operation Anthropoid', Holocaust Encyclopedia, accessed 31 May 2019, https://encyclopedia.ushmm.org/content/en/article/lidice; Nick Fagge, 'I Despise Them. Germany Is the Enemy: The Greek Survivors of Nazi Massacre Who Say "No" Vote Wasn't Just about Austerity but Continued Resistance Against "Occupation"', *Daily Mail*, 8 July 2015, accessed 30 May 2019, https://www.dailymail.co.uk/news/article-3152216/I-despise-Germany-enemy-Greek-survivors-Nazi-massacre-say-No-vote-wasn-t-just-austerity-continued-resistance-against-occupation.html; '1944 Massacre in France: German Police Raid Homes of Six Former SS Soldiers', *Spiegel Online*, 6 December 2011, accessed 31 May 2019, https://www.spiegel.de/international/germany/1944-massacre-in-france-german-police-raid-homes-of-six-former-ss-soldiers-a-802019.html.
73 Al-Hayat Media Center, *Rumiyah*, Issue 9 (May 2017), pp. 47–51, 56; *Rumiyah*, Issue 5 (Jan., 2017); Al-Malahem Media, *Inspire* (Winter 2010), p. 7.
74 Ulam, *Prophets and Conspirators*, p. 99; Chaliand and Blin, *The History of Terrorism*, p. 137; *Obshchina*, No. 1, 1 September 1870, London. Document No. 14, in Evgenia L. Rudnitskaia, ed., *Revoliutsionnii radikalizm v Rossii: deviatnadtsatii vek* (Moscow: Arkheograficheskii Tsentr, 1997), pp. 291–292; 'Program of Zemlia i Volia', May 1878, in Rudnitskaia, *Revoliutsionnii radikalizm*, p. 395.

75 Sergei Kravchinskii, 'Smert' za smert' [Death for a Death], in Rudnitskaia, *Revoliutsionnii radikalizm*, pp. 402–403; Editorial published in the newspaper *Zemlia i Volia*, No. 1, 25 October 1878, in Rudnitskaia, *Revoliutsionnii radikalizm*, p. 408; 'Ot tsentral'nogo komiteta P.S.-R. Po voprosu ob agrarnom i fabrichnom terrore' [From the Central Committee of the PSR. On the question of agrarian and factory terror], *Znamia Truda*, No. 3, 1 August 1907, in Nikolai D. Erofeev, *Partiia sotsialistov-revoliutsionerov*, p. 35; 'Program for Issues and Drafts of Resolutions Subject to Discussion at the Forthcoming Conference and [Meeting of the] Council', *Protocols of the First PSR All-Party Conference*, Paris, August 1908, in Nikolai D. Erofeev, *Partiia sotsialistov-revoliutsionerov*, pp. 43–46.
76 Alfred Rosenberg, 'Der Weltparasit', *Völkischer Beobachter*, 6 June 1943.
77 See footnote 73. Also, see Al-Hayat Media Center, *Dabiq*, Issue 10 (Jun., Jul., 2015), pp. 50, 53.
78 See Chapters 4 and 7 in this volume.
79 Sergei Gennadievich Nechaev, 'Katekhizis revoliutsionera', in Evgenia L. Rudnitskaia, ed., *Revoliutsionnii radikalizm v Rossii: deviatnadtsatii vek* (Moscow: Arkheograficheskii Tsentr, 1997), pp. 244–245.
80 Vladimir I. Lenin, 'The Constituent Assembly Elections and the Dictatorship of the Proletariat', 16 December 1919, *Collective Works*, Volume 30 (Moscow: Progress Publishers, 1965), pp. 253–275, accessed 2 June 2019, https://www.marxists.org/archive/lenin/works/1919/dec/16.htm. In this article, Lenin ridicules concepts such as equality, democracy and universal suffrage, advocating the principle of the dictatorship of the proletariat as the only revolutionary solution for societies suffering under bourgeois oppression and exploitation.
81 'Program of the Executive Committee', *Narodnaia Volia* No. 3, 1 January 1880, in Rudnitskaia, *Revolutsionnii radikalizm*, pp. 417–419; 'Programma partii sotsialistov-revoliutsionerov' [Program of the Party of Socialist Revolutionaries] *His95*, 2002, accessed 3 June 2019, http://his95.narod.ru/party/eser.htm.
82 See Chapters 4–7 in this volume.
83 Reichsorganisationsleiter Dr. Robert Ley, 'Die Entwicklung der Parteiorganisation' [Development of the Party Organization], *Völkischer Beobachter*, 24 February 1943.
84 See the detailed analysis presented in Chapters 4–7 in this volume.

Bibliography

Baldwin, Marshall W., ed. *A History of the Crusades*. Madison: University of Wisconsin Press, 1969, I.
Bawabat al-harika al-Islamiyya. "Antar al-Zouabri, "dhabbah" jama'at GIA al-jazai'r' ['Antar Zouabri, the Butcher of Algeria's GIA], accessed 10 May 2015. Accessed 24 December 2016. http://islamist-movements.com/28316.
Beranek, Ondrej and Pavel Tupek. 'From Visiting Graves to their Destruction: The Question of Ziyara through the Eyes of Salafis'. Crown Paper 2, July 2009, *Crown Center for Middle East Studies*. Accessed 24 January 2018. https://www.brandeis.edu/crown/publications/cp/CP2.pdf.
Broido, Vera. *Apostles into Terrorists: Women and the Revolutionary Movement in the Russia of Alexander II*. New York, NY: Viking Press, 1977.
Budnitskii, Oleg V. *Terrorizm: ideologiia, etika, psikhologiia (vtoraia polovina xix – nachalo xx veka)* [Terrorism: Ideology, Ethics and Psychology (Second Half of the Nineteenth and Early Twentieth Centuries]. Moscow: ROSSPEN, 2000.

Chaliand, Gérard and Arnaud Blin. 'Introduction'. In Gérard Chaliand and Arnaud Blin, eds. *The History of Terrorism: From antiquity to Al Qaeda*. Berkeley: University of California Press, 2009, pp. 1–11.

Chehab, Zaki. *Inside Hamas: The Untold Story of the Militant Islamic Movement*. New York, NY: Nation Books, 2007.

Clarke, Colin P. 'ISIS Is So Desperate It's Turning to the Drug Trade'. *Fortune*, 24 July 2017. Accessed 30 May 2019. http://fortune.com/2017/07/24/isis-mosul-defeated-news-territory-islamic-state-drugs/.

Commins, David. *The Wahhabi Mission and Saudi Arabia*. London: I.B. Tauris, 2006. Accessed 24 January 2018. http://asrdiplomacy.ir/wp-content/uploads/2017/03/The-Wahhabi-Mission-and-Saudi-Arabia-Book-1.pdf.

Dabiq.

Daftary, Farhad. *The Isma'ilis: Their History and Doctrines*. Cambridge: Cambridge University Press, 1990.

Daly, Jonathan. *Autocracy under Siege: Security Police and Opposition in Russia 1866–1905*. DeKalb: Northern Illinois University Press, 1998.

Daly, Jonathan. *The Watchful State: Security Police and Opposition in Russia 1906–1917*. DeKalb: Northern Illinois University Press, 2004.

Dearden, Lizzie. 'Isis Is Using Far More Child Soldiers than the World Realised'. *Independent*, 19 February 2016. Accessed 28 May 2019. https://www.independent.co.uk/news/world/middle-east/isis-using-more-child-fighters-than-feared-as-suicide-bombers-and-soldiers-after-brainwashing-at-a6883626.html.

DeLong-Bas, Natana J. *Wahhabi Islam: From Revival and Reform to Global Jihad*. New York: Oxford University Press, 2004.

Fortune (New York).

Gannon, Kathy and Rahim Faiez. 'Taliban Infiltrate Afghan Army to Target Foreign Troops'. *The Associated Press*, 18 June 2017. Accessed 9 March 2019. https://www.militarytimes.com/news/your-military/2017/06/18/q-a-taliban-infiltrate-afghan-army-to-target-foreign-troops/.

Hengel, Martin. *The Zealots: Investigations into the Jewish Freedom Movement in the Period from Herod I until 70 A.D.*, trans. David Smith. Edinburgh: T. & T. Clark, 1989.

Hernandez, Vladimir and Stephanie Hagarty. 'Made-up to Look Beautiful. Sent Out to Die. The Young Women Sent into Crowds to Blow Themselves Up'. *BBC*. Accessed 28 May 2019. https://www.bbc.co.uk/news/resources/idt-sh/made_up_to_look_beautiful_sent_out_to_die.

Hitler, Adolf. *Mein Kampf* [My Struggle]. Munich: Zentralverlag der NSDAP, Frz. Eher Nachf., G.m.b.H., 1943 (first published 1925, Vol. 1 and 1927, Vol. 2).

Hodgson, Marshall G. S. *The Secret Order of Assassins: The Struggle of the Early Nizari Isma'ilis against the Islamic World*. Philadelphia: University of Pennsylvania Press, 2005, first published 1955.

Horsley, Richard. 'The Sicarii: Ancient Jewish "Terrorists"'. *The Journal of Religion*, Vol. 59, No. 4 (October 1979), pp. 435–58.

The International Bible Society. 'Exodus 22- New International Version'. *Biblica*. Accessed 17 May 2019. https://www.biblica.com/bible/niv/exodus/22/.

International Institute for Counter-Terrorism. 'Abu Yahya Al-Libi: Profile of an Al-Qaeda Leader', March 2012. Accessed 10 April 2018. https://www.ict.org.il/UserFiles/Abu%20Yahya%20al-Libi.pdf.

Kershner, Isabel. 'Israeli Dies as Palestinian Attackers Stage Assaults in Jerusalem'. *New York Times*, 16 June 2017. Accessed 20 May 2019. https://www.nytimes.com/2017/06/16/world/middleeast/israel-palestinians-attack-jerusalem.html.

Knight, Amy. 'Female Terrorists in the Russian Socialist Revolutionary Party'. *The Russian Review*, Vol. 38, No. 2 (April 1979), pp. 139–59.

Kravchinskii, Sergei. 'Smert' za smert' [A Death for a Death]. In Rudnitskaia, ed., *Revoliutsionnii radikalizm v Rossii: deviatnadtsatii vek*. Moscow: Arkheograficheskii Tsentr, 1997, pp. 397–404.

Kucukcan, Talip. 'Some Reflections on the Wahhabiyah Movement'. *As-Sunnah Foundation of America*. Accessed January 24, 2018. http://sunnah.org/wp/2012/12/26/reflections-wahhabiyah-movement/.

Landers, Neil Grant. *Representing the Algerian Civil War: Literature, History, and the State* (Dissertation). Accessed 29 April 2018. http://digitalassets.lib.berkeley.edu/etd/ucb/text/Landers_berkeley_0028E_13922.pdf.

Law, Randall D. *Terrorism: A History*. Cambridge: Polity Press, 2009.

Lenin, Vladimir I. 'The Constituent Assembly Elections and the Dictatorship of the Proletariat', 16 December 1919, *Collected Works*, Volume 30. Moscow: Progress Publishers, 1965. Accessed 13 February 2018. https://www.marxists.org/archive/lenin/works/1919/dec/16.htm.

Lewis, Bernard. 'The Ismāʿīlites and the Assassins'. In Marshall W. Baldwin, ed. *A History of the Crusades*. Madison: University of Wisconsin Press, 1969, I, second edition.

Ley, Reichsorganisationsleiter Robert. 'Die Entwicklung der Parteiorganisation' [Development of the Party Organization]. *Völkischer Beobachter*. 24 February 1943.

Malek, Redha. 'Islamist Terrorism in Algeria: An Experience to Ponder'. In Walter Laqueur, ed. *Voices of Terror: Manifestos, Writings and Manuals of Al Qaeda, Hamas, and Other Terrorists from Around the World and throughout the Ages*. Naperville: Sourcebooks, Inc., 2004, pp. 439–46.

Michael, George. 'The Legend and Legacy of Abu Musab al-Zarqawi'. *Defense Studies*, Vol. 7, No. 3 (September 2007), pp. 338–57.

Narodnaia Volia. No. 3, 1 January 1880. 'Programma ispolnitel'nogo komiteta' [Program of the Executive Committee]. In Rudnitskaia, *Revolutsionnii radikalizm v Rossii: deviatna'dtsatii vek*. Moscow: Arkheograficheskii Tsentr, 1997, pp. 417–19.

National Archives and Records Administration (NARA, USA).

Nechaev, Sergei Gennadievich. 'Katekhizis revoliutsionera' [Catechism of the Revolutionist]. In E. L. Rudnitskaia, ed. *Revoliutsionnii radikalizm v Rossii: deviatnadtsatii vek*. Moscow: Arkheograficheskii Tsentr, 1997, pp. 244–45.

Obshchina (London).

Okhrana Records. *Hoover Institution*. Palo Alto, CA: Stanford University.

Ottaway, David B. 'Algeria: Bloody Past and Fractious Factions'. 27 August 2015. *Wilson Center*. Accessed 18 January 2017. https://www.wilsoncenter.org/article/algeria-bloody-past-and-fractious-factions.

Otten, Cathy. 'Slaves of Isis: The Long Walk of the Yazidi Women'. *The Guardian*, 25 July 2017. Accessed 30 May 2019. https://www.theguardian.com/world/2017/jul/25/slaves-of-isis-the-long-walk-of-the-yazidi-women.

Party of Socialist Revolutionaries. 'Programma Voprosov i Proekty Rezoliutsii, Podlezhashchikh Obsuzhdeniiu na Predstoiashchikh Konferentsii i Sovete' [Program for Issues and Drafts of Resolutions Subject to Discussion at the

Forthcoming Conference and [Meeting of the] Council]. *Protocols of the first PSR All-Party Conference*, Paris, August 1908, in Nikolai D. Erofeev, *Partiia sotsialistov-revoliutsionerov*, pp. 43–46.

Party of Socialist Revolutionaries. 'Programma partii sotsialistov-revoliutsionerov' [Program of the Party of Socialist Revolutionaries] *His95*, 2002. http://his95.narod.ru/party/eser.htm.

Pillalamarri, Akhilesh. 'Revealed: Why ISIS Hates the Taliban'. *The Diplomat*, 29 January 2016. Accessed 29 May 2019. https://thediplomat.com/2016/01/revealed-why-isis-hates-the-taliban/.

Pipes, Richard. *The Degaev Affair: Terror and Treason in Tsarist Russia*. New Haven, CT: Yale University Press, 2003.

'Podgotovitel'naia Rabota Partii' [Preparatory Work of the Party]. *Kalendar' Narodnoi Voli 1883-go goda'* [1883 Almanac of Narodnaia Volia]. Geneva. In Rudnitskaia, ed. *Revoliutsionnii radikalizm v Rossii: deviatnadtsatii vek*. Moscow: Arkheograficheskii Tsentr, 1997, pp. 420–27.

Pomper, Philip, *Sergei Nechaev*. New Brunswick, NJ: Rutgers University Press, 1979.

Qutb, Sayyid. *Ma'alim fi'l-tariq* [Milestones]. SIME ePublishing Services (distributor). Accessed 21 July 2018. http://majallah.org/2017/01/qutbs-milestone.html.

Rapoport, David C. 'Fear and Trembling: Terrorism in Three Religious Traditions'. *The American Political Science Review*, Vol. 78, No. 3 (September 1984), pp. 658–77.

Rhoads, David M. *Israel in Revolution: 6–74 C.E.: A Political History Based on the Writings of Josephus*. Philadelphia: Fortress Press, 1976.

Robinson, Bruce A. 'Religious Intolerance in Afghanistan'. *Religious Tolerance*, 20 November 2001. Accessed 29 May 2019. http://www.religioustolerance.org/rt_afgha.htm.

Rosenberg, Alfred. *Der Mythus des 20. Jahrhunderts: Eine Wertung der seelisch-geistigen Gestaltungskaempfe unserer Zeit* [The Myth of the Twentieth Century: An Assessment of Creativity Struggles of Our Time as They Relate to Mind and Spirit]. Munich: Hoheneichen Verlag, 1939.

Rosenberg, Alfred. 'Der Weltparasit'. *Völkischer Beobachter*, 6 June 1943.

Rumiyah.

Savinkov, Boris. *Vospominania terrorista* [Memoirs of a Terrorist]. Moscow: Vagrius, 2006. First published in 1909. *Lib.ru/Klassika*. Accessed 7 September 2015. http://az.lib.ru/s/sawinkow_b_w/text_0010.shtml.

Sheikh-Dilthey, Helmtraut. 'Dariyyah: Das Herz Saudi-Arabiens' [Darriyya: Heart of Saudi Arabia]. *Anthropos*, Vol. 84, No. 1/3 (1989), pp. 141-154.

Spiegel Online. 6 December 2011. '1944 Massacre in France: German Police Raid Homes of Six Former SS Soldiers'. Accessed 31 May 2019. https://www.spiegel.de/international/germany/1944-massacre-in-france-german-police-raid-homes-of-six-former-ss-soldiers-a-802019.html.

Stone, Martin. *The Agony of Algeria*. New York, NY: Columbia University Press, 1997.

Strenski, Ivan. 'Sacrifice, Gift and the Social Logic of Muslim "Human Bombers"'. *Library of Social Science*. Accessed 22 May 2016. https://www.libraryofsocialscience.com/essays/strenski-sacrifice.html.

Ulam, Adam B. *Prophets and Conspirators: Prerevolutionary Russia*. New Brunswick and London: Transaction Publishers, 1998 (first published in 1977 by Viking Press).

United States Holocaust Memorial Museum. 'Operation Anthropoid'. *Holocaust Encyclopedia*. Accessed 31 May 2019. https://encyclopedia.ushmm.org/content/en/article/lidice.

Virani, Shafique N. 'The Eagle Returns: Evidence of Continued Isma'ili Activity at Alamut and in the South Caspian Region Following the Mongol Conquests'. *Journal of the American Oriental Society*, Vol. 123, No. 2 (April - June 2003), pp. 351-370.

Wahhab, Muhammad Ibn Abdul. *Kitab at-Tawheed Explained*. Explanation compiled and translated by Sameh Strauch. Riyadh: International Islamic Publishing House, 2000, second edition.

Weiss, Michael and Hassan Hassan. *ISIS: Inside the Army of Terror*. New York, NY: Regan Arts, 2015.

Woody, Christopher. 'Heroin Is Driving a Sinister Trend in Afghanistan'. *Business Insider*, 30 October 2017. Accessed 30 May 2019. https://www.businessinsider.com/taliban-control-of-heroin-drug-production-trafficking-in-afghanistan-2017-10.

Zavarzin, Pavel Pavlovich. *Zhandarmy i Revoliutsionery: Vospominaniia* [Gendarmes and Revolutionaries: A Memoir]. Paris: Published by the author [izdanie avtora] 1930.

Zeitlin, Solomon. 'Masada and the Sicarii'. *The Jewish Quarterly Review*, Vol. 55, No. 4 (April 1965), pp. 299-317.

Zemlia i Volia.

Zemlia i Volia. 'Programma Zemli i Voli' [Program of Zemlia i Volia]. May 1878. In Evgenia L. Rudnitskaia. *Revoliutsionnii radikalizm v Rossii: deviatnadtsatii vek*. Moscow: Arkheograficheskii Tsentr, 1997, pp. 395-97?.

Znamia Truda.

Conclusion

The multidisciplinary approach of this study – historical, linguistic, rhetorical and religious – to the phenomenon of terrorism has provided ample evidence in support of its three main assumptions – continuity with regard to ideology and methodology, the flaws of extremist propaganda and the fears of terrorist leaders. Based upon the research findings presented in this volume, one can conclude that an historical approach to the subject of this study reveals a pattern of considerable continuity as to the ideologies and methodologies of extremist militant groups, organizations and states despite the centuries which separate earlier forms of terrorism from more recent examples of violent ideologies and interpretations of religions. Second, the detailed analysis of terrorist propaganda has demonstrated that it is a double-edged sword, which will boomerang on the propagandist unless handled with extreme caution. Third, this book has confirmed that terrorists, like their victims, have fears, albeit mostly different than those of their targets. The fears of the former have received much lesser attention than those of the latter despite the fact that it could be argued that they are at least as important as the fears of civilians and governments since familiarity with these weaknesses enables educational institutions, law enforcement and intelligence agencies to adopt more effective measures in the war on terror.

The striking similarities evinced by terrorist organizations operating in different centuries and distinctly different social and cultural milieus indicate that totalitarian ideologies and extremist interpretations of religion are to some degree predictable, particularly since they display commonalities pertaining to ideology, modus operandi, strengths and weaknesses. This predictability places a powerful weapon in the hands of societies which strive to adopt measures to counter the influence of terrorist groups. Examples of continuity are the Sicarii and Nizaris, who had a common methodology concerning the implementation of their agenda. Both movements resorted to terror carried out by individual perpetrators using daggers to eliminate their targets. These two movements and the Muwahhidun, who created the Saʿudi state, shared exclusivist, though not identical, approaches to human interaction and interpretations of religion, resulting

DOI: 10.4324/9781003260943-14

in restrictions being imposed on both social interaction and religious life. Additionally, the Sicarii and Nizaris were both generally selective with regard to targets, whereas anyone who disagreed with the Muwahhid interpretation of Islam ran the risk of being labeled an apostate or 'polytheist' as a result of saint worship. Furthermore, the violence to which these three movements resorted in order to realize their politico-religious agenda was justified by reference to a higher power. This reference presumably served to create a direct link between the movement and God, legitimating its actions as taken 'for the cause of God'. The connection with a 'higher power' – be it the '*narod*' (people) for Russian terrorists, the mystic concept of the 'Volk' for the Nazis or 'God' for the GIA (Groupe Islamique Armée) and Islamic State – has consistently filled the same function of legitimizing any action taken by a militant organization examined in this work.

If obvious similarities are found in earlier and later terrorist organizations despite considerable cultural differences, such as between nineteenth-century Russia and late twentieth-century Middle East, it suggests that direct interaction and cultural affinity are not necessarily decisive determinants in the context of explaining existing similarities in ideologies and methodologies of terrorist groups and states. Sergei Nechaev argues that the revolutionary has severed all ties to traditional society and morality, a contention which places him above the law. Concomitantly, this allows him to justify any act which, in his mind, serves the revolution as good and any act which constitutes an obstacle to establishing the new order as evil. Conversely, Antar Zouabri's contention that only one law exists; God's law, at first glance, differs from the Russian claim since it is not Zouabri's or his group's law, but that of a higher power. This presumably places the GIA within the pale of Islamic law, a reasonable but nevertheless an erroneous conclusion. Zouabri insisted that most Muslims' interpretation of Islam was flawed and in violation of God's law. This was, of course, a claim as arbitrary as that of Nechaev, actually placing Zouabri outside the law of his Islamic society since he was paying lip service only to God's law, replacing it with his personal interpretation which was embraced by a tiny minority of the Algerian population and rejected by most extremists as well. The above comparison leads one to conclude that manipulation and arbitrary interpretation of sources drastically reduces the gap between secular and 'religious' terrorism despite what may appear as fundamental conceptual differences.

This work has demonstrated the crucial role of propaganda for totalitarian regimes such as the Nazi party in Germany and the 'Caliphate' of the Islamic State in Iraq and Syria. The National Socialist Workers Party of Germany (NSDAP) preferred method of propaganda was based on the premise that the 'Aryan' people was facing an existential threat emanating from Jewish Germans and Jews residing in other countries. The purpose of this myth was to instill a deep fear in 'Aryans' to make them submit to the totalitarian rule of the party and persuade them to become the willing instruments of the regime's aspirations to world domination. It was believed that the only way to achieve this goal was to engage in an apocalyptic war against the enemy. This worldview is closely mirrored in Daʿish's terrorist interpretation of Islam. Like the Nazi party, the Islamic State rejects parliamentary democracy, albeit for a different reason. The National Socialists argued that, when too many voices speak, the result is confusion in society. The Islamic State justification for its form of totalitarianism is that democracy is a manmade system of government and therefore illegitimate since all activities in any society have to be in accordance with God's law as defined by the 'Caliph'. Democracy is thus a flawed system which usurps God's authority. The religious rhetoric notwithstanding, this myth fails to conceal the similar outlook of both totalitarian systems. The rationale for the Nazi state is to prevent the looming disaster of the purity of the 'Aryan' race from becoming diluted by *Untermenschen* (subhumans), whereas that of the Islamic State is to restore Islam to its original purity, defending it against external aggression and 'innovations' (bidʿa) introduced by Muslims gone astray. Both regimes paint a very bleak prospect of survival unless citizens surrender their individuality to the 'greater good' of society, that is, the State's obligation to ensure 'purity', racial in one case and religious in the other.

Propaganda oftentimes comes at a price, namely, reduced credibility and legitimacy. Like dynamite, propaganda has the potential to have very negative consequences beyond the control of its author once it has been conveyed to the public since it can blow up in the face of the propagandist. The meticulous analysis in this volume of Nazi and Islamic State manipulation of information has revealed that propaganda intended to conceal negative consequences of certain policies is very often fraught with incorrect claims and flawed argumentation, the latter a result of the absence of evidence in support of arguments advanced by the propagandist and quotes from authoritative sources taken out of context and interpreted in a way which disregards the historical context and fits the ideological agenda of the author. Both regimes have made use of hyperbole, creation of myths and untrue statements in their propaganda, making the task of exposing the aforementioned flaws comparatively easy for a reader who has acquired the basic skills of critical thinking. The question is whether a message with so many weaknesses can still be effective. Unfortunately, the answer is yes. The answer suggests that the analyst needs to look for the reason in the target audience. If the reader, listener or viewer for one reason or another is not prepared to subject the message to critical analysis, it can be embraced despite its weaknesses. The audience therefore constitutes the weakest link in a society, ready to be exploited by the extremist propagandist.

The emphasis on emotive argumentation in Nazi and Islamic State propaganda evidences the significance which these two states attributed to converting the public to their cause. It is obvious from Nazi and Daʿish propaganda that their ideologues and propagandists firmly believed in the effectiveness of emotive argumentation. Furthermore, their publications reveal that this rhetorical device is used when solid evidence cannot be found to back up a specific claim or when it is believed to strengthen a weak claim. The purpose of resorting to emotive argumentation is to steer the reader, listener or viewer away from critical thinking toward an emotive reaction. If this reaction can be linked to an existing prejudice, no evidence needs to be provided since the audience's reaction will not be based upon reasoning. Needless to say, the frequency with which this rhetorical device is used demonstrates what kind of audience is being targeted. Moreover, it shows that authors have doubts about the effectiveness of other types of propaganda and that their propaganda does not work without a constant infusion of manipulated information intended to provoke a particular emotional reaction. The depiction of the 'enemy' is part of this tactic. In order to provoke as negative as possible an emotion, the 'enemy' is demonized and accused of various crimes which do not have to be substantiated since propagandists most likely believe that a natural prejudice against someone 'identified' as the enemy will suffice to persuade people to embrace the propaganda. Emotive argumentation can be quite effective if the audience does not engage in critical thinking or is reluctant to do so for fear of negative consequences.

Cultural 'appropriation' is another tactic often resorted to by totalitarian organizations for the purpose of strengthening their appeal to the public and claim to legitimacy by associating themselves with historical individuals held in high esteem by society. Nazi propagandists and Islamic militants alike have exploited the reputation of prominent scientists and cultural luminaries in the former case and renowned religious scholars in the latter case to benefit from establishing links, no matter how dubious, to highly respected historical personalities. Needless to say, the 'appropriation' of such individuals sometimes presents difficulties for propagandists, particularly for the NSDAP, which was not known before the end of the First World War, though some of the ideas embraced by the Nazis such as Social Darwinism and scientific racism circulated widely in nineteenth-century Western societies. This constitutes less of a problem for Islamic militants since the religious scholars to whom they refer all operated within the same Islamic context. Two examples of scholars whom the Nazis 'appropriated' are Nikolaus Kopernikus and Friedrich Nietzsche. The National Socialists could for obvious reasons not prove that Kopernikus was a Nazi, so they established a link between the great astronomer and their ideology by arguing that they, like Kopernikus, fought for the truth, without going into detail about what the latter was. Neither could the Nazis provide evidence that Nietzsche was a Nazi, so they referred to the philosopher's warning against the 'barbarians in the east', that is, the Russians, a warning which fit perfectly into the Nazi agenda. Islamic militants have embraced a similar approach to great Islamic scholars in their eagerness to 'prove' the legitimacy of their extremist cause despite the disparity between Ibn Taymiyya's and their interpretation of jihad and Muhammad Ibn 'Abd al-Wahhab's and their own approach to dissent.

The obviously best way that a society can protect itself against militant extremism is to address a root of the problem, not just a symptom. This is an approach which demands early intervention, instead of waiting until a convert has already planned or perpetrated a terrorist act. The conclusion one can draw from the argument that the terrorists' target audience in a society constitutes the weakest link of that society is that education must play a major role in any endeavor which aims at neutralizing propaganda which incites to violence. One of the best approaches to terrorism is thus to inoculate the population against extremist propaganda. The earlier such measures are taken the better, if the goal is to make citizens more or less impervious to hate and violence mongering ideologies by providing effective means which prevent people from embracing violence as an argument. Efforts to teach students critical thinking should begin no later than in junior high school and continue until the student graduates. Critics might argue that one needs more than basic critical thinking skills to navigate the traps set by propagandists. The analysis in this study reveals that some flaws in propaganda published by terrorist organizations are easily discovered by anyone with an elementary knowledge of critical thinking. This point confirms the great importance of early education in the principles of critical thinking.

A common denominator of violent extremist ideologies is the concept of exclusivism, which has played a prominent role as a motivator for terrorism from the ancient Sicarii to Da'ish. Totalitarian regimes and groups have recognized the usefulness of this concept because it can be exploited to create strong cohesion, a sense of belonging and legitimacy for a state or an organization. A simple way to achieve such an effect is to draw very clear distinction between friend and foe, a task normally achieved by demonization of anyone who disagrees with a totalitarian ideology. Furthermore, by creating a myth that the totalitarian entity is under constant attack and has to resort to violence to counter the 'injustice and hostility' of external forces, a group or state is able to maintain the desired level of fear and hatred among its followers or citizens. Typically, sophistication is not required to instill such an idea in the minds of followers. Nineteenth-century Russian terrorists, German National Socialists and Islamic terrorists have all depicted the enemy in broad brush strokes since it makes their task to create the image of the enemy as representing inhuman behavior easier. If the foe can be described as a monolithic creature, there is no need for propagandists to make efforts to address individual differences. A more nuanced image of the enemy will make it more difficult for leaders to drive home the point that the foe is a monster and not a human being. It is worth noting that the same approach has been used by belligerents, both democratic and totalitarian, in twentieth-century world wars.

Use of somewhat similar methodology by terrorist organizations and their main adversaries, law enforcement agencies, is both a strength and a weakness. It is a strength because the former's operations can be predicted to a degree and a weakness because the latter suffer from some of the same vulnerabilities as the former. Law enforcement can surveille terrorists' activities on social media and adopt countermeasures accordingly. At the same time, terrorists can hack computer networks operated by the police, thereby causing disruption. Furthermore, the former can through their own surveillance, as revealed in the chapters on Russian terrorism, gain access to information by direct observation which, in turn, can be used to plan attacks on law enforcement officials. International cooperation is another method which has been applied by both terrorists and police agencies at least since the nineteenth century. Exchange of intelligence among agencies in different countries and cooperation in international organizations such as Interpol is a common practice. Unfortunately, the same approach has also been adopted by terrorist organizations such as the Russian Narodnaia Volia and the Party of Socialist Revolutionaries and Al-Qa'ida and the Taliban. Russian militant groups exchanged information with similar groups in Western Europe and planned joint operations with militant groups among Russia's ethnic minorities. However, the good news is that the situation appears to be brighter for international cooperation among governments because of the large number of law enforcement agencies and the relative ease with which such cooperation can be established. Conversely, the most extreme terrorist organizations such as the GIA and the Islamic State are oftentimes not inclined to engage in cooperation with other groups unless the latter recognize their subservience to the former by swearing *bai'a* (allegiance) to the leader of the former group. An example of such a relationship is the one between Boko Haram and the Islamic State. Fortunately, for intelligence agencies, such cooperation does not exist between Al-Qa'ida and Da'ish or between the latter and the Taliban.

Works on terrorism generally devote much attention to the fears which terrorist organizations and states strive to instill in people, whereas the fears of terrorists themselves constitute an aspect of terrorism which has attracted much less interest. In order to be able to formulate effective counterterrorism strategies, government agencies have to be conversant with the fears of the terrorists themselves. In their own propaganda, jihadis strive to create an impression that they have one fear only, the fear of God, but a close examination of their publications reveals that they have multiple other fears as well. The rationale of jihadi propaganda is to create an image of invincibility by establishing a direct link between their cause and God's law, which, in their mind, is one and the same. However, when subjected to scrutiny, many Islamic militant publications yield valuable information about fears which jihadis themselves strive to conceal, but which are sometimes revealed unintentionally. Researchers can thus establish that some of these fears are obvious vulnerabilities since they can be exploited by an adversary. The possibility of espionage and infiltration is taken very seriously by Islamic terrorists as demonstrated by the fact that the jihadi ideologue Abu Yahya al-Libi has published a whole book devoted to the subject. The book, entitled *Al-Mu'allim fi hukm al-jasus al-muslim* (Guidance on the Ruling of the Muslim Spy), warns the mujahid of the negative consequences in which a lack of vigilance can result. Fear of internal division is another weakness which can be exploited by intelligence and law enforcement agencies. The summary executions with which such division has been met by GIA and Islamic State leaders constitute proof of the fear dissent and division instill in leading terrorists. The critical discussion in this study of the above and other fears demonstrates that familiarity with these vulnerabilities is of fundamental importance for the formulation of effective counterterrorism policies.

A final point which needs to be made in this concluding chapter is whether it is possible to rank terrorist organizations based upon the forms of violence to which they resort. The short answer is yes, and it provides food for thought for Muslims and non-Muslims alike since much of the violence in recent decades has occurred in the Middle East and has been perpetrated by Islamic extremist groups. Concurrently, it is important to be mindful of the fact that terrorism is a common phenomenon in many non-Middle Eastern societies. Furthermore, news media's focus on the unimaginable violence perpetrated by the Islamic State might lead the public to conclude that this level of brutality is unprecedented in recent human history. The analysis of Islamic extremism in this work has shown that Da'ish, despite the impression created in media, is not the 'worst' Islamic terrorist organization, but that this dubious title belongs to the GIA. This Algerian group can convincingly be labeled the 'worst' Islamic terrorist organization, owing to its *takfir* (excommunication) of the whole Muslim population of Algeria. This is an act unheard of in Islamic history. So, does this fact finally settle the matter of the most brutal and violent terrorist organization? No, it does not because this title belongs to the NSDAP, whose ideological, propagandistic and physical violence was worse than that of the GIA. The reason is that, if you embraced the GIA's interpretation of Islam and supported the group, you would not be targeted by its leaders. In the case of the National Socialists, that was not an option. If you were a non-'Aryan' or 'unfit to live', it was of no importance whether you embraced Nazi ideology or not since you would be sentenced to eternal slavery or extermination. Being a Jew was a capital offense under the Nazi regime.

Glossary

Action dirècte: French, 'direct action', revolution by terrorist means.
'Alim, pl. 'ulama, Arabic: Islamic religious scholar.
Der Angriff: German, Attack, Nazi newspaper.
Ansar: Arabic, supporter; Medinans who converted to Islam, following Muhammad's hijra (migration) to Medina.
'Aql: Arabic, reason.
Aya, pl. -t: Arabic, Quranic verse.
Bai'a: Arabic, swearing of allegiance.
Batin: Arabic, hidden, secret.
Berliner Arbeiterzeitung: German, *The Berlin Workers Paper*, Nazi newspaper.
Bezmotivnik: Russian, proponent of the idea that terrorism does not have to be justified.
Bid'a: Arabic, (heretical) innovation.
Chistii adres: Russian, 'clean address', address of individual above suspicion.
Crusader: Term denoting Christians used by extremist Muslims.
Dabiq: Town in Syria, believed by extremist Muslims in particular to be the site of a future decisive battle between Muslims and Christians out of which the former will emerge victorious; a magazine formerly published by the Islamic State in a number of languages.
Da'ish: Arabic, the Islamic State, ISIS, the 'Caliphate'.
Dar al-harb: Arabic, 'abode of war', non-Muslim majority country.
Dar al-Islam: Arabic, 'abode of Islam', Muslim majority country.
Dashnak: Armenian, member of an Armenian revolutionary party in imperial Russia.
Dunya: Arabic, world; concepts and phenomena reflective of the temporal world.
Endlösung: German, Final Solution. The Nazi policy which resulted in the Holocaust.
Fardh kifaya: Arabic, collective duty to fight a jihad.
Fardh 'ain: Arabic, individual duty to fight a jihad.
Faris: Arabic, knight.

Fatwa, pl. fatawa: Arabic, religious ruling.
Fida'i, Arabic, pl. –yun: He who sacrifices himself.
Filior: Russian, detective.
Fi sabil Allah: Arabic, 'in the path of Allah', recurring phrase used as justification for violent jihad.
Führerprinzzip: German, leader principle, the idea of unconditional loyalty to the Führer.
Gauverband: German, gau (Nazi regional administrative) unit.
Ghanima: Arabic, spoils of jihadi warfare.
Hadd, pl. hudud: Arabic, Islamic legal punishment.
Haqiqa: Arabic, ultimate reality.
Harb: Arabic, regular warfare, as opposed to jihad.
Herem: Hebrew, Jewish jihad.
Herrenvolk: German, master race.
Hijra: Arabic, Muhammad's escape from Mecca to Medina. Term used by modern jihadis in the sense of migration to a truly Islamic state.
Houri: Young beautiful woman believed to accompany a good Muslim in Paradise.
Hujja: Arabic, proof of God; evidence.
Hukm: Arabic, rule.
Ijtihad: Arabic, independent religious reasoning.
Imama: Arabic, Islamic leadership.
Inspire: Magazine published by Al-Qaʿida.
Intihar: Arabic, suicide.
Ismaʿili Nizaris: Assassins.
Istishhad: Arabic, martyrdom.
ʿId al-adhha: Arabic, Feast of Immolation.
Jahili: Arabic, originally a term used in reference to pre-Islamic society. Now a term used by Muslim extremists about their opponents to discredit them.
Jamaʿa: Arabic, Islamic community.
Jihad akbar: Arabic, Greater Jihad against one's lower self.
Jihad asghar: Arabic, Lesser Jihad, military operations 'in the path of Allah'.
Jihadi: Arabic, individual who fights a jihad.
Jizya: Arabic, formerly a poll tax paid by Christians, Jews and Zoroastrians living under Muslim rule.
Kafir, pl. kuffar: Arabic, unbeliever.
Katekhizis Revoliutsionera: Russian, Catechism of the Revolutionist, terrorist pamphlet authored by Sergei Nechaev.
Khalifa: Arabic, caliph.
Khimicheskii tekst: Russian, invisible ink.
Khozhdenie v narod: Russian, 'going to the people', a movement the goal of which was to incite uprisings against the tsarist regime among Russia's peasants.

Lebensraum: German, 'living space', territory the Nazis believed Germany had to control in order to prosper.
Majlis al-shura: Arabic, consultative assembly.
Metatel'nii snariad: Russian, bomb that can be thrown at a target.
Milla: Arabic, religion.
Mir: Russian, peasant administrative unit.
Muhajir, pl. –un: Arabic, emigrant; a Muslim who migrated to Medina to join Muhammad.
Mujahid, pl. –un: Arabic, an individual who fights a jihad.
Mushrik, pl. –un: Arabic, polytheist, idolater.
Muwahhid, pl. –un: Arabic, Wahhabi.
Narodnaia Rasprava: Russian, People's Retribution, Russian terrorist organization.
Narodnaia Volia: Russian, 'People's Will', a terrorist organization.
Narodnik, pl. -i: Russian, nineteenth-century Russian revolutionary populists.
Nifaq: Arabic, hypocrisy.
Novoe Vremia: Russian, 'New Time', conservative newspaper.
Oblast': Russian, region.
Ordensrat: German, Council of the Order.
Ovod: Russian, 'Gadfly', satirical journal.
Partia sotsialistov-revoliutsionerov: Russian, Party of Socialist Revolutionaries, a political party and terrorist organization.
Propaganda of the deed: Revolution by terrorism.
Qiyama: Arabic, resurrection.
Reichsführer: German, Reich leader, commander of the SS.
Reichsorganisationsleiter: German, 'Reich Organization Leader'. Nazi administrative title.
Ri'a': Arabic, hypocrisy.
Rumiyah: Arabic, Rome, a magazine published by the Islamic State.
Salaf: Arabic, early generations of Muslims, believed to represent 'pure' Islam.
Salafi: Arabic, pertaining to early Islam.
Sayyid: Title of a descendant of the Prophet Muhammad.
Shahada: Arabic, Muslim profession of faith: 'There is no god but God, and Muhammad is the Messenger of God'.
Sica: Latin, dagger.
Sicarii: Movement based on the 'fourth philosophy'.
Sonderfahndungsliste: German, a wanted list drawn up by the Nazis for the arrest of leading anti-Nazis in countries they planned to occupy.
Streng geheim: German, top secret.
Sura: Arabic, Quranic chapter.
Takfir: Arabic, excommunication.
Taqlid: Arabic, imitation of the past.
Tawhid: Arabic, oneness of God.

Tret'e Otdelenie: Russian, 'Third Department', predecessor of the Okhrana.
Untermensch: German, 'subhuman'.
Vernichtung: German, eradication.
Vestnik Narodnoi Voli: Russian, *Journal of Narodnaia Volia*, journal published by Narodnaia Volia.
La Voix des Belges: French, *Voice of Belgium*, underground anti-Nazi newspaper.
Volk und Rasse: German, *People and Race*, Nazi magazine.
Völkisch: German, national, ethnic, völkisch, Nazi nationalist ideological term referring to the German nation.
Völkischer Beobachter: German, *Völkisch Observer*, official organ of the Nazi party.
Volksgemeinschaft: German, 'people's community', German society under the Nazi regime.
Volksgenosse: German, literally 'people's comrade', citizen of the Nazi state.
Die Wahrheit: German, *Truth*, underground German-language Belgian periodical.
Weltherrschaft: German, 'world domination', a desire attributed to Jews by National Socialists, suspiciously similar to their own geopolitical agenda.
Wunderwaffe: German, 'miracle weapon'.
Zahir: Arabic, manifest; external
Zakat: Arabic, charitable tax.
Zeal: Duty to implement Jewish law.
Zealot: Member of ancient Jewish sect, which resisted Roman rule.
Zemlia i Volia: Russian, Land and Freedom, a revolutionary movement; a revolutionary newspaper.
Ziyara: Arabic, the act of visiting the tomb of a saint.
Znamia Truda: Russian, *Banner of Labor*, newspaper published by the Party of Socialist Revolutionaries.

Index

Note: Page numbers followed by "n" denote endnotes.

action dirècte 33
Afghanistan 155
ahl al-kitab *see* people of the Book
ahl al-tawhid *see* Muwahhidun
AIS 156–157, 162, 232
Aleksandr II 27, 36, 62
Aleksandr III 62–63
Alexander *see* Aleksandr
anarchists 52
L'Armée islamique du salut *see* AIS
Assassins *see* Nizaris
Azef, Evno 56, 64, 65; the Azef affair 38
'Azzam, 'Abdullah Yusuf *see* Al-Qa'ida

bai'a 190
Bakr, Caliph Abu 206–207
Bakunin, Mikhail A. 28–29, 31–32; the Committee 245
Boko Haram 250
Burtsev, Vladimir L. 64

continuity 2, 7, 241, 246–247, 250, 255, 265
counterterrorism 137, 179, 235–236, 248–250
Crusaders 205, 212
Crusades 128
cultural appropriation 268

Dabiq: apocalyptic battle 184–185, 230
Da'ish 127–128, 227, 230, 243–244, 253–255; attacks on co-religionists and other religions 209–212; counterpropaganda 213–214; cult of personality 200–201; democracy 206–207; emotive argumentation 267–268; hijra 185–187; killing Americans 211–212; legitimacy 200–203; nationalism 207–208; propaganda 180–183, 245–246, 252–255; prophecy 230; removal of markers and symbols 209–211, 217; socialism 208; strength of propaganda 180–182, 183–187, 190–195, 205–206; weakness of propaganda 179–180, 187–189, 204–208, 210–211, 214–216
Dar al-Ifta' al-Misriyya 129, 143–144; dar al-harb 185–186
Dar al-Islam 185–186
democracy 228–229; *see also* Da'ish and democracy
Département du renseignement et sécurité *see* DRS
DRS 160–162
Duma 40, 63

education, and terrorism 1–2, 269
Emancipation Edict 27
excommunication *see* takfir

Farag, Muhammad 'Abd al-Salam 125–126, 141–142
fardh 'ain *see* jihad, individual duty
fardh kifaya *see* jihad, collective duty
faris *see* knight
fears: of adversity 222–223; of challenged legitimacy 232–235; of democracy, nationalism, and socialism 228–229; of de-radicalization and self-de-radicalization 235; of enemy propaganda 232; of espionage/ infiltration 223–226; of God 222–223; of internal division 226–227; of loss of popular support 227–228; of

loss of revenue 233–234; of reduced recruitment 231; of terrorists 3, 236; see also Al-Qaʿida, and Abu Yahya al-Libi
FIS 154–157, 162
FLN 154, 155
Front de Liberation Nationale see FLN
Front Islamique du Salut see FIS

Ghanima 123, 145
GIA 138–139, 155–159, 226–227, 229, 232–233, 270–271; Algerian elections 155; alienation of Algerians 158, 162; ʿAntar Zouabri 157–158, 227–228, 233; hijra wa takfir 158–159
Going to the people see khozhdenie v narod
Groupe Islamique Armée see GIA
GSPC 156, 159, 226–227

Hamza, Abu 158–159
herem 13, 242
hijra 185–187, 230–231
Himmler, Heinrich 79, 81, 89, 101, 112–114
Hitler, Adolf: in the cause of the creator 183; *Mein Kampf* 180–181, 182–183
holy war see jihad

ijtihad 148–149
immutability 130–132
Inspire 164–169; Americans killing Muslims 168; analysis of weaknesses and strengths 169; confounding democracy with dictatorship 167; discrimination of Muslims in the West 167; hyperbole and deception 168; West's war on Islam 166–167
Inter-Services Intelligence see ISI
IS, Islamic State see Daʿish
ISI 156
Islamic League for the Daʿwa and Jihad see LIDD
Islamic State in Iraq and Greater Syria see Daʿish
istishhad see martyrdom

Jabhat al-Nusra see Nusra Front
jihad: collective duty 121, 125; conversion 122; defensive 121, 123; eternal struggle 140; individual duty 121, 125 ; killing Christians 139, 141; killing Muslims 141; mushrikun (polytheists) 140–141, 144; offensive 121, 122; Paradise 145–147; slavery 139; takfir 139; tawhid 148
jihad akbar see jihad, greater
jihad asghar see jihad, lesser

Katekhizis Revoliutsionera see Nechaev and Catechism of a Revolutionist
khozhdenie v narod 27–28
knight 205–206
Kravchinskii, Sergei M. 34–35, 43

Bin Laden, Osama see Al-Qaʿida
Land and Freedom see Zemlia i Volia
al-Libi, Abu Yahya see Al-Qaʿida
LIDD 156

Macchiavelli, Niccoló 30; *The Prince* 30
Maktab al-Khidmat see Al-Qaʿida, Services Bureau
al-malhama al-kubra (the great battle) see Dabiq
martyrdom (istishhadi) operations 145–147, 246–247
Masada 14
Mezentsev, Nikolai V 34
Mongols 126
Morozov, Nikolai A. 35–37, 37n41
muhajirun (emigrants) 187
mujahidun 120, 123, 127, 158–159, 205–206
mushrikun 140, 142–145, 147–148
Muwahhidun 19–22, 242–243, 248, 265–266; bidʿa 17; control of territory 18; state terrorism 20

Naji, Abu Bakr 124, 126; jihad 141
Narodnaia Volia (NV) 28, 32–33, 51, 54–55, 245, 254; the Executive Committee 33, 59; explosives 51; future society 41–42; prison escapes 54–55
Narodniki 44n3, 245
National Socialism: argumentation 77–79; Bolshevism 79, 82, 86; conspiracy theory 99–103; defeat of 1918 81–82, 103–104; education 84; enemy propaganda 107–108; euthanasia 88; geopolitics 85–86; Germanization 84; Herrenvolk (master race) 83; Holocaust 5–6; labour recruitment 108–110; morale 110–114; propaganda 98–101; propaganda and adversity 104–107;

race 75–79, 244, 253–254; radio propaganda 103–104; rejection of democracy 83–84; religion 88–91; the State 75–77, 251; survival 114–116; terrorism 98–99, 253–254; Untermensch (subhuman) 79, 267, 75–77, 244; war and peace 86–87
National Socialist propaganda 75–76, 254
Nechaev, Sergei 28–32; Catechism of the Revolutionist 28–30, 254
Nihilists 44n8
Nizaris: Alamut 15; assassination 16; Hasan-i Sabbah 15–16; Marco Polo 14; Nizar 15

OAS 155
Okhrana 33–34; explosives 55–58; firearms 58; funding of the Party of Socialist Revolutionaries 60–61; informants 64; international intelligence cooperation 67; perlustration 52–53; smuggled literature 53–54
Organisation de l'Armée Secret see OAS

Pakistan 155
Partiia sotsialistov-revoliutsionerov see Party of Socialist Revolutionaries
Party of Socialist Revolutionaries (PSR) 33–34, 37; Central Committee (CC) 38–39; the Combat Organization (CO) 38; conciliatory SRs 39–40; cooperation with parties of national minorities) 61; dynamite 50–51, 55, 65; factory terror 37–38; justification of terrorism 29; peasants 27–28; Regional International Committee 38
Princip, Gavrilo 102
propaganda 2, 4, 179–182, 230, 231–232, 236, 267–268
Prophet Muhammad 166

Al-Qa'ida 25; 'Azzam, 'Abdullah Yusuf 164; derailments 165; justifications for jihad 164–165; Abu Yahya al-Libi 164–165, 223–224, 232; in Mesopotamia 170–171; open source jihad (OSJ) 165; Services Bureau 163; Osama Bin Laden 163; volunteers 156, 163; Aiman al-Zawahiri 209
Quran 143–144, 187; peace 143
Sayyid Qutb 121–122; jihad 139–141; slavery 139

Romanov dynasty 31
Rosenberg, Alfred 77–78, 85, 89–91
Rumiyah 144–147, 231
Russian anarchists: assassination 52; international reach 52
Russian civil war 254
Russian counterterrorism: effectiveness 64–67
Russian terrorism: effectiveness 62–64

Salafism 129–130, 154, 203
Salafist Group for Preaching and Combat see GSPC
Saqifa 206–207
Savinkov, Boris: evasive action 54; explosives 55–57
Seljuqs 16
Serebrennikov, Vladimir 30–31
Setmarian, Mustafa see Abu Mus'ab al-Suri
Shi'is 242–243, 252
Shin Bet 225
shirk (polytheism) 228–229
Sicarii 13–14; death 14; the fourth philosophy 12–13; Judas of Galilee (Judas the Galilean) 12; Menahem 12
Strasser, Otto 86–87
Sudeikin, Georgii P. 66–67
Sufis 125
Suicide bombings see martyrdom operations
al-Suri, Abu Mus'ab 126–127; Christians 138; non-Muslim places of worship 139

takfir 158–159, 163
Taliban 209, 233, 251–252, 270
tawhid 203, 207, 244; tawhid banner 244
al-Tawhid wa'l-Jihad see Abu Mus'ab al-Zarqawi
Ibn Taymiyya 120, 126, 128–130, 146, 148, 232
terrorism: causes 241–242; children 249–250; deception 248–249; definitions 3–6; enemy espionage 270–271; exclusivism 242–243, 269; fear 270–271; ideology 242–245; international cooperation 270; Islamic definition 3; methodology 245–248, 265–266; the people 244, 266; predictability 265–266; propaganda 252–255; Russian 242, 244–250; of the state 250–252; totalitarianism 244
Third Department 34, 248
Tikhomirov, Lev A. 41–42

al-Tirmidhi, Abu 'Isa 125
Tret'e Otdelenie *see* Third Department
Twelver (Ithna 'Ashari) Shi'ism 194

universities 27

Volkhovskii, Feliks V. 39
Völkischer Beobachter 80

Muhammad Ibn 'Abd al-Wahhab: Dar'iyya 18; ijtihad 19; jihad 147–148; killing of Shi'is 19–20; methodology 19–20; mushrikun (idolaters) 19; shirk 20; taqlid 19; tawhid 20–21; 'ulama 18
Wahhabis *see* Muwahhidun
Wehrmacht 82
Weimar Republic 83, 101

zakat (charitable tax) 208
al-Zarqawi, Abu Mus'ab 154, 163, 234, 241–242; civil war in Iraq 170; criticism of Usama Bin Ladin 170; criticized by his mentor al-Maqdisi 170; financial support 170–171
Zavarzin, Pavel P. 52–53; female Okhrana agents 59
al-Zawahiri, Aiman *see* Al-Qa'ida
Zeal 13
Zealots 11–12, 243–244
Zemlia i Volia 32, 34–35
Zitouni, Jamal *see* GIA
Znamia Truda 39
Zouabri, 'Antar *see* GIA